Angel Sanctuary

story and art by Kaori Yuki   vol. 19

The Story Thus Far

High school boy Setsuna Mudo's life is hellish. He's always been a troublemaker, and his worst sin was falling incestuously in love with his beautiful sister Sara. But his troubles are preordained—Setsuna is the reincarnation of the Lady Alexiel, an angel who rebelled against Heaven and led the demons of Hell in a revolt. Sara, in turn, is a manifestation of the angel Jibril.

Sara has been driven mad by Sandalphon's nightmare, and a vestige of Sandalphon's soul is still hiding inside Sara's mind, looking for one last chance to reincarnate himself through her.

On the main plane of Heaven, the Third War of Heaven and Hell is raging. Rosiel has ordered his troops to win no matter the cost—even if it means destroying Heaven itself.

Rosiel has absorbed all of Sandalphon's power, but it had the unexpected side-effect of causing the rapid decay of his own body. He now has set off with Lucifer for the Gate of Heaven, which is the only entrance to the plane of Atziluth, in the center of which is Etenamenki, the Tower of God. Inside the tower is the Tablet of God, which can grant any wish. Rosiel plans to use it to heal his corrupted flesh, merge with Alexiel, and become beautiful for eternity.

Hearing that Rosiel and Lucifer are headed there, Setsuna and his allies also race toward the Gate of Heaven to stop them. But when they arrive, they find Lucifer has slaughtered the gatekeepers, and Rosiel has opened the gate. Battling Lucifer's demons as they go, Setsuna and company make a desperate attempt to enter, as the gate begins to close. They make it only through the heroism of Kato, who sacrifices his life so the others can enter.

Contents

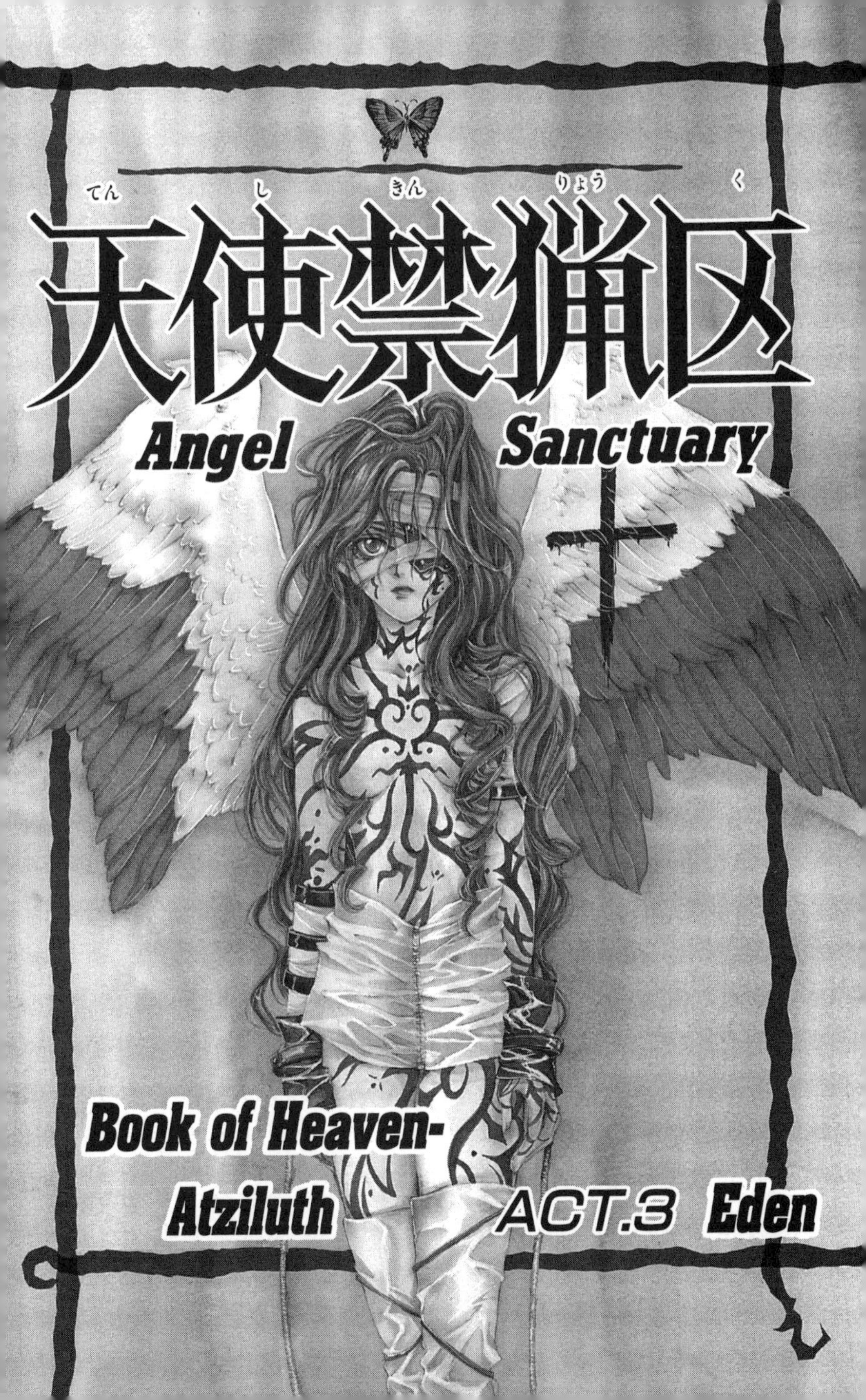
天使禁猟区
Angel Sanctuary
Book of Heaven-Atziluth
ACT.3 Eden

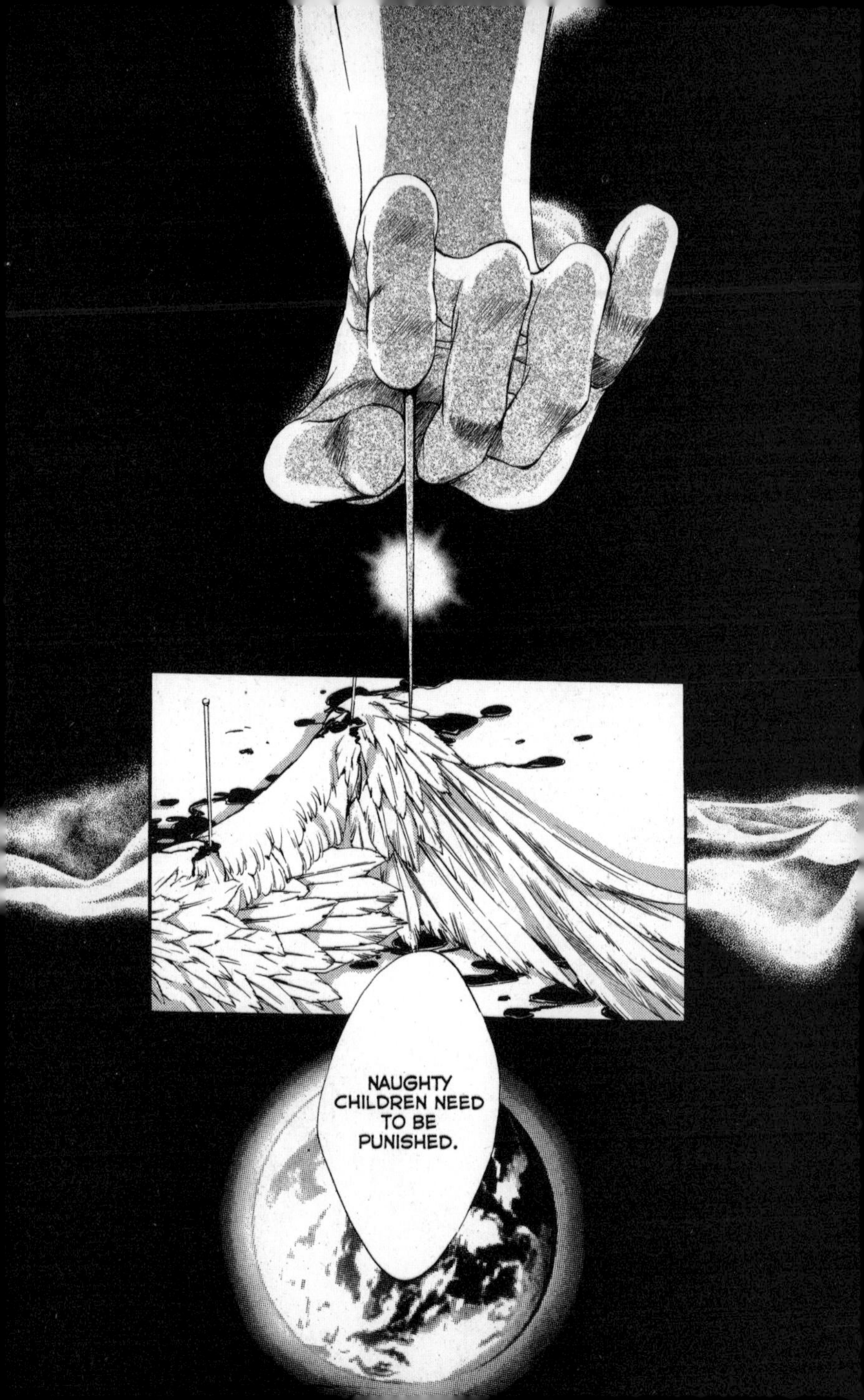
NAUGHTY CHILDREN NEED TO BE PUNISHED.

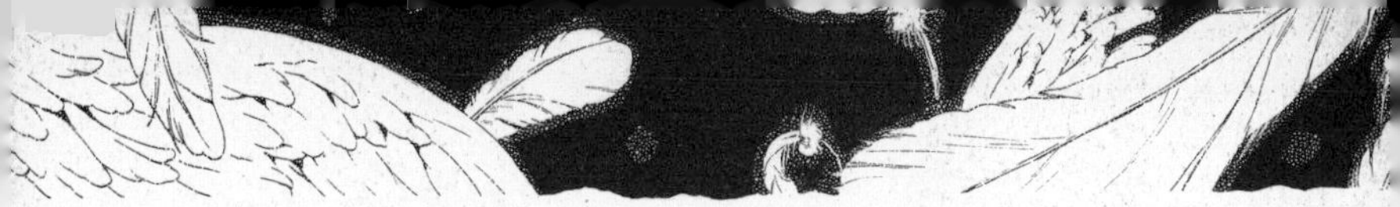

UNDER AN IMPERFECT SUN, CLINGING TO AN IMPERFECT LONGING...

INSIDE THIS LITTLE ASPHALT GARDEN, DENYING MYSELF LIKE AN IMITATION CREATURE,
I THINK OF YOU.

MY CORPULENT HEART IS ABOUT TO BURST, AND MY CONSCIOUSNESS IS DISTORTED.
SOON THE CRYSTAL WILL CRUMBLE FROM ECHOING, AND FLOAT TO THE GROUND.

HOW MANY THOUSAND THINGS BECOME BROKEN FRAGMENTS OF MEMORY...
I WANT TO HOLD YOU, HUMMING A MELANCHOLY TUNE.

FOREVER AND EVER, I WANT TO CARESS YOU UNTIL YOU FALL ASLEEP.
ALTHOUGH I MAY NO LONGER HOLD YOU IN MY HANDS,
I HOPE MY PRAYERS MAY REACH YOU.

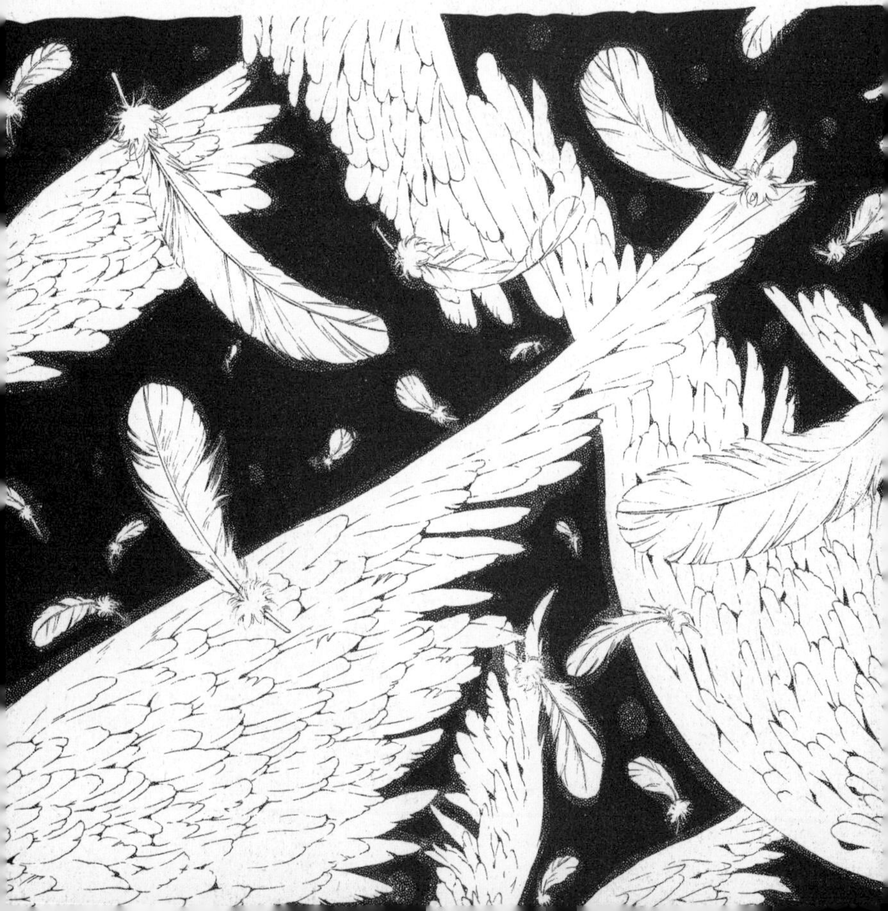

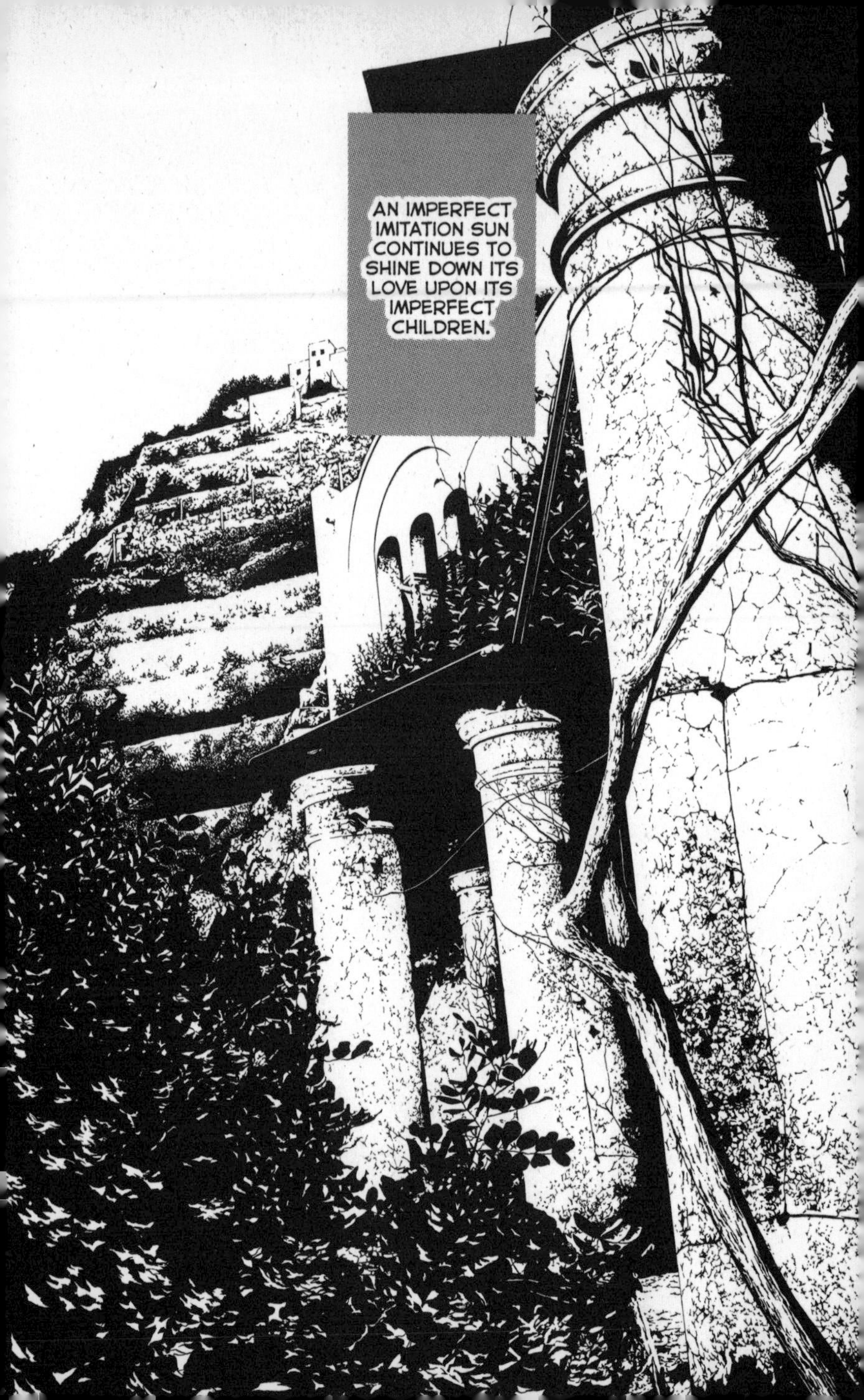
AN IMPERFECT IMITATION SUN CONTINUES TO SHINE DOWN ITS LOVE UPON ITS IMPERFECT CHILDREN.

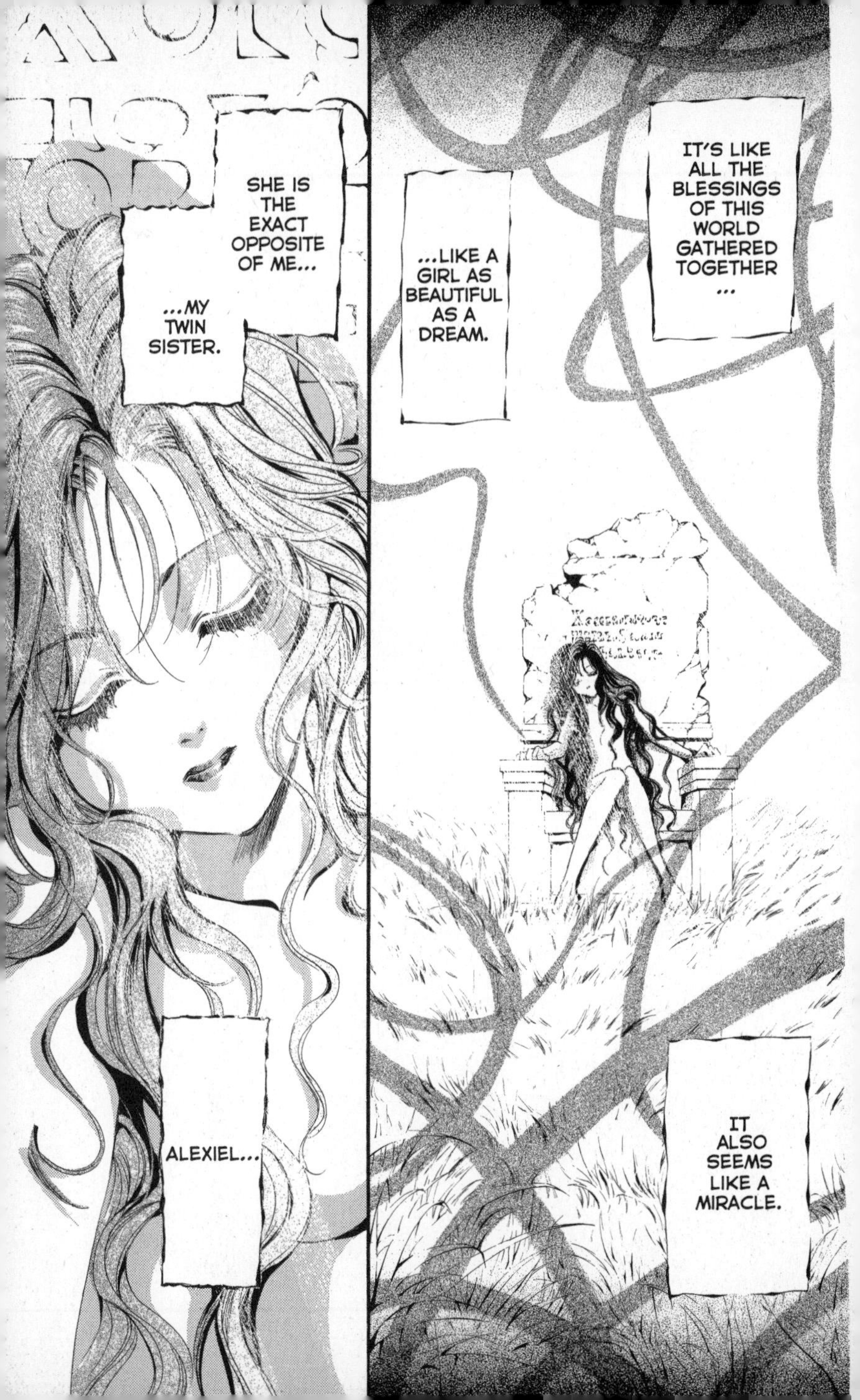
IT'S LIKE ALL THE BLESSINGS OF THIS WORLD GATHERED TOGETHER ...
...LIKE A GIRL AS BEAUTIFUL AS A DREAM.
IT ALSO SEEMS LIKE A MIRACLE.
SHE IS THE EXACT OPPOSITE OF ME...
...MY TWIN SISTER.
ALEXIEL...

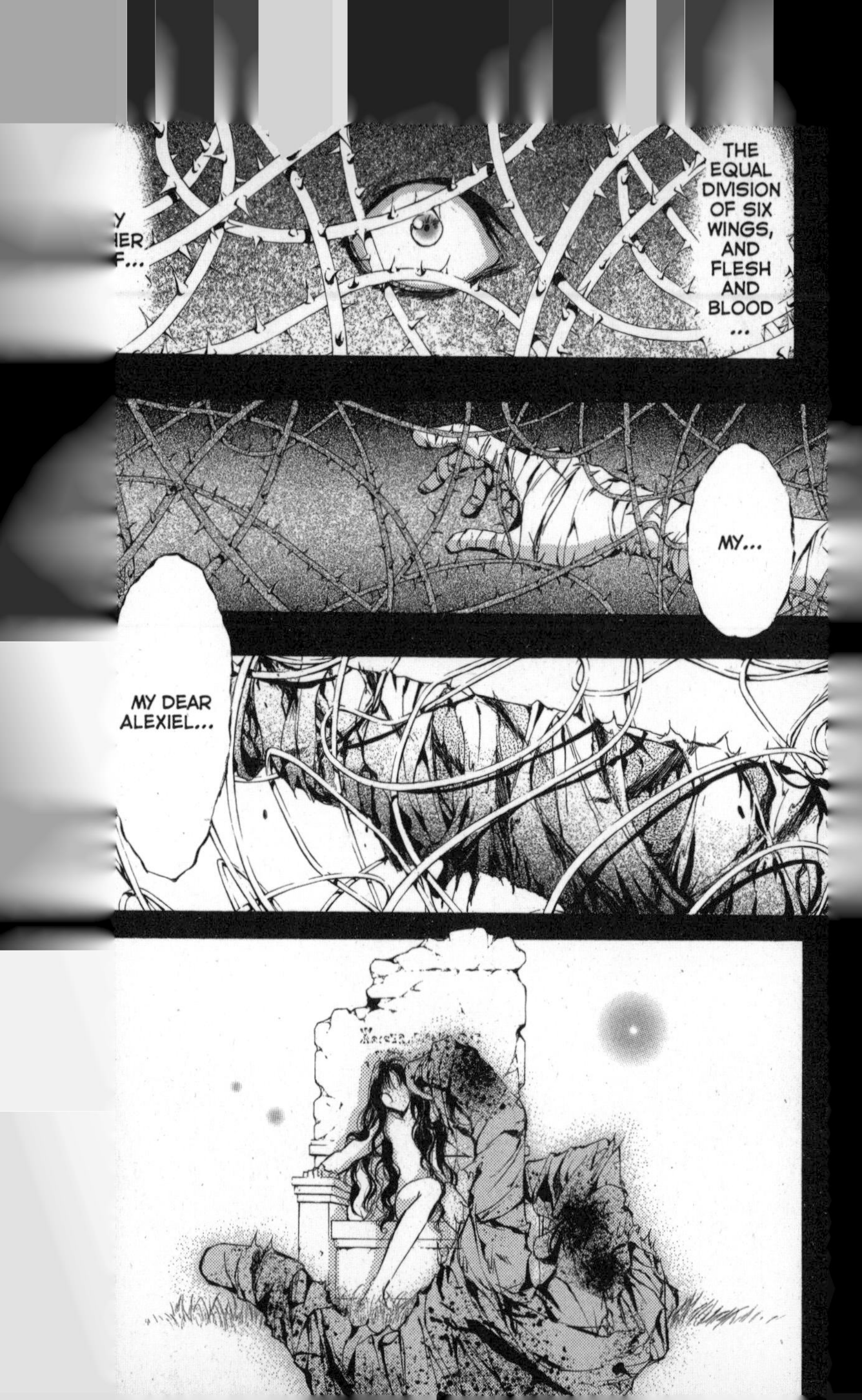
THE EQUAL DIVISION OF SIX WINGS, AND FLESH AND BLOOD ...
MY...
MY DEAR ALEXIEL...

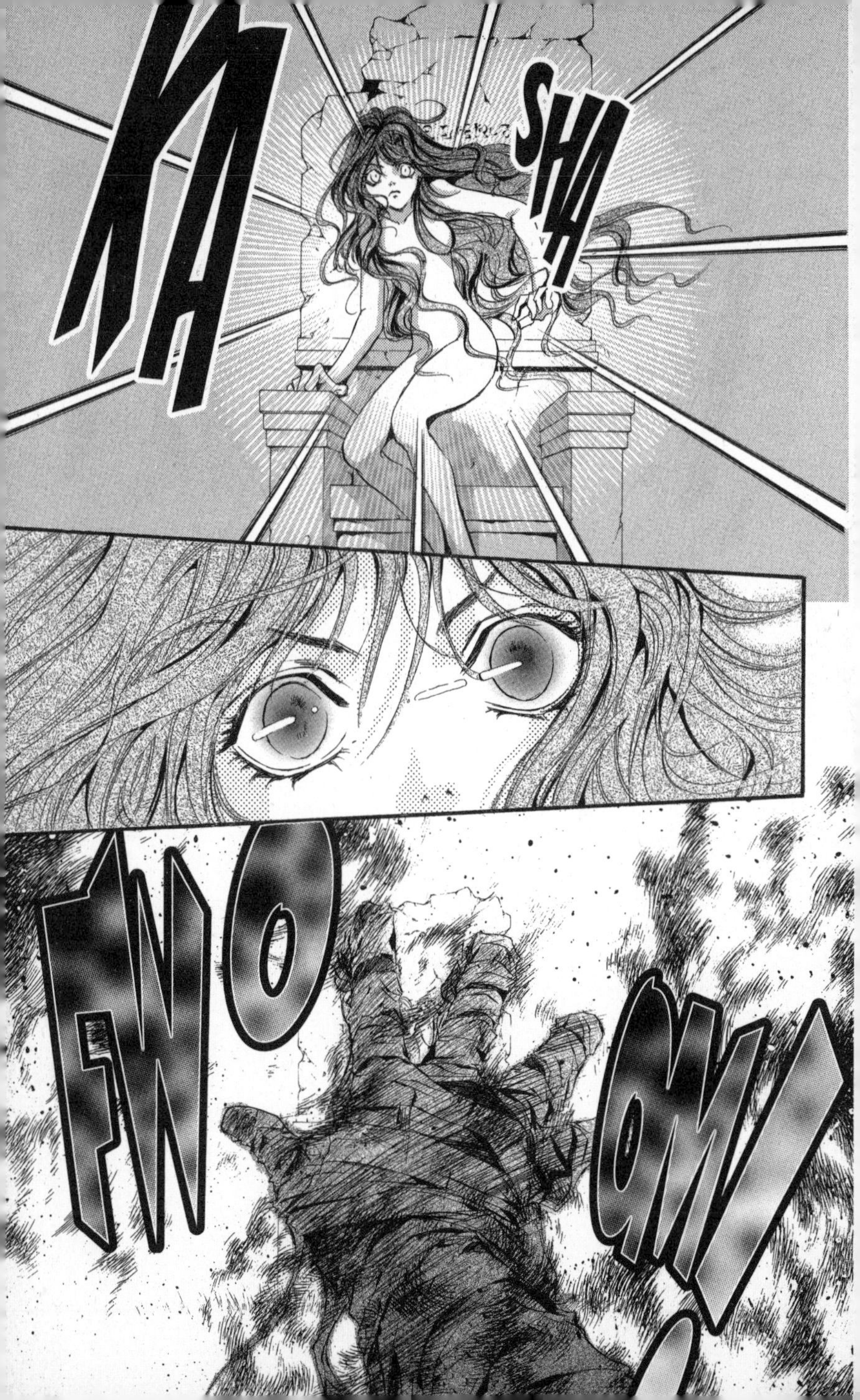
KA
SHA
FWOOM

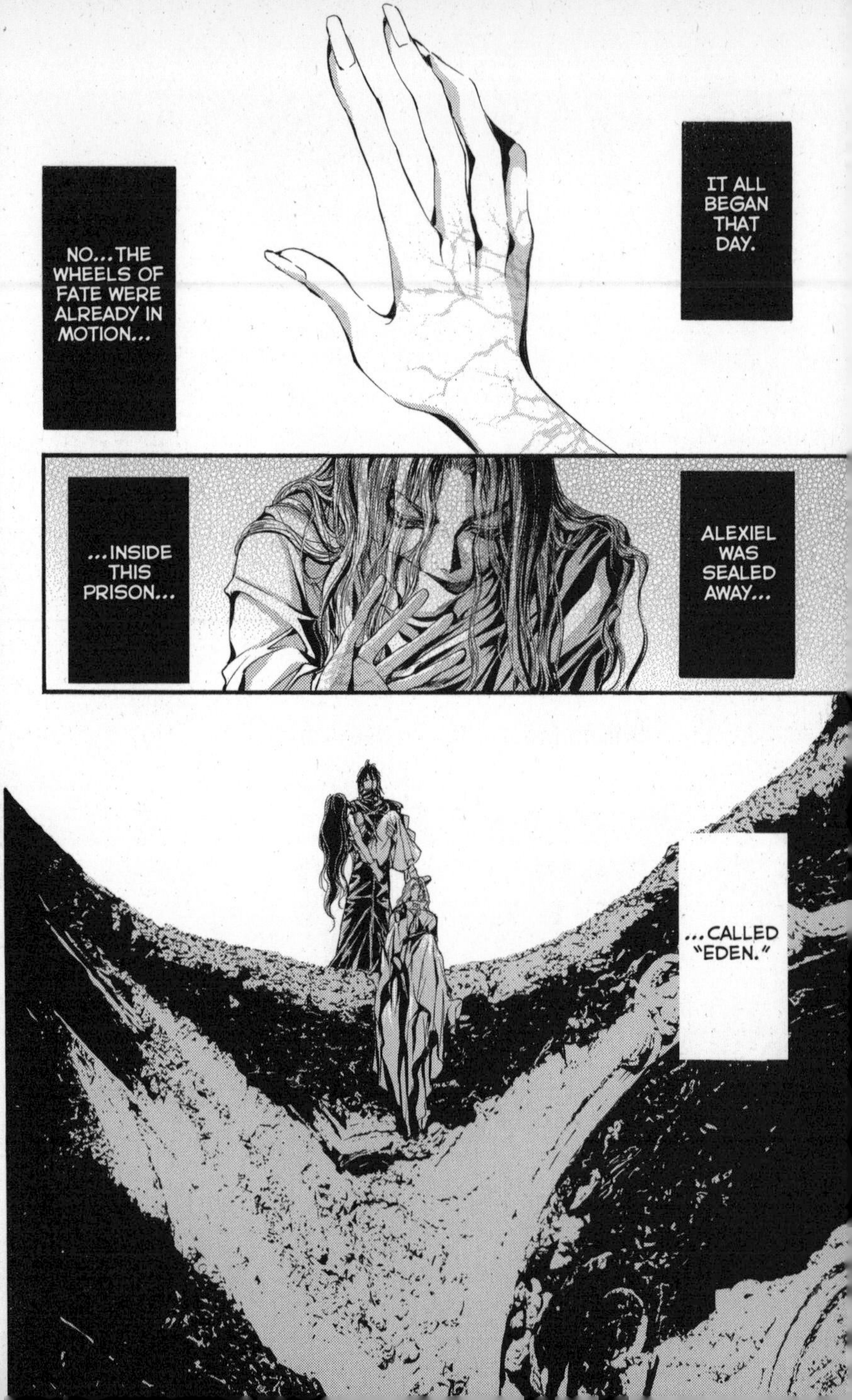
IT ALL BEGAN THAT DAY.
NO... THE WHEELS OF FATE WERE ALREADY IN MOTION...
ALEXIEL WAS SEALED AWAY...
...INSIDE THIS PRISON...
...CALLED "EDEN."

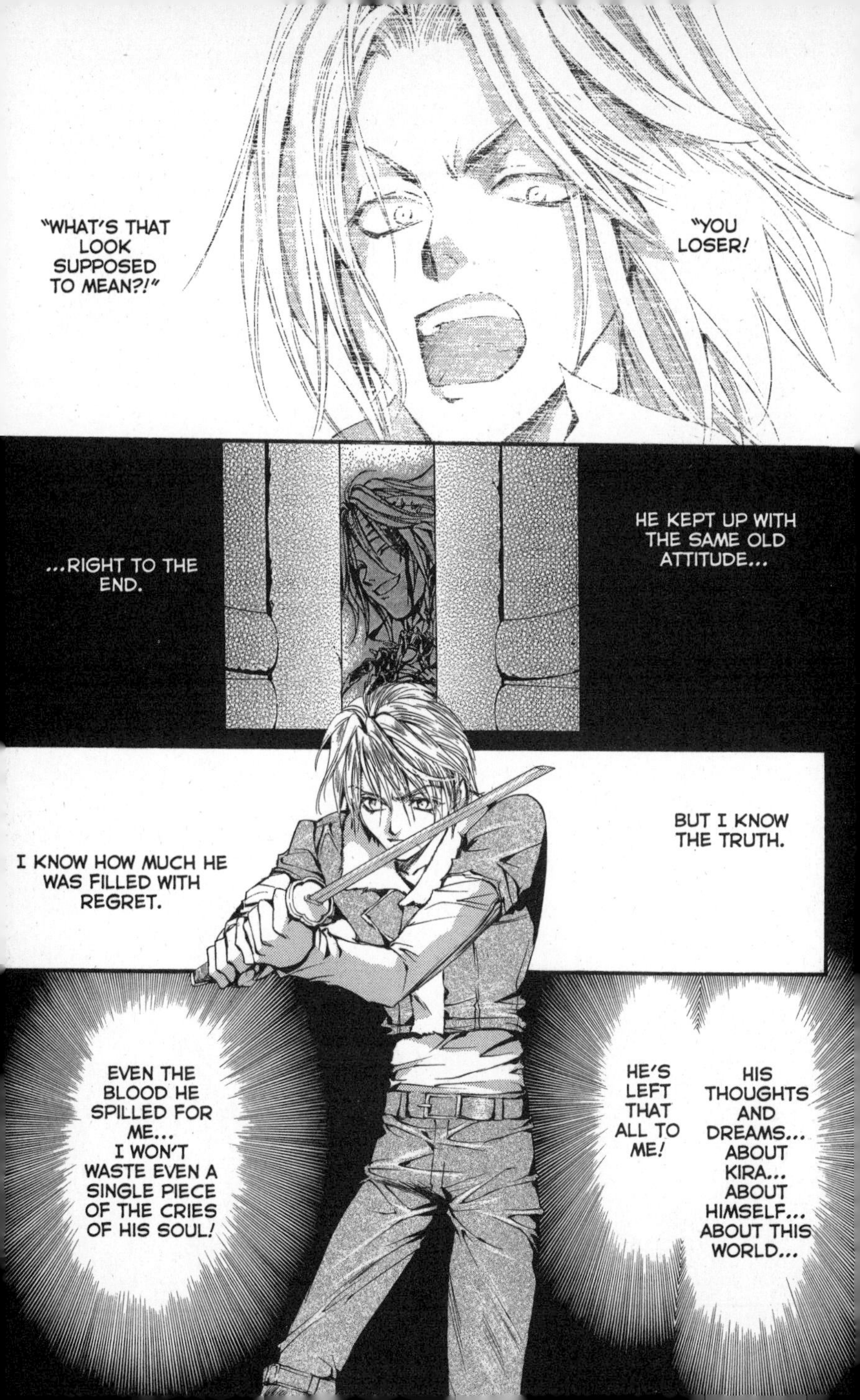
"YOU LOSER!
"WHAT'S THAT LOOK SUPPOSED TO MEAN?!"
HE KEPT UP WITH THE SAME OLD ATTITUDE...
...RIGHT TO THE END.
BUT I KNOW THE TRUTH.
I KNOW HOW MUCH HE WAS FILLED WITH REGRET.
HIS THOUGHTS AND DREAMS... ABOUT KIRA... ABOUT HIMSELF... ABOUT THIS WORLD...
HE'S LEFT THAT ALL TO ME!
EVEN THE BLOOD HE SPILLED FOR ME... I WON'T WASTE EVEN A SINGLE PIECE OF THE CRIES OF HIS SOUL!

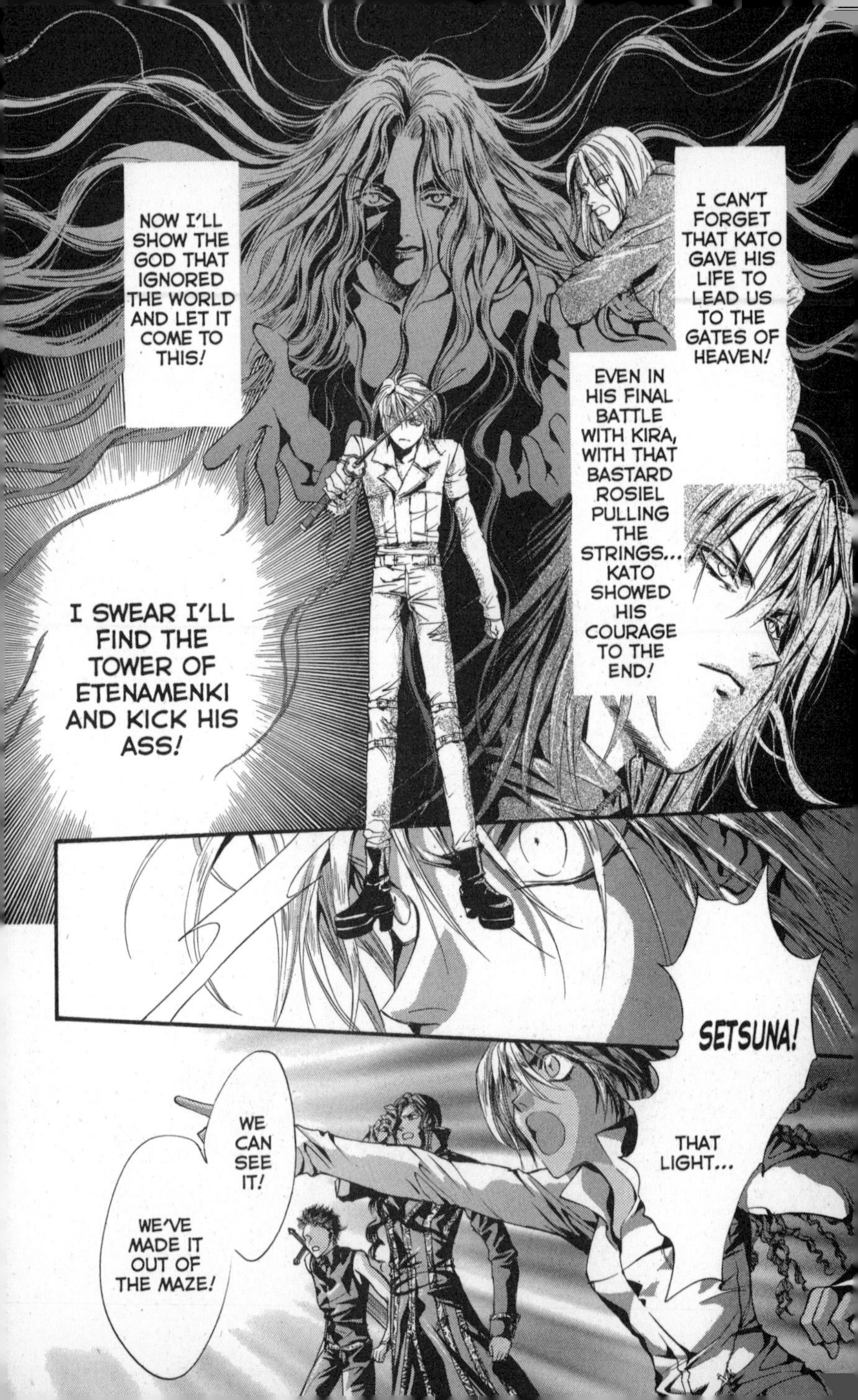
I CAN'T FORGET THAT KATO GAVE HIS LIFE TO LEAD US TO THE GATES OF HEAVEN!
EVEN IN HIS FINAL BATTLE WITH KIRA, WITH THAT BASTARD ROSIEL PULLING THE STRINGS... KATO SHOWED HIS COURAGE TO THE END!
NOW I'LL SHOW THE GOD THAT IGNORED THE WORLD AND LET IT COME TO THIS!
I SWEAR I'LL FIND THE TOWER OF ETENAMENKI AND KICK HIS ASS!
SETSUNA!
THAT LIGHT...
WE CAN SEE IT!
WE'VE MADE IT OUT OF THE MAZE!

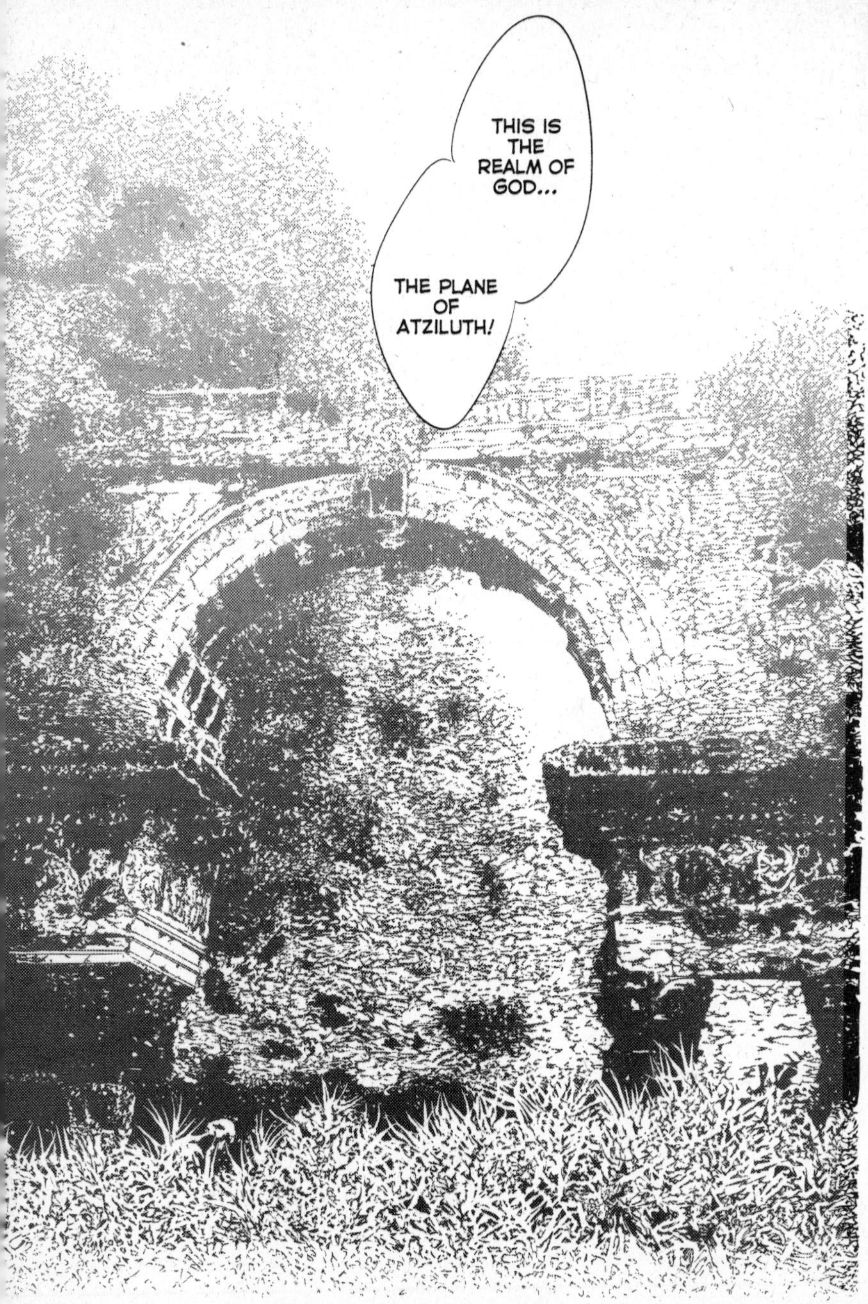
THIS IS THE REALM OF GOD...
THE PLANE OF ATZILUTH!

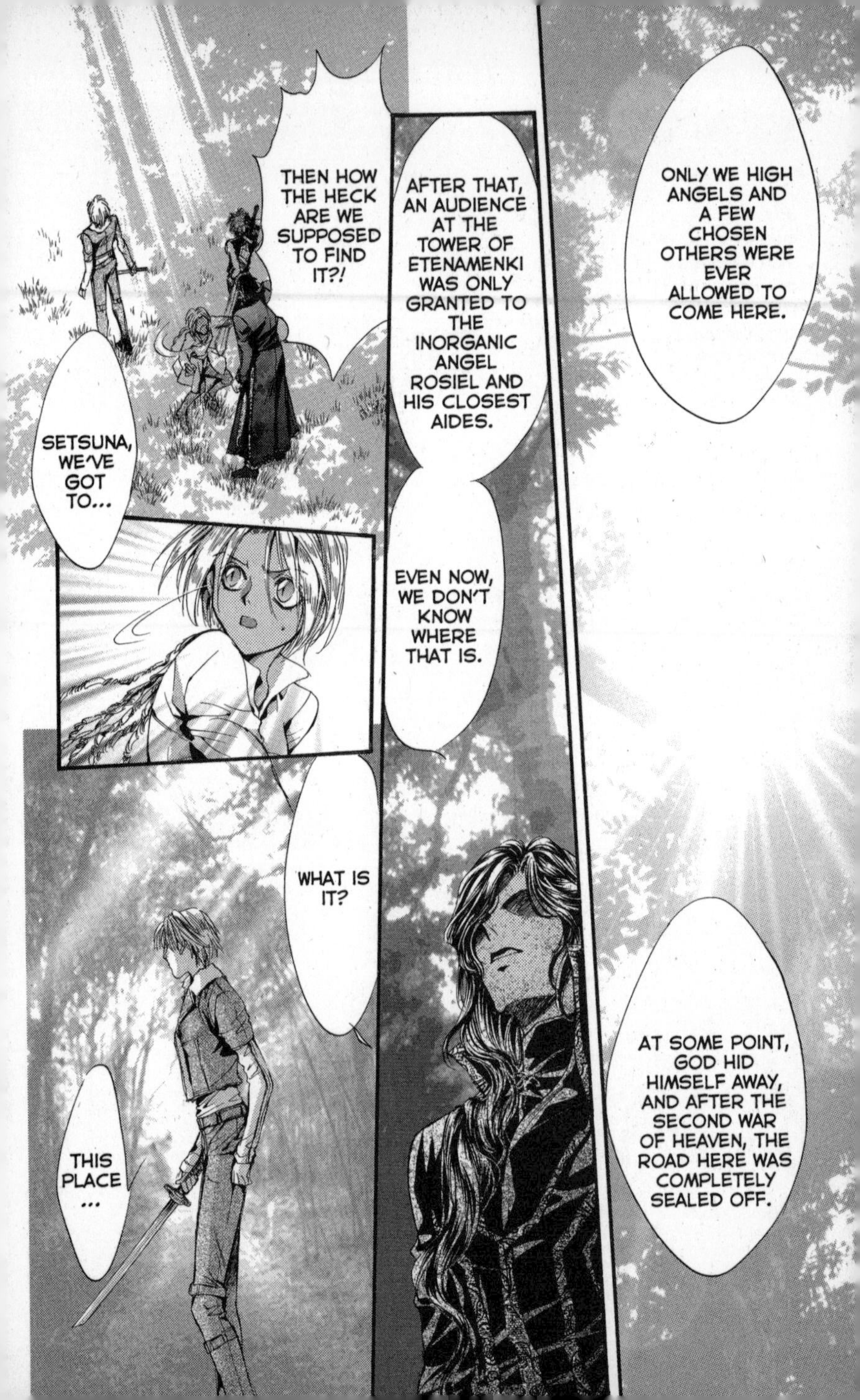
ONLY WE HIGH ANGELS AND A FEW CHOSEN OTHERS WERE EVER ALLOWED TO COME HERE.
AT SOME POINT, GOD HID HIMSELF AWAY, AND AFTER THE SECOND WAR OF HEAVEN, THE ROAD HERE WAS COMPLETELY SEALED OFF.
AFTER THAT, AN AUDIENCE AT THE TOWER OF ETENAMENKI WAS ONLY GRANTED TO THE INORGANIC ANGEL ROSIEL AND HIS CLOSEST AIDES.
EVEN NOW, WE DON'T KNOW WHERE THAT IS.
THEN HOW THE HECK ARE WE SUPPOSED TO FIND IT?!
SETSUNA, WE'VE GOT TO...
WHAT IS IT?
THIS PLACE ...

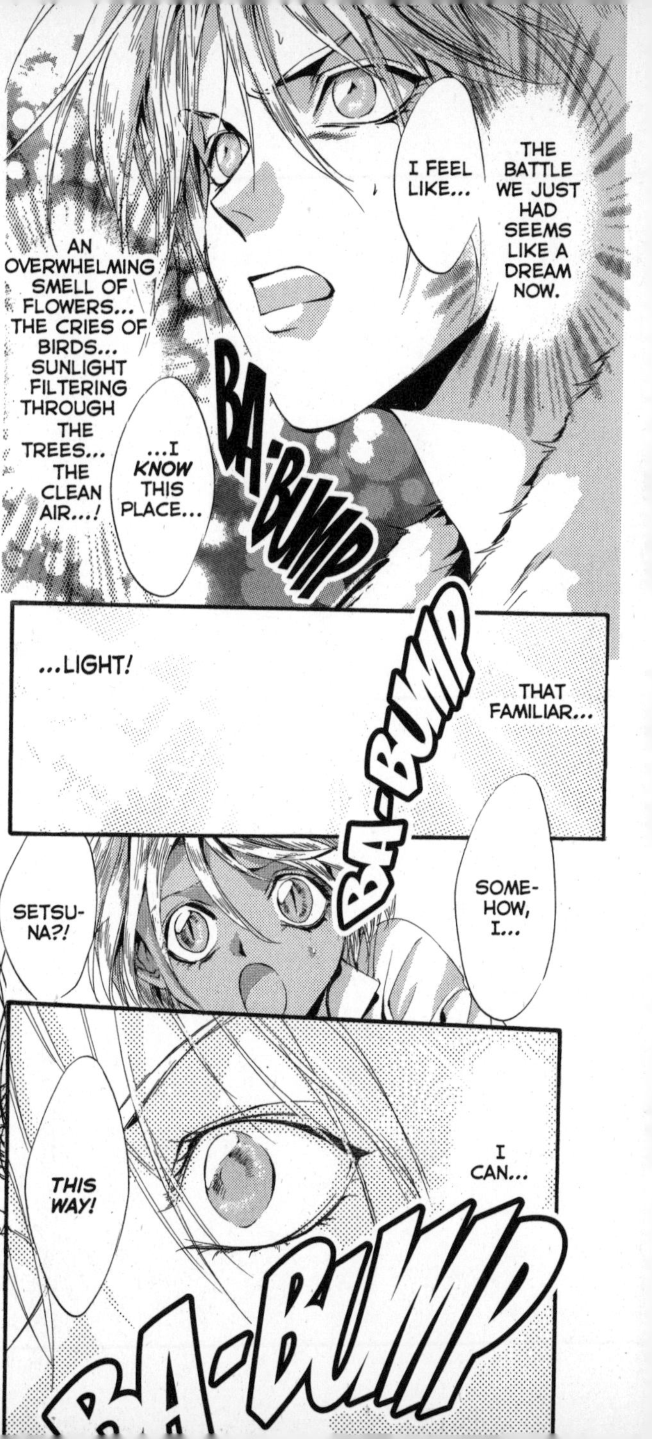
THE BATTLE WE JUST HAD SEEMS LIKE A DREAM NOW.
I FEEL LIKE...
AN OVERWHELMING SMELL OF FLOWERS... THE CRIES OF BIRDS... SUNLIGHT FILTERING THROUGH THE TREES... THE CLEAN AIR...!
...I *KNOW* THIS PLACE...
BA-BUMP
THAT FAMILIAR...
...LIGHT!
BA-BUMP
SOME-HOW, I...
SETSU-NA?!
I CAN...
THIS WAY!
BA-BUMP

Hey!
It's volume 19!
So next is 20...the end of the series! Wow! We're really building towards the final climax. As I write this text, I've got two more episodes to draw, and then I'm done. What's it been...five or six years? Now that I'm here, I can't tell if feels like a long time or a fleeting moment. I myself feel like, "Wow. It's finally over." Up till now I was too busy to think about it, but now that I'm here, it's really hitting me. I get a lot of letters saying, "We don't want it to end...but we want to see how it comes out." That's a real dilemma, isn't it?

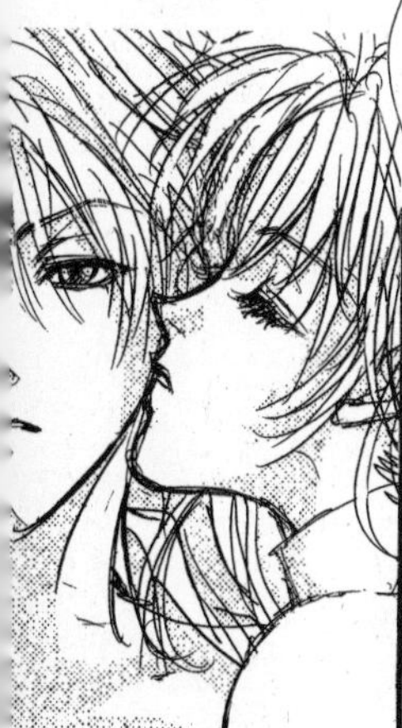

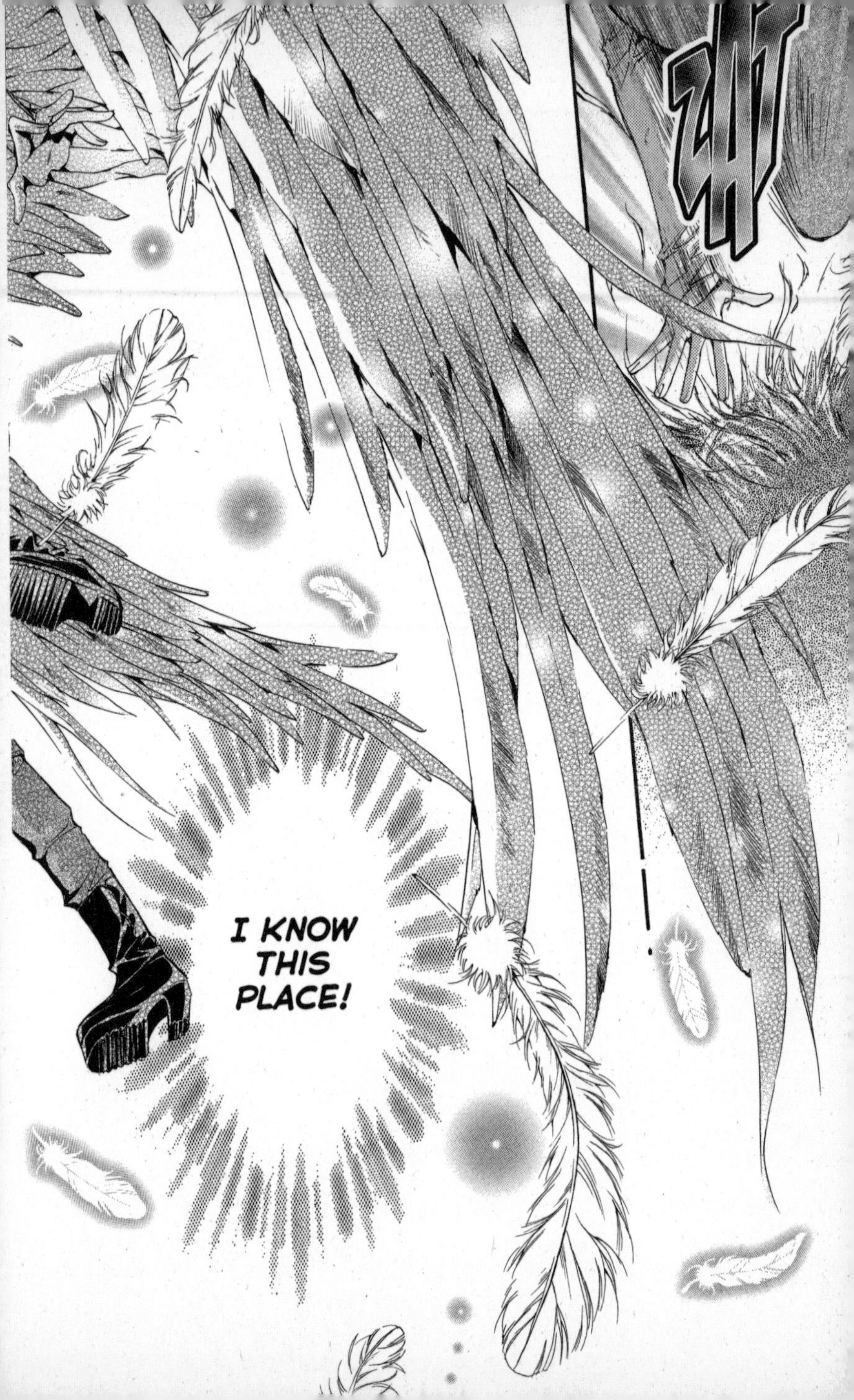
I KNOW THIS PLACE!

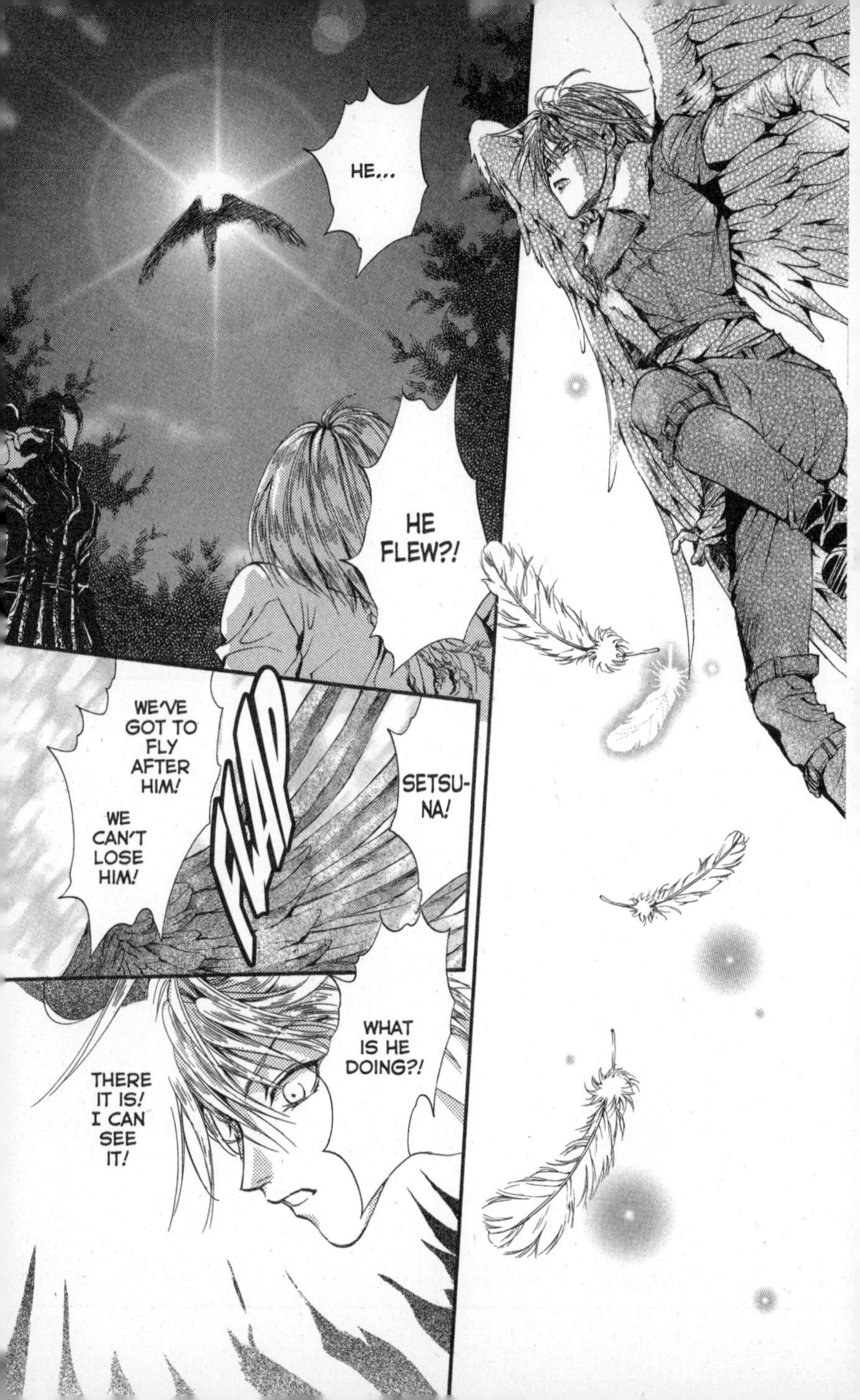
HE...
HE FLEW?!
SETSU-NA!
WE'VE GOT TO FLY AFTER HIM!
WE CAN'T LOSE HIM!
WHAT IS HE DOING?!
THERE IT IS! I CAN SEE IT!

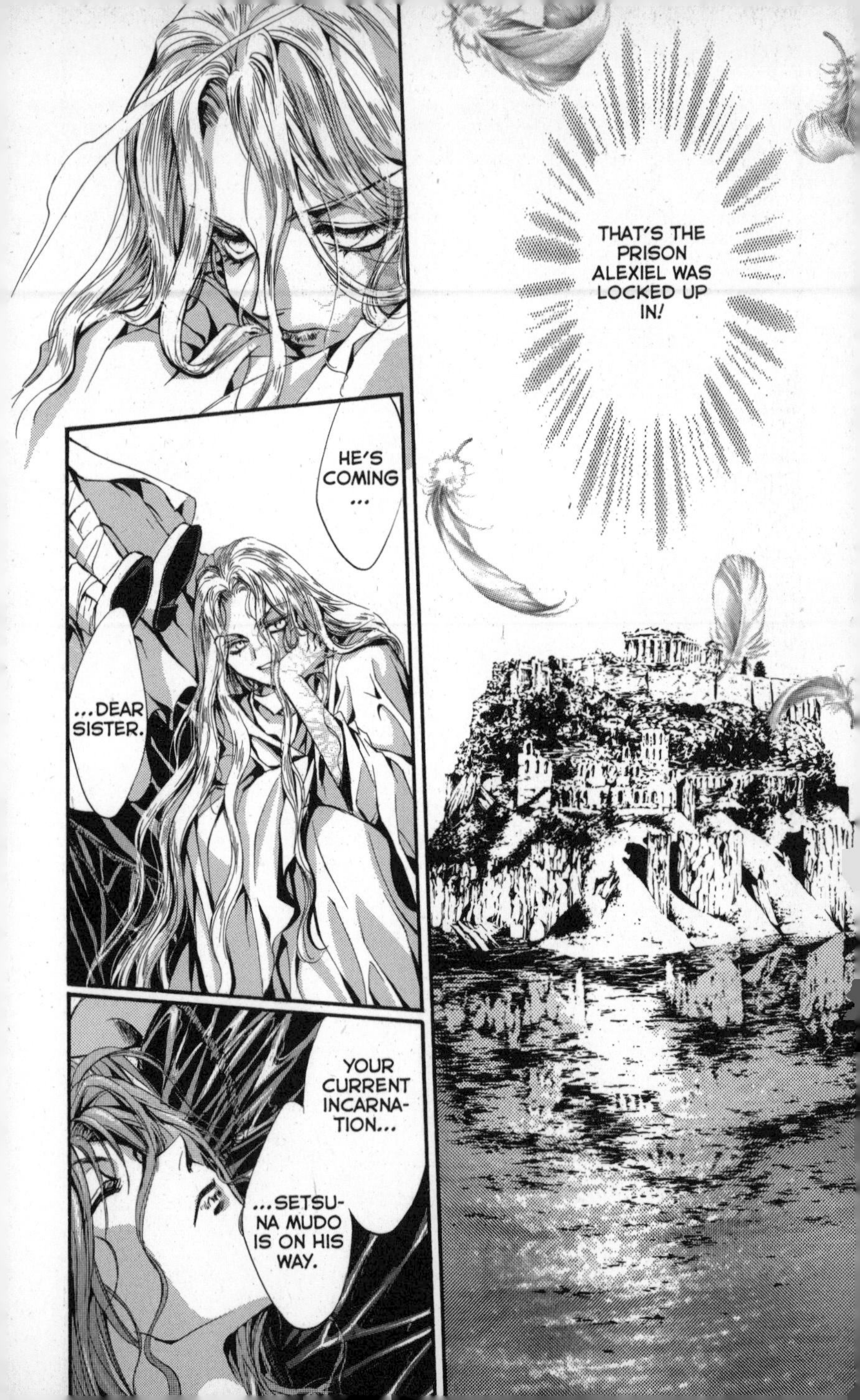
THAT'S THE PRISON ALEXIEL WAS LOCKED UP IN!
HE'S COMING ...
...DEAR SISTER.
YOUR CURRENT INCARNA-TION...
...SETSU-NA MUDO IS ON HIS WAY.

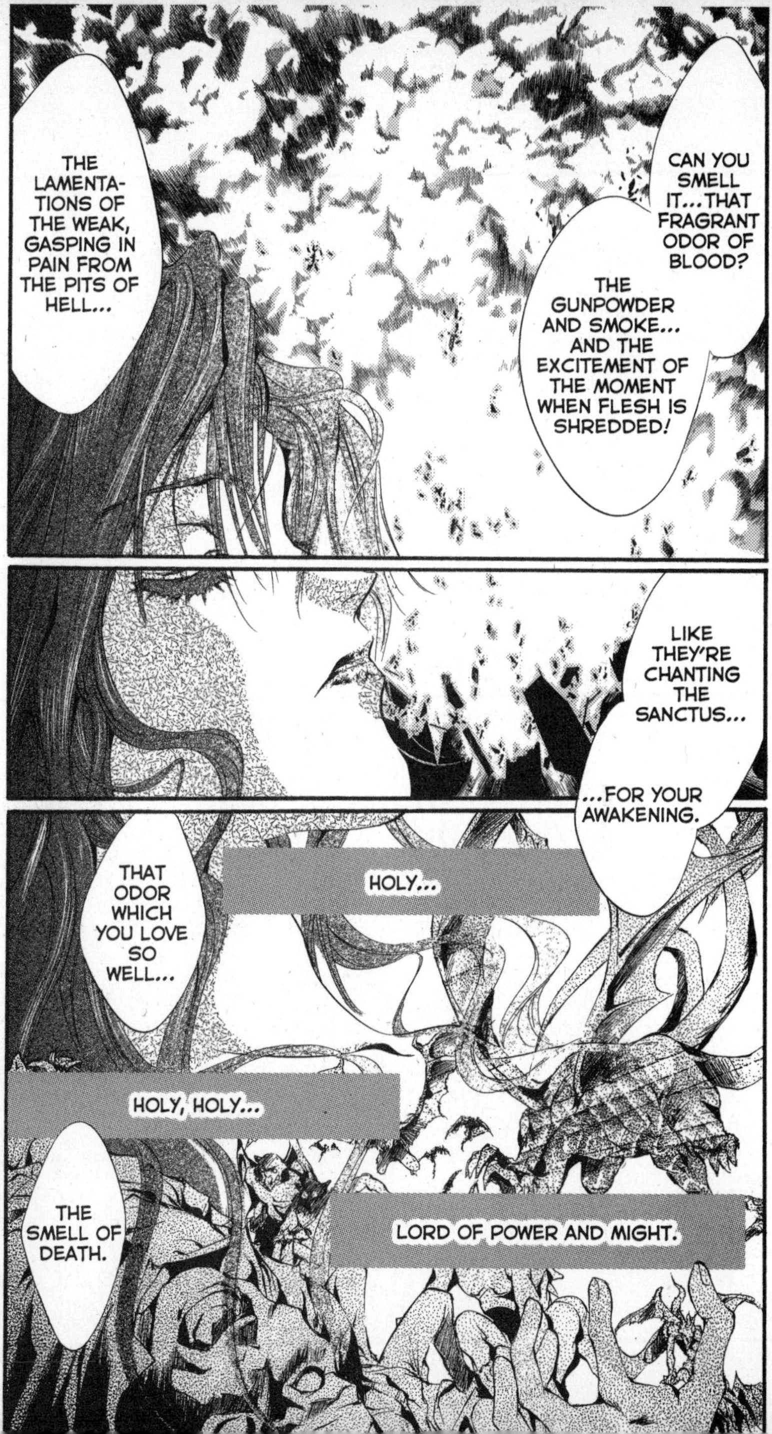
CAN YOU SMELL IT...THAT FRAGRANT ODOR OF BLOOD?
THE GUNPOWDER AND SMOKE... AND THE EXCITEMENT OF THE MOMENT WHEN FLESH IS SHREDDED!
THE LAMENTATIONS OF THE WEAK, GASPING IN PAIN FROM THE PITS OF HELL...
LIKE THEY'RE CHANTING THE SANCTUS...
...FOR YOUR AWAKENING.
HOLY...
THAT ODOR WHICH YOU LOVE SO WELL...
HOLY, HOLY...
LORD OF POWER AND MIGHT.
THE SMELL OF DEATH.

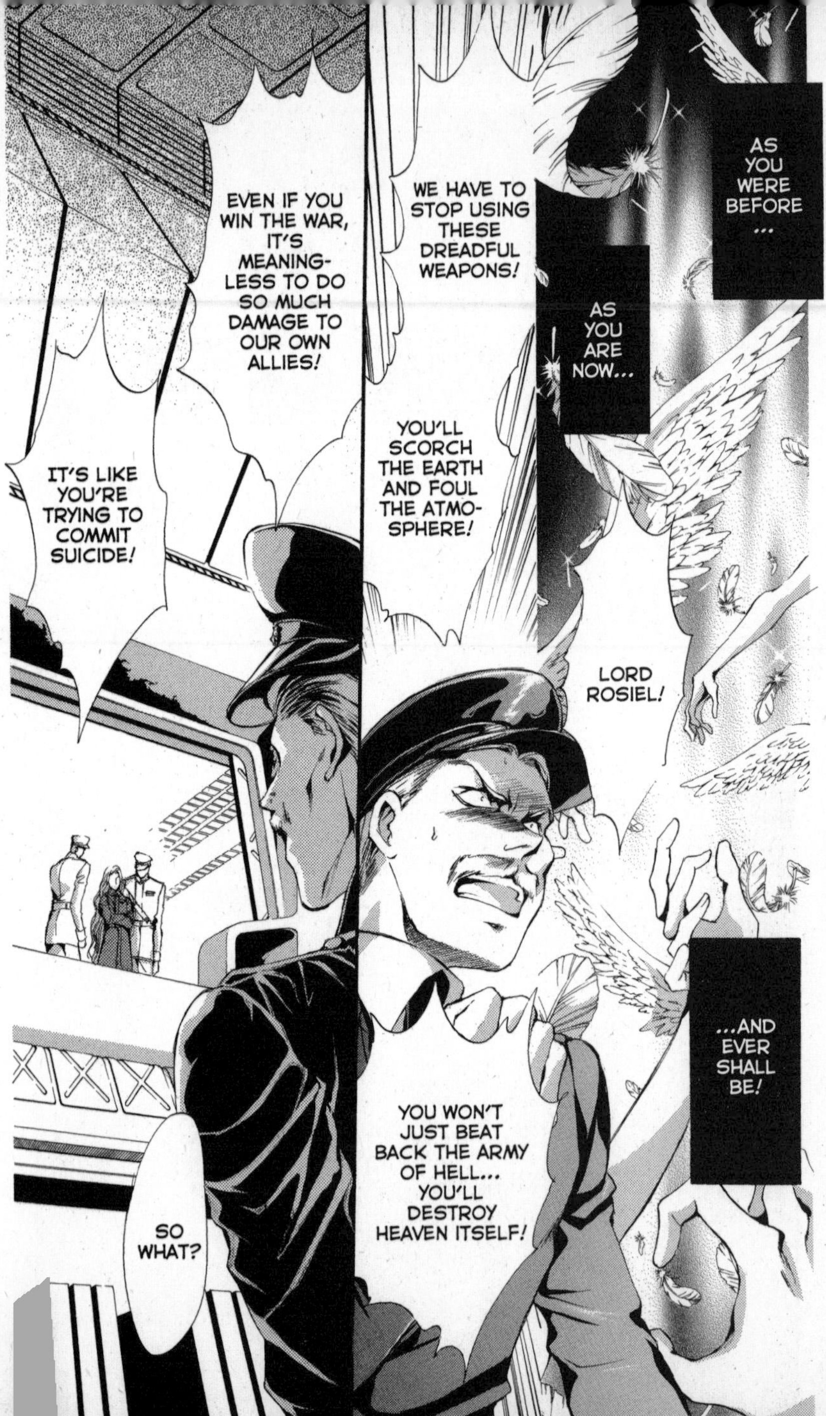
AS YOU WERE BEFORE...
AS YOU ARE NOW...
LORD ROSIEL!
...AND EVER SHALL BE!
WE HAVE TO STOP USING THESE DREADFUL WEAPONS!
YOU'LL SCORCH THE EARTH AND FOUL THE ATMOSPHERE!
YOU WON'T JUST BEAT BACK THE ARMY OF HELL... YOU'LL DESTROY HEAVEN ITSELF!
EVEN IF YOU WIN THE WAR, IT'S MEANINGLESS TO DO SO MUCH DAMAGE TO OUR OWN ALLIES!
IT'S LIKE YOU'RE TRYING TO COMMIT SUICIDE!
SO WHAT?

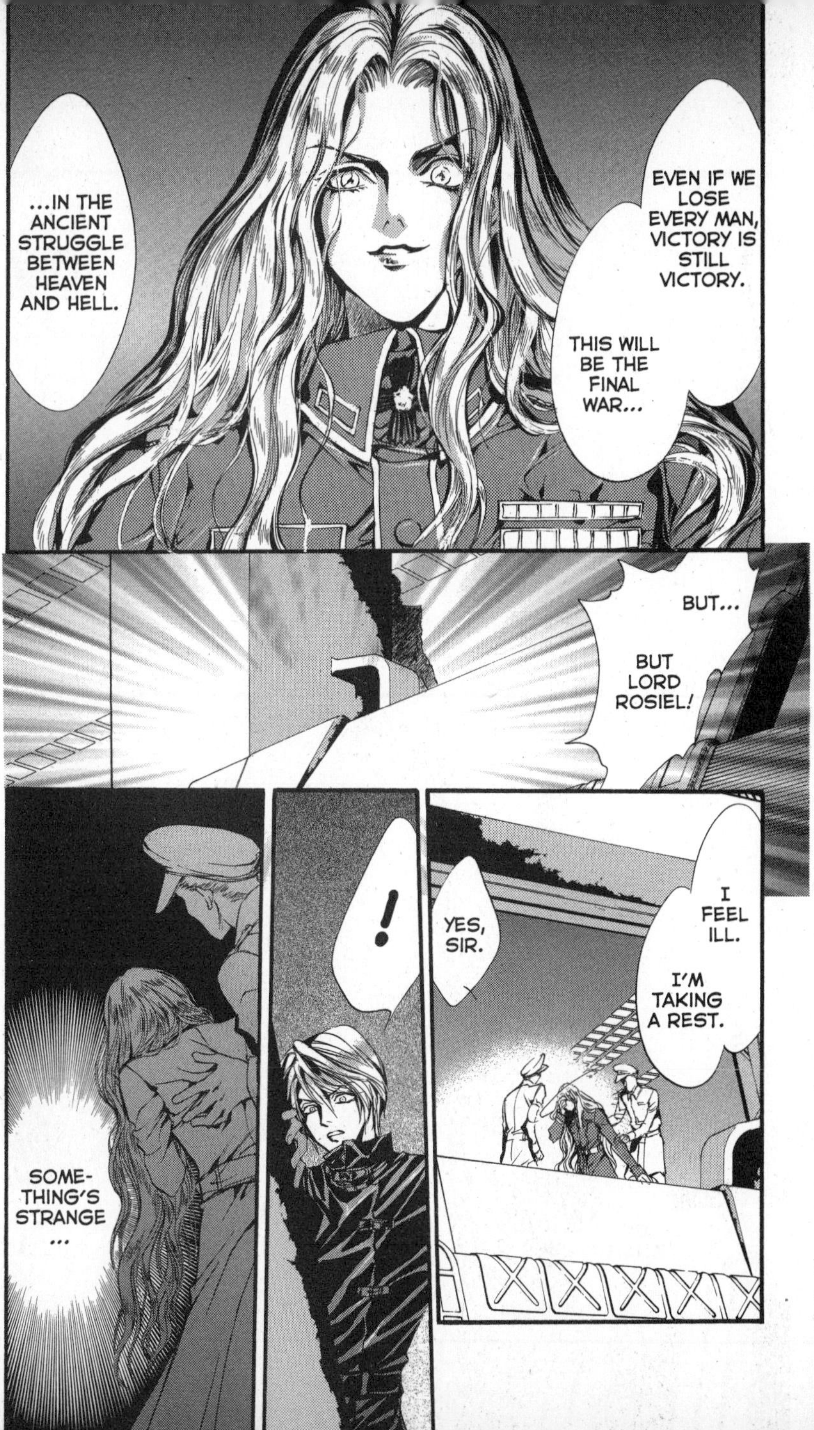
EVEN IF WE LOSE EVERY MAN, VICTORY IS STILL VICTORY.
THIS WILL BE THE FINAL WAR...
...IN THE ANCIENT STRUGGLE BETWEEN HEAVEN AND HELL.
BUT...
BUT LORD ROSIEL!
I FEEL ILL.
I'M TAKING A REST.
YES, SIR.
!
SOME-THING'S STRANGE...

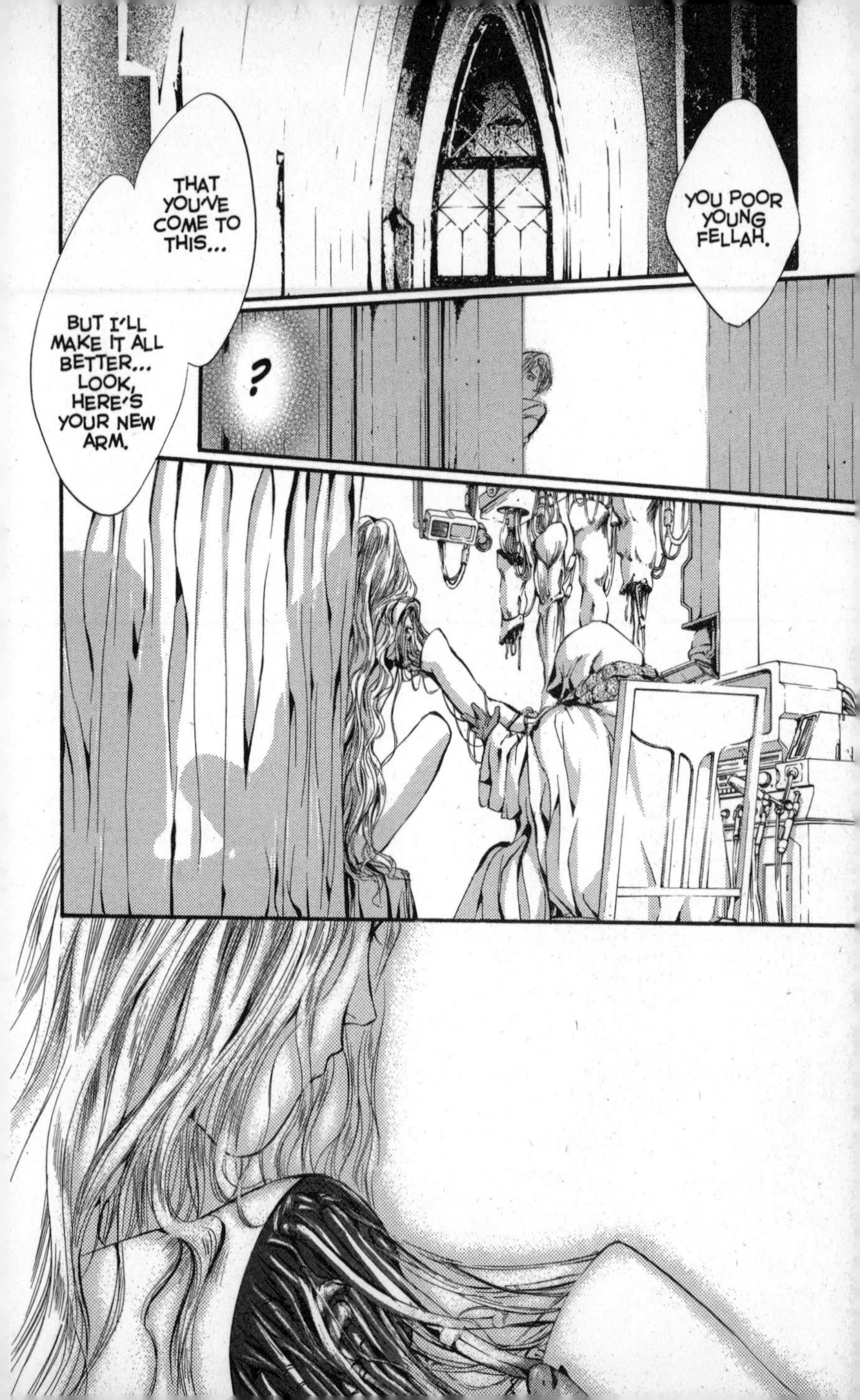
YOU POOR YOUNG FELLAH.
THAT YOU'VE COME TO THIS...
?
BUT I'LL MAKE IT ALL BETTER... LOOK, HERE'S YOUR NEW ARM.

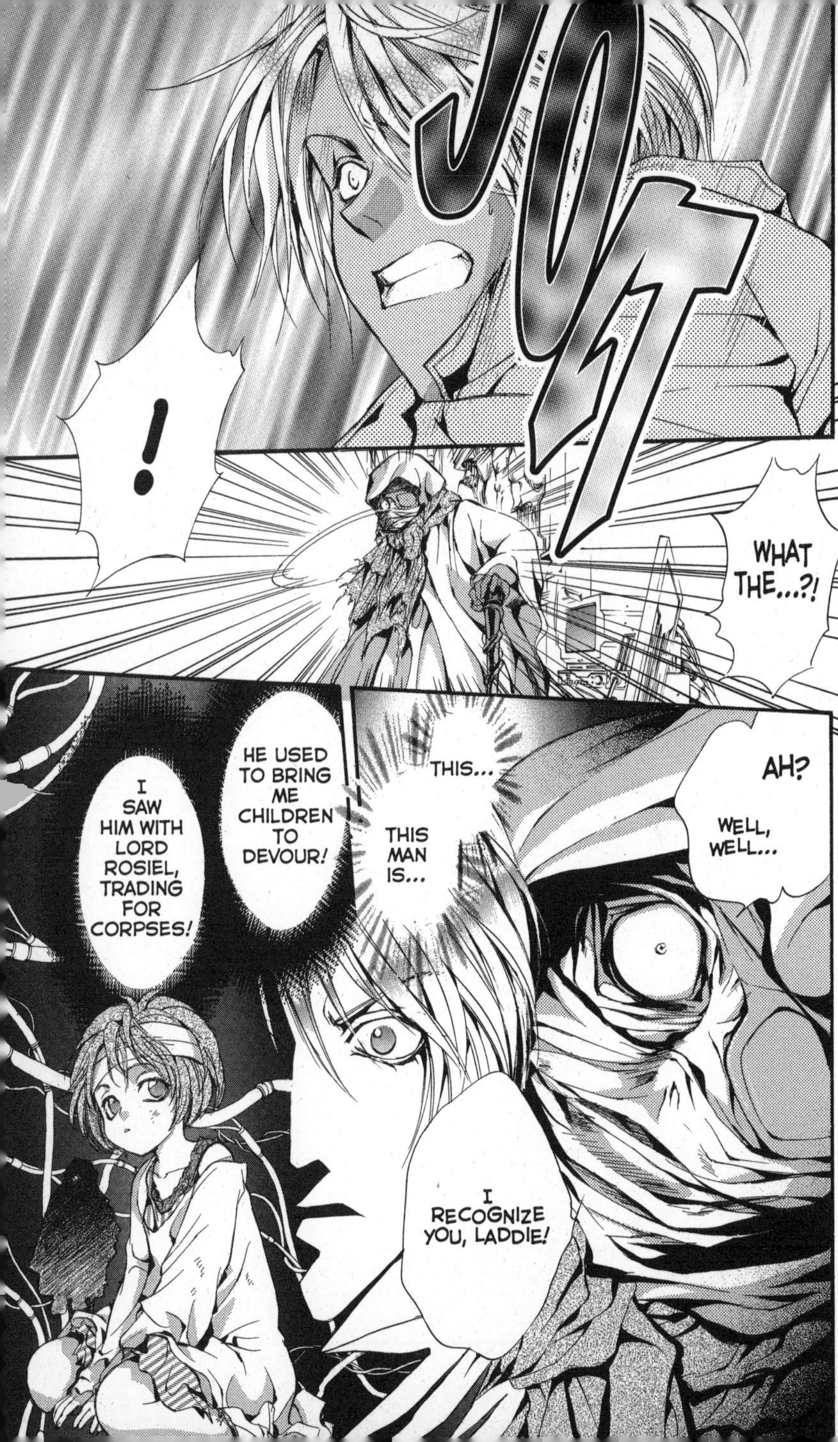
!
WHAT THE...?!
AH?
WELL, WELL...
I RECOGNIZE YOU, LADDIE!
THIS...
THIS MAN IS...
HE USED TO BRING ME CHILDREN TO DEVOUR!
I SAW HIM WITH LORD ROSIEL, TRADING FOR CORPSES!

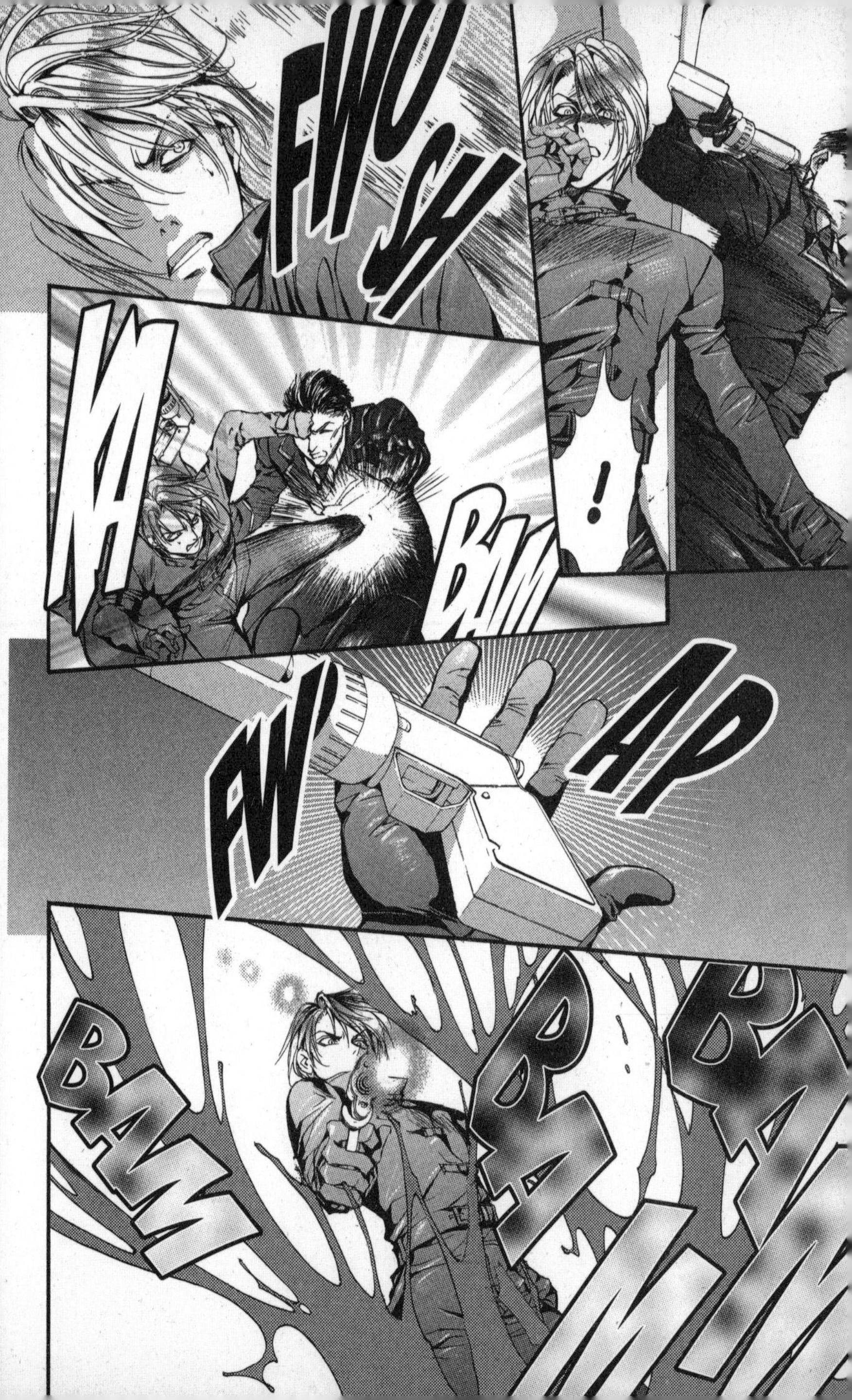
!
FWOSH
BAM
FWAP
BAM
BAM
BAM

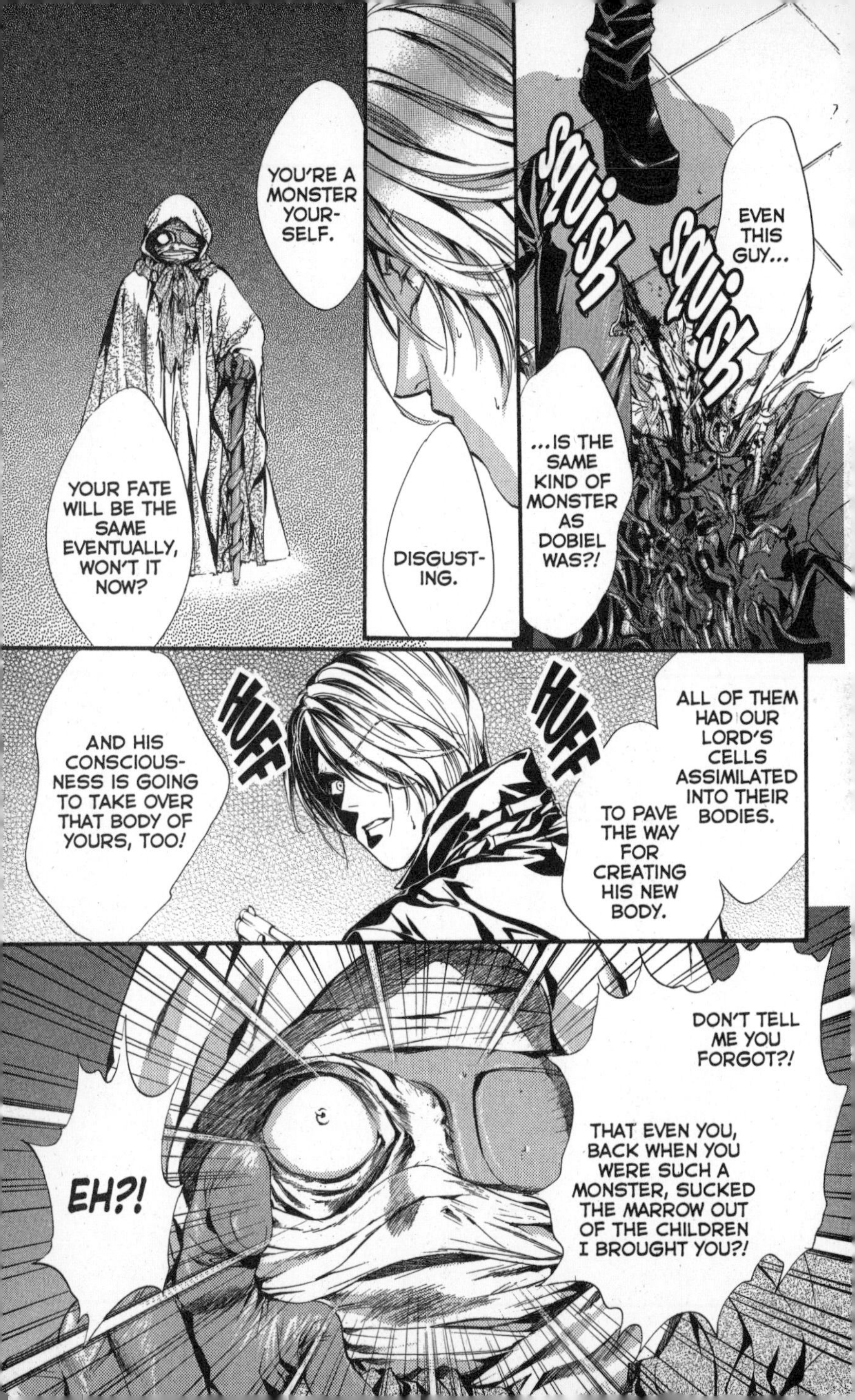

EVEN THIS GUY...
SQUISH
SQUISH
...IS THE SAME KIND OF MONSTER AS DOBIEL WAS?!
DISGUSTING.
YOU'RE A MONSTER YOURSELF.
YOUR FATE WILL BE THE SAME EVENTUALLY, WON'T IT NOW?
ALL OF THEM HAD OUR LORD'S CELLS ASSIMILATED INTO THEIR BODIES.
TO PAVE THE WAY FOR CREATING HIS NEW BODY.
HUFF
HUFF
AND HIS CONSCIOUSNESS IS GOING TO TAKE OVER THAT BODY OF YOURS, TOO!
DON'T TELL ME YOU FORGOT?!
THAT EVEN YOU, BACK WHEN YOU WERE SUCH A MONSTER, SUCKED THE MARROW OUT OF THE CHILDREN I BROUGHT YOU?!
EH?!

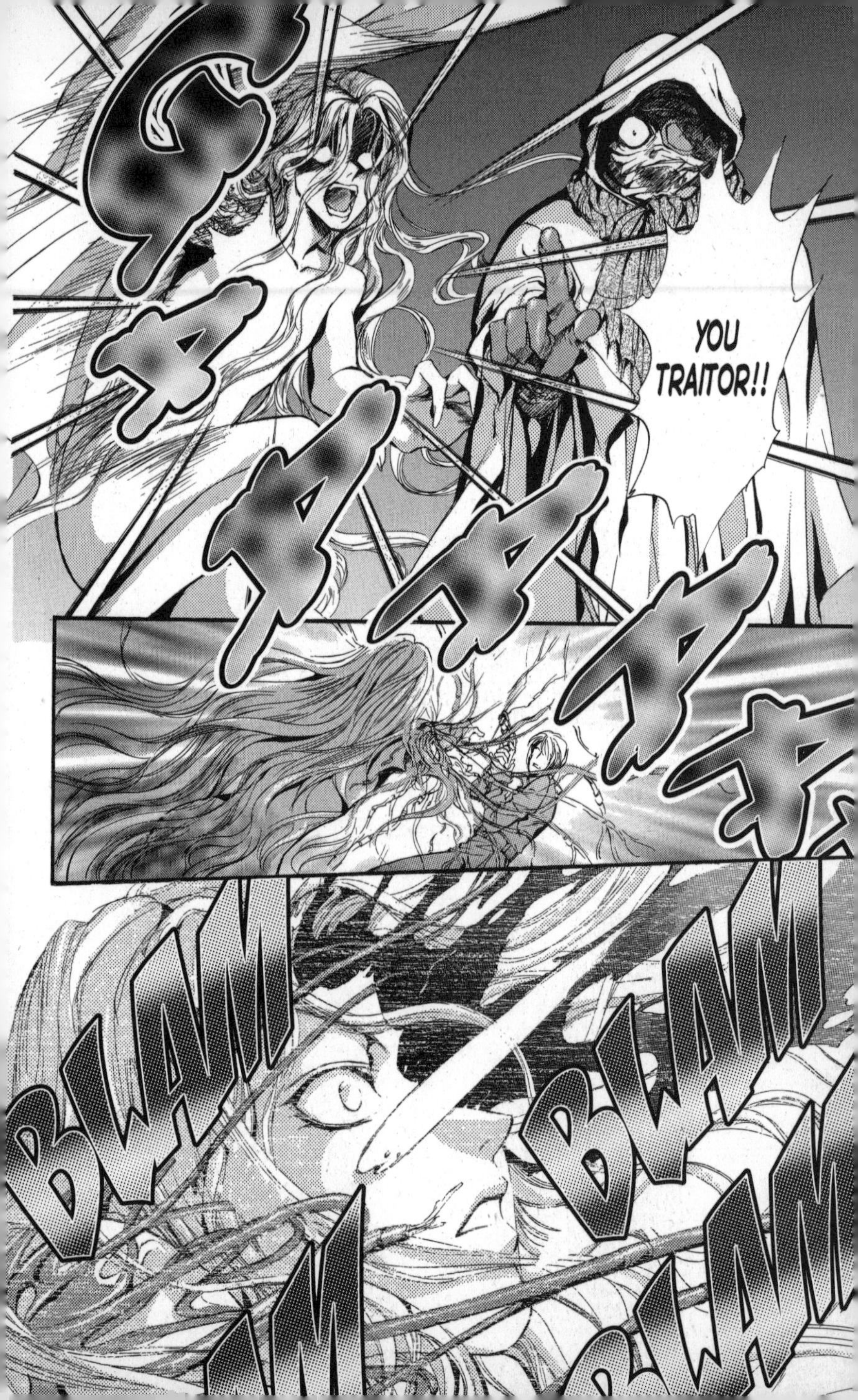
YOU TRAITOR!!
BLAM
BLAM

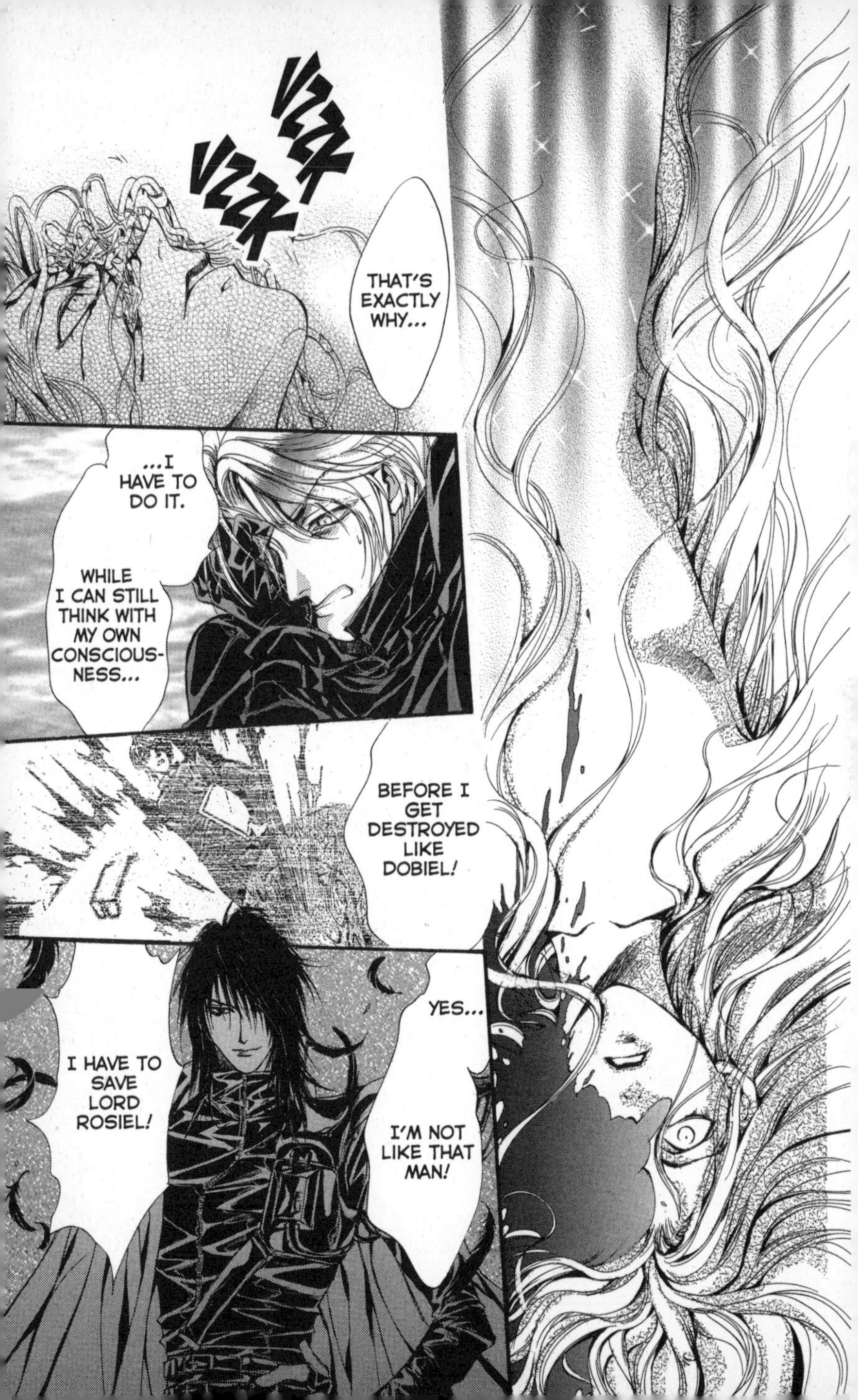
VZZK
VZZK
THAT'S EXACTLY WHY...
...I HAVE TO DO IT.
WHILE I CAN STILL THINK WITH MY OWN CONSCIOUS-NESS...
BEFORE I GET DESTROYED LIKE DOBIEL!
YES...
I'M NOT LIKE THAT MAN!
I HAVE TO SAVE LORD ROSIEL!

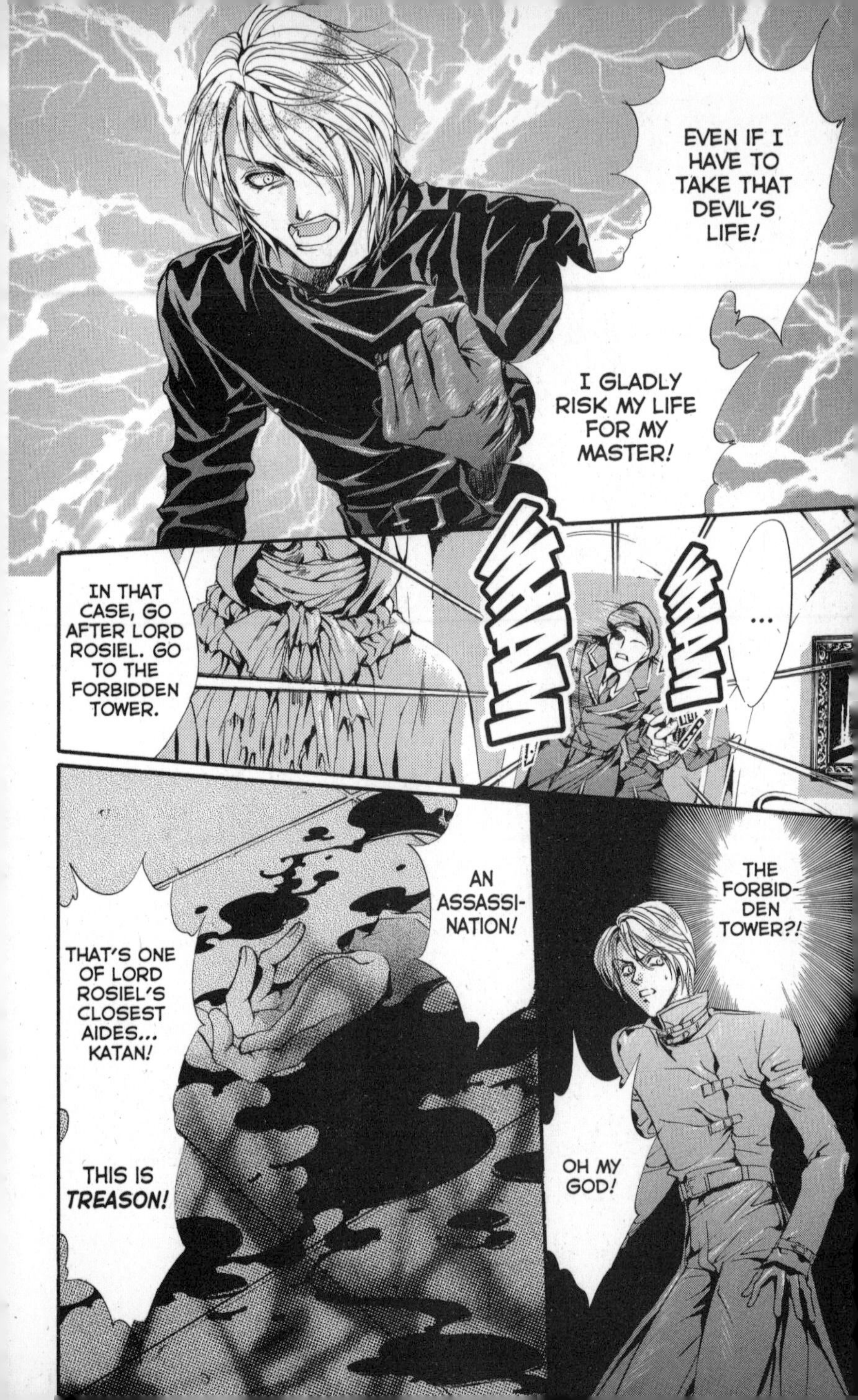
EVEN IF I HAVE TO TAKE THAT DEVIL'S LIFE!
I GLADLY RISK MY LIFE FOR MY MASTER!
...
WHAM
WHAM
IN THAT CASE, GO AFTER LORD ROSIEL. GO TO THE FORBIDDEN TOWER.
THE FORBID-DEN TOWER?!
OH MY GOD!
AN ASSASSI-NATION!
THAT'S ONE OF LORD ROSIEL'S CLOSEST AIDES... KATAN!
THIS IS *TREASON!*

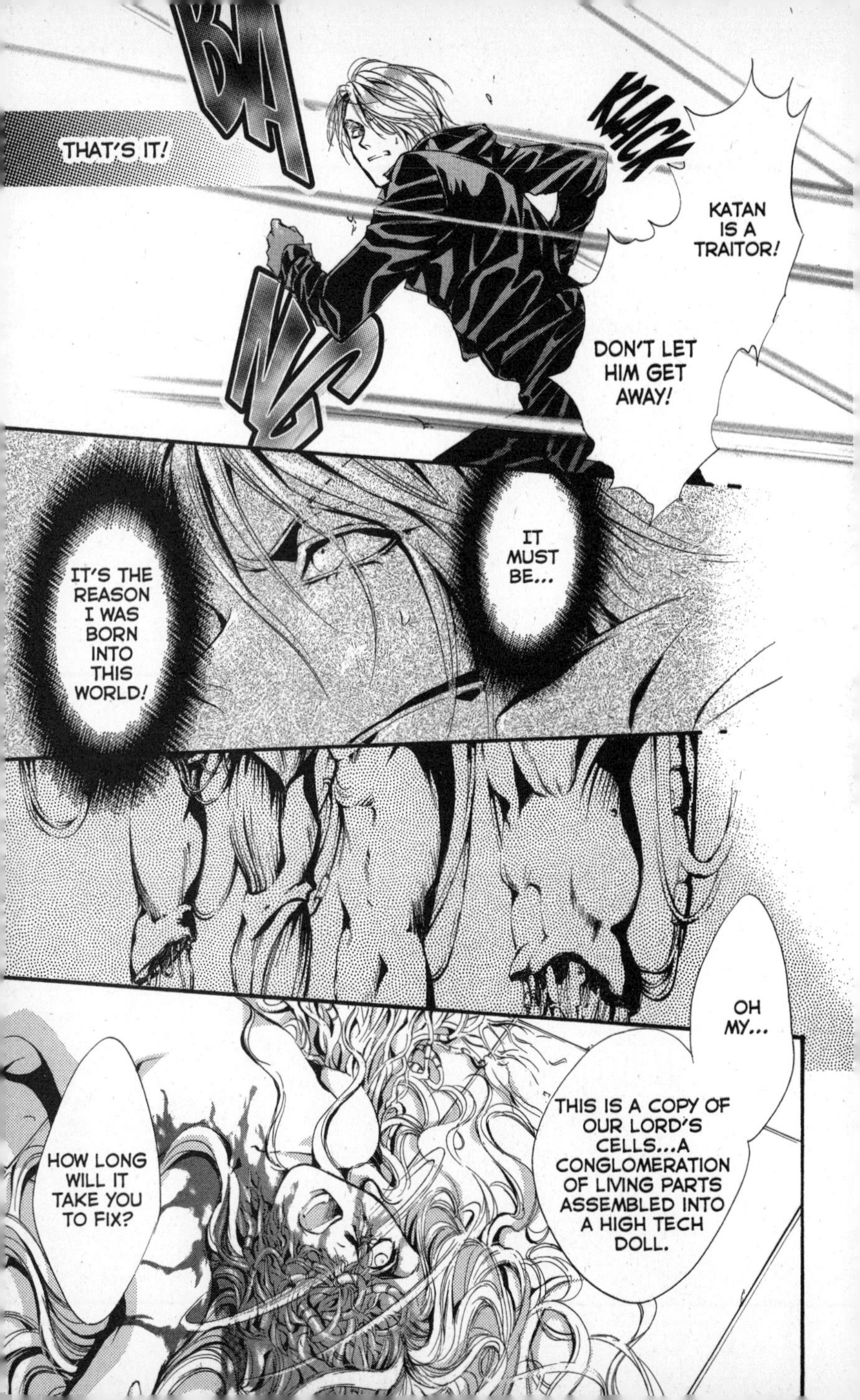
KATAN IS A TRAITOR!
DON'T LET HIM GET AWAY!
KLACK
BANG
THAT'S IT!
IT MUST BE...
IT'S THE REASON I WAS BORN INTO THIS WORLD!
OH MY...
THIS IS A COPY OF OUR LORD'S CELLS...A CONGLOMERATION OF LIVING PARTS ASSEMBLED INTO A HIGH TECH DOLL.
HOW LONG WILL IT TAKE YOU TO FIX?

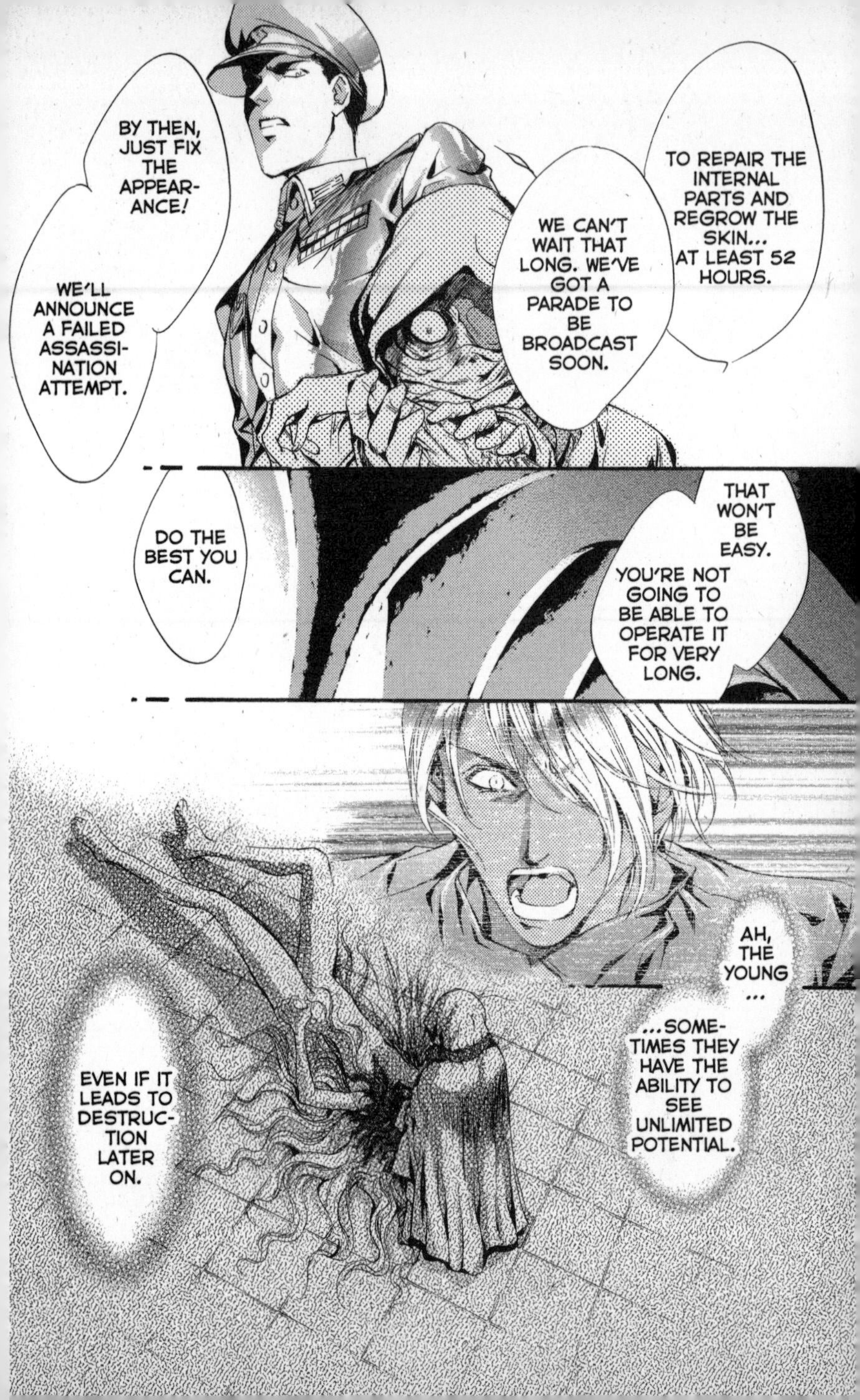
TO REPAIR THE INTERNAL PARTS AND REGROW THE SKIN... AT LEAST 52 HOURS.
WE CAN'T WAIT THAT LONG. WE'VE GOT A PARADE TO BE BROADCAST SOON.
BY THEN, JUST FIX THE APPEARANCE!
WE'LL ANNOUNCE A FAILED ASSASSINATION ATTEMPT.
THAT WON'T BE EASY.
YOU'RE NOT GOING TO BE ABLE TO OPERATE IT FOR VERY LONG.
DO THE BEST YOU CAN.
AH, THE YOUNG...
...SOMETIMES THEY HAVE THE ABILITY TO SEE UNLIMITED POTENTIAL.
EVEN IF IT LEADS TO DESTRUCTION LATER ON.

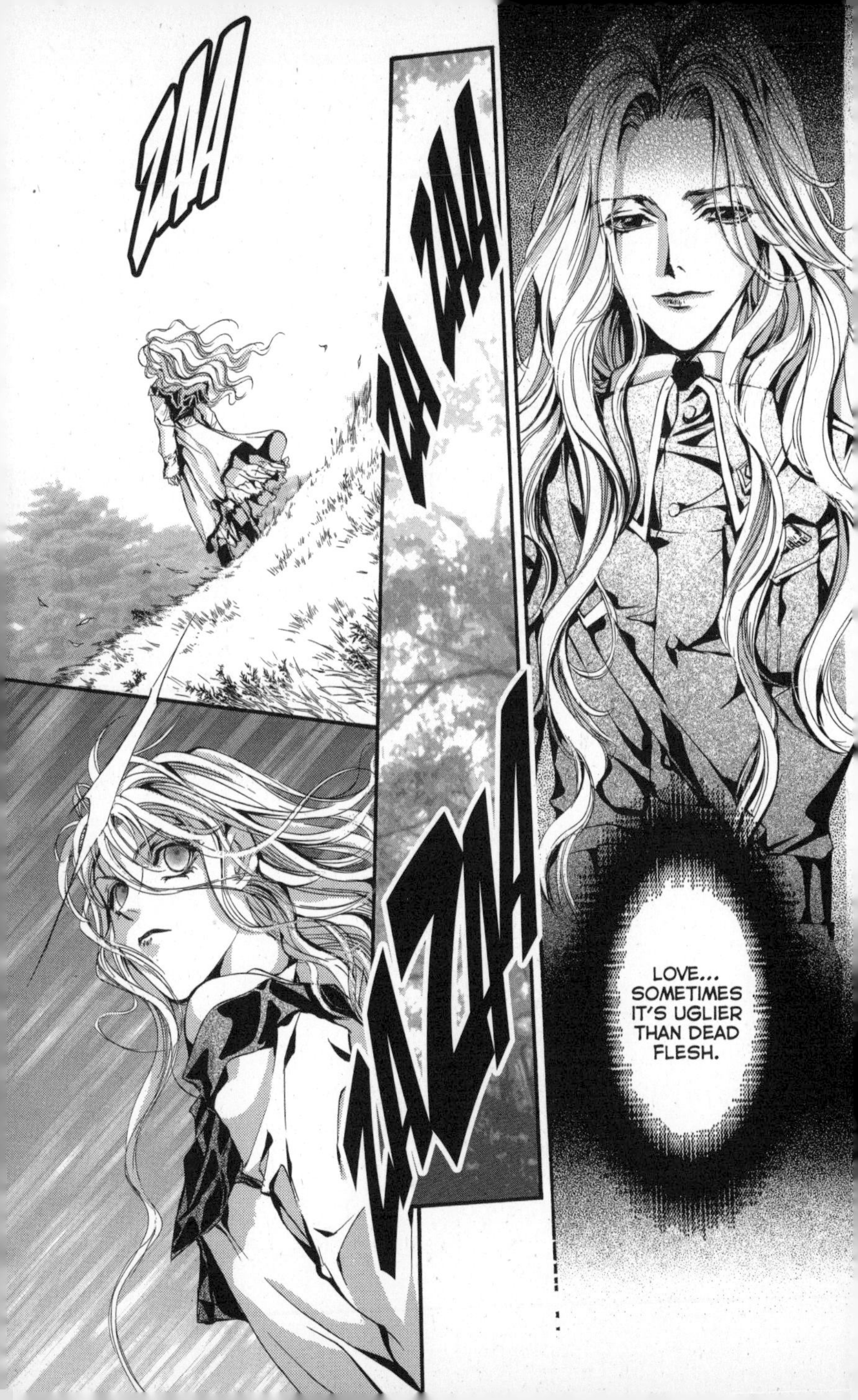
LOVE... SOMETIMES IT'S UGLIER THAN DEAD FLESH.
ZA ZAA
ZAA

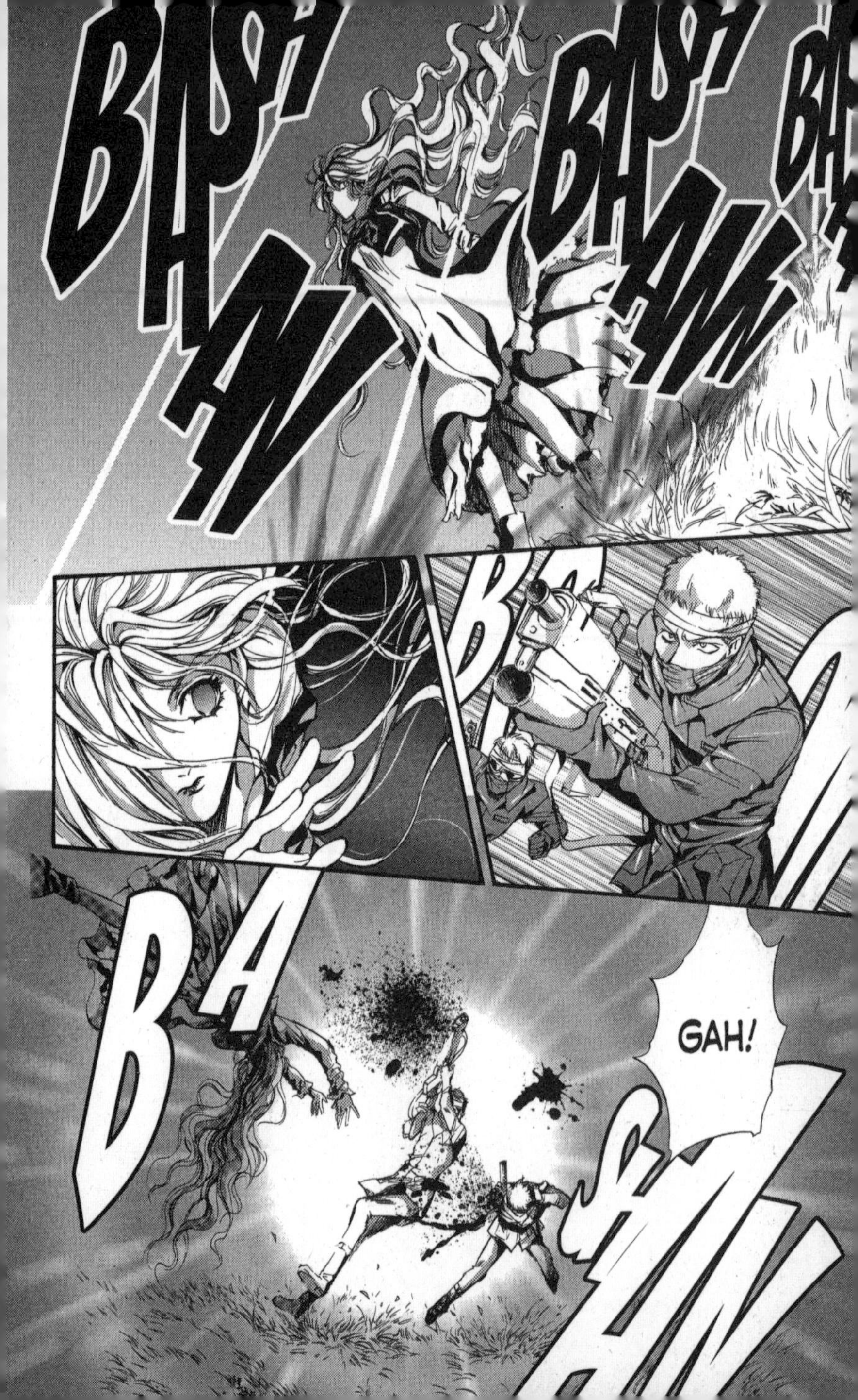
GAH!

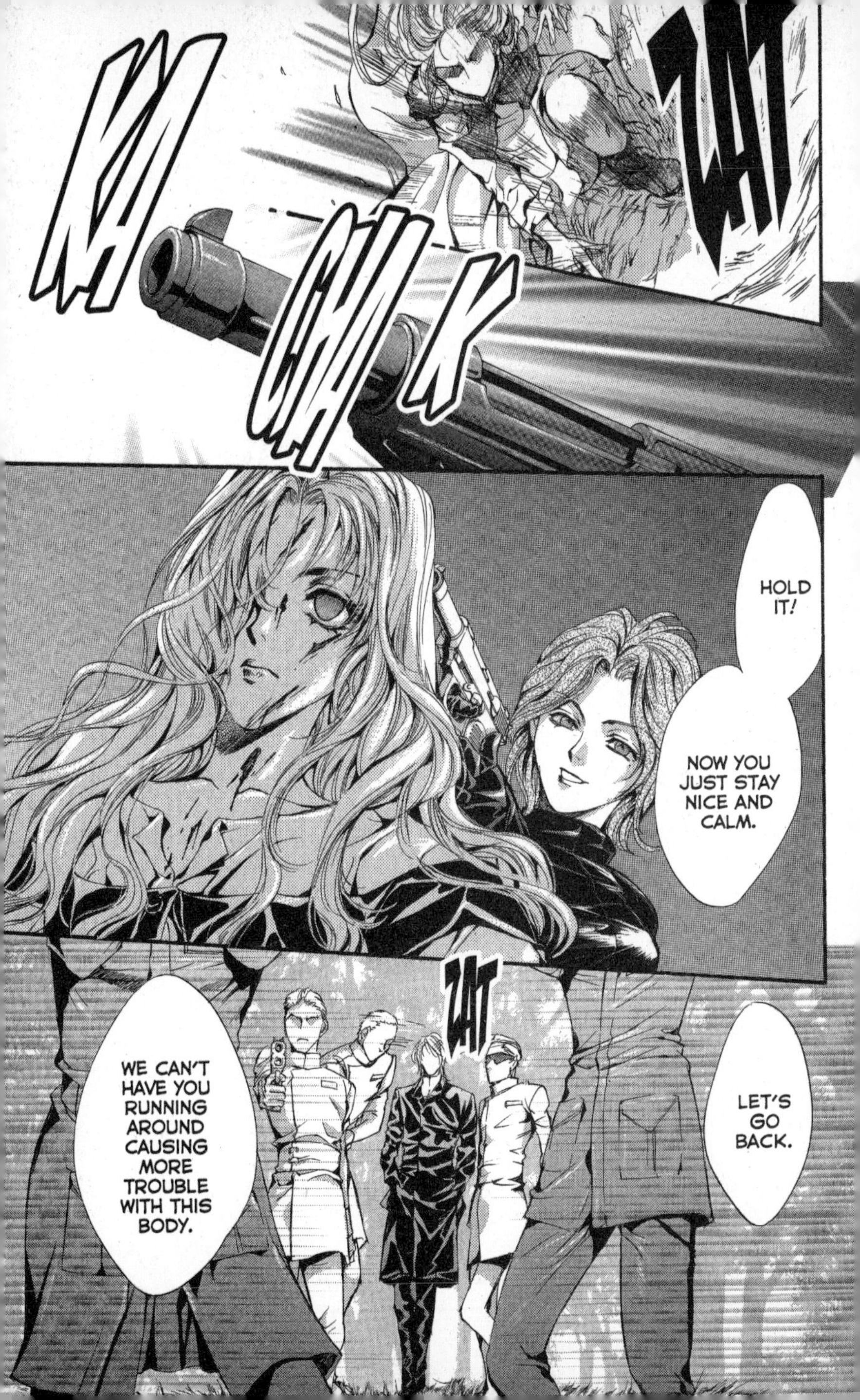
ZAT
KA
CHAK
HOLD IT!
NOW YOU JUST STAY NICE AND CALM.
LET'S GO BACK.
ZAT
WE CAN'T HAVE YOU RUNNING AROUND CAUSING MORE TROUBLE WITH THIS BODY.

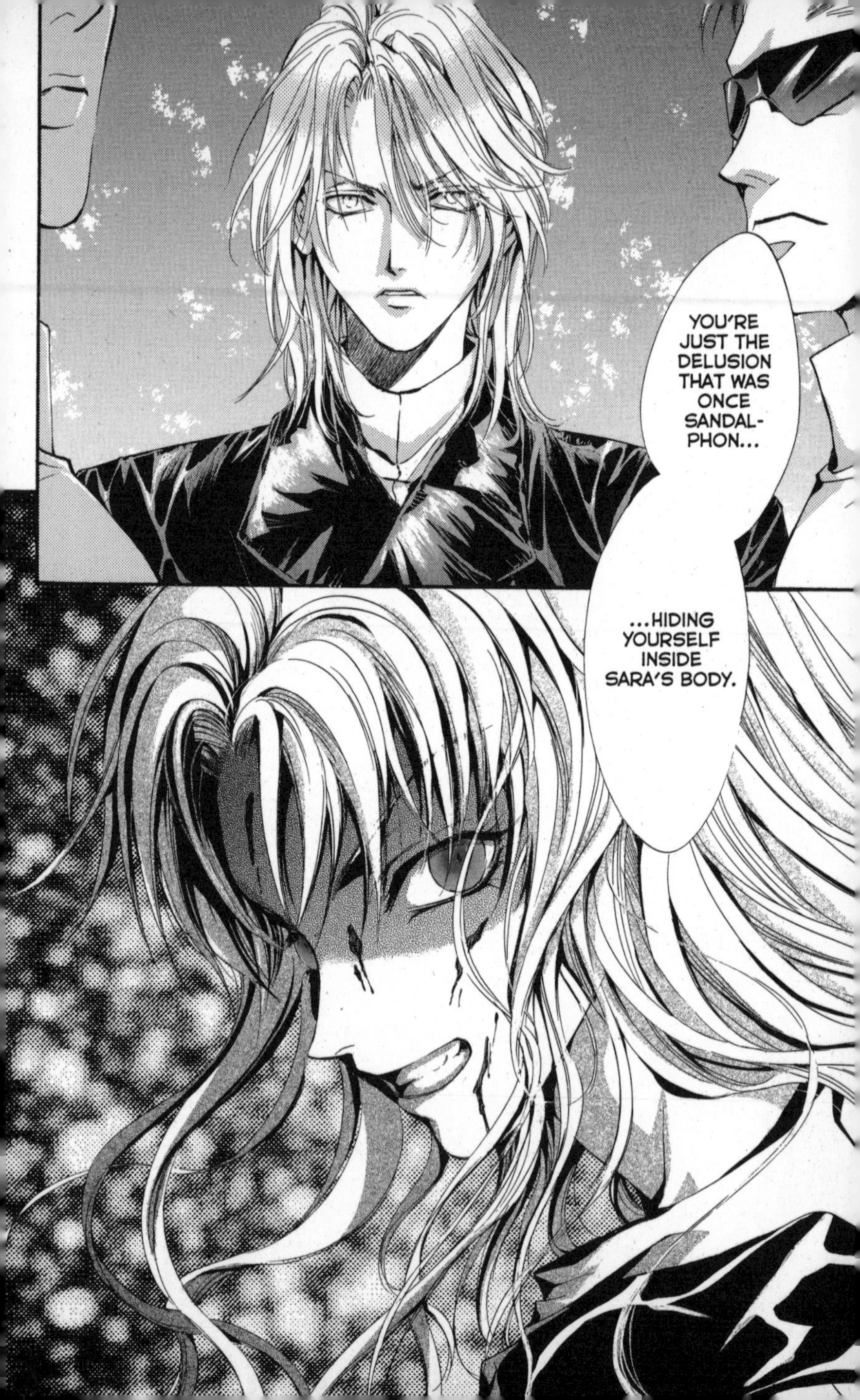
YOU'RE JUST THE DELUSION THAT WAS ONCE SANDAL-PHON...
...HIDING YOURSELF INSIDE SARA'S BODY.

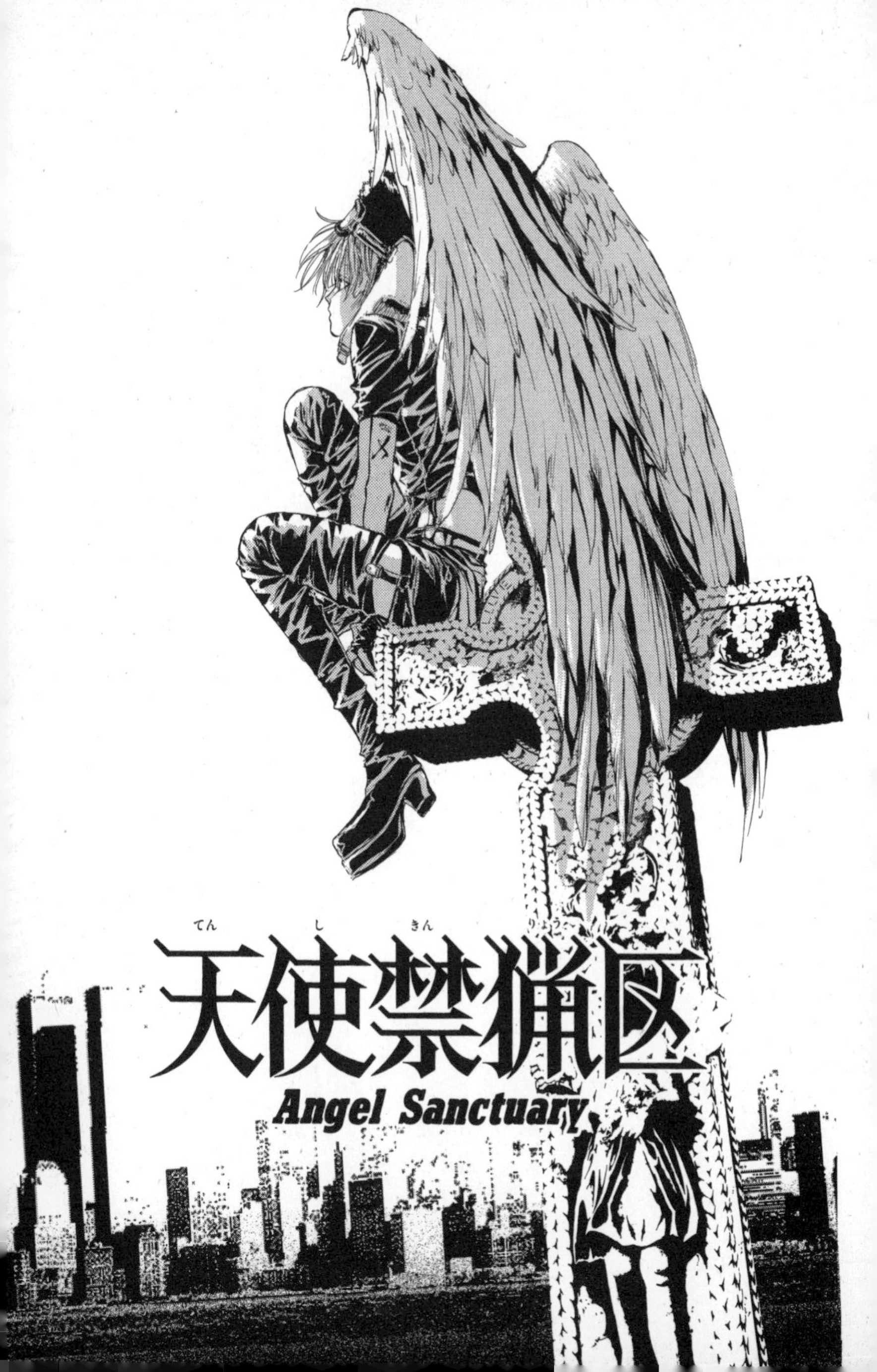
天使禁猟区
Angel Sanctuary

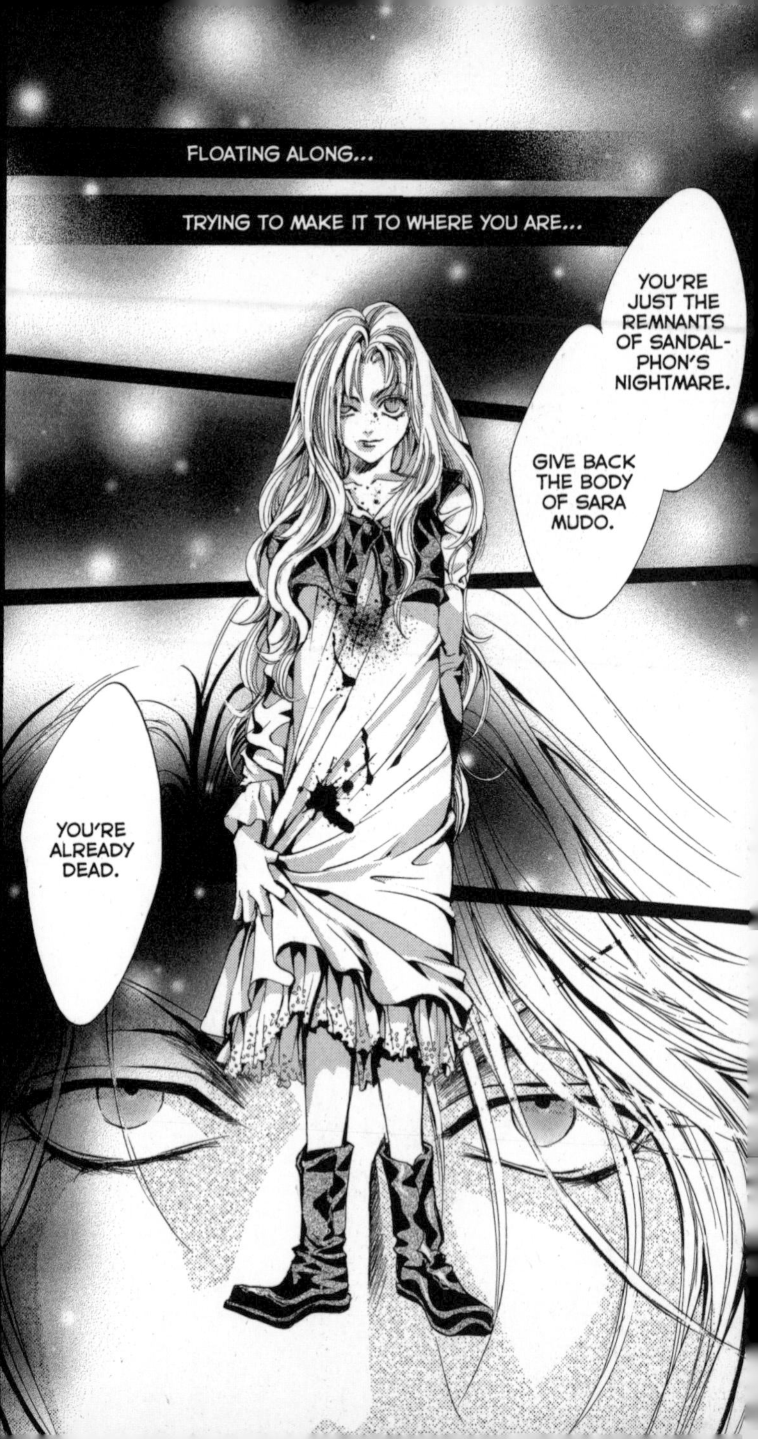
FLOATING ALONG...
TRYING TO MAKE IT TO WHERE YOU ARE...
YOU'RE JUST THE REMNANTS OF SANDAL-PHON'S NIGHTMARE.
GIVE BACK THE BODY OF SARA MUDO.
YOU'RE ALREADY DEAD.

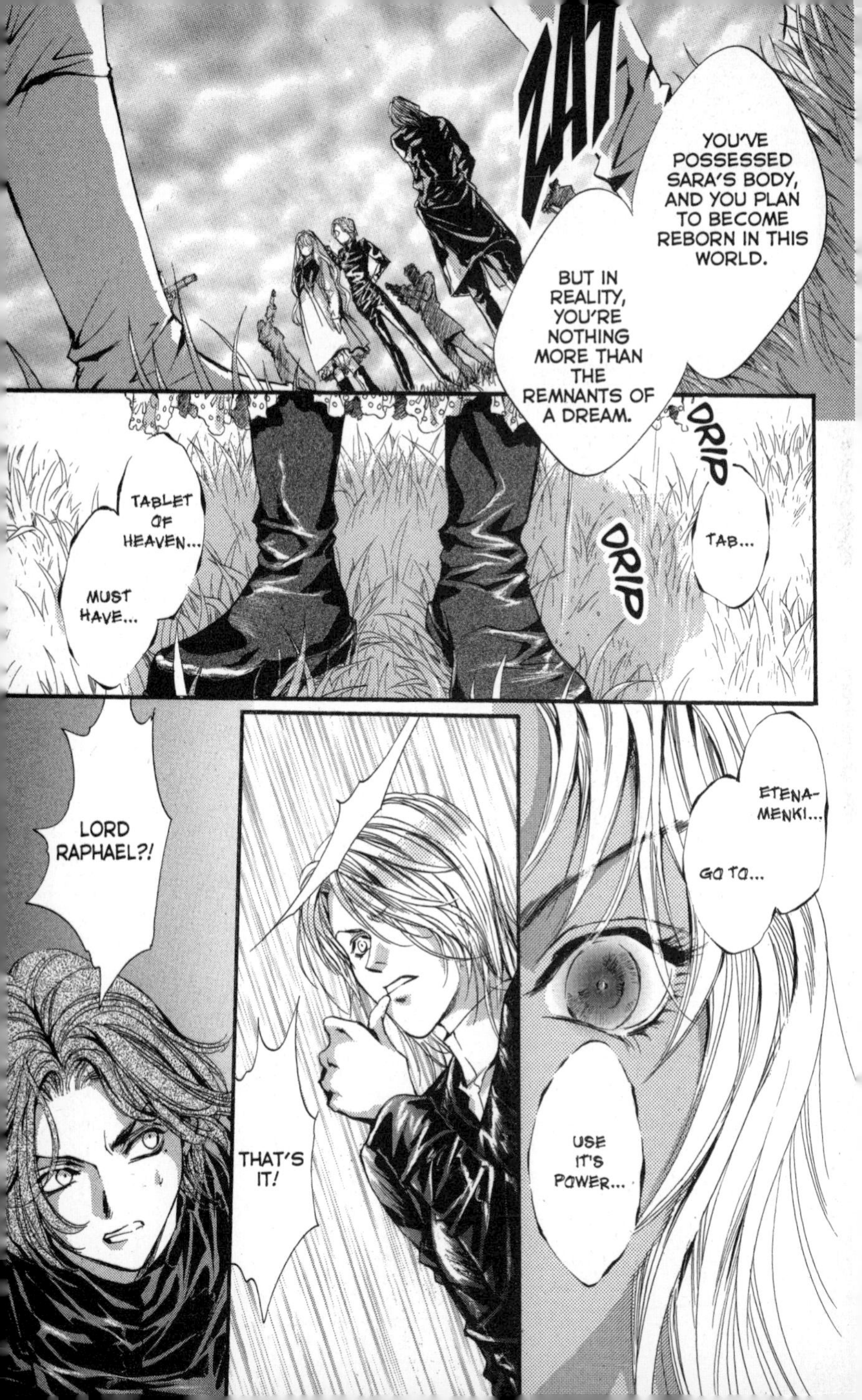
ZAP
YOU'VE POSSESSED SARA'S BODY, AND YOU PLAN TO BECOME REBORN IN THIS WORLD.
BUT IN REALITY, YOU'RE NOTHING MORE THAN THE REMNANTS OF A DREAM.
DRIP
DRIP
TAB...
TABLET OF HEAVEN...
MUST HAVE...
ETENA-MENKI...
GO TO...
USE IT'S POWER...
THAT'S IT!
LORD RAPHAEL?!

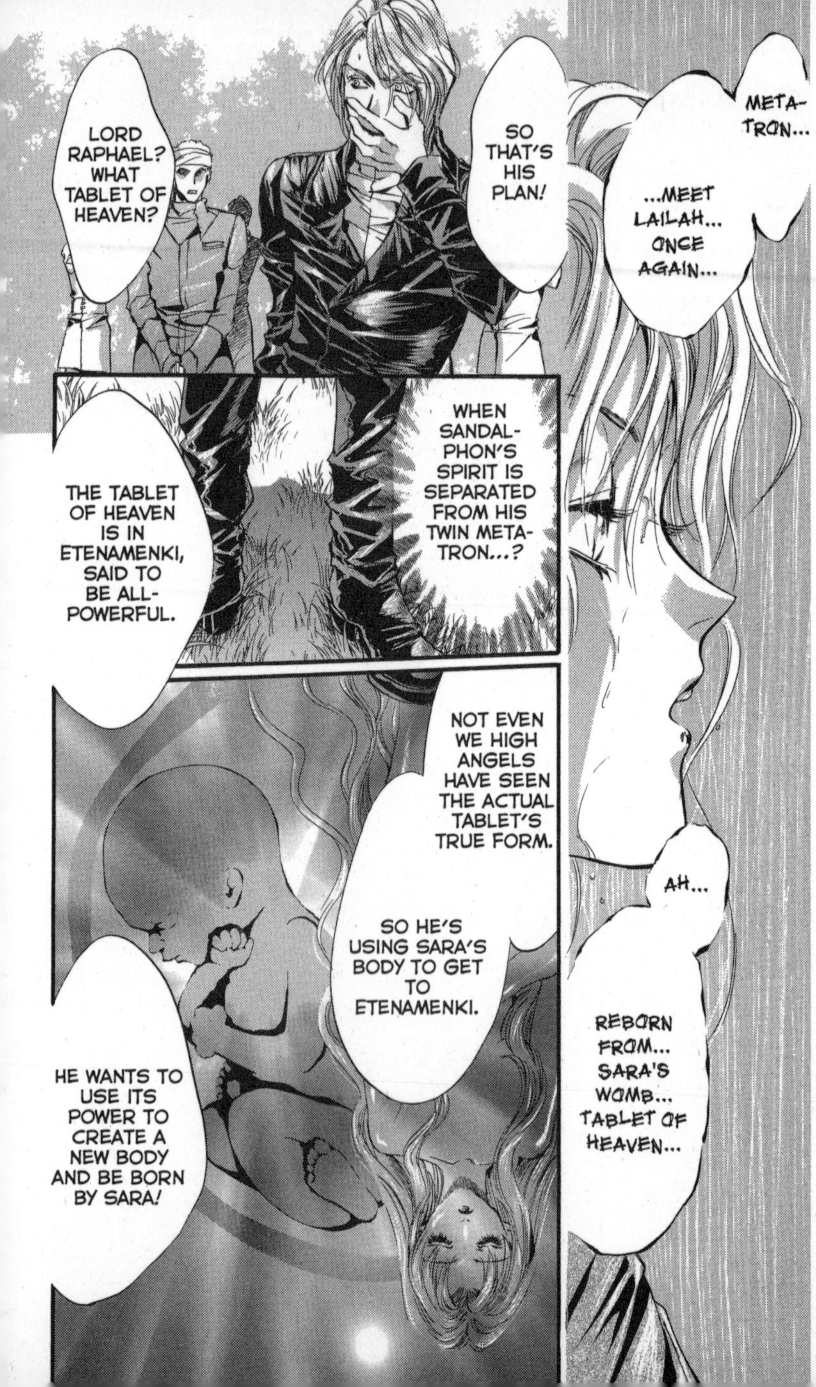
METATRON...
...MEET LAILAH... ONCE AGAIN...
AH...
REBORN FROM... SARA'S WOMB... TABLET OF HEAVEN...
SO THAT'S HIS PLAN!
LORD RAPHAEL? WHAT TABLET OF HEAVEN?
WHEN SANDALPHON'S SPIRIT IS SEPARATED FROM HIS TWIN METATRON...?
THE TABLET OF HEAVEN IS IN ETENAMENKI, SAID TO BE ALL-POWERFUL.
NOT EVEN WE HIGH ANGELS HAVE SEEN THE ACTUAL TABLET'S TRUE FORM.
SO HE'S USING SARA'S BODY TO GET TO ETENAMENKI.
HE WANTS TO USE ITS POWER TO CREATE A NEW BODY AND BE BORN BY SARA!

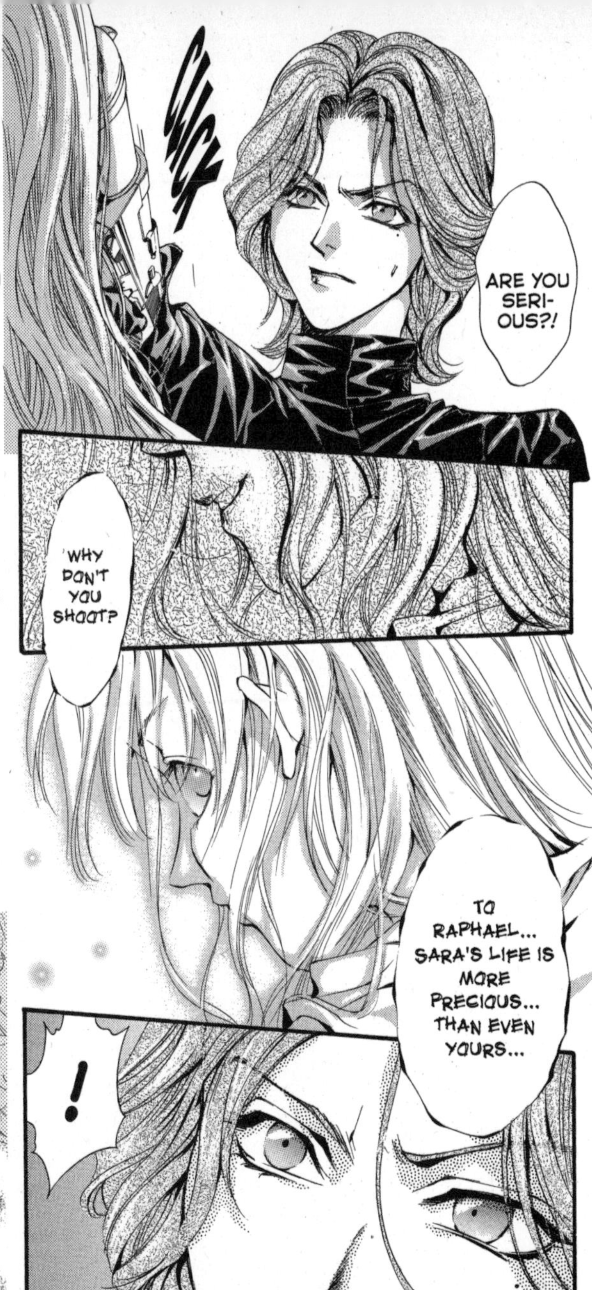
CLICK
ARE YOU SERI-OUS?!
WHY DON'T YOU SHOOT?
TO RAPHAEL... SARA'S LIFE IS MORE PRECIOUS... THAN EVEN YOURS...
!

To those of you who also bought the OVA, thanks! It was expensive, wasn't it? I went to see the voice recording three times, but I didn't really have much to do, so I just sat there and watched. The climax in the second tape had some really loud emotion sound effects, since it's anime. But even though it was Setsuna's body, when Alexiel possessed him, the voice was Alexiel's. Kinda strange, huh? The voice actor for Adam Kadamon wasn't quite feminine enough, I think. Maybe it's a difference of interpretation. But I'm impressed that the anime could keep up with this whacked-out story as well as it did. My gratitude goes out to the entire staff.

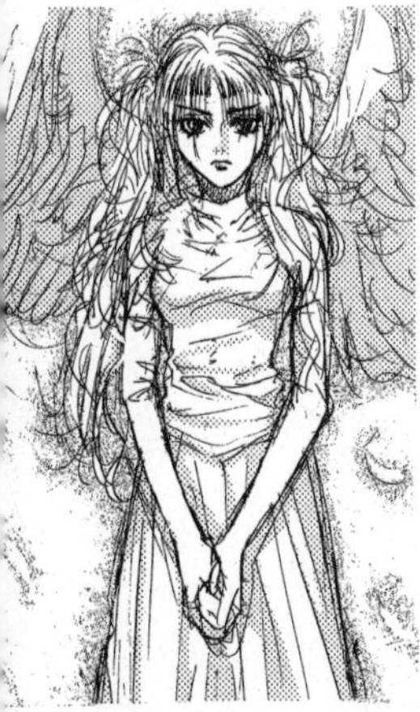

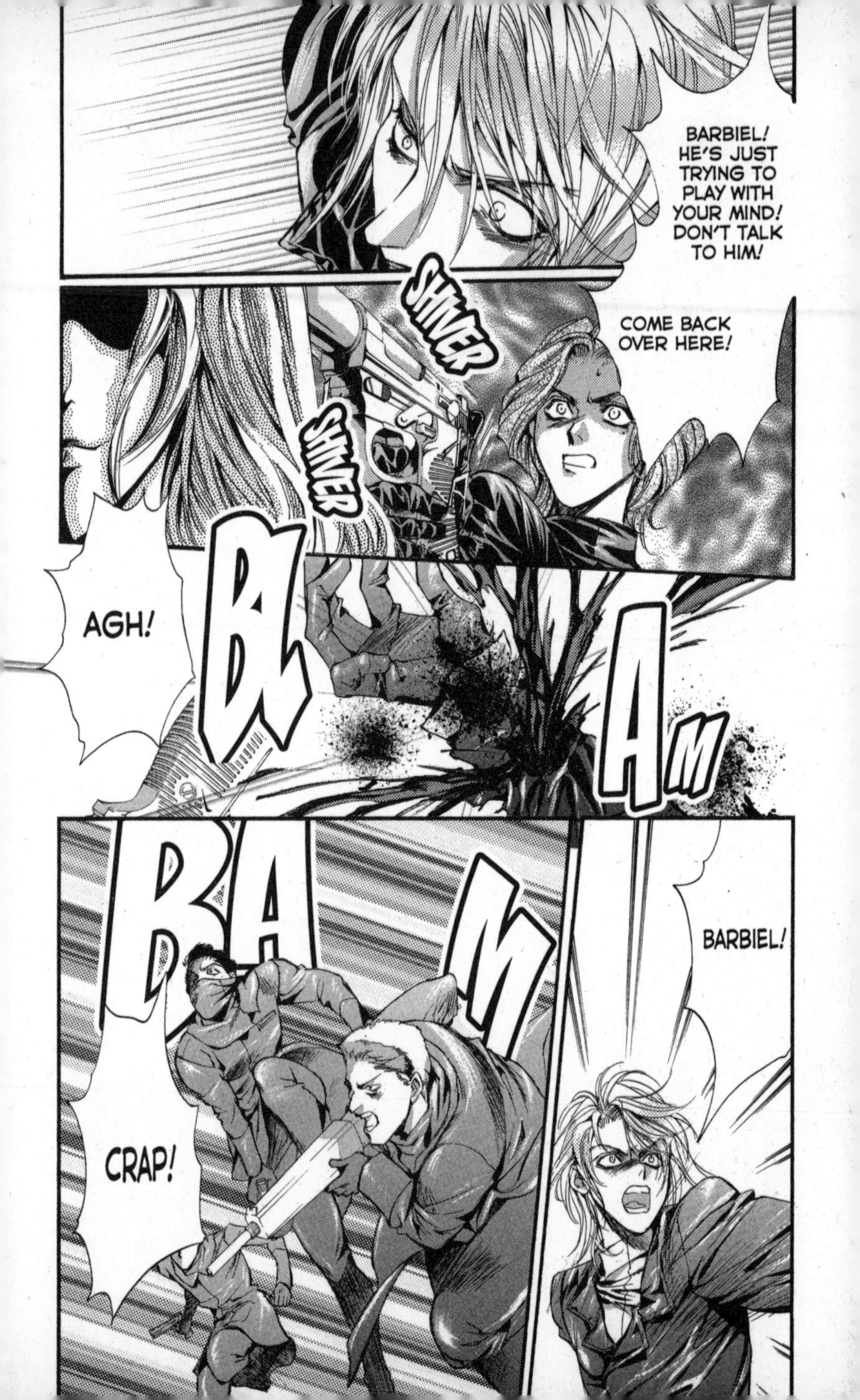
BARBIEL! HE'S JUST TRYING TO PLAY WITH YOUR MIND! DON'T TALK TO HIM!
COME BACK OVER HERE!
SHIVER
SHIVER
BLAM
AGH!
BARBIEL!
BAM
CRAP!

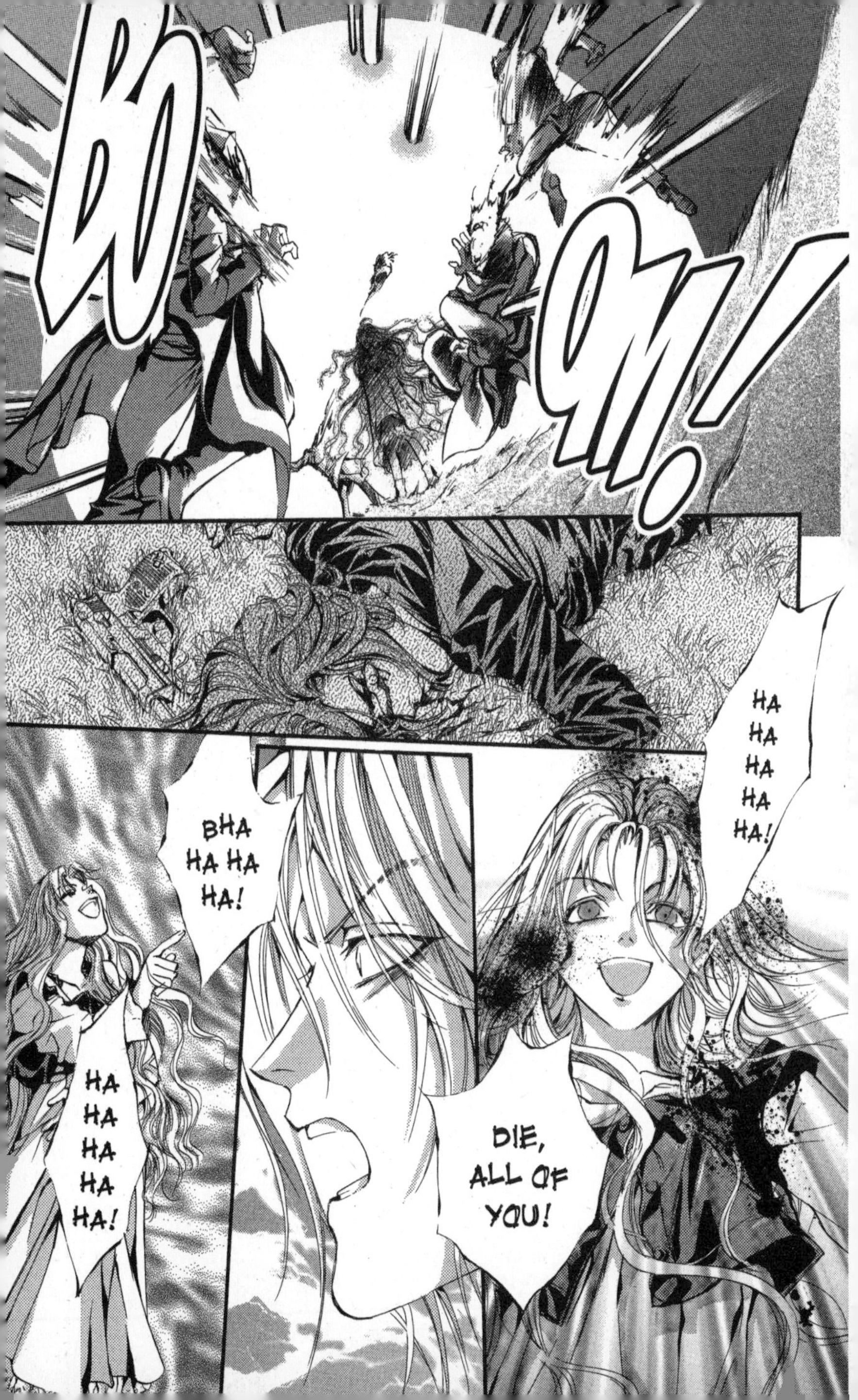
HA HA HA HA HA!
DIE, ALL OF YOU!
BHA HA HA HA!
HA HA HA HA HA!

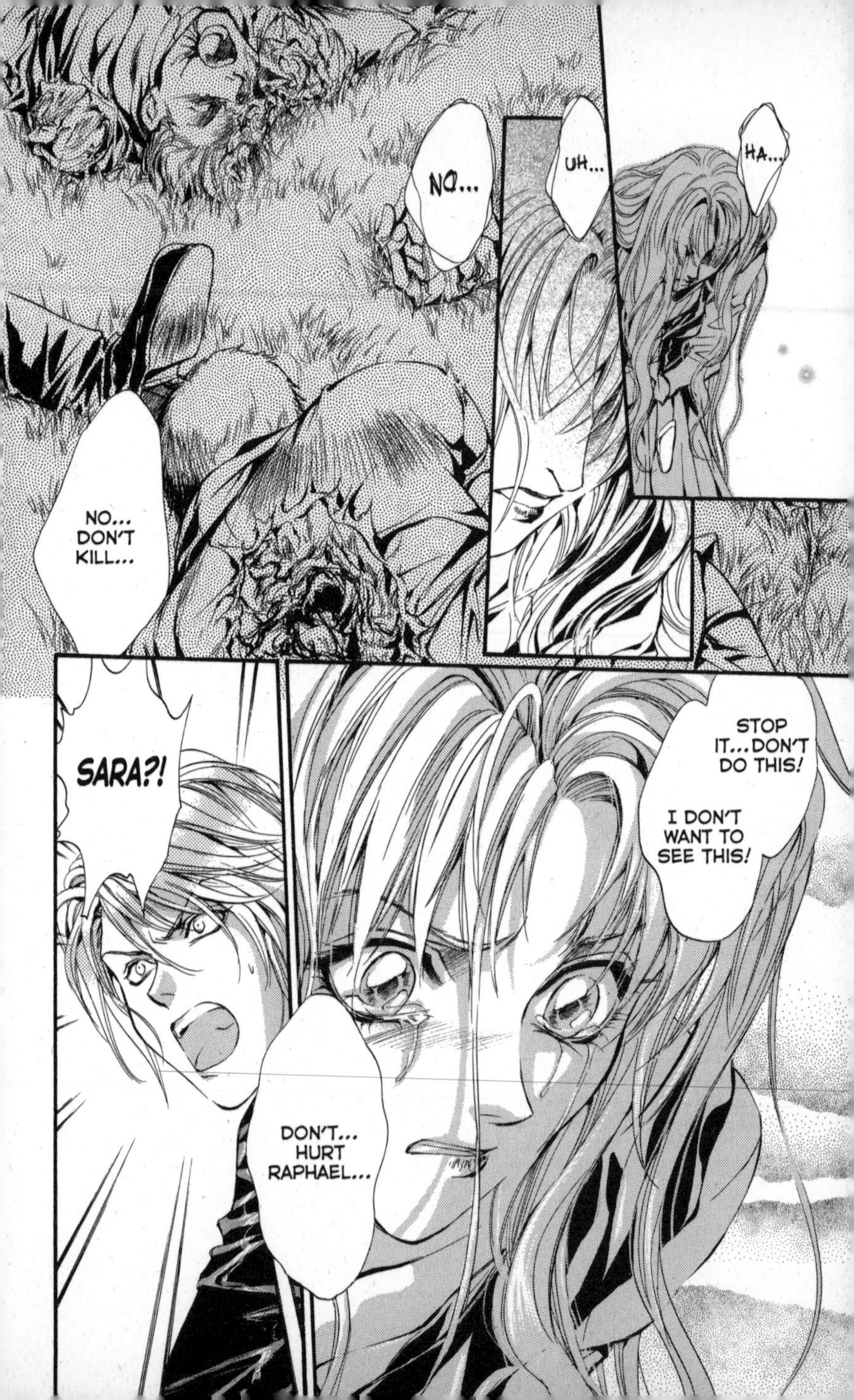
HA...
UH...
NO...
NO... DON'T KILL...
STOP IT... DON'T DO THIS!
I DON'T WANT TO SEE THIS!
DON'T... HURT RAPHAEL...
SARA?!

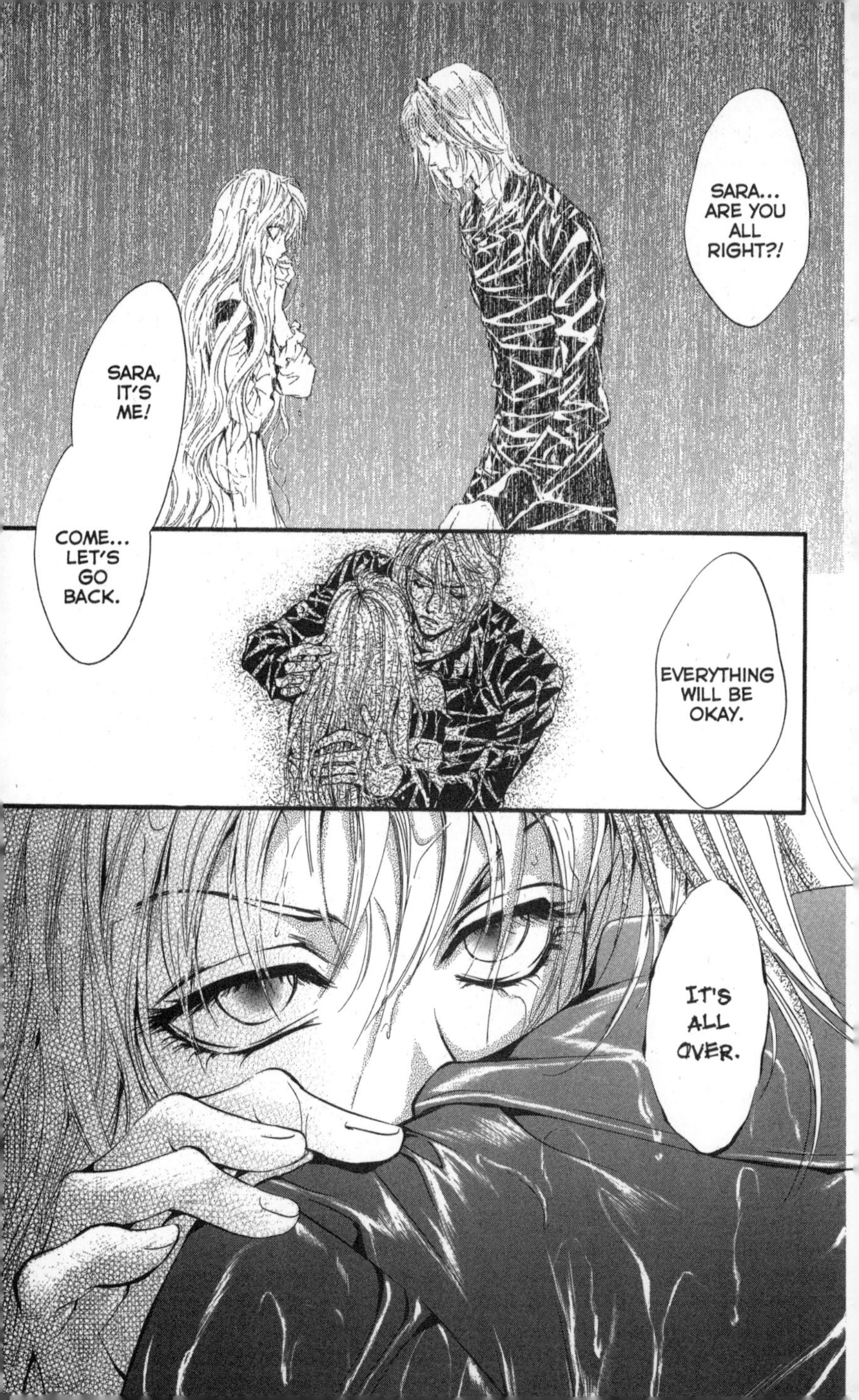
SARA... ARE YOU ALL RIGHT?!
SARA, IT'S ME!
COME... LET'S GO BACK.
EVERYTHING WILL BE OKAY.
IT'S ALL OVER.

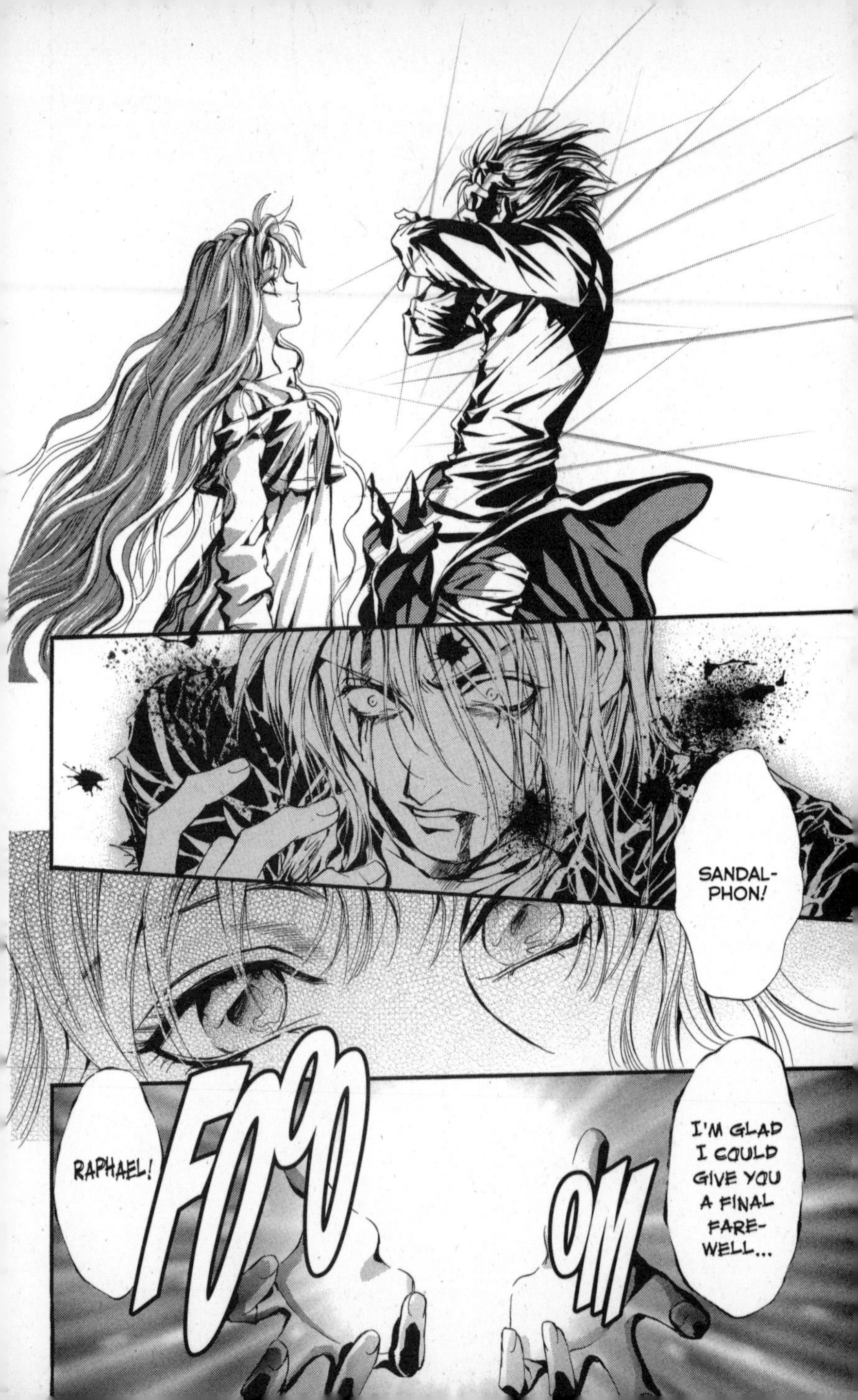
SANDAL-
PHON!
I'M GLAD I COULD GIVE YOU A FINAL FARE-WELL...
FOOOM
RAPHAEL!

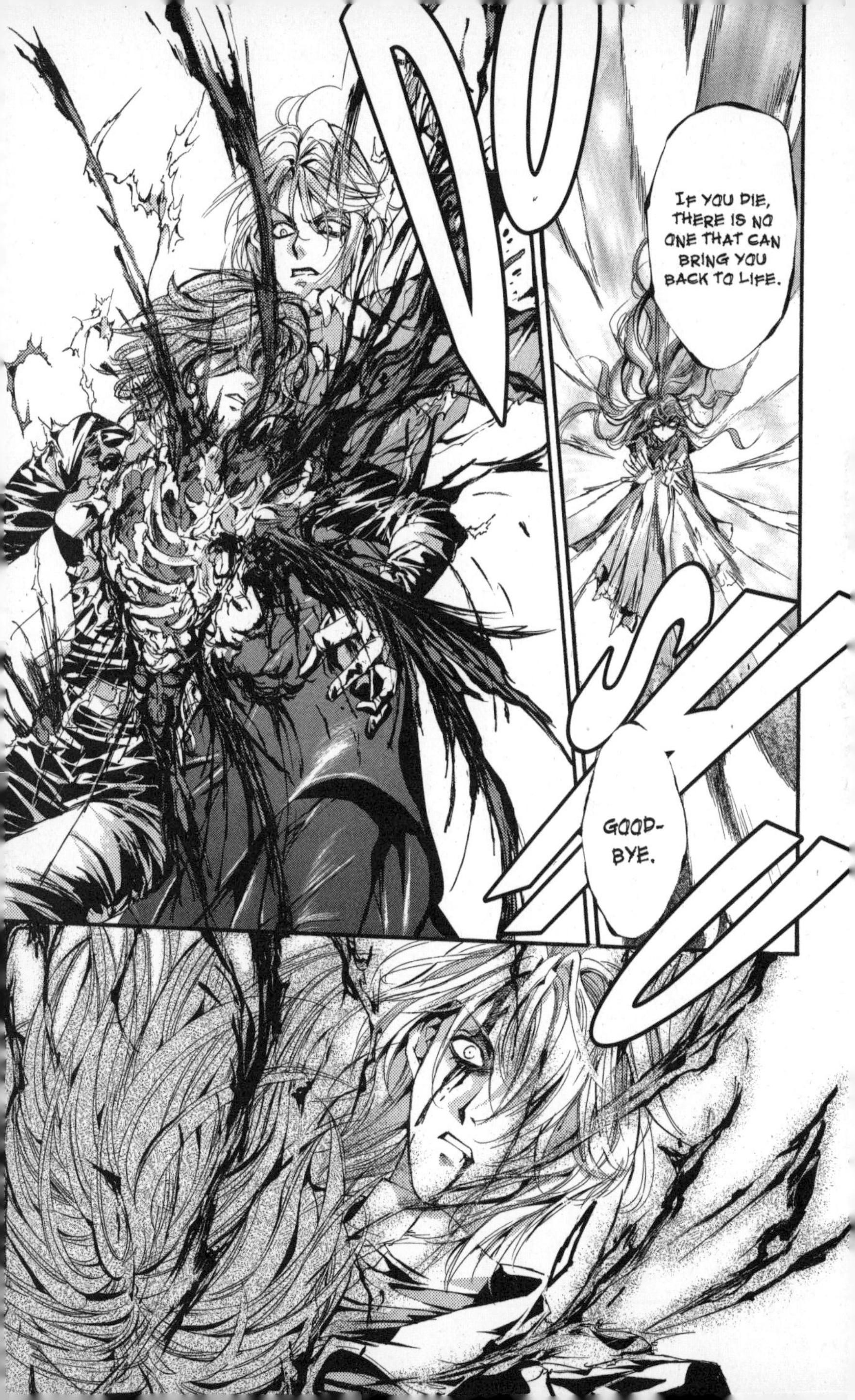
IF YOU DIE, THERE IS NO ONE THAT CAN BRING YOU BACK TO LIFE.
GOOD-BYE.

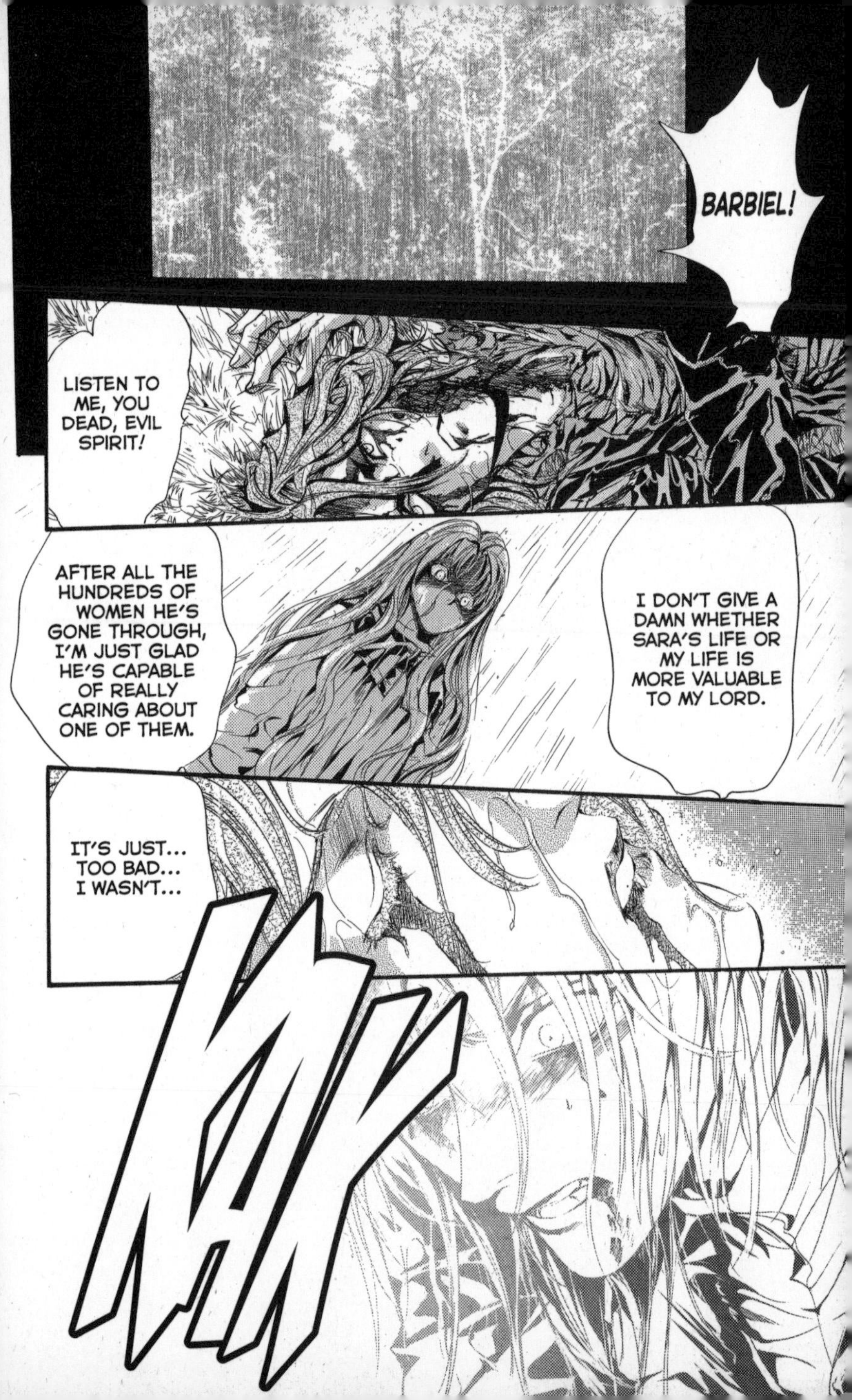
BARBIEL!
LISTEN TO ME, YOU DEAD, EVIL SPIRIT!
I DON'T GIVE A DAMN WHETHER SARA'S LIFE OR MY LIFE IS MORE VALUABLE TO MY LORD.
AFTER ALL THE HUNDREDS OF WOMEN HE'S GONE THROUGH, I'M JUST GLAD HE'S CAPABLE OF REALLY CARING ABOUT ONE OF THEM.
IT'S JUST... TOO BAD... I WASN'T...

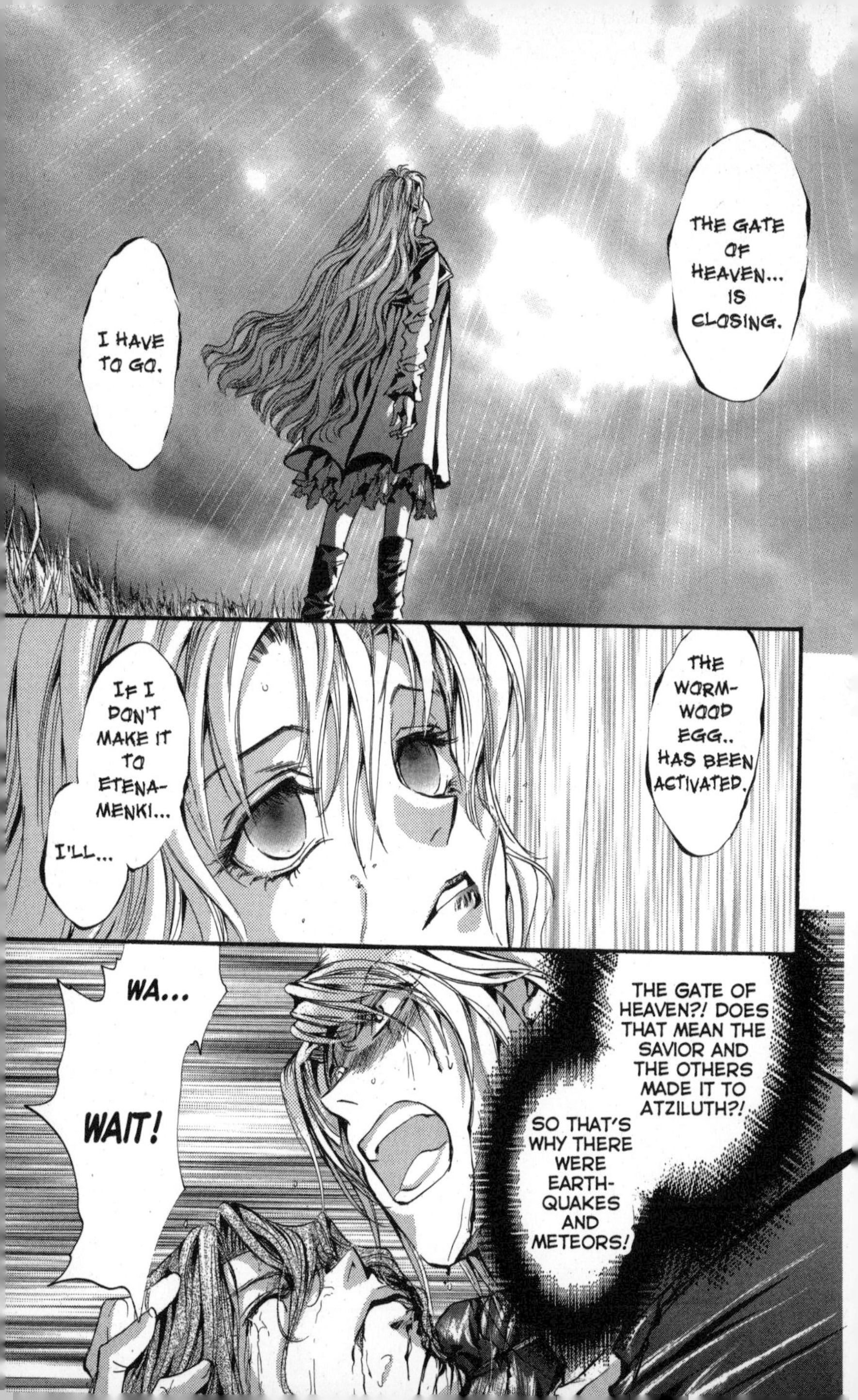
THE GATE OF HEAVEN... IS CLOSING.
I HAVE TO GO.
THE WORM-WOOD EGG.. HAS BEEN ACTIVATED.
IF I DON'T MAKE IT TO ETENA-MENKI...
I'LL...
THE GATE OF HEAVEN?! DOES THAT MEAN THE SAVIOR AND THE OTHERS MADE IT TO ATZILUTH?!
SO THAT'S WHY THERE WERE EARTH-QUAKES AND METEORS!
WA...
WAIT!

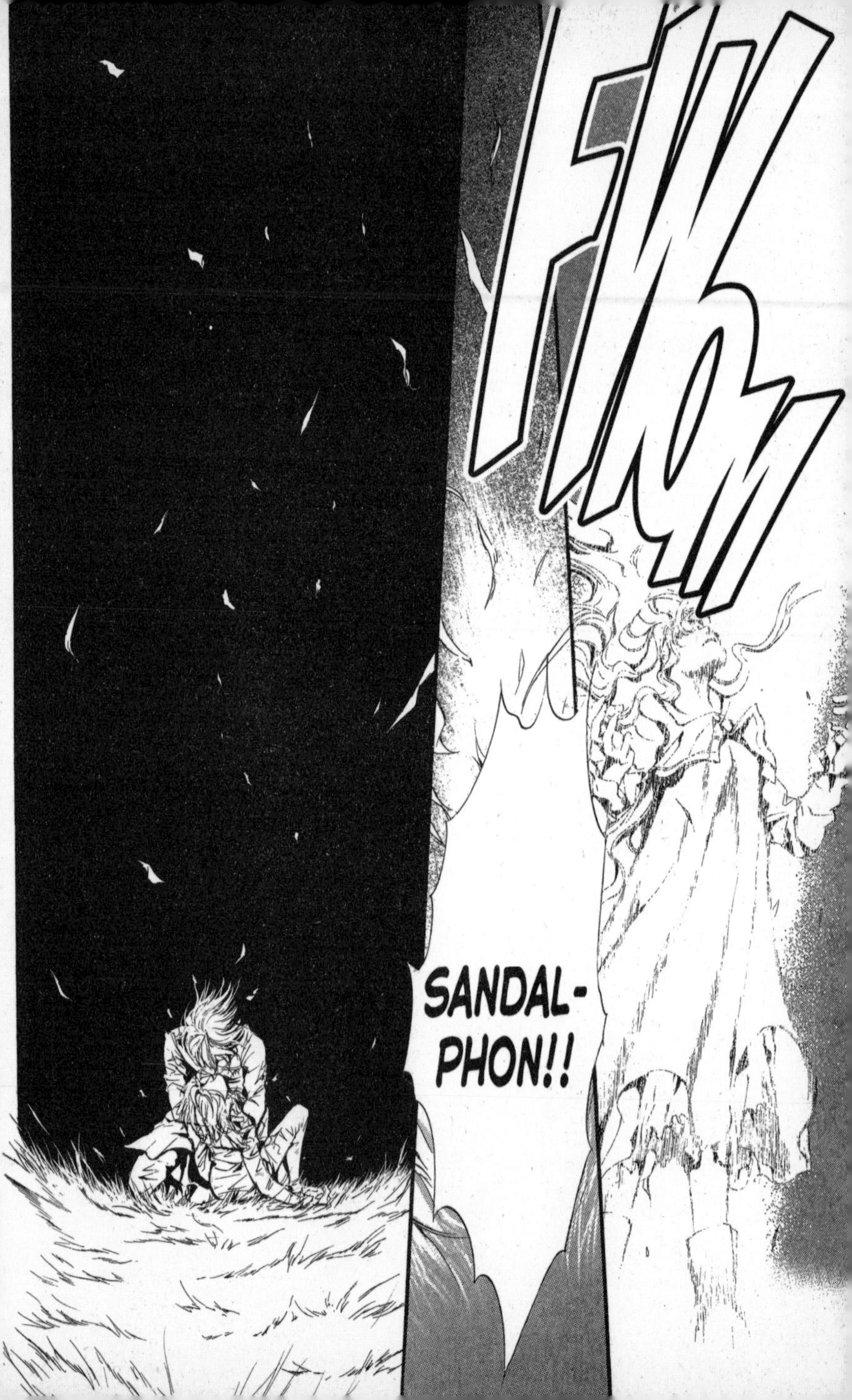
SANDAL-
PHON!!

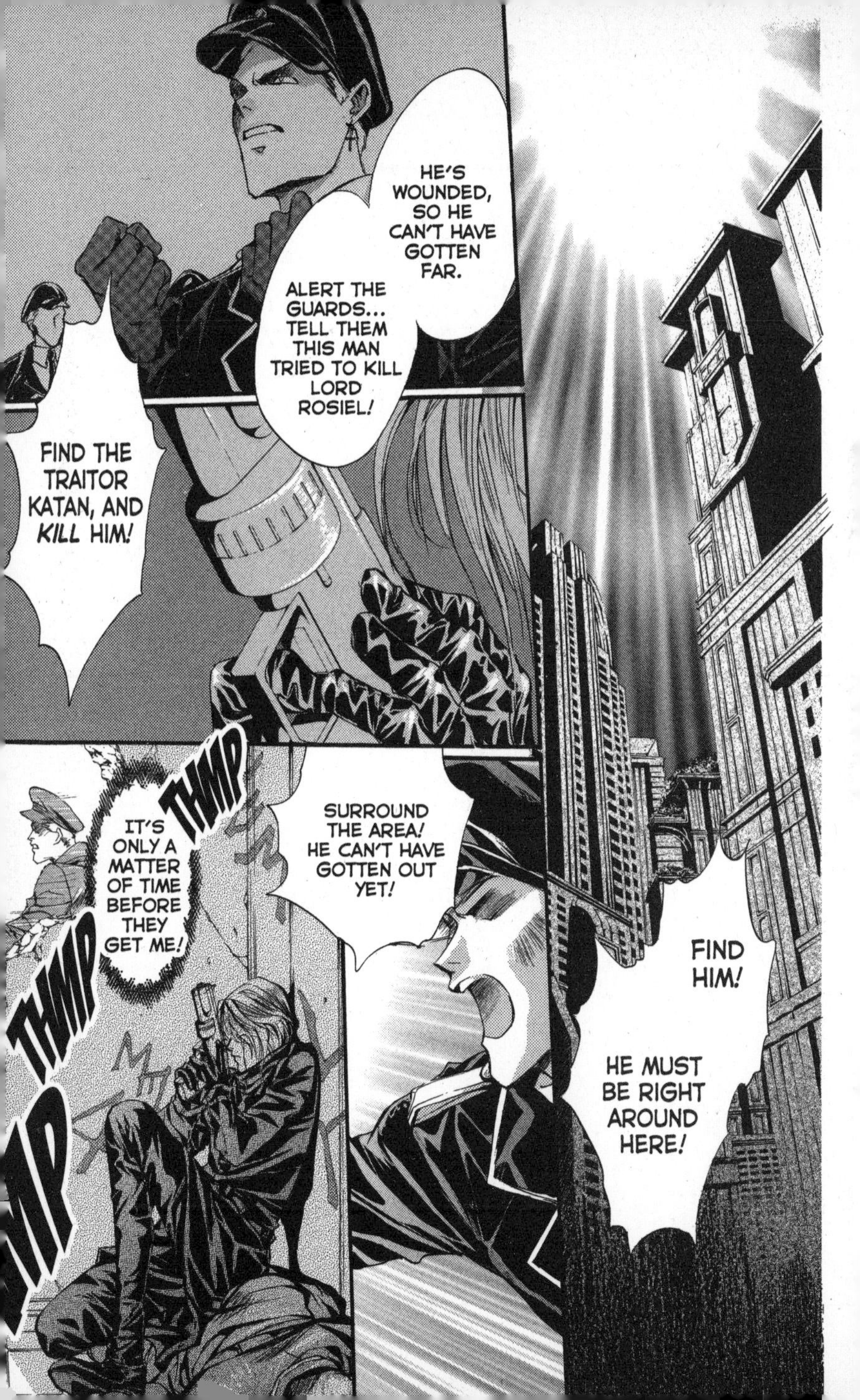
FIND HIM!
HE MUST BE RIGHT AROUND HERE!
HE'S WOUNDED, SO HE CAN'T HAVE GOTTEN FAR.
ALERT THE GUARDS... TELL THEM THIS MAN TRIED TO KILL LORD ROSIEL!
FIND THE TRAITOR KATAN, AND *KILL* HIM!
SURROUND THE AREA! HE CAN'T HAVE GOTTEN OUT YET!
THMP
IT'S ONLY A MATTER OF TIME BEFORE THEY GET ME!
THMP
THMP

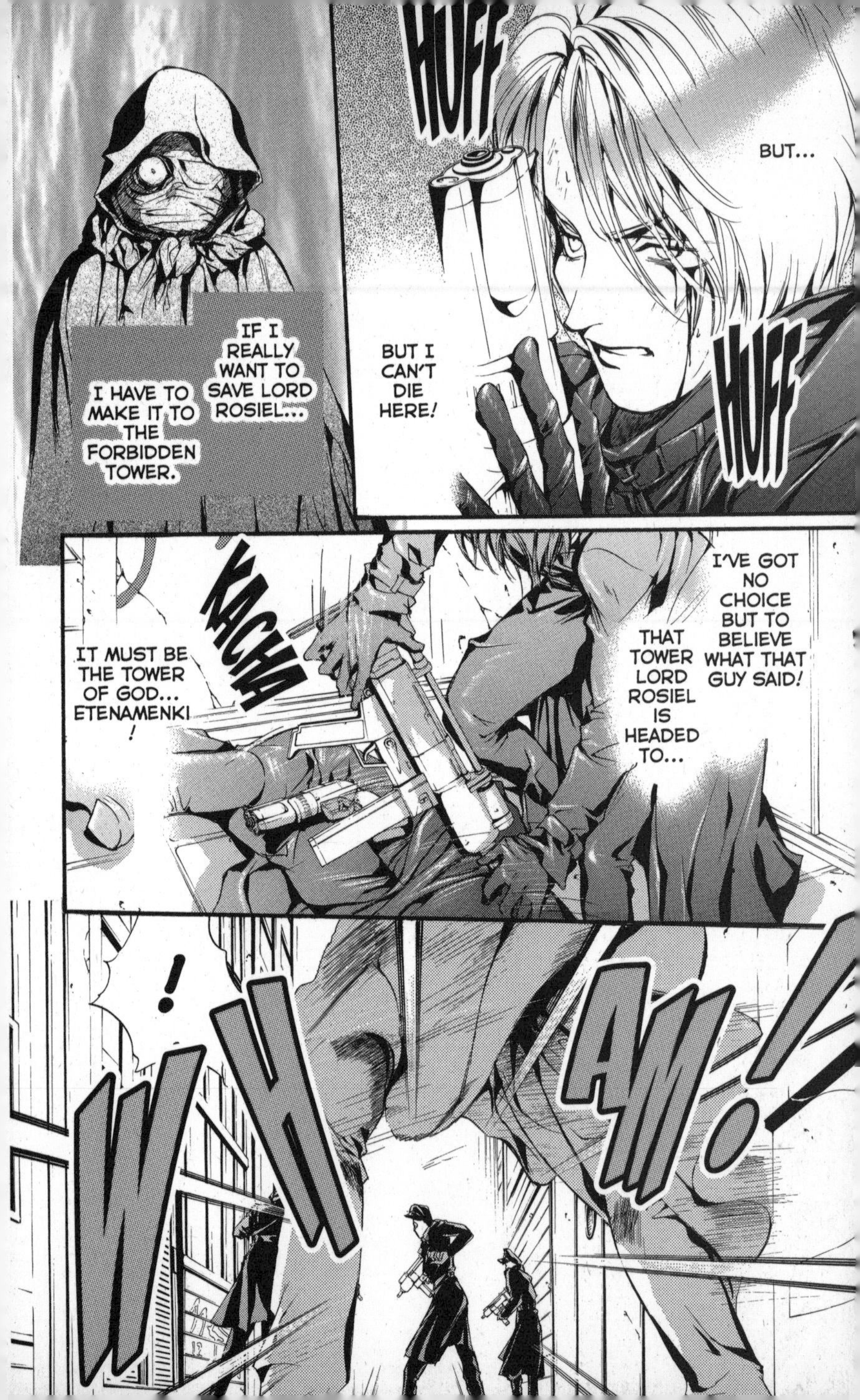

HUFF
BUT...
HUFF
BUT I CAN'T DIE HERE!
IF I REALLY WANT TO SAVE LORD ROSIEL...
I HAVE TO MAKE IT TO THE FORBIDDEN TOWER.
KACHA
I'VE GOT NO CHOICE BUT TO BELIEVE WHAT THAT GUY SAID!
THAT TOWER LORD ROSIEL IS HEADED TO...
IT MUST BE THE TOWER OF GOD... ETENAMENKI!
!
WHAM!!

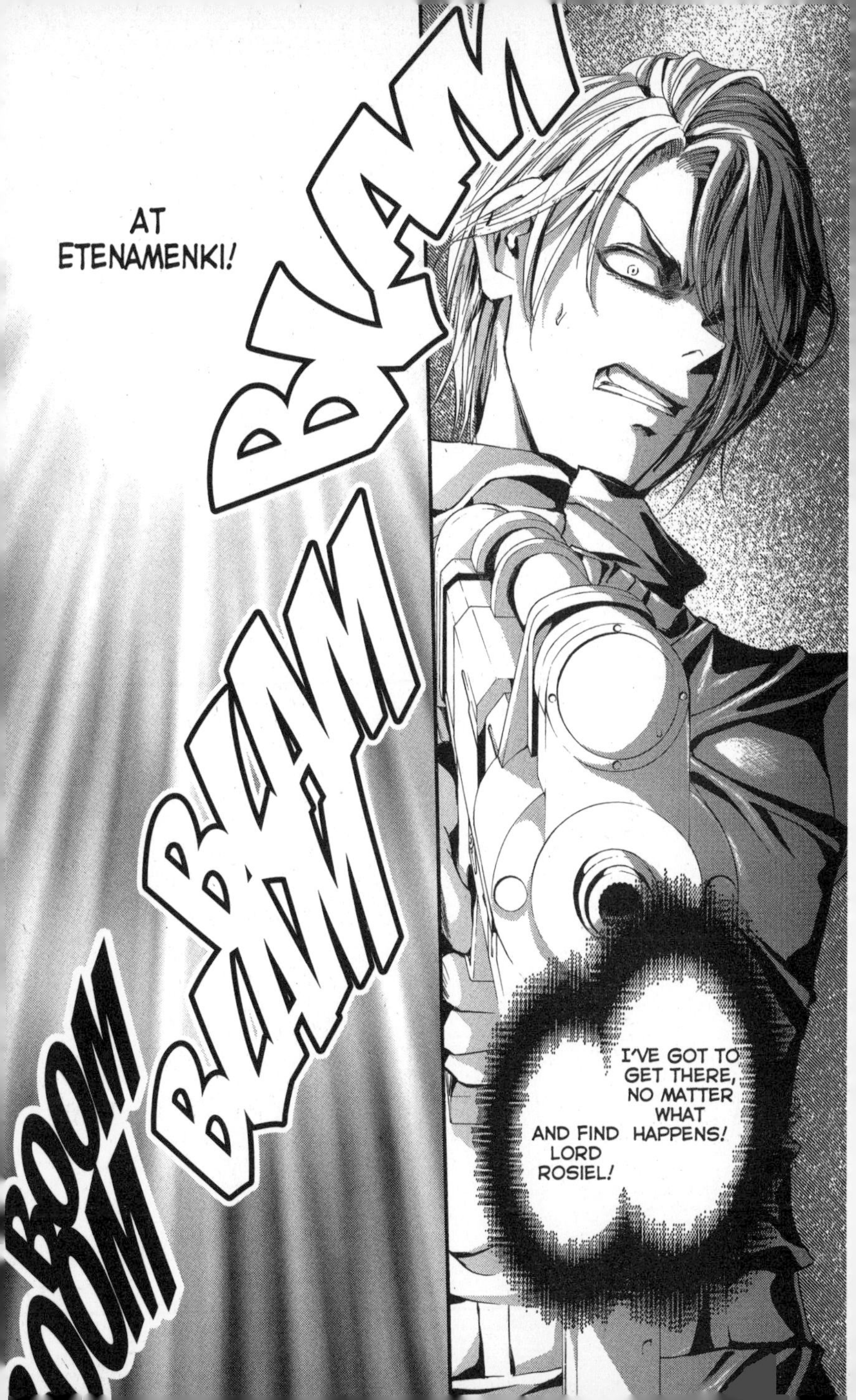
I'VE GOT TO GET THERE, NO MATTER WHAT HAPPENS!
AND FIND LORD ROSIEL!
BLAM
BLAM BLAM
BOOM BOOM
AT ETENAMENKI!

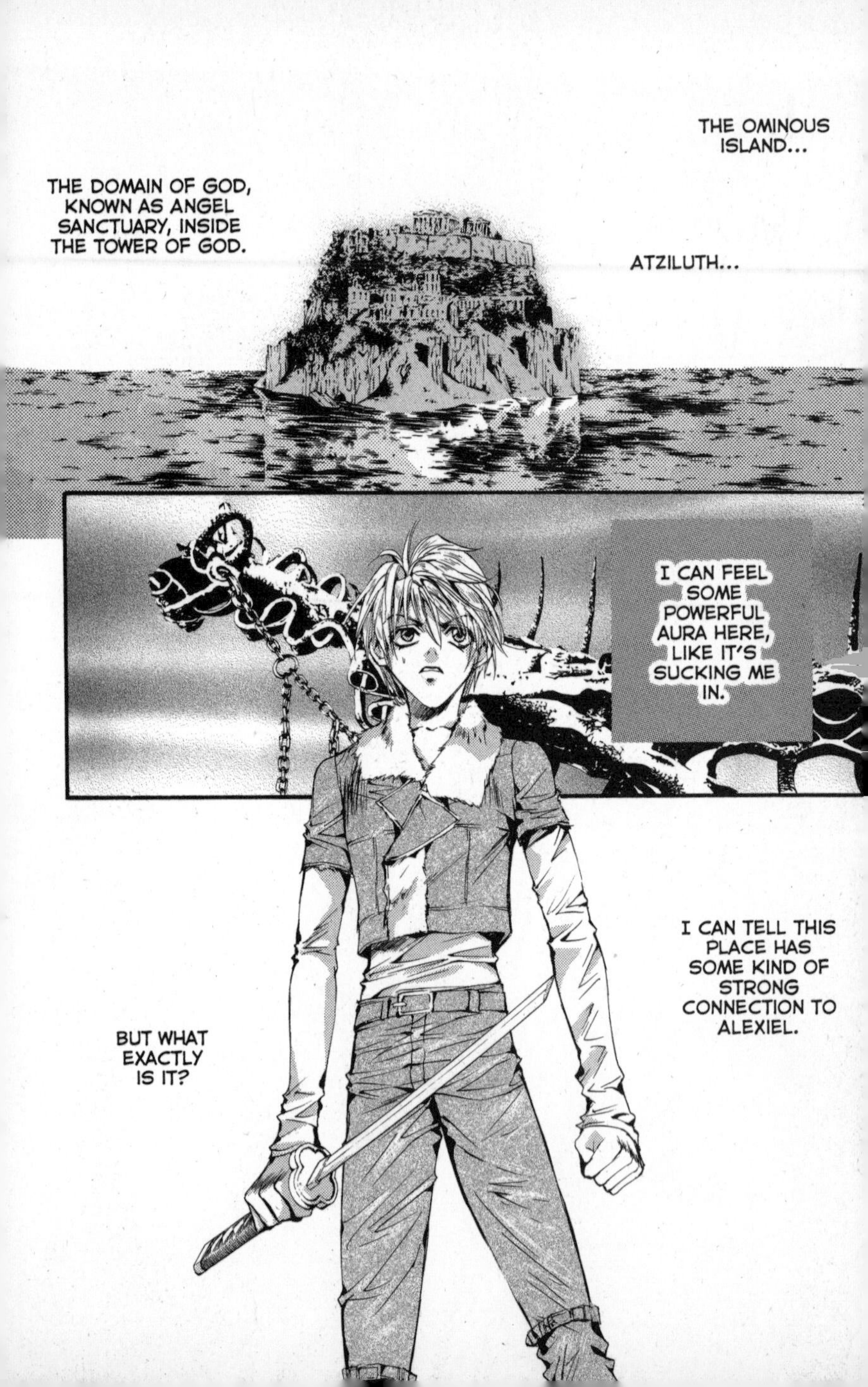
THE OMINOUS ISLAND...
ATZILUTH...
THE DOMAIN OF GOD, KNOWN AS ANGEL SANCTUARY, INSIDE THE TOWER OF GOD.
I CAN FEEL SOME POWERFUL AURA HERE, LIKE IT'S SUCKING ME IN.
I CAN TELL THIS PLACE HAS SOME KIND OF STRONG CONNECTION TO ALEXIEL.
BUT WHAT EXACTLY IS IT?

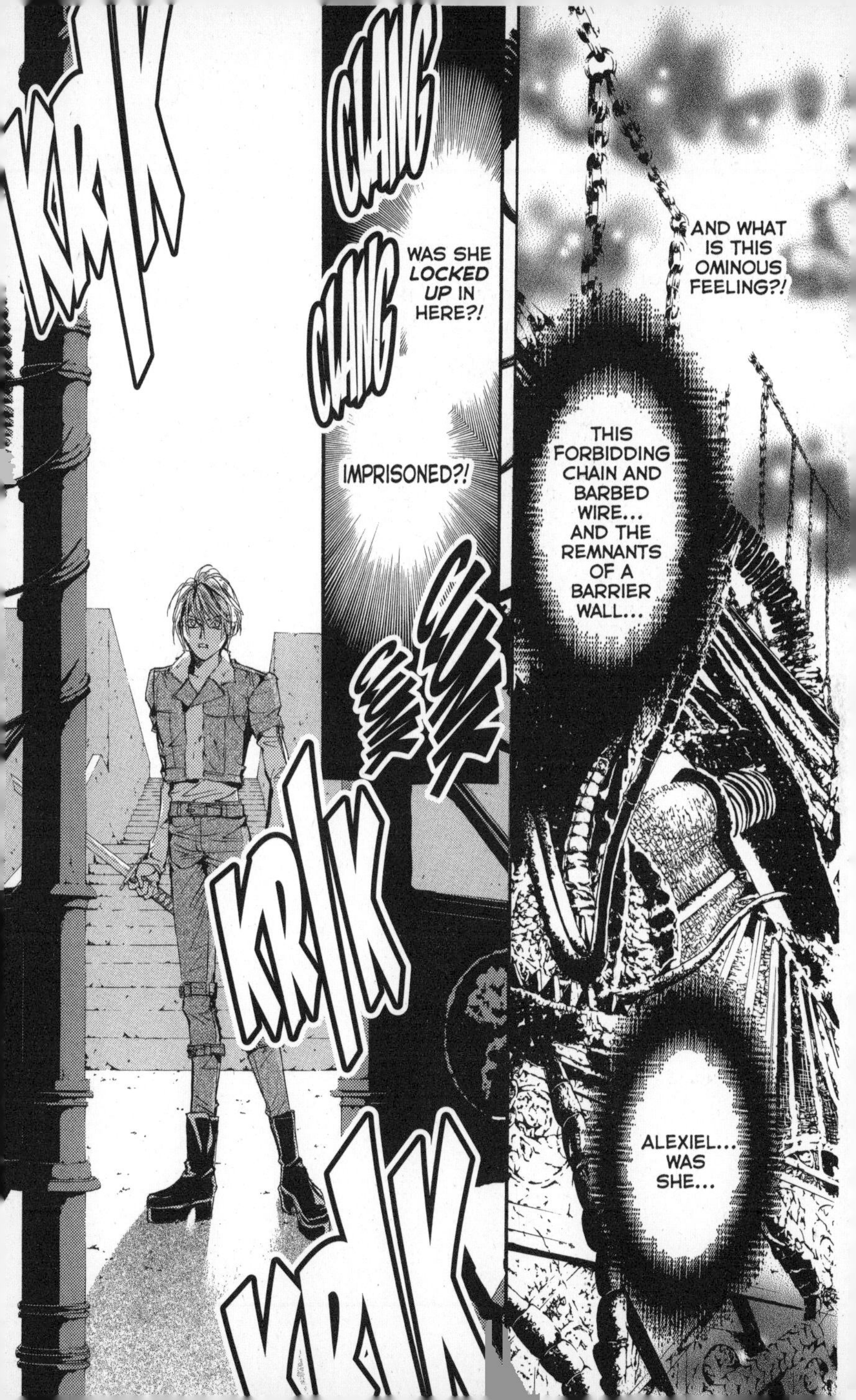
AND WHAT IS THIS OMINOUS FEELING?!
THIS FORBIDDING CHAIN AND BARBED WIRE... AND THE REMNANTS OF A BARRIER WALL...
ALEXIEL... WAS SHE...
CLANG
CLANG
WAS SHE LOCKED UP IN HERE?!
IMPRISONED?!
KRIK
KRIK

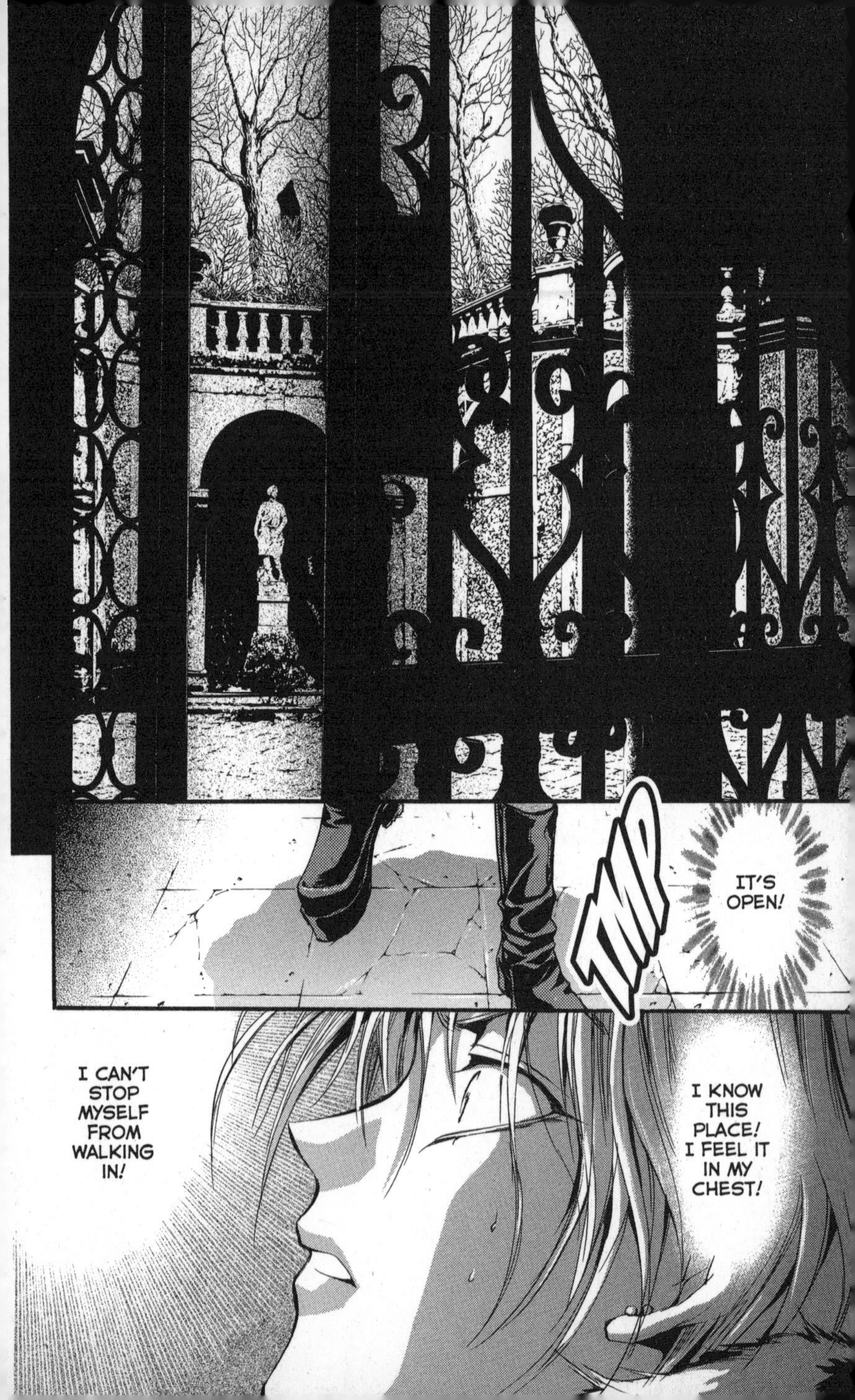
IT'S OPEN!
TMP
I KNOW THIS PLACE! I FEEL IT IN MY CHEST!
I CAN'T STOP MYSELF FROM WALKING IN!

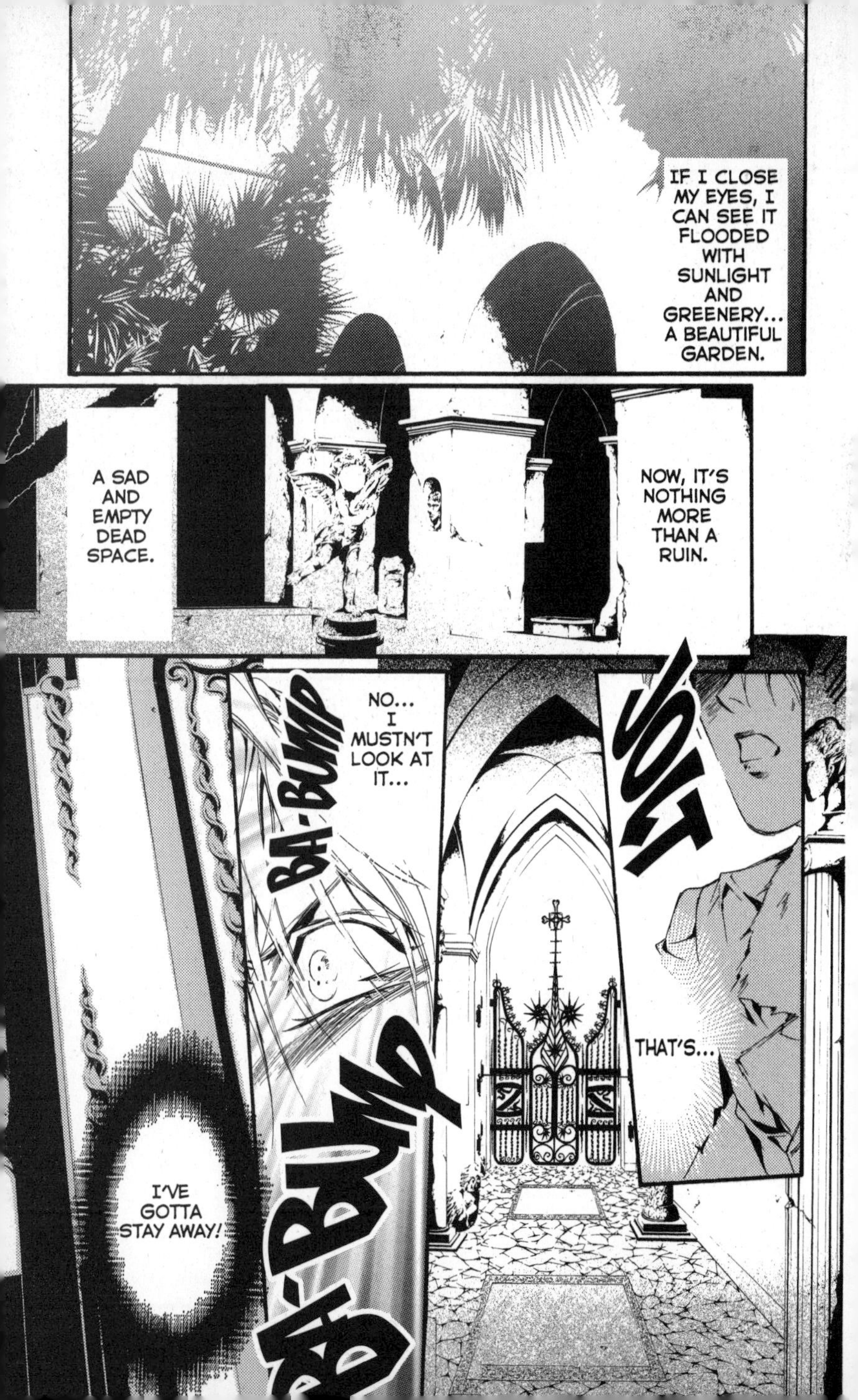
IF I CLOSE MY EYES, I CAN SEE IT FLOODED WITH SUNLIGHT AND GREENERY... A BEAUTIFUL GARDEN.
NOW, IT'S NOTHING MORE THAN A RUIN.
A SAD AND EMPTY DEAD SPACE.
JOLT
THAT'S...
NO... I MUSTN'T LOOK AT IT...
BA-BUMP
BA-BUMP
I'VE GOTTA STAY AWAY!

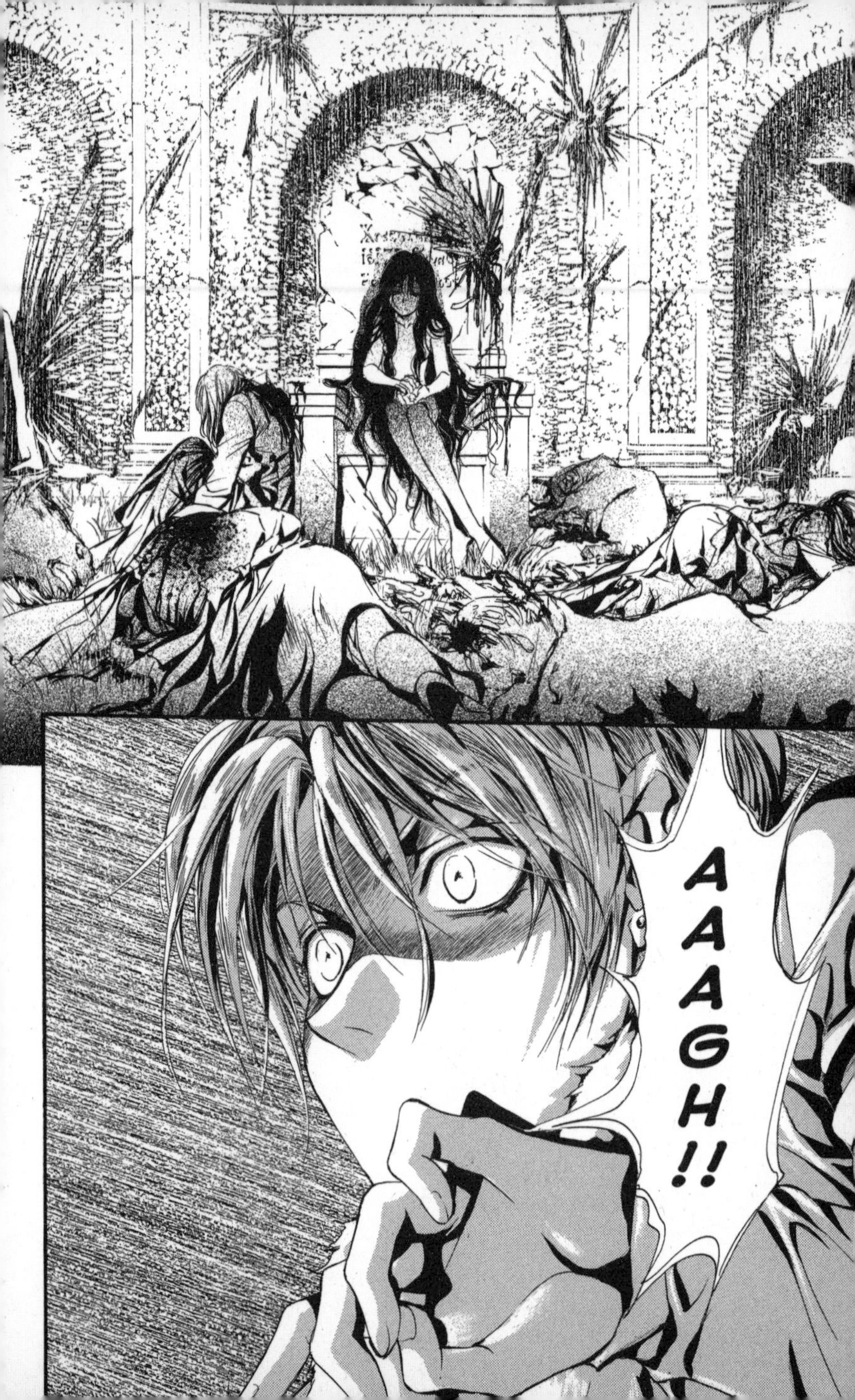
AAAGH!!

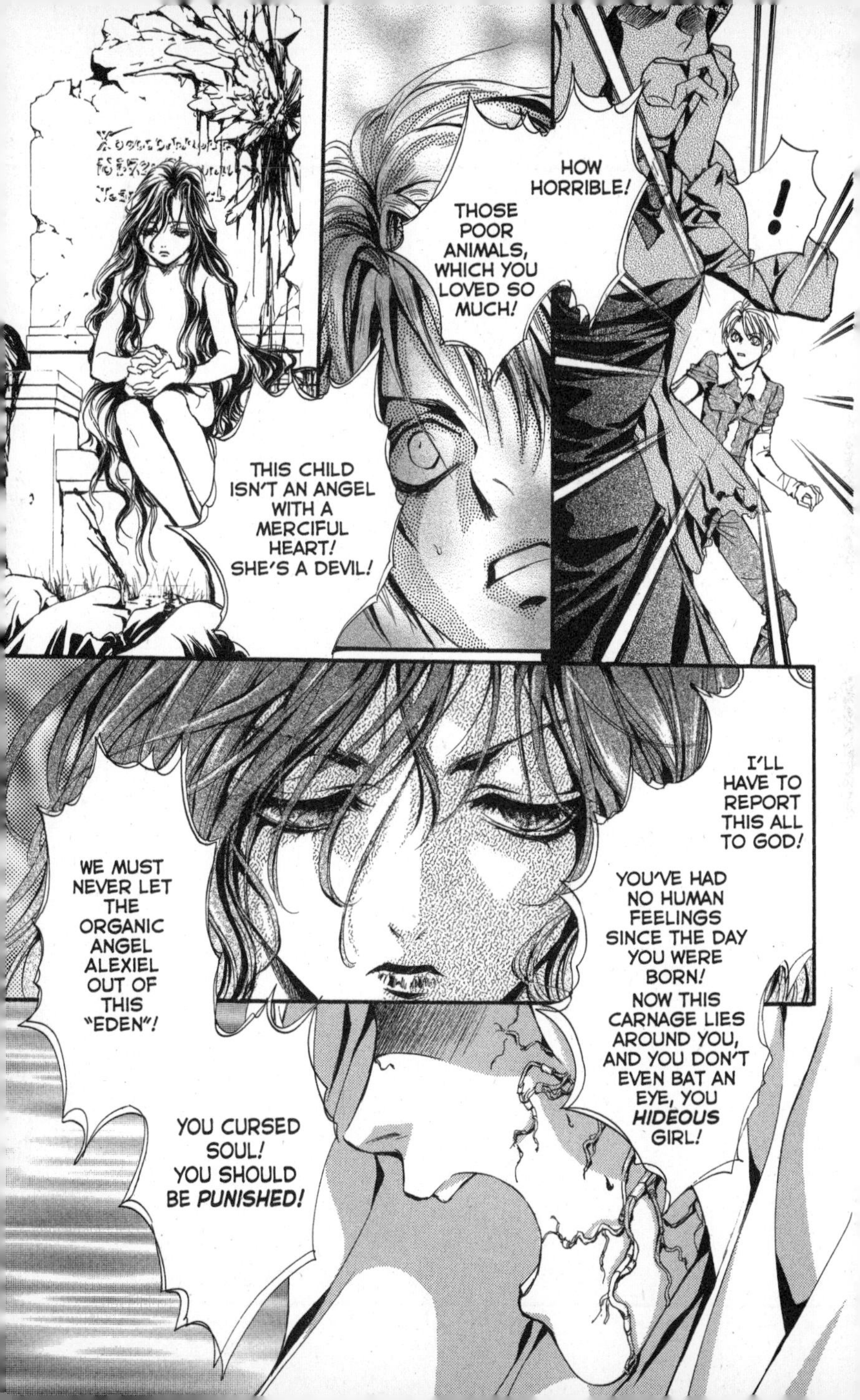
!
HOW HORRIBLE!
THOSE POOR ANIMALS, WHICH YOU LOVED SO MUCH!
THIS CHILD ISN'T AN ANGEL WITH A MERCIFUL HEART! SHE'S A DEVIL!
I'LL HAVE TO REPORT THIS ALL TO GOD!
YOU'VE HAD NO HUMAN FEELINGS SINCE THE DAY YOU WERE BORN!
NOW THIS CARNAGE LIES AROUND YOU, AND YOU DON'T EVEN BAT AN EYE, YOU *HIDEOUS* GIRL!
WE MUST NEVER LET THE ORGANIC ANGEL ALEXIEL OUT OF THIS "EDEN"!
YOU CURSED SOUL! YOU SHOULD BE *PUNISHED!*

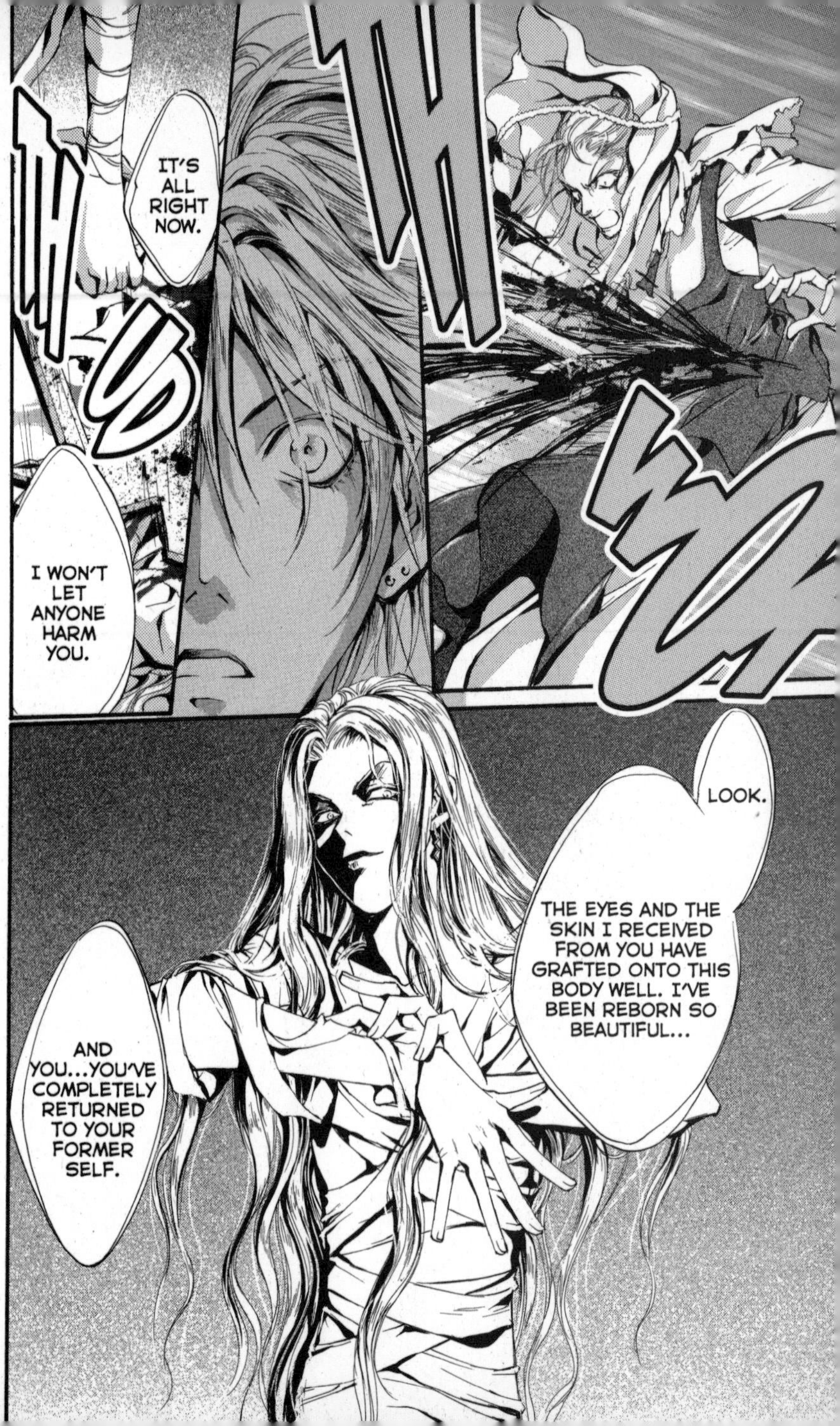
IT'S ALL RIGHT NOW.
I WON'T LET ANYONE HARM YOU.
LOOK.
THE EYES AND THE SKIN I RECEIVED FROM YOU HAVE GRAFTED ONTO THIS BODY WELL. I'VE BEEN REBORN SO BEAUTIFUL...
AND YOU...YOU'VE COMPLETELY RETURNED TO YOUR FORMER SELF.

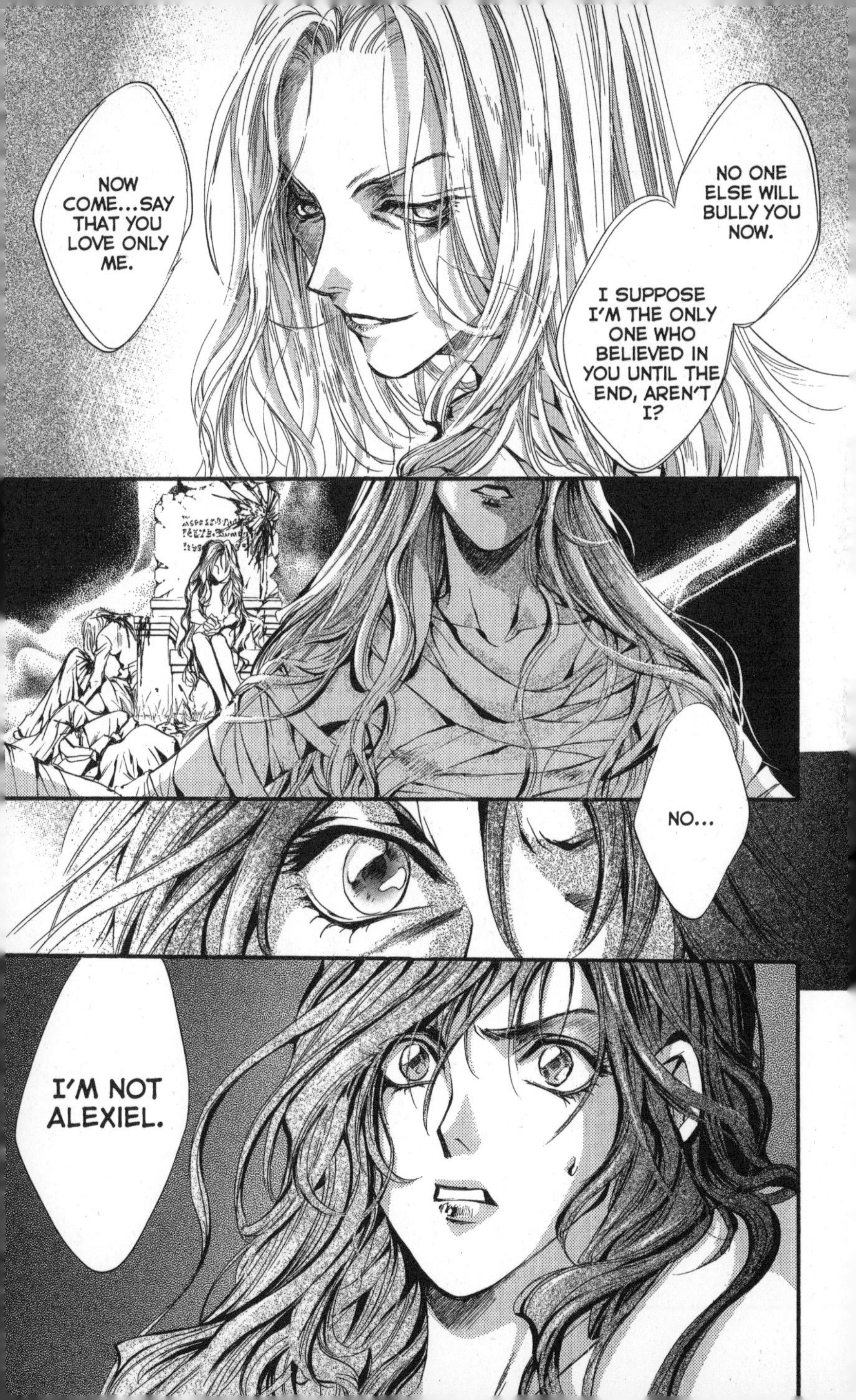
NO ONE ELSE WILL BULLY YOU NOW.
I SUPPOSE I'M THE ONLY ONE WHO BELIEVED IN YOU UNTIL THE END, AREN'T I?
NOW COME...SAY THAT YOU LOVE ONLY ME.
NO...
I'M NOT ALEXIEL.

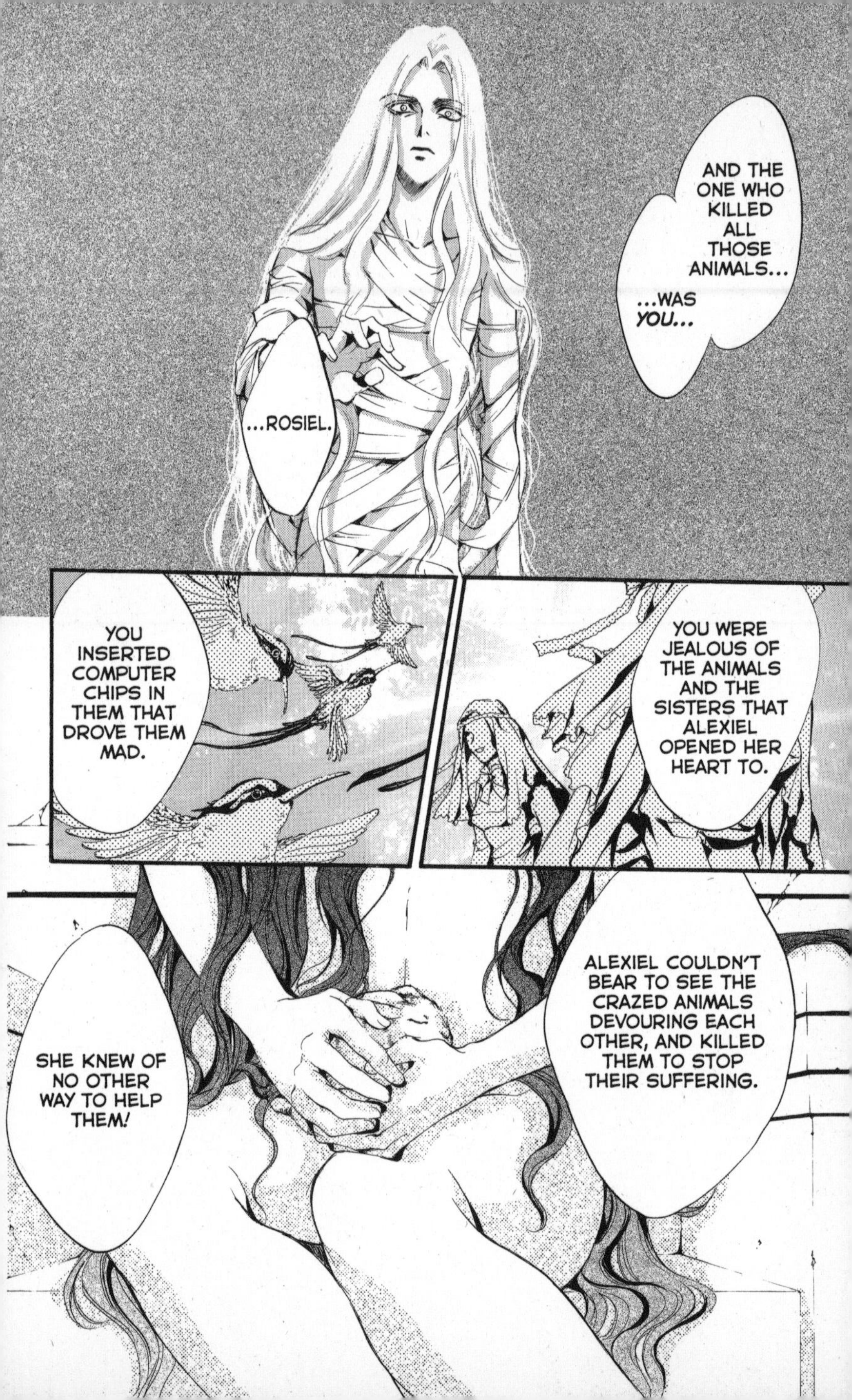
AND THE ONE WHO KILLED ALL THOSE ANIMALS...
...WAS *YOU*...
...ROSIEL.
YOU WERE JEALOUS OF THE ANIMALS AND THE SISTERS THAT ALEXIEL OPENED HER HEART TO.
YOU INSERTED COMPUTER CHIPS IN THEM THAT DROVE THEM MAD.
ALEXIEL COULDN'T BEAR TO SEE THE CRAZED ANIMALS DEVOURING EACH OTHER, AND KILLED THEM TO STOP THEIR SUFFERING.
SHE KNEW OF NO OTHER WAY TO HELP THEM!

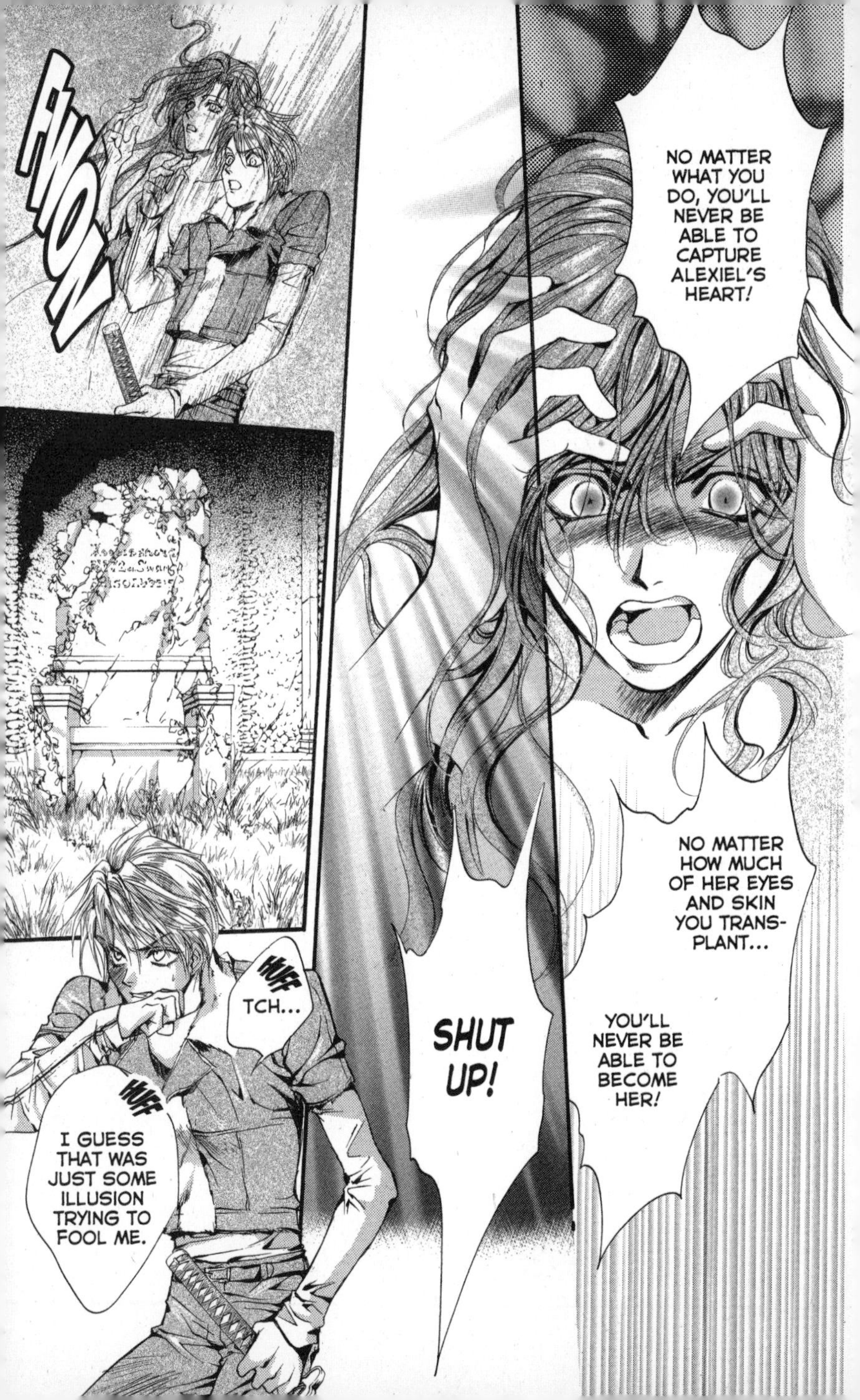
NO MATTER WHAT YOU DO, YOU'LL NEVER BE ABLE TO CAPTURE ALEXIEL'S HEART!
NO MATTER HOW MUCH OF HER EYES AND SKIN YOU TRANS-PLANT...
YOU'LL NEVER BE ABLE TO BECOME HER!
SHUT UP!
FWOM
HUFF
TCH...
HUFF
I GUESS THAT WAS JUST SOME ILLUSION TRYING TO FOOL ME.

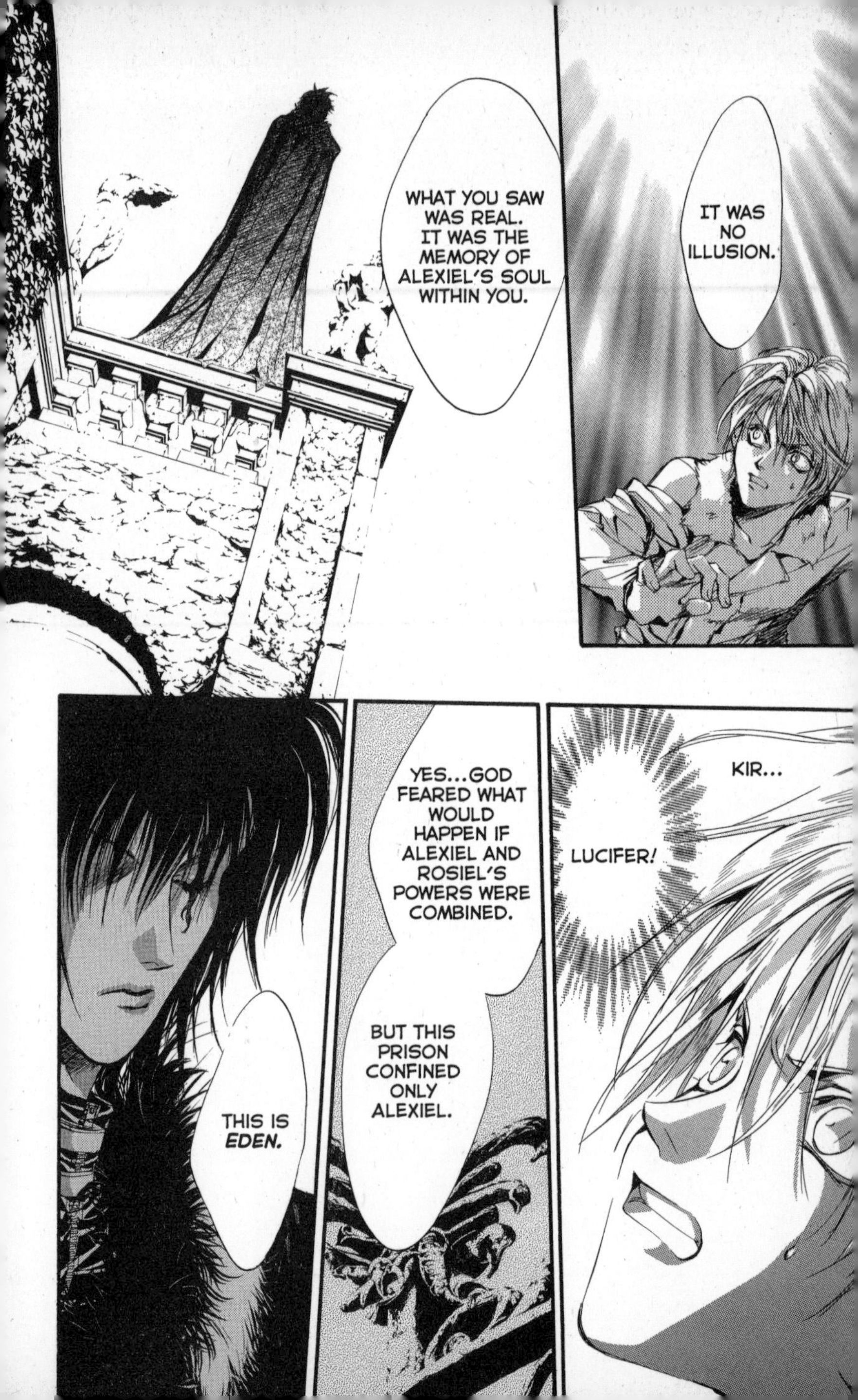
IT WAS NO ILLUSION.
WHAT YOU SAW WAS REAL. IT WAS THE MEMORY OF ALEXIEL'S SOUL WITHIN YOU.
KIR...
LUCIFER!
YES...GOD FEARED WHAT WOULD HAPPEN IF ALEXIEL AND ROSIEL'S POWERS WERE COMBINED.
BUT THIS PRISON CONFINED ONLY ALEXIEL.
THIS IS *EDEN.*

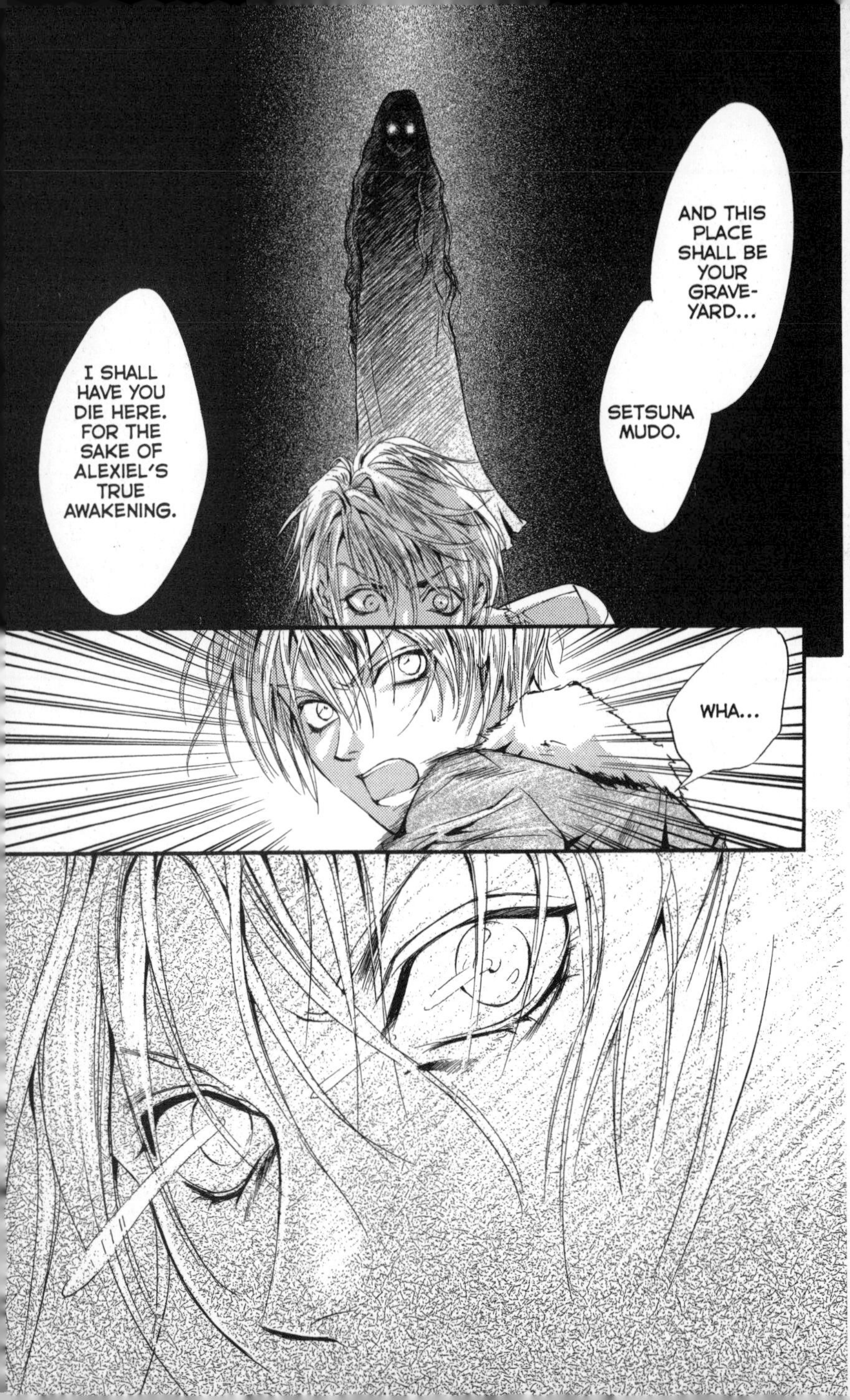
AND THIS PLACE SHALL BE YOUR GRAVE-YARD...
SETSUNA MUDO.
I SHALL HAVE YOU DIE HERE. FOR THE SAKE OF ALEXIEL'S TRUE AWAKENING.
WHA...

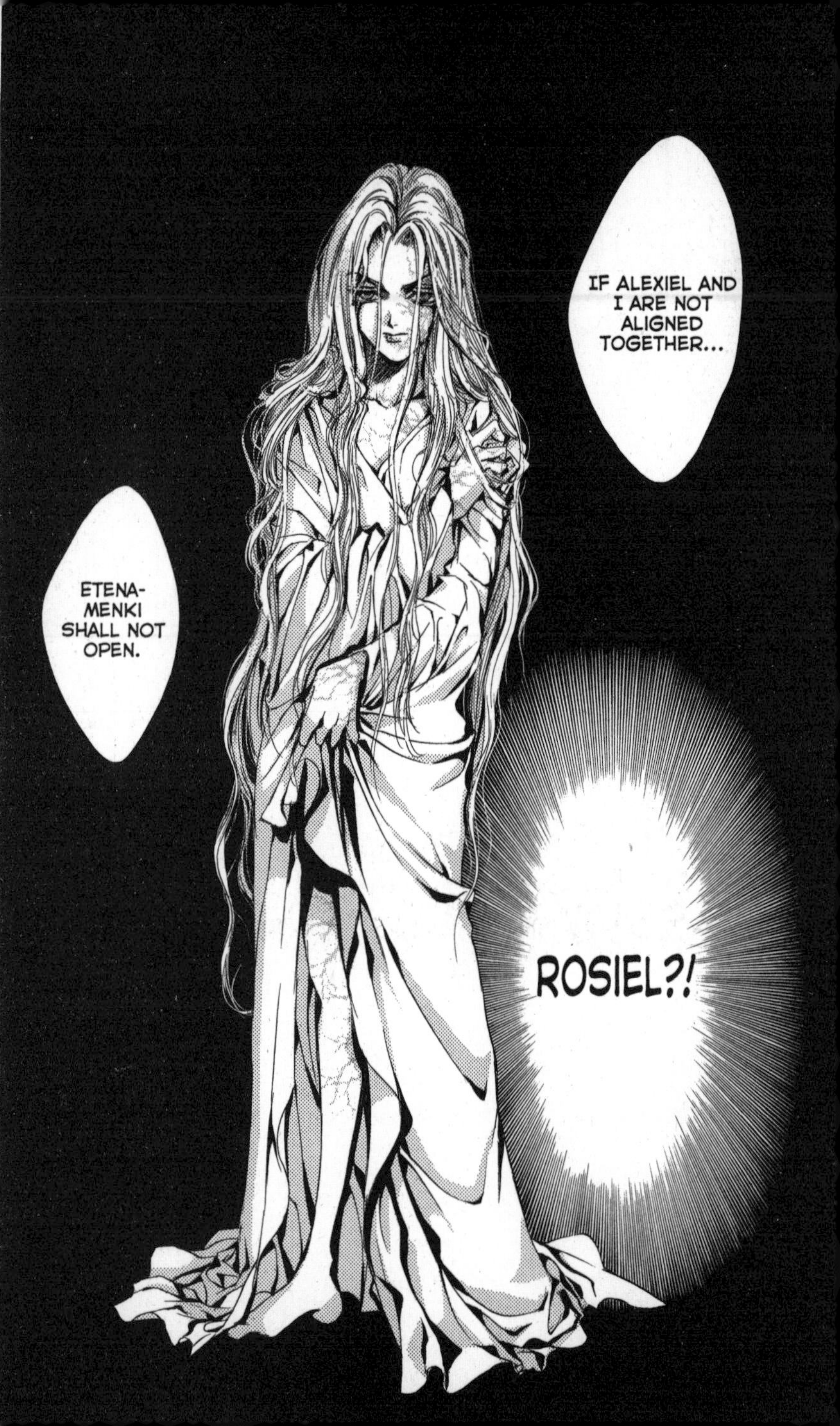
IF ALEXIEL AND I ARE NOT ALIGNED TOGETHER...
ETENA-MENKI SHALL NOT OPEN.
ROSIEL?!

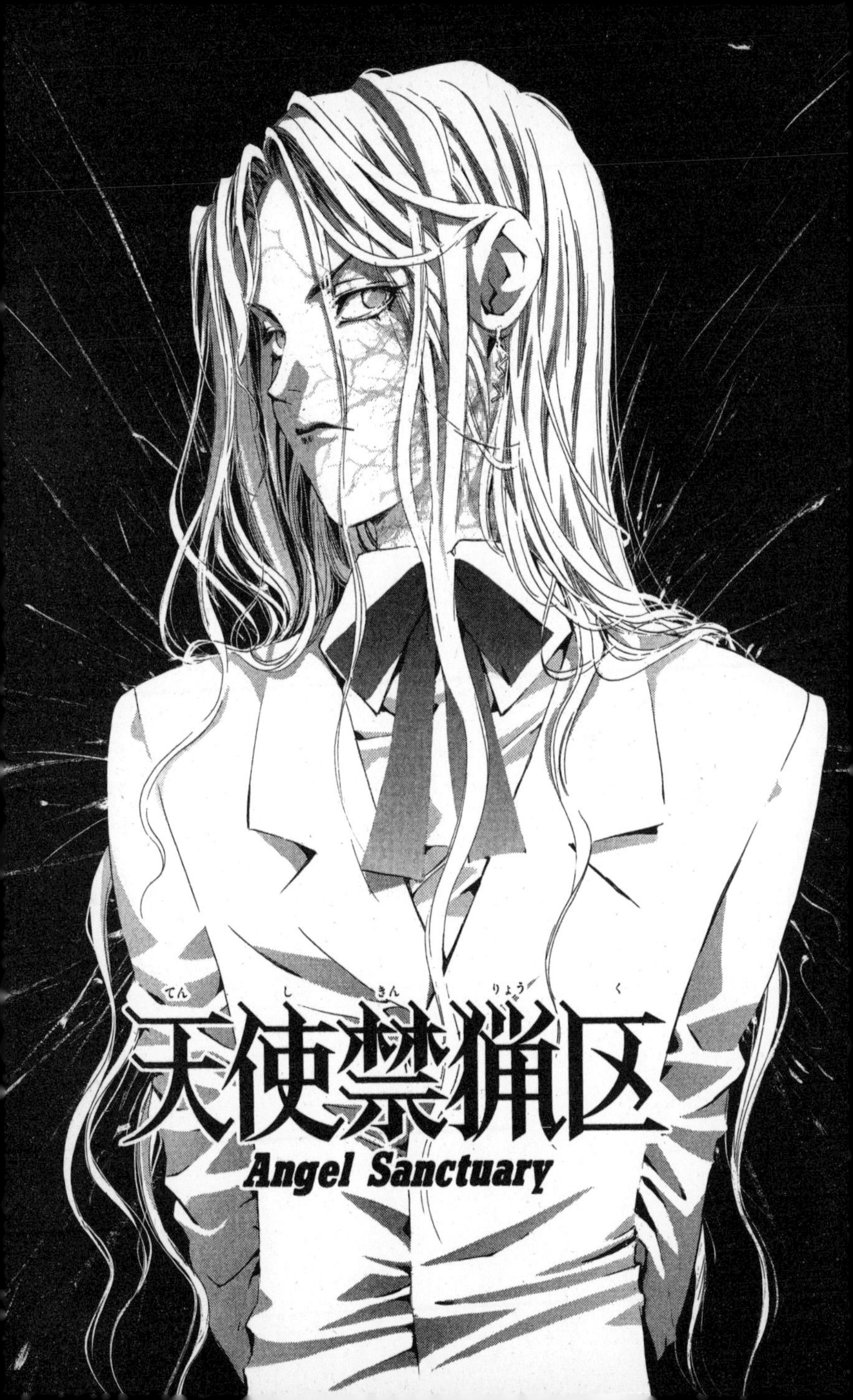
天使禁猟区
Angel Sanctuary

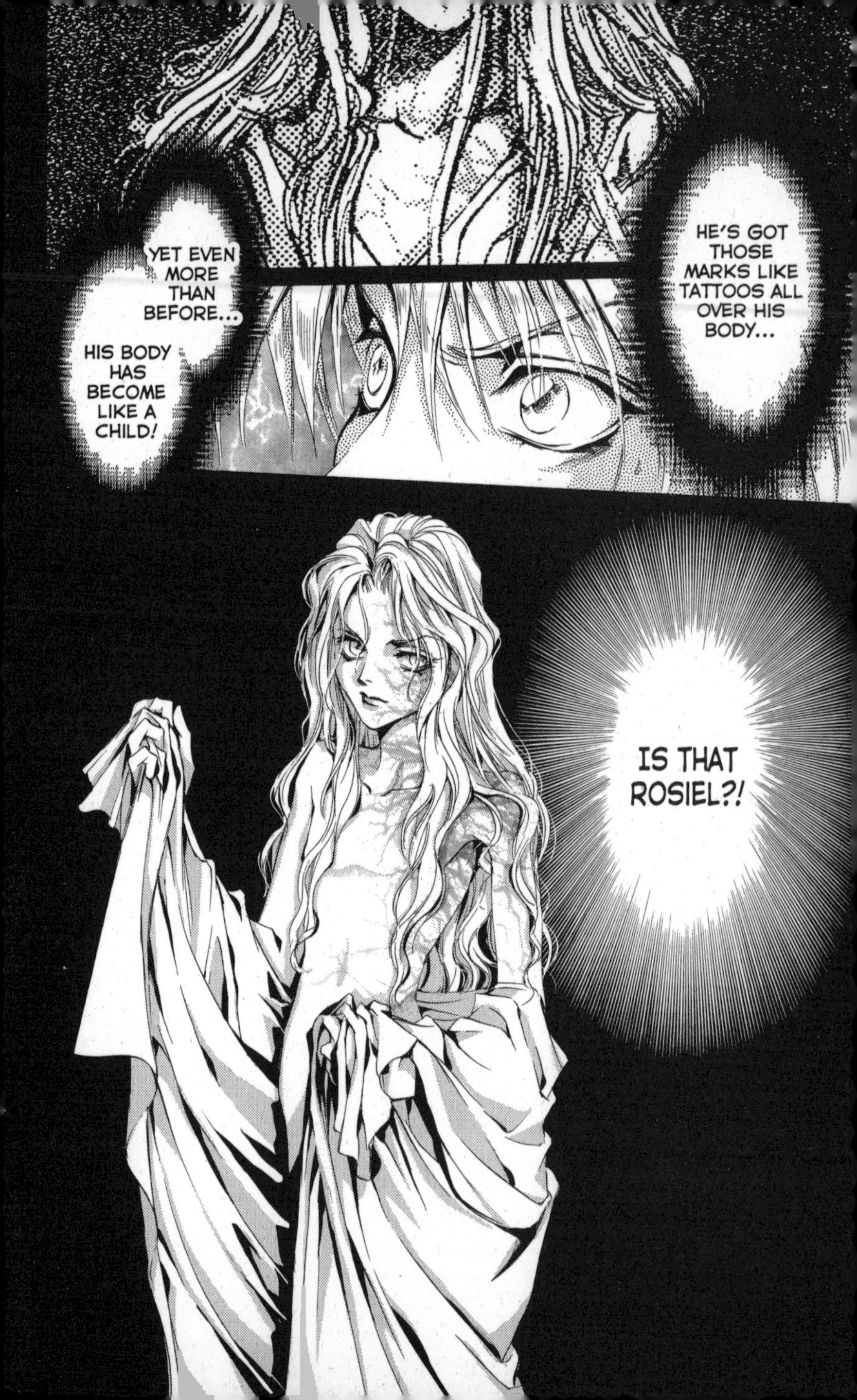
HE'S GOT THOSE MARKS LIKE TATTOOS ALL OVER HIS BODY...
YET EVEN MORE THAN BEFORE...
HIS BODY HAS BECOME LIKE A CHILD!
IS THAT ROSIEL?!

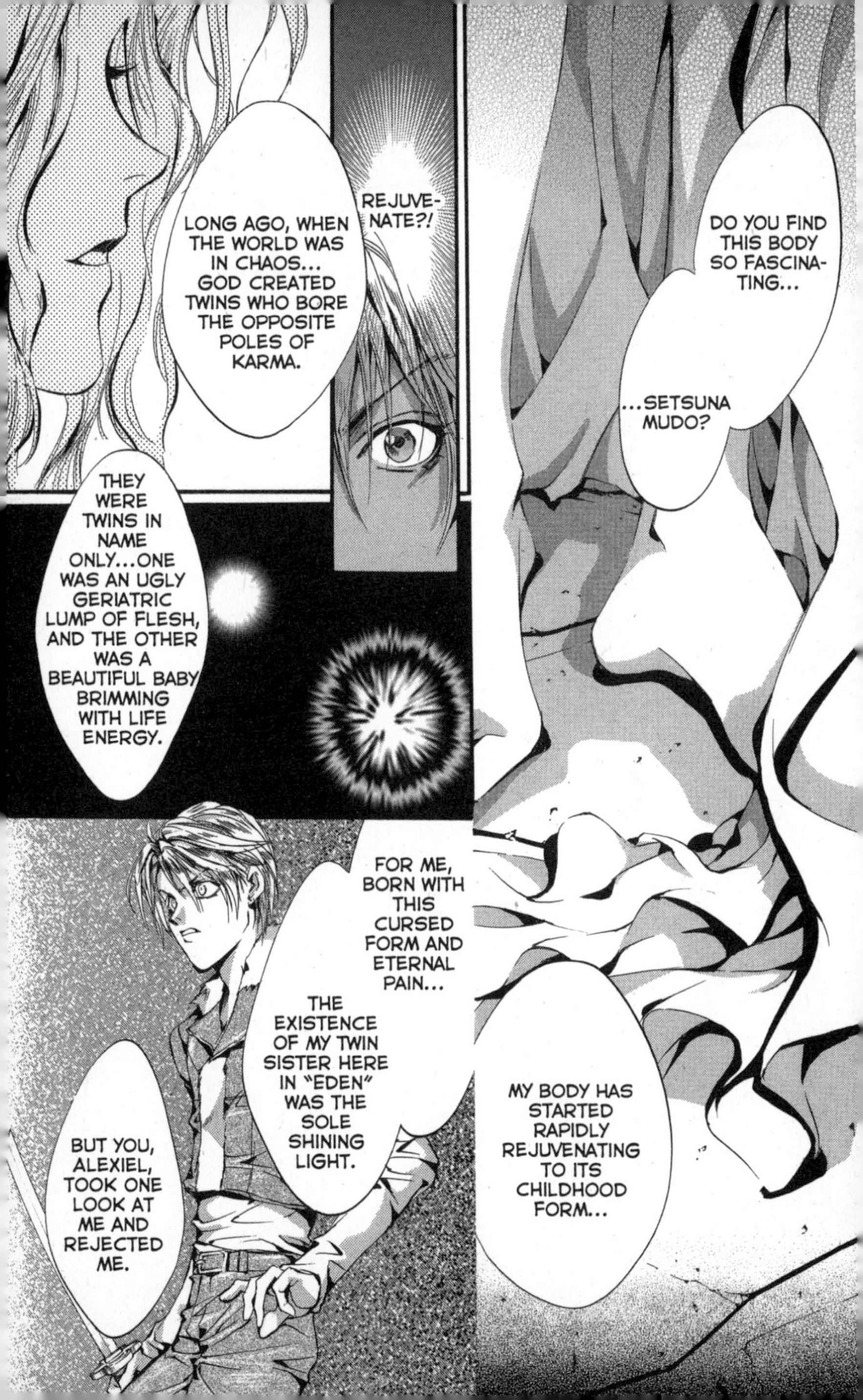
DO YOU FIND THIS BODY SO FASCINATING...
...SETSUNA MUDO?
MY BODY HAS STARTED RAPIDLY REJUVENATING TO ITS CHILDHOOD FORM...
REJUVENATE?!
LONG AGO, WHEN THE WORLD WAS IN CHAOS... GOD CREATED TWINS WHO BORE THE OPPOSITE POLES OF KARMA.
THEY WERE TWINS IN NAME ONLY...ONE WAS AN UGLY GERIATRIC LUMP OF FLESH, AND THE OTHER WAS A BEAUTIFUL BABY BRIMMING WITH LIFE ENERGY.
FOR ME, BORN WITH THIS CURSED FORM AND ETERNAL PAIN...
THE EXISTENCE OF MY TWIN SISTER HERE IN "EDEN" WAS THE SOLE SHINING LIGHT.
BUT YOU, ALEXIEL, TOOK ONE LOOK AT ME AND REJECTED ME.

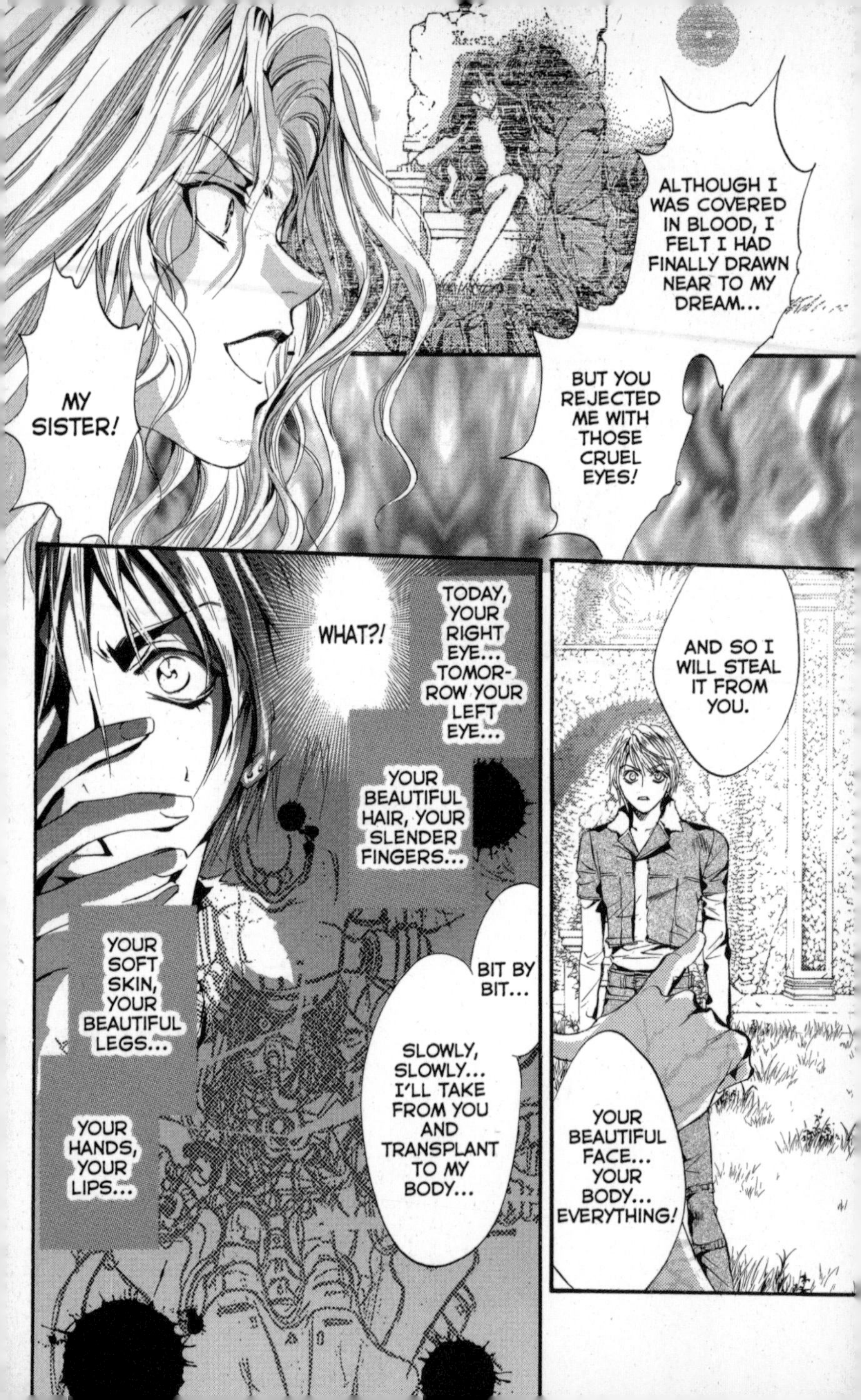
ALTHOUGH I WAS COVERED IN BLOOD, I FELT I HAD FINALLY DRAWN NEAR TO MY DREAM...
BUT YOU REJECTED ME WITH THOSE CRUEL EYES!
MY SISTER!
AND SO I WILL STEAL IT FROM YOU.
YOUR BEAUTIFUL FACE... YOUR BODY... EVERYTHING!
WHAT?!
TODAY, YOUR RIGHT EYE... TOMOR-ROW YOUR LEFT EYE...
YOUR BEAUTIFUL HAIR, YOUR SLENDER FINGERS...
YOUR SOFT SKIN, YOUR BEAUTIFUL LEGS...
YOUR HANDS, YOUR LIPS...
BIT BY BIT...
SLOWLY, SLOWLY... I'LL TAKE FROM YOU AND TRANSPLANT TO MY BODY...

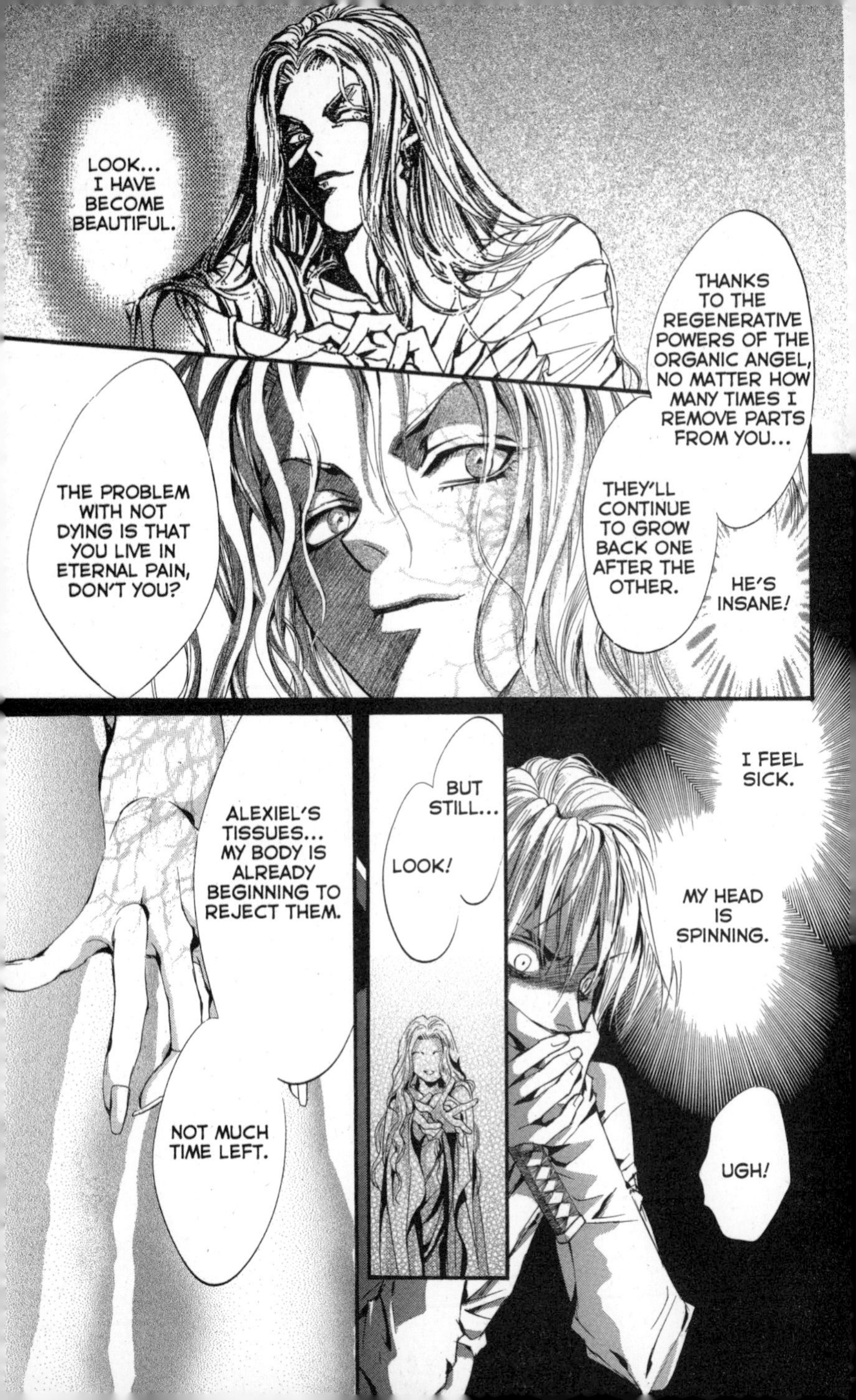
LOOK... I HAVE BECOME BEAUTIFUL.
THANKS TO THE REGENERATIVE POWERS OF THE ORGANIC ANGEL, NO MATTER HOW MANY TIMES I REMOVE PARTS FROM YOU...
THEY'LL CONTINUE TO GROW BACK ONE AFTER THE OTHER.
HE'S INSANE!
THE PROBLEM WITH NOT DYING IS THAT YOU LIVE IN ETERNAL PAIN, DON'T YOU?
I FEEL SICK.
MY HEAD IS SPINNING.
UGH!
BUT STILL...
LOOK!
ALEXIEL'S TISSUES... MY BODY IS ALREADY BEGINNING TO REJECT THEM.
NOT MUCH TIME LEFT.

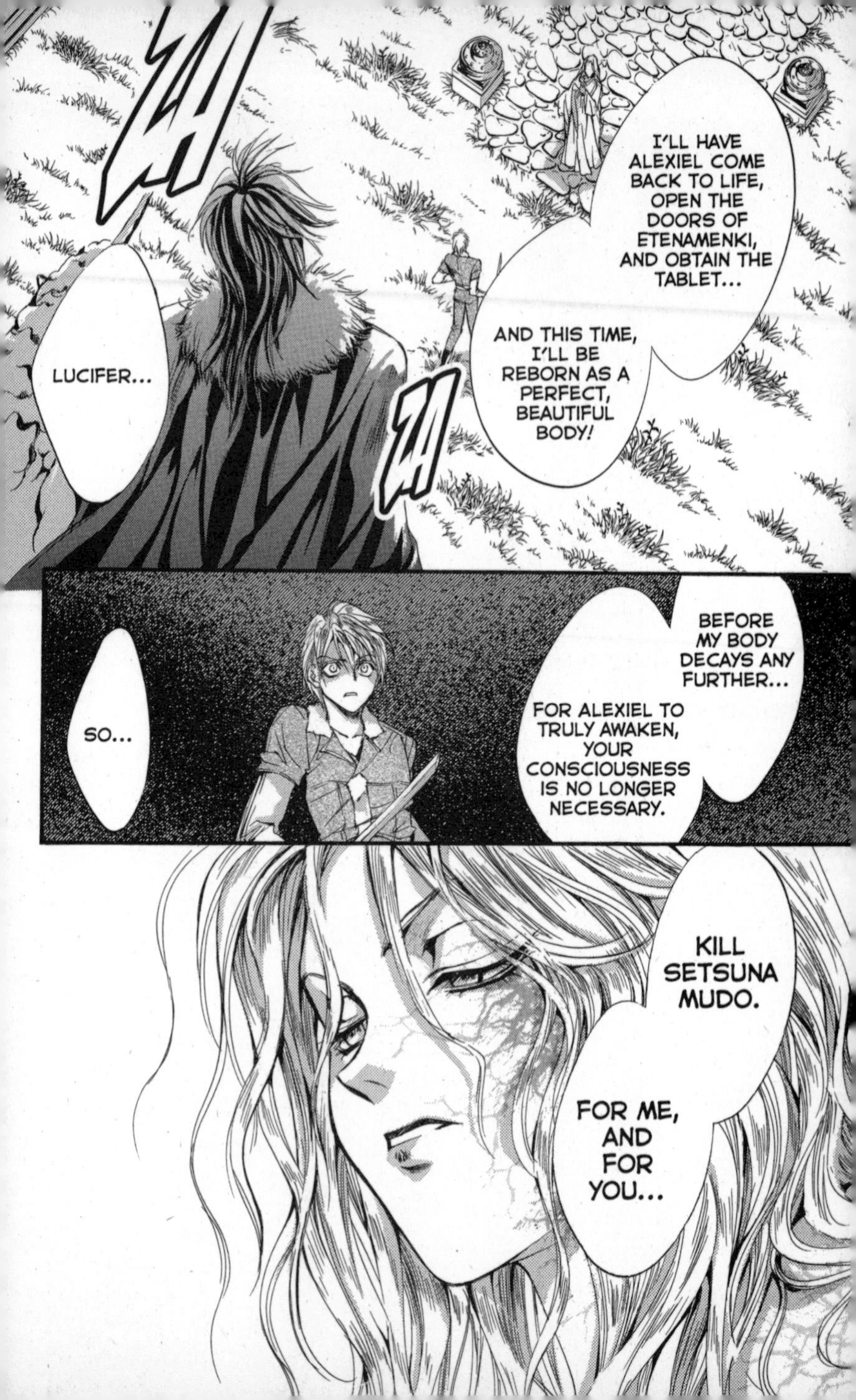
I'LL HAVE ALEXIEL COME BACK TO LIFE, OPEN THE DOORS OF ETENAMENKI, AND OBTAIN THE TABLET...
AND THIS TIME, I'LL BE REBORN AS A PERFECT, BEAUTIFUL BODY!
ZA
ZA
LUCIFER...
BEFORE MY BODY DECAYS ANY FURTHER...
FOR ALEXIEL TO TRULY AWAKEN, YOUR CONSCIOUSNESS IS NO LONGER NECESSARY.
SO...
KILL SETSUNA MUDO.
FOR ME, AND FOR YOU...

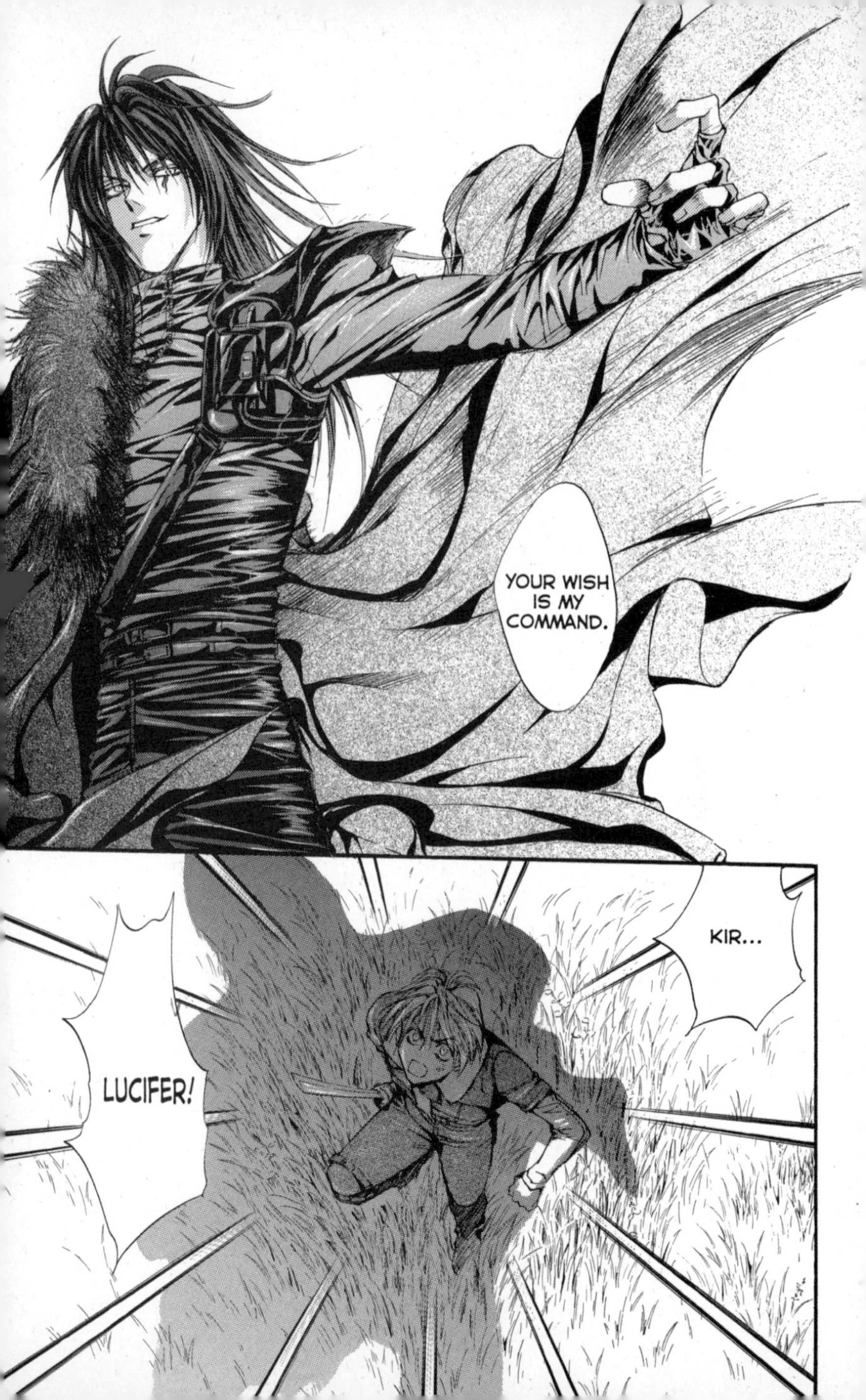
YOUR WISH IS MY COMMAND.
KIR...
LUCIFER!

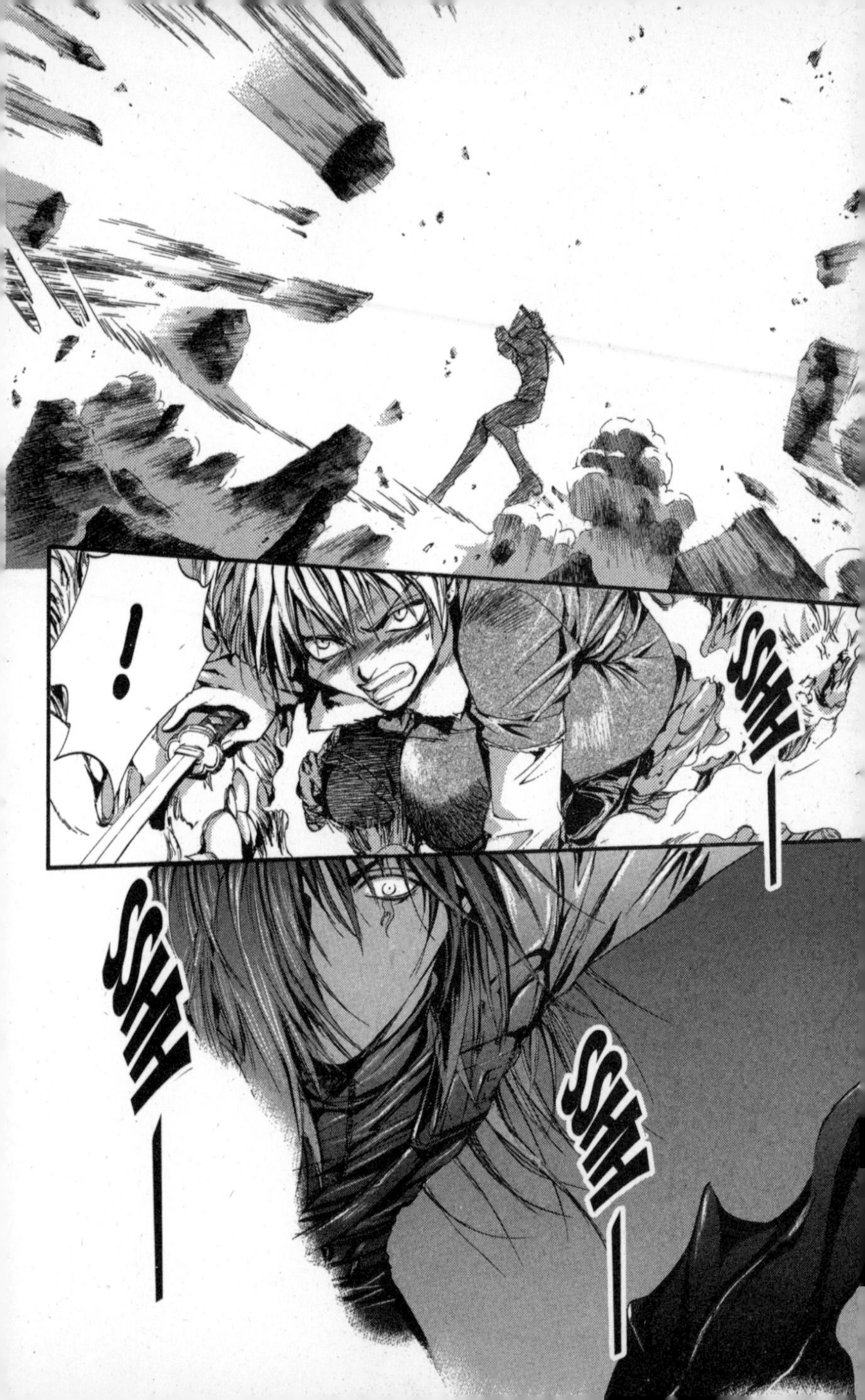
SSHH
!
SSHH
SSHH

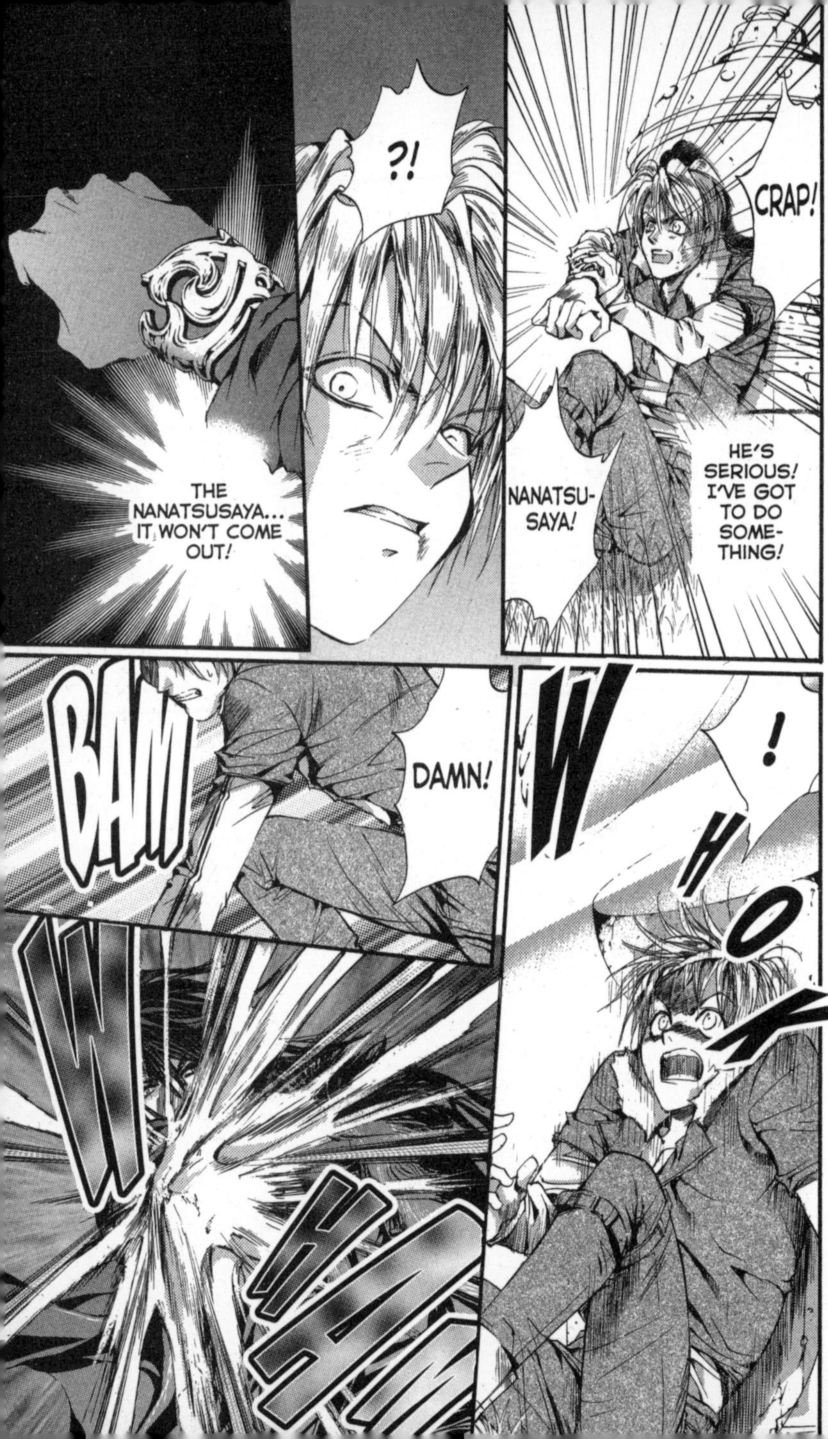
CRAP!
HE'S SERIOUS! I'VE GOT TO DO SOME-THING!
NANATSU-SAYA!
?!
THE NANATSUSAYA... IT WON'T COME OUT!
W H O K
!
BAM
DAMN!

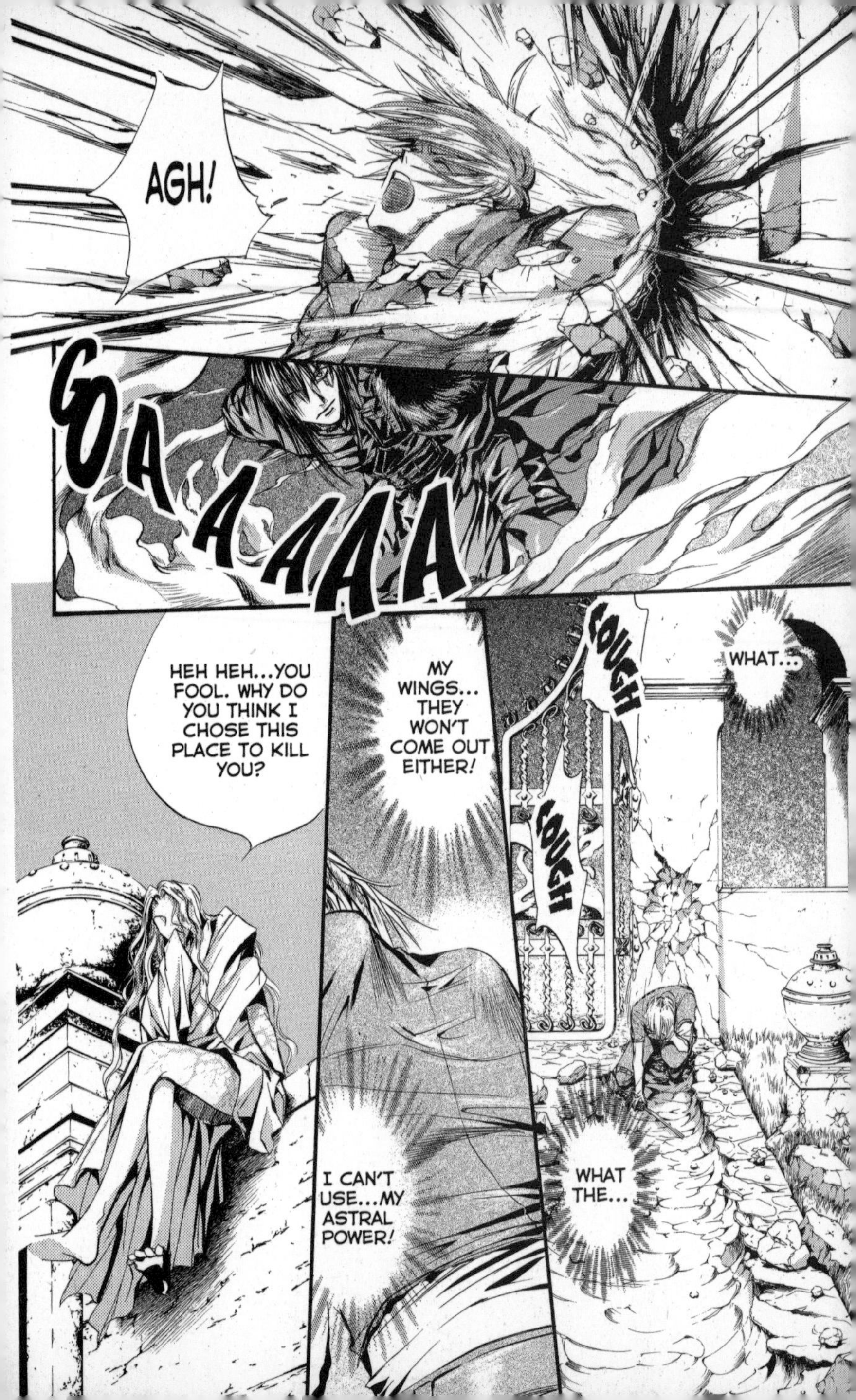
AGH!
GOAAAAAA
WHAT...
COUGH
COUGH
WHAT THE...
MY WINGS... THEY WON'T COME OUT EITHER!
I CAN'T USE...MY ASTRAL POWER!
HEH HEH...YOU FOOL. WHY DO YOU THINK I CHOSE THIS PLACE TO KILL YOU?

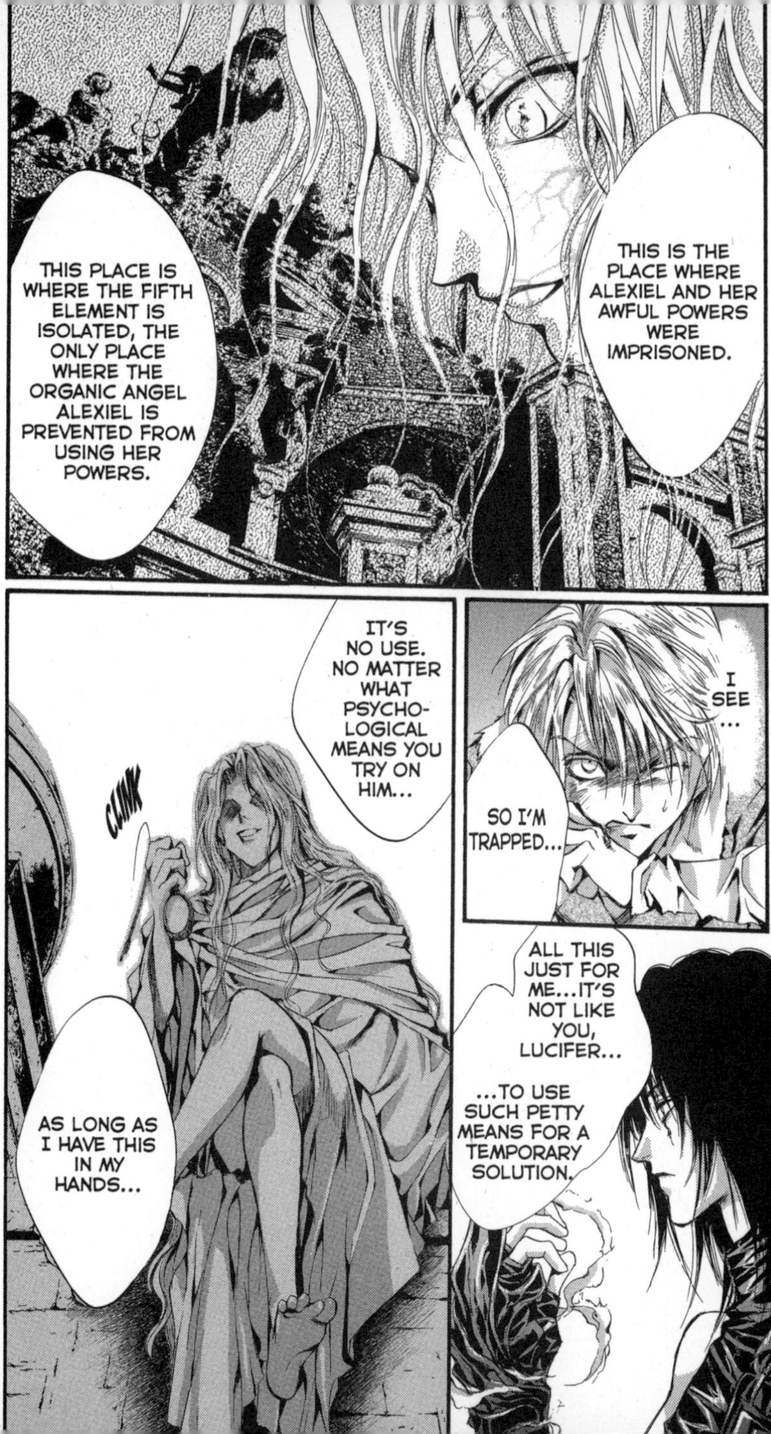
THIS IS THE PLACE WHERE ALEXIEL AND HER AWFUL POWERS WERE IMPRISONED.
THIS PLACE IS WHERE THE FIFTH ELEMENT IS ISOLATED, THE ONLY PLACE WHERE THE ORGANIC ANGEL ALEXIEL IS PREVENTED FROM USING HER POWERS.
I SEE...
SO I'M TRAPPED...
ALL THIS JUST FOR ME...IT'S NOT LIKE YOU, LUCIFER...
...TO USE SUCH PETTY MEANS FOR A TEMPORARY SOLUTION.
IT'S NO USE. NO MATTER WHAT PSYCHO-LOGICAL MEANS YOU TRY ON HIM...
CLINK
AS LONG AS I HAVE THIS IN MY HANDS...

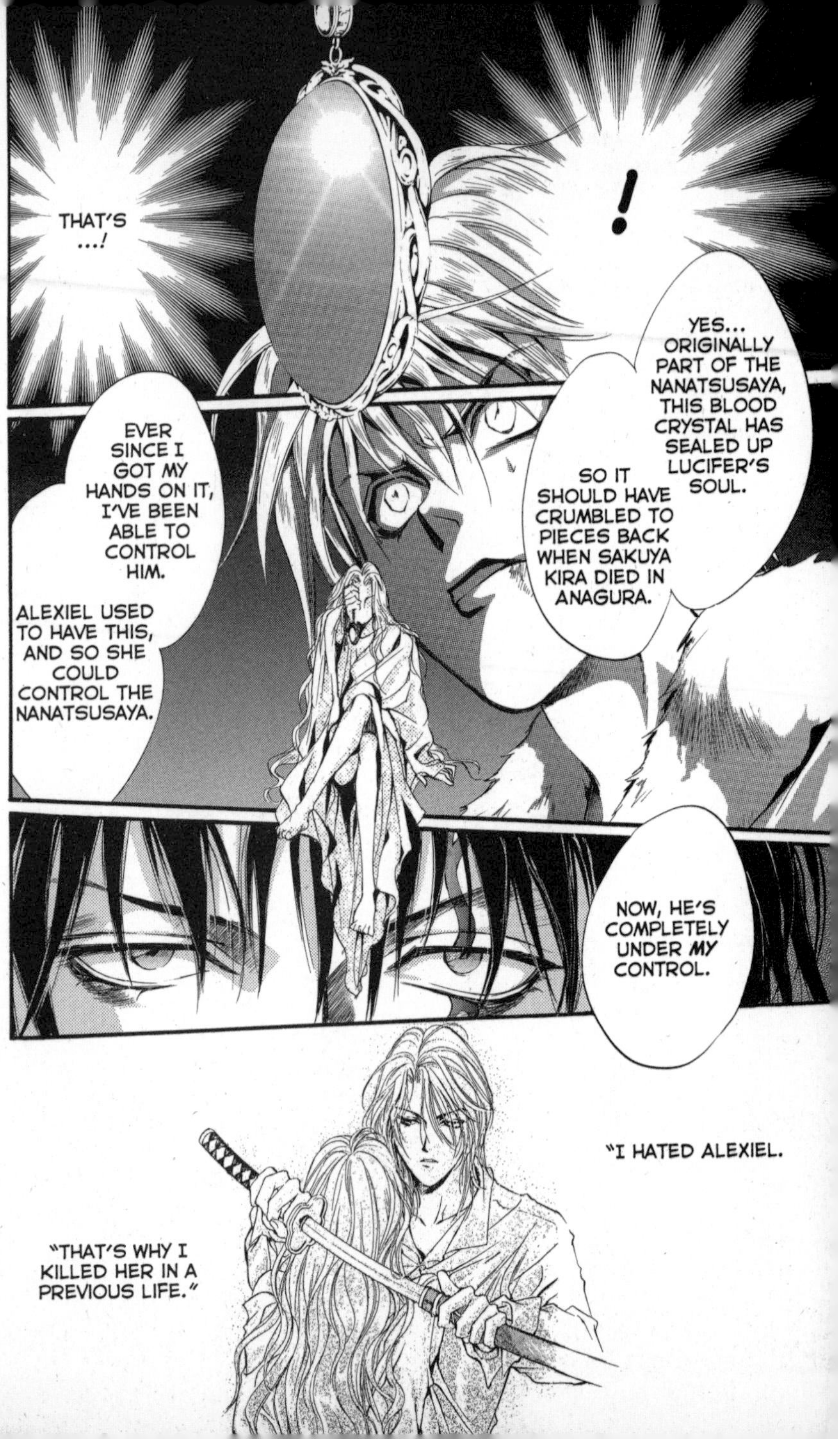
!
THAT'S ...!
YES... ORIGINALLY PART OF THE NANATSUSAYA, THIS BLOOD CRYSTAL HAS SEALED UP LUCIFER'S SOUL.
SO IT SHOULD HAVE CRUMBLED TO PIECES BACK WHEN SAKUYA KIRA DIED IN ANAGURA.
EVER SINCE I GOT MY HANDS ON IT, I'VE BEEN ABLE TO CONTROL HIM.
ALEXIEL USED TO HAVE THIS, AND SO SHE COULD CONTROL THE NANATSUSAYA.
NOW, HE'S COMPLETELY UNDER *MY* CONTROL.
"I HATED ALEXIEL.
"THAT'S WHY I KILLED HER IN A PREVIOUS LIFE."

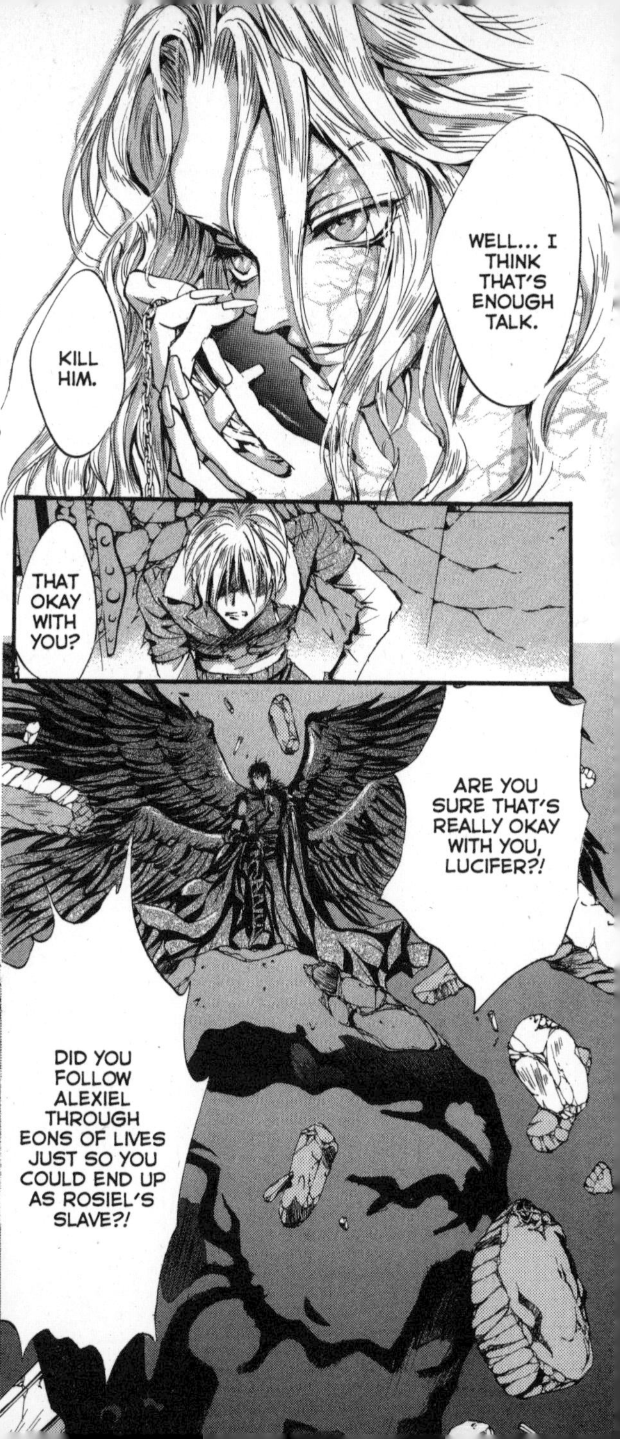
WELL... I THINK THAT'S ENOUGH TALK.
KILL HIM.
THAT OKAY WITH YOU?
ARE YOU SURE THAT'S REALLY OKAY WITH YOU, LUCIFER?!
DID YOU FOLLOW ALEXIEL THROUGH EONS OF LIVES JUST SO YOU COULD END UP AS ROSIEL'S SLAVE?!

Actually, we plan to keep putting out the CDs as a continuation of the Book of the Material World. The CD of the Book of Hades is already on sale, and doing pretty well. I don't know why, but the voice cast changed a bit, and now it's more like the OVA. And it's so well made, you don't notice any differences. The Book of Hades is sort of like "Kato on Parade," and Ueda-san did a great job on Kato's voice, although it was a little more mature than I imagined Kato. Rosiel's voice sounded a little perverted, but that actually gave it more dignity.

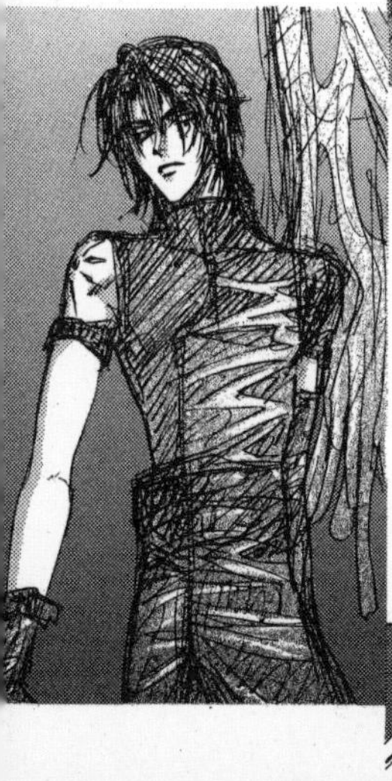

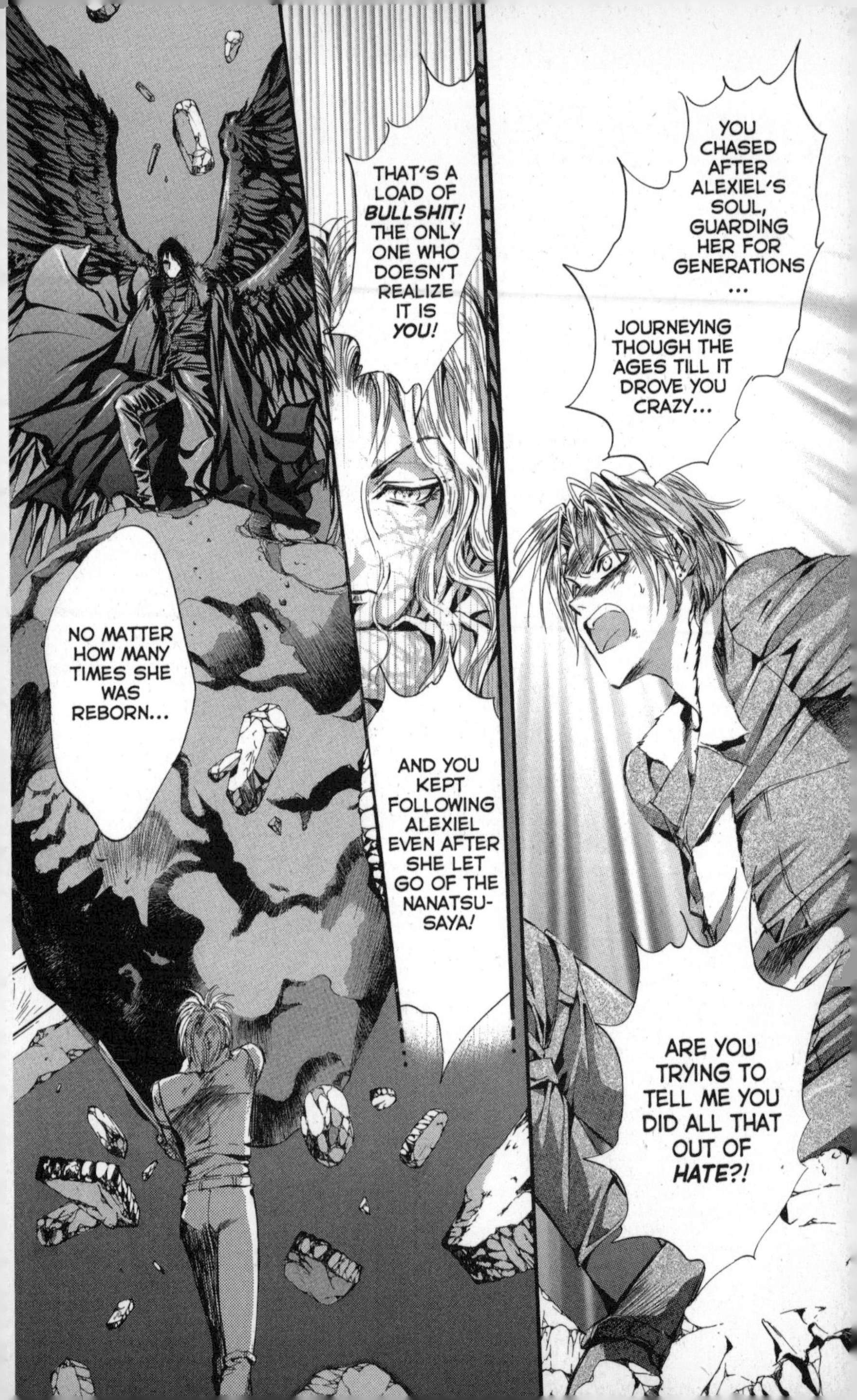
YOU CHASED AFTER ALEXIEL'S SOUL, GUARDING HER FOR GENERATIONS...
JOURNEYING THOUGH THE AGES TILL IT DROVE YOU CRAZY...
NO MATTER HOW MANY TIMES SHE WAS REBORN...
AND YOU KEPT FOLLOWING ALEXIEL EVEN AFTER SHE LET GO OF THE NANATSU-SAYA!
ARE YOU TRYING TO TELL ME YOU DID ALL THAT OUT OF *HATE?!*
THAT'S A LOAD OF *BULLSHIT!* THE ONLY ONE WHO DOESN'T REALIZE IT IS *YOU!*

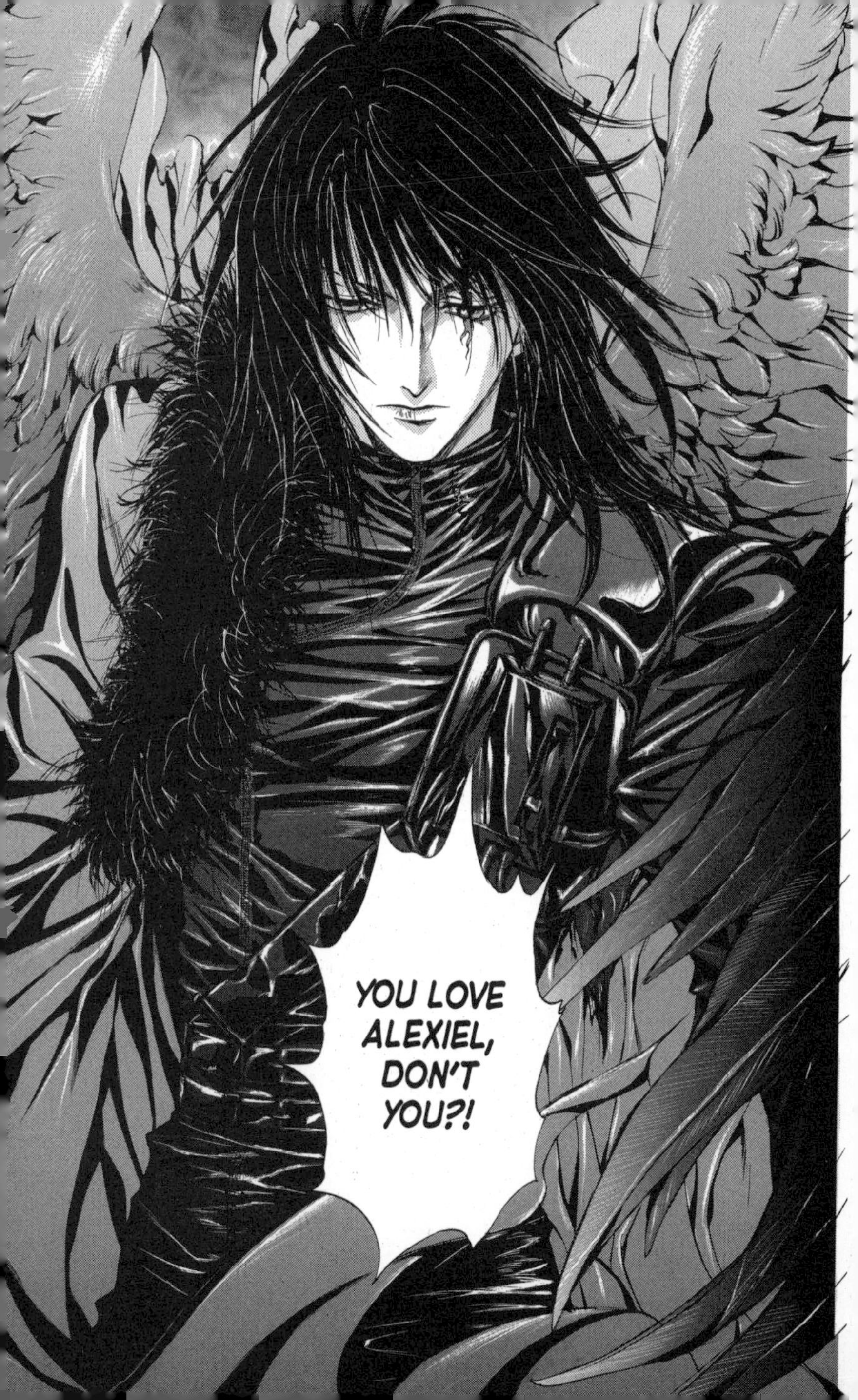
YOU LOVE ALEXIEL, DON'T YOU?!

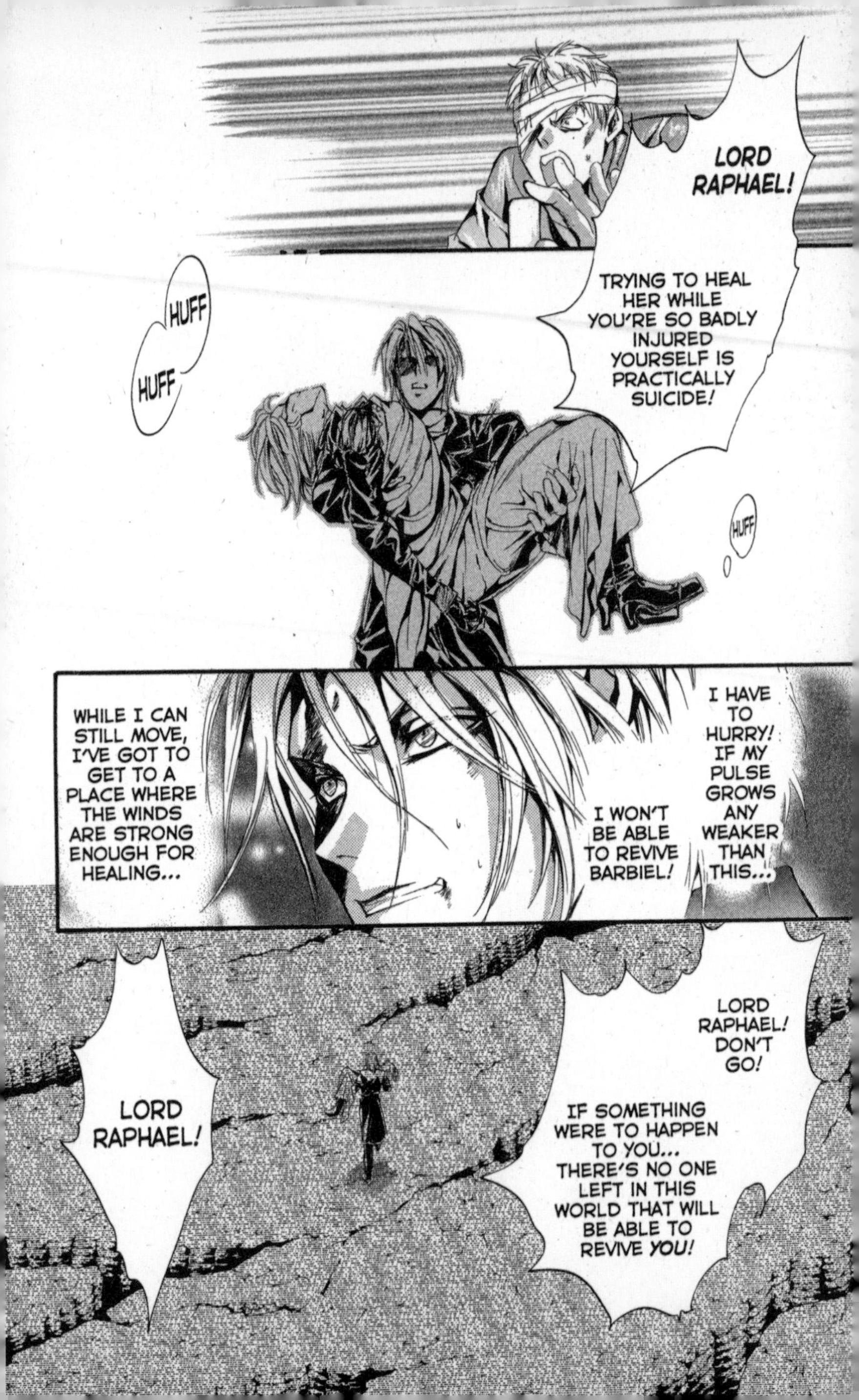
LORD RAPHAEL!
TRYING TO HEAL HER WHILE YOU'RE SO BADLY INJURED YOURSELF IS PRACTICALLY SUICIDE!
HUFF
HUFF
HUFF
I HAVE TO HURRY! IF MY PULSE GROWS ANY WEAKER THAN THIS...
I WON'T BE ABLE TO REVIVE BARBIEL!
WHILE I CAN STILL MOVE, I'VE GOT TO GET TO A PLACE WHERE THE WINDS ARE STRONG ENOUGH FOR HEALING...
LORD RAPHAEL! DON'T GO!
IF SOMETHING WERE TO HAPPEN TO YOU... THERE'S NO ONE LEFT IN THIS WORLD THAT WILL BE ABLE TO REVIVE *YOU*!
LORD RAPHAEL!

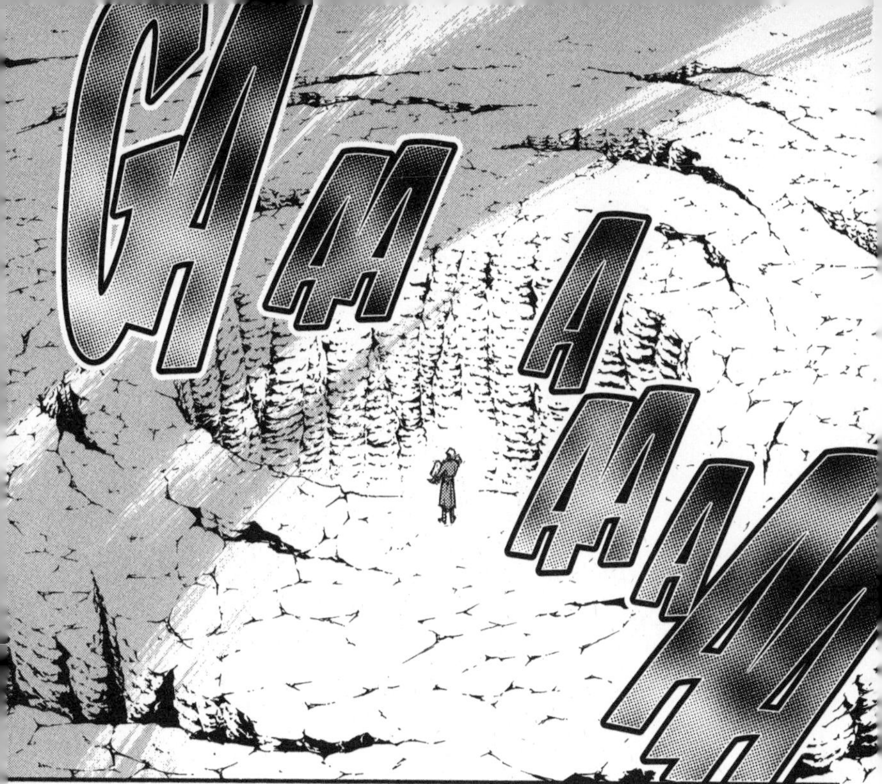
GAAAAAAAAH

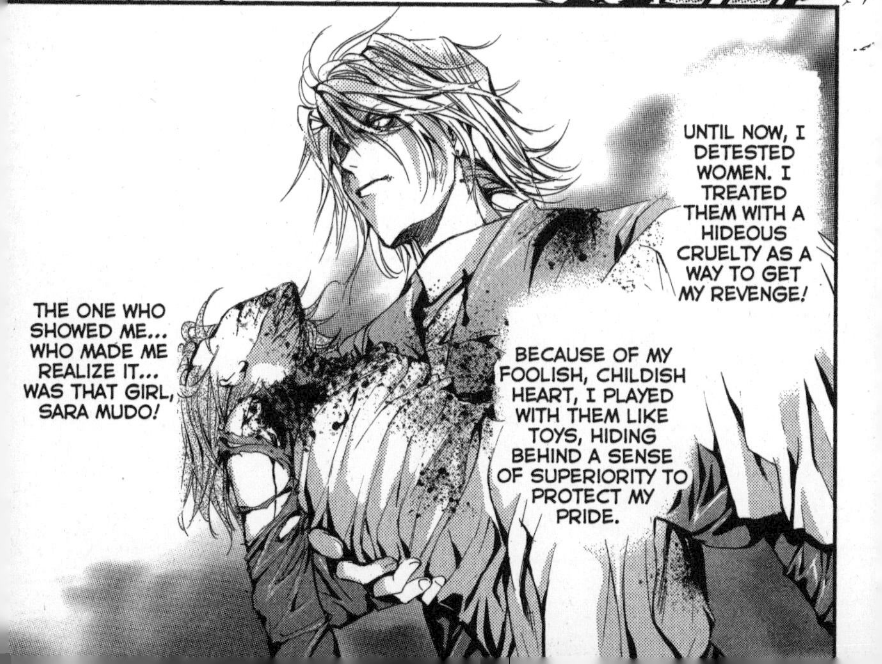
UNTIL NOW, I DETESTED WOMEN. I TREATED THEM WITH A HIDEOUS CRUELTY AS A WAY TO GET MY REVENGE!
BECAUSE OF MY FOOLISH, CHILDISH HEART, I PLAYED WITH THEM LIKE TOYS, HIDING BEHIND A SENSE OF SUPERIORITY TO PROTECT MY PRIDE.
THE ONE WHO SHOWED ME... WHO MADE ME REALIZE IT... WAS THAT GIRL, SARA MUDO!

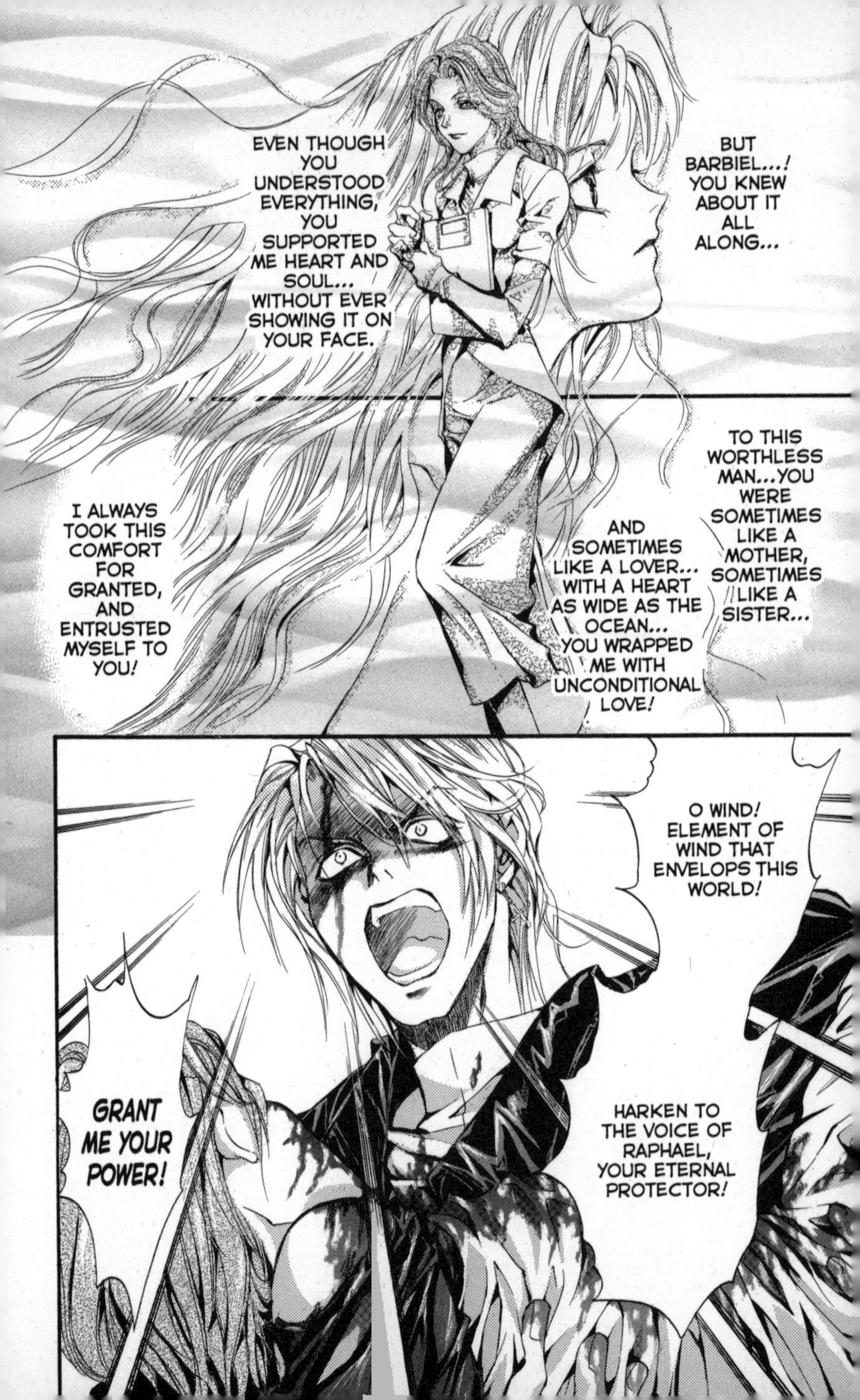
BUT BARBIEL...! YOU KNEW ABOUT IT ALL ALONG...
EVEN THOUGH YOU UNDERSTOOD EVERYTHING, YOU SUPPORTED ME HEART AND SOUL... WITHOUT EVER SHOWING IT ON YOUR FACE.
TO THIS WORTHLESS MAN...YOU WERE SOMETIMES LIKE A MOTHER, SOMETIMES LIKE A SISTER...
AND SOMETIMES LIKE A LOVER... WITH A HEART AS WIDE AS THE OCEAN... YOU WRAPPED ME WITH UNCONDITIONAL LOVE!
I ALWAYS TOOK THIS COMFORT FOR GRANTED, AND ENTRUSTED MYSELF TO YOU!
O WIND! ELEMENT OF WIND THAT ENVELOPS THIS WORLD!
HARKEN TO THE VOICE OF RAPHAEL, YOUR ETERNAL PROTECTOR!
GRANT ME YOUR POWER!

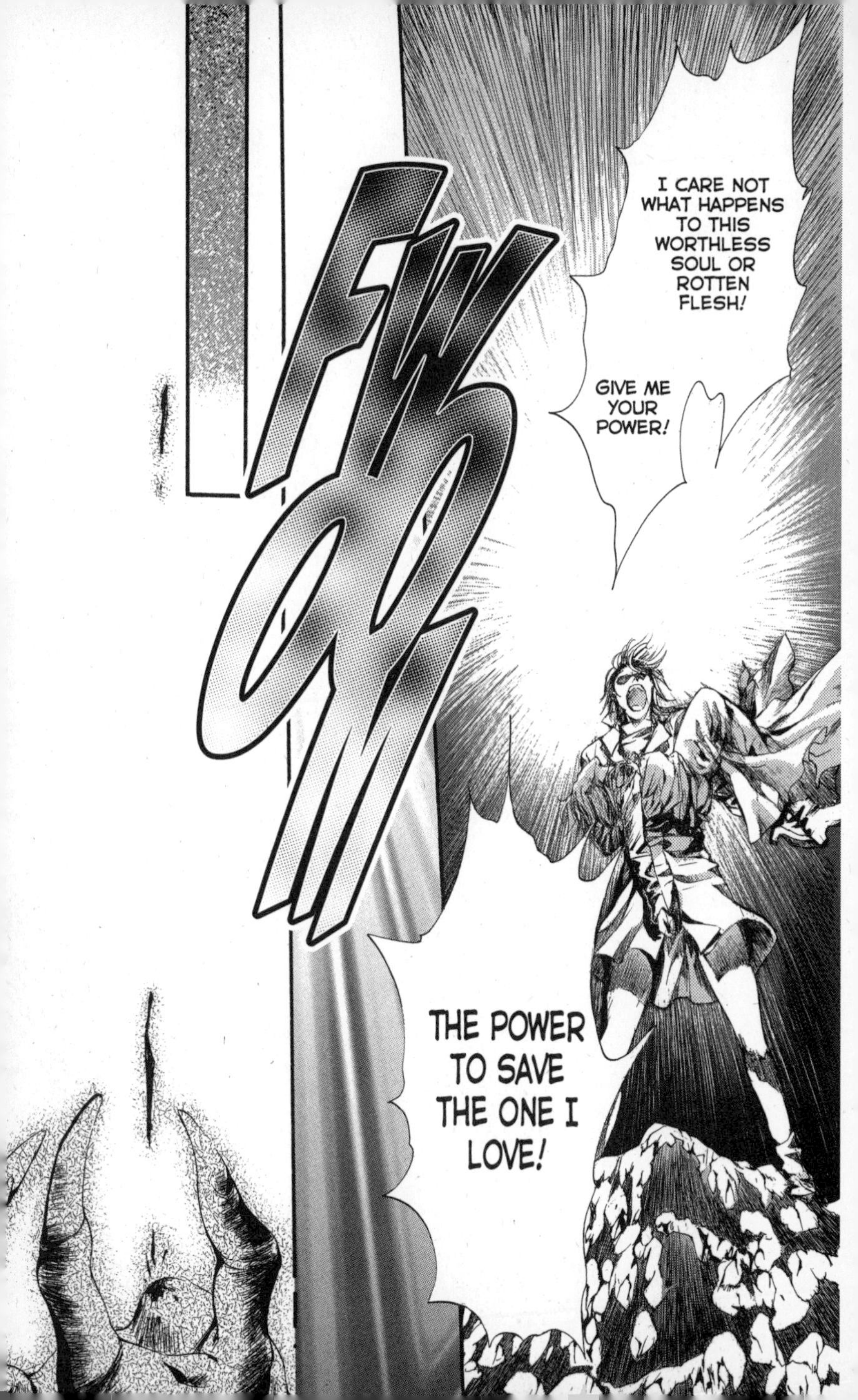
I CARE NOT WHAT HAPPENS TO THIS WORTHLESS SOUL OR ROTTEN FLESH!
GIVE ME YOUR POWER!
THE POWER TO SAVE THE ONE I LOVE!

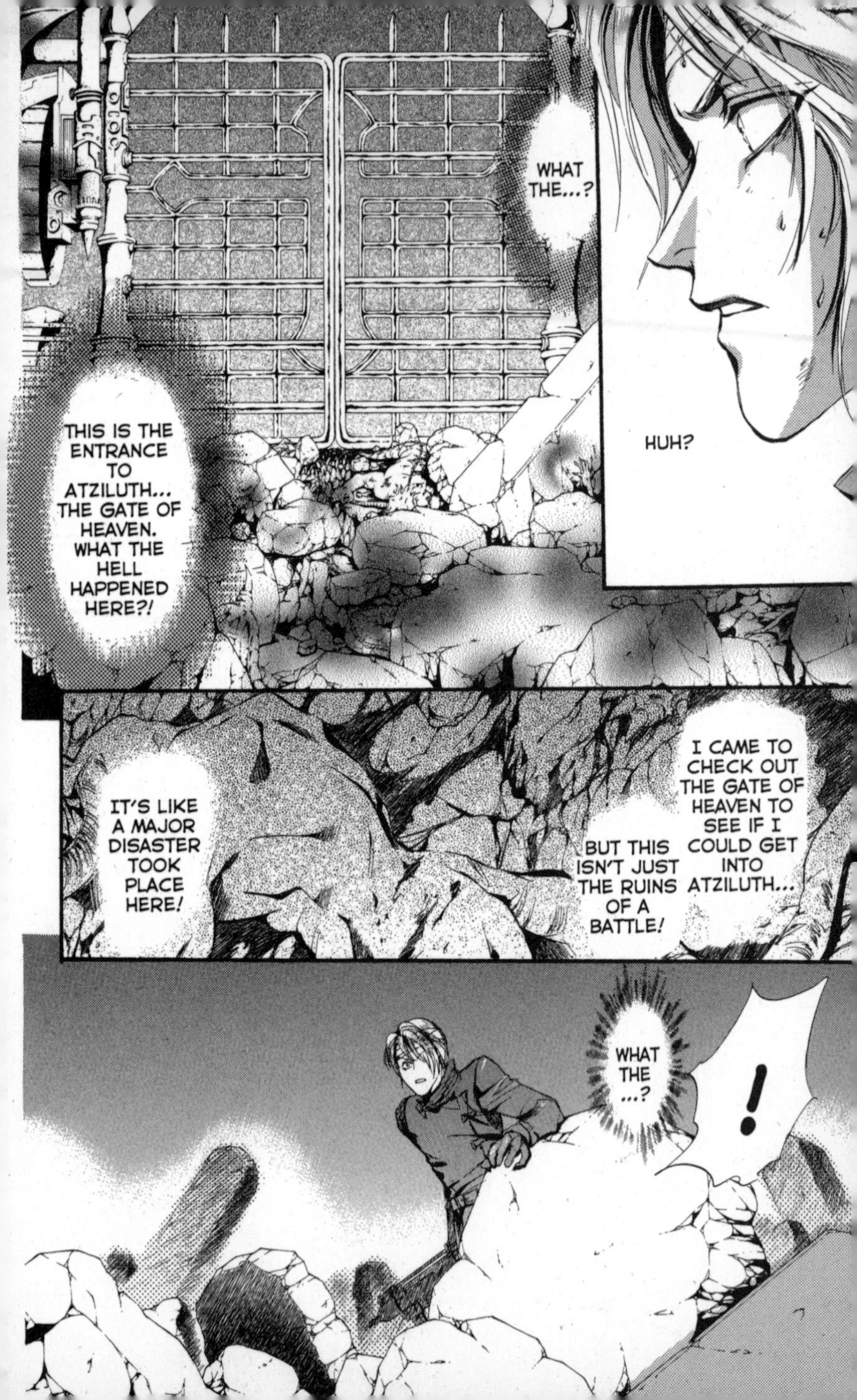
WHAT THE...?
HUH?
THIS IS THE ENTRANCE TO ATZILUTH... THE GATE OF HEAVEN. WHAT THE HELL HAPPENED HERE?!
I CAME TO CHECK OUT THE GATE OF HEAVEN TO SEE IF I COULD GET INTO ATZILUTH...
BUT THIS ISN'T JUST THE RUINS OF A BATTLE!
IT'S LIKE A MAJOR DISASTER TOOK PLACE HERE!
WHAT THE ...?
!

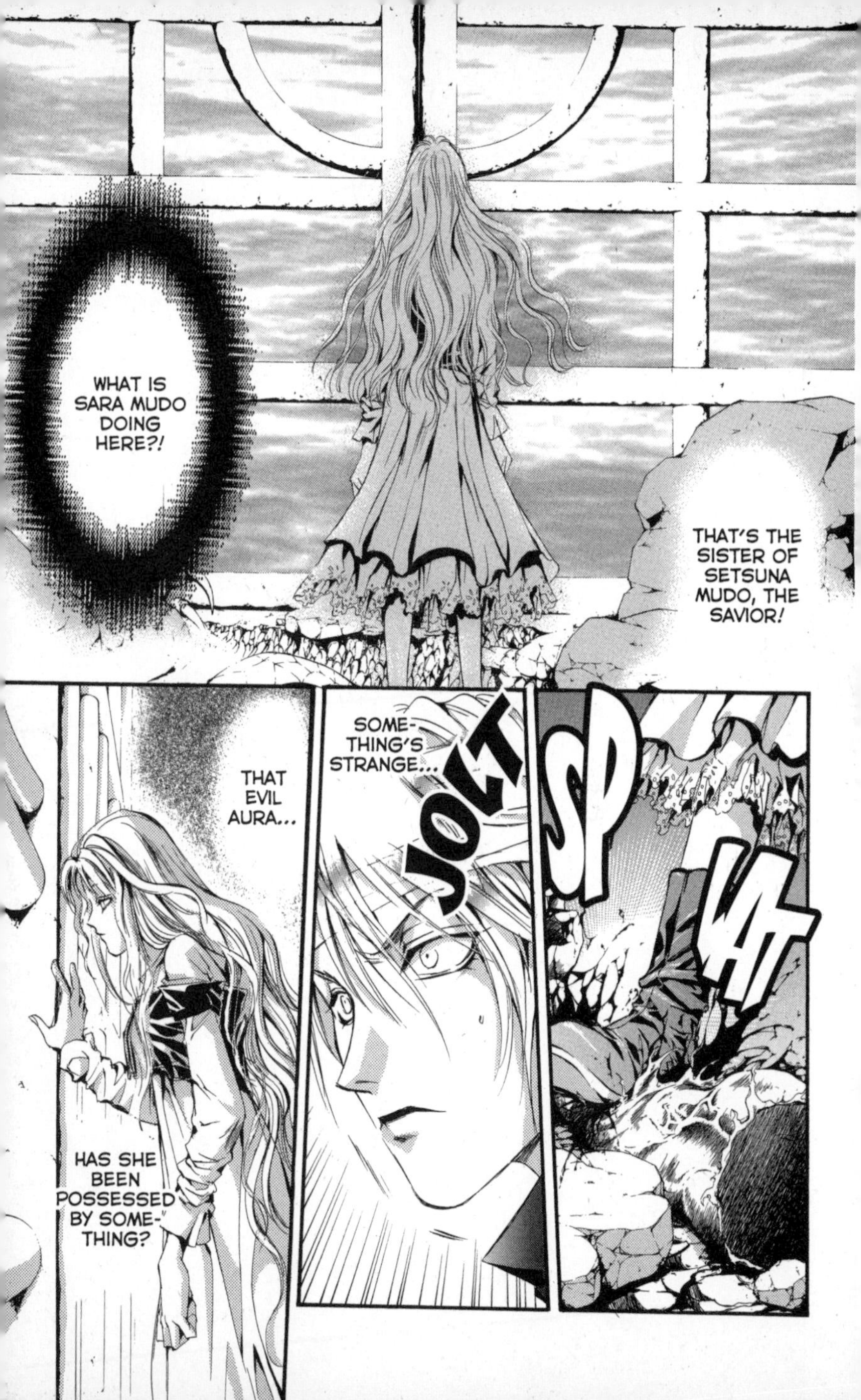
THAT'S THE SISTER OF SETSUNA MUDO, THE SAVIOR!
WHAT IS SARA MUDO DOING HERE?!
SPLAT
JOLT
SOME-THING'S STRANGE...
THAT EVIL AURA...
HAS SHE BEEN POSSESSED BY SOME-THING?

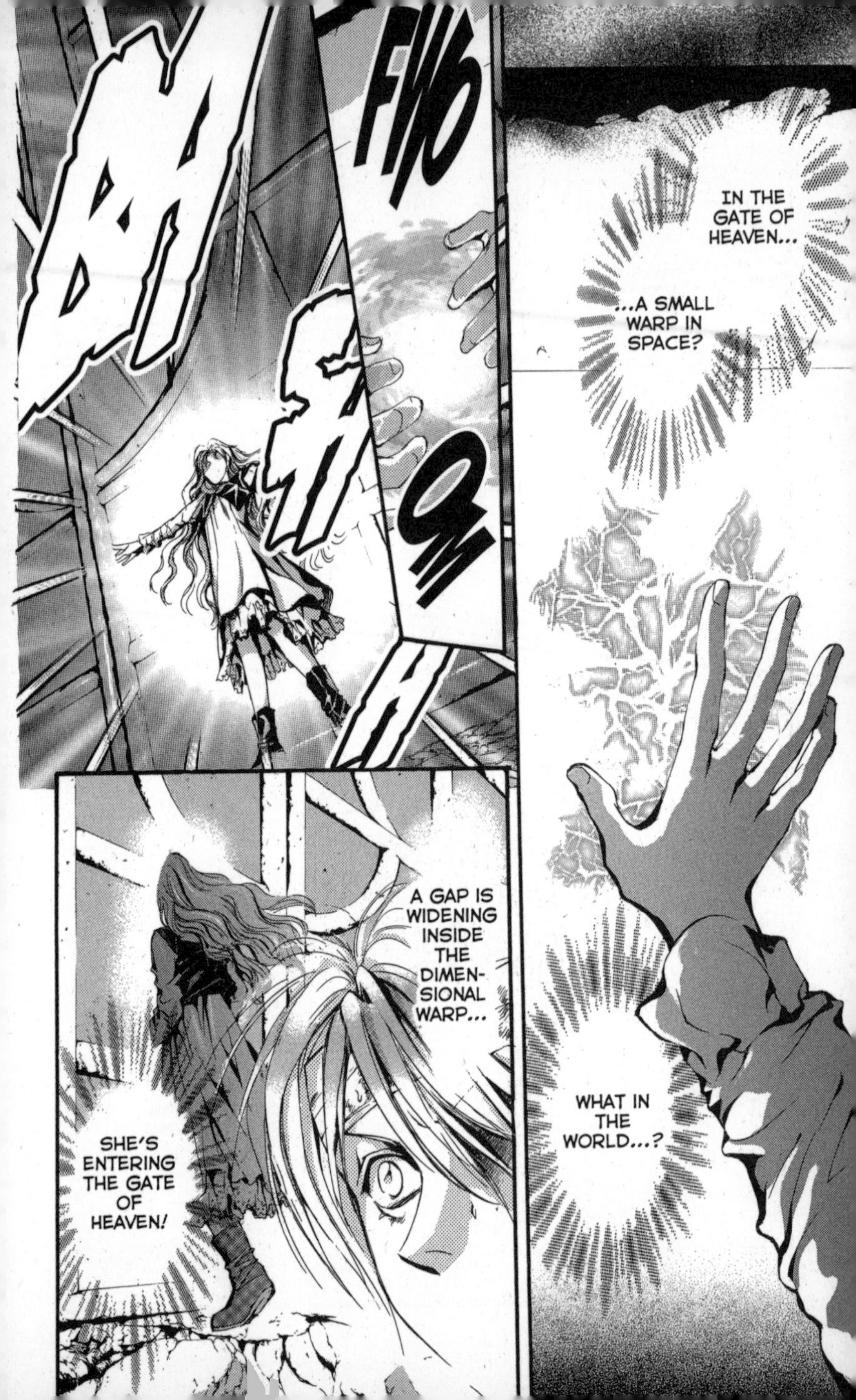
IN THE GATE OF HEAVEN...
...A SMALL WARP IN SPACE?
WHAT IN THE WORLD...?
FWO
OM
A GAP IS WIDENING INSIDE THE DIMEN-SIONAL WARP...
SHE'S ENTERING THE GATE OF HEAVEN!

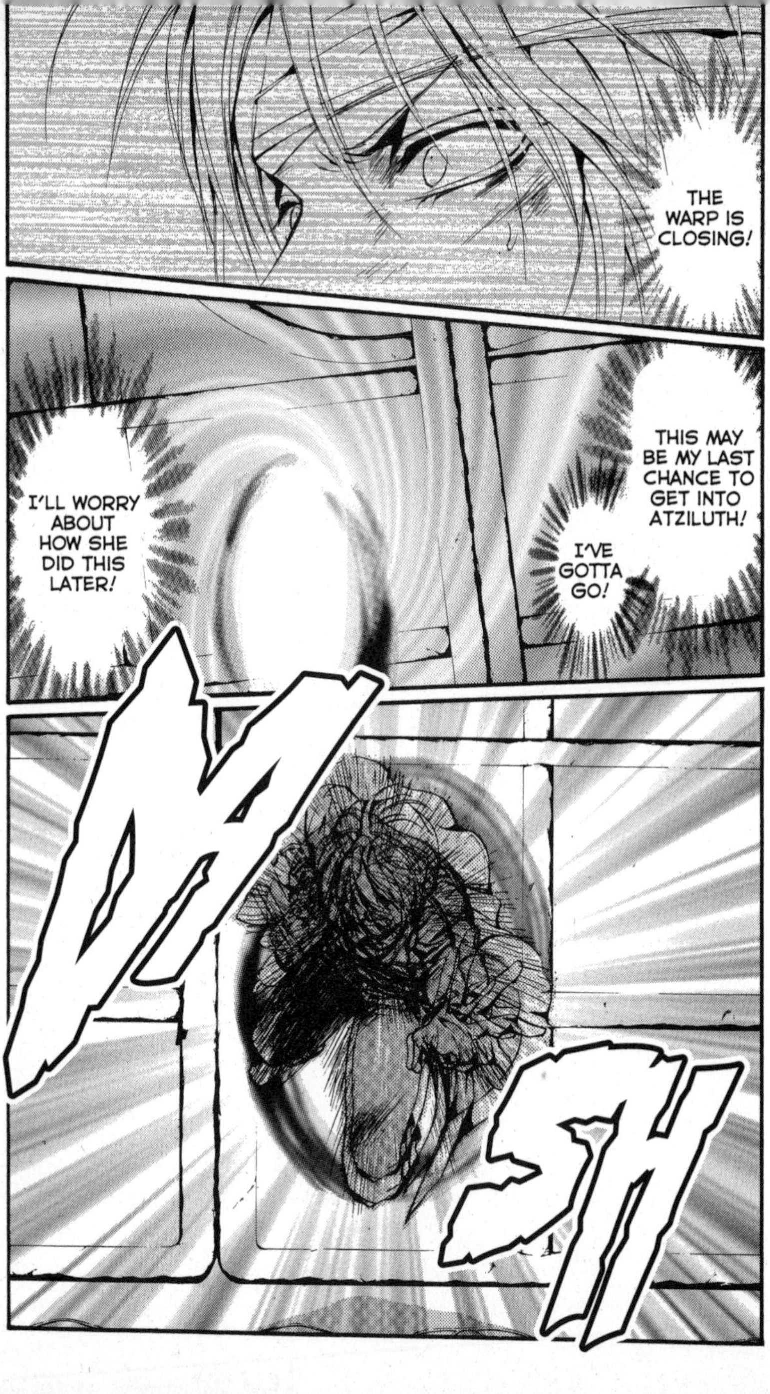
THE WARP IS CLOSING!
THIS MAY BE MY LAST CHANCE TO GET INTO ATZILUTH!
I'VE GOTTA GO!
I'LL WORRY ABOUT HOW SHE DID THIS LATER!
DASH

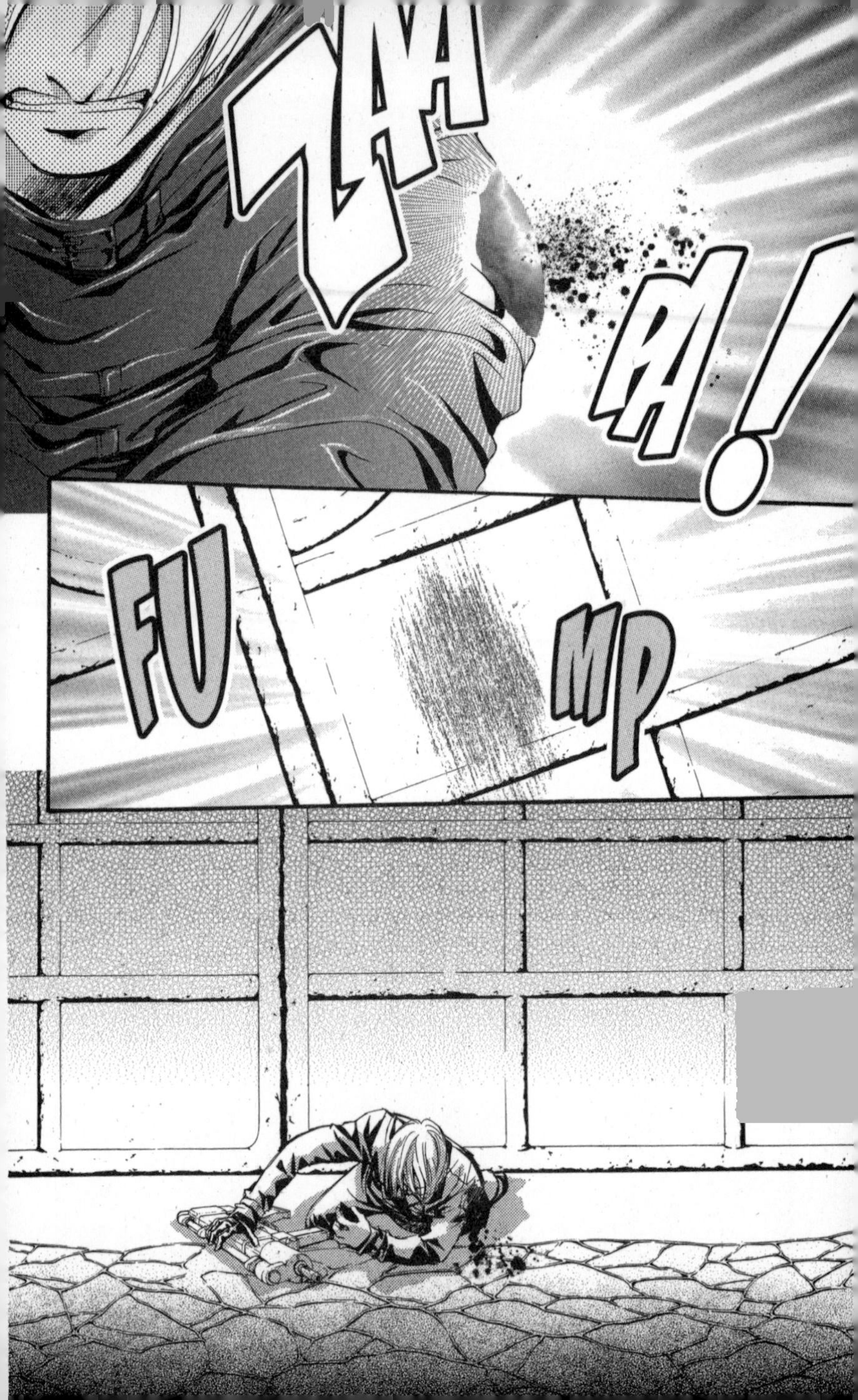
ZAA
PA!
FU
MP

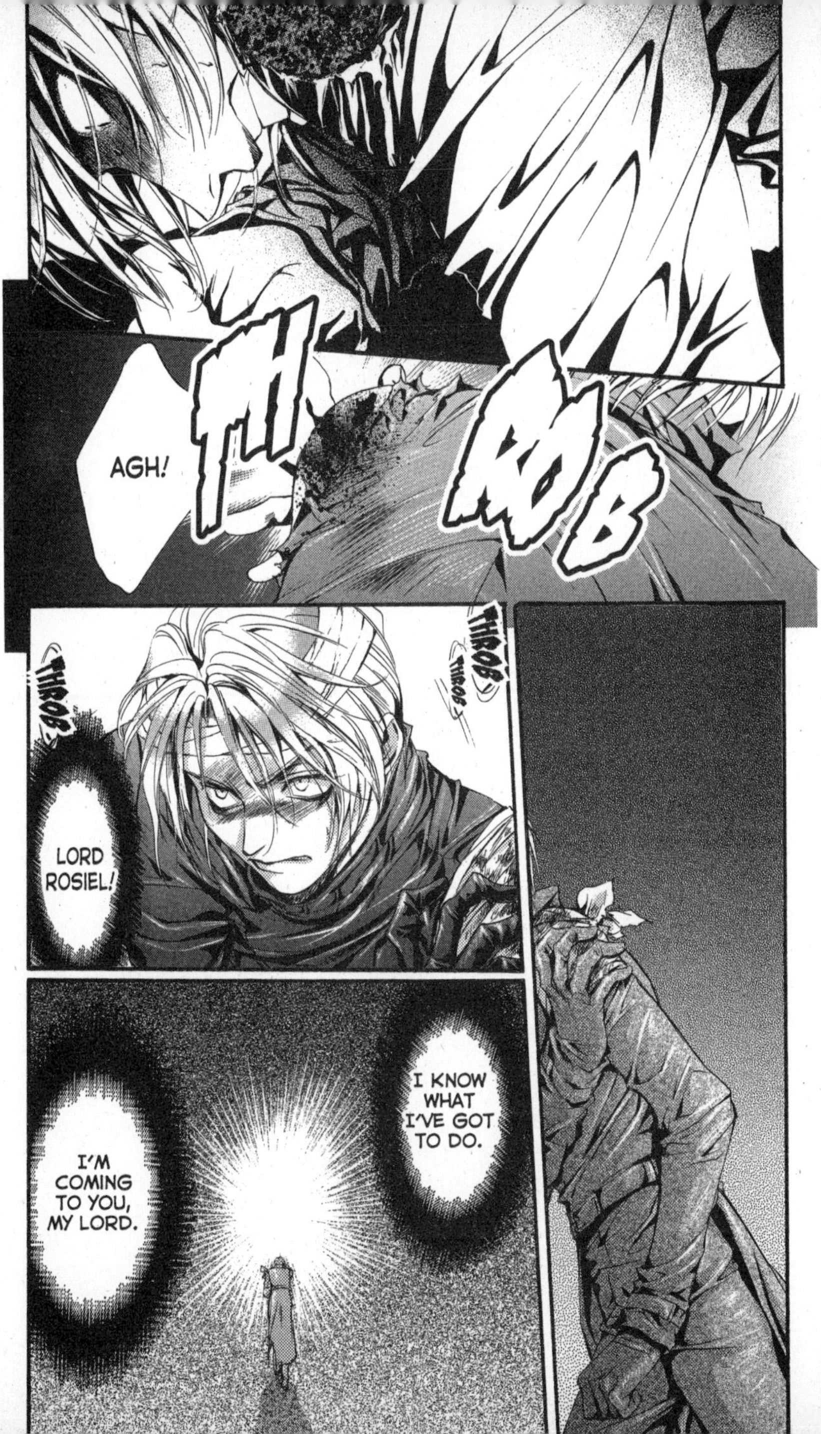
THROB
AGH!
THROB THROB
THROB
LORD ROSIEL!
I KNOW WHAT I'VE GOT TO DO.
I'M COMING TO YOU, MY LORD.

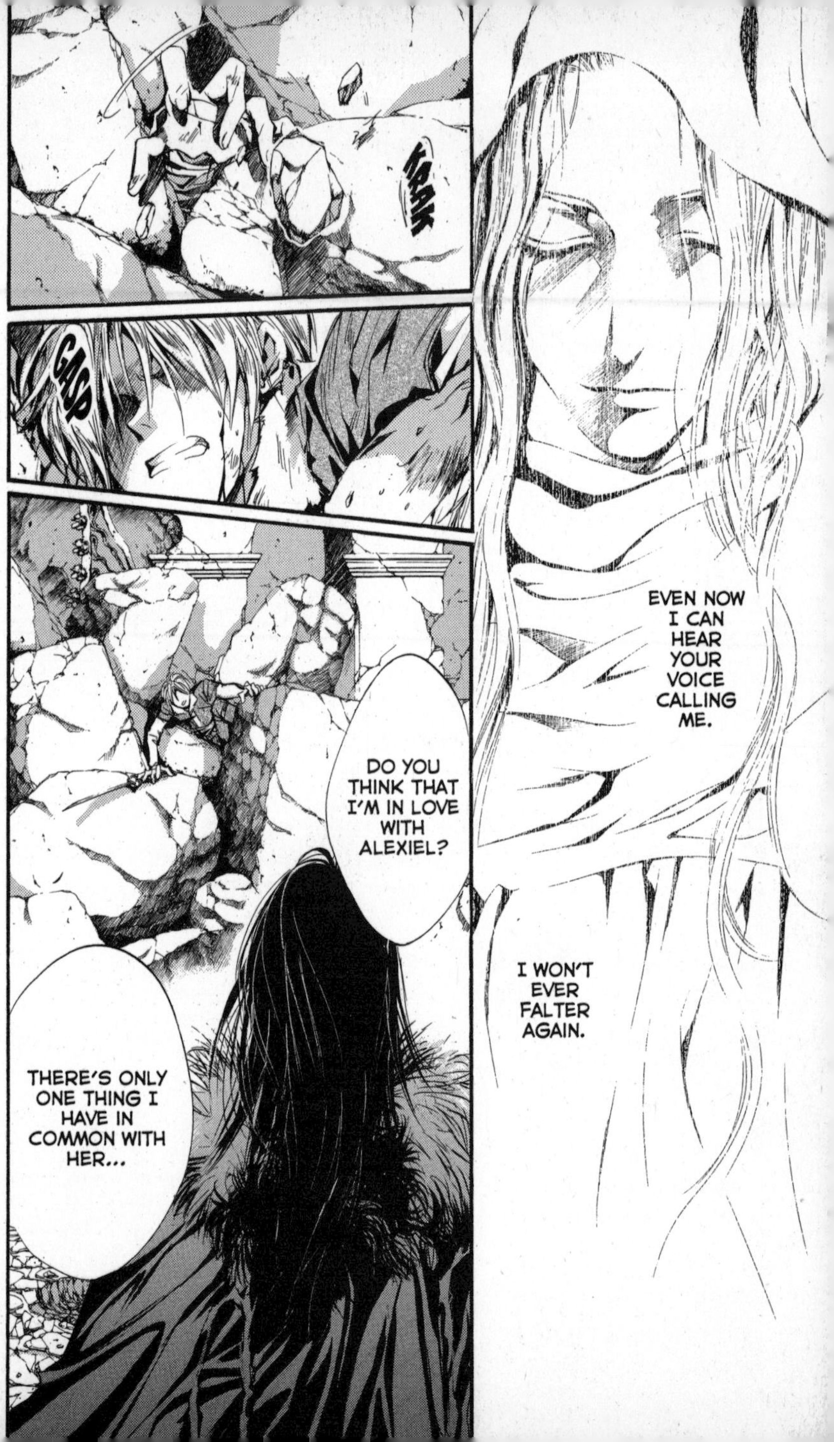
EVEN NOW I CAN HEAR YOUR VOICE CALLING ME.
I WON'T EVER FALTER AGAIN.
KRAAK
GASP
DO YOU THINK THAT I'M IN LOVE WITH ALEXIEL?
THERE'S ONLY ONE THING I HAVE IN COMMON WITH HER...

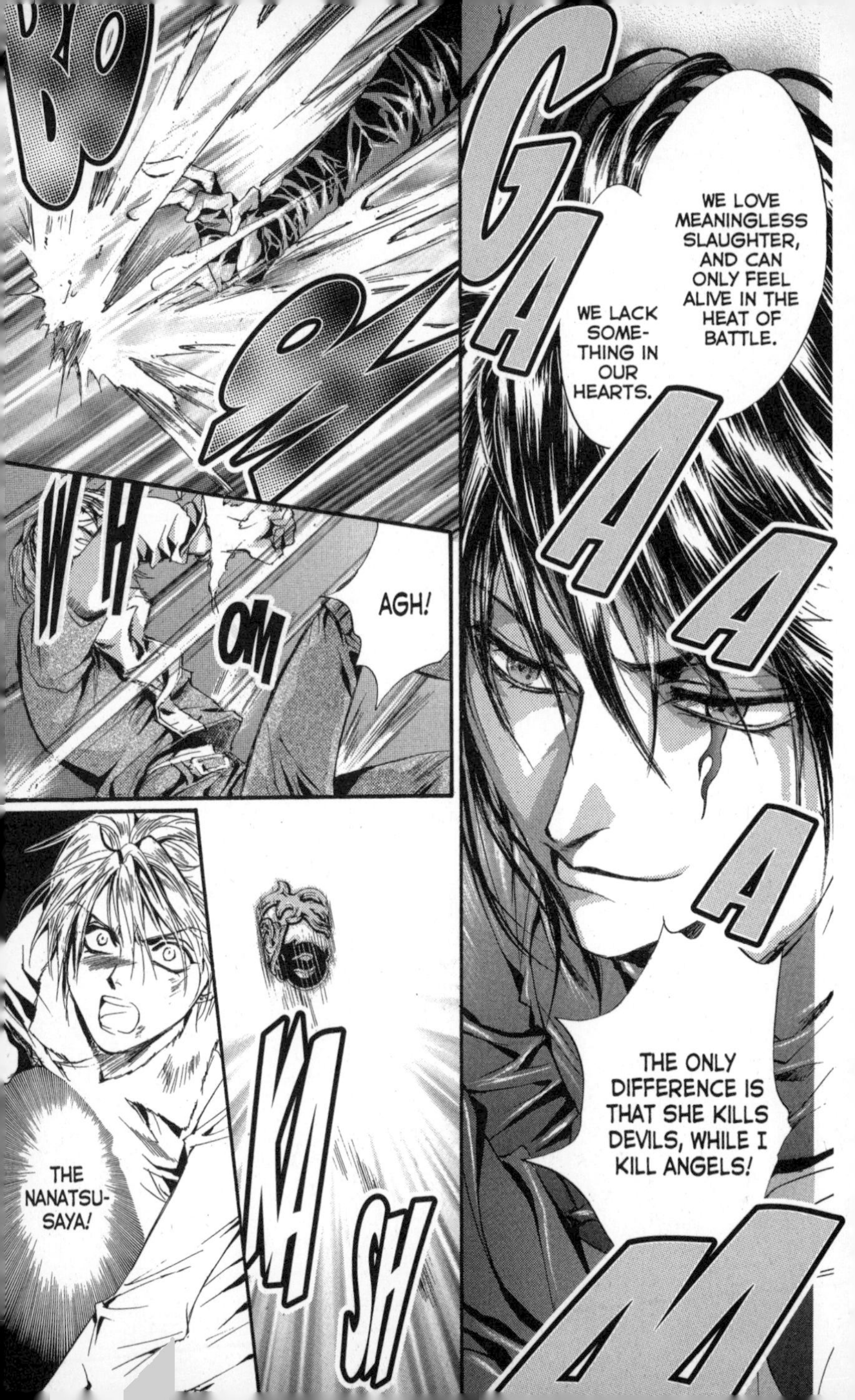
WE LOVE MEANINGLESS SLAUGHTER, AND CAN ONLY FEEL ALIVE IN THE HEAT OF BATTLE.
WE LACK SOME-THING IN OUR HEARTS.
THE ONLY DIFFERENCE IS THAT SHE KILLS DEVILS, WHILE I KILL ANGELS!
AGH!
THE NANATSU-SAYA!

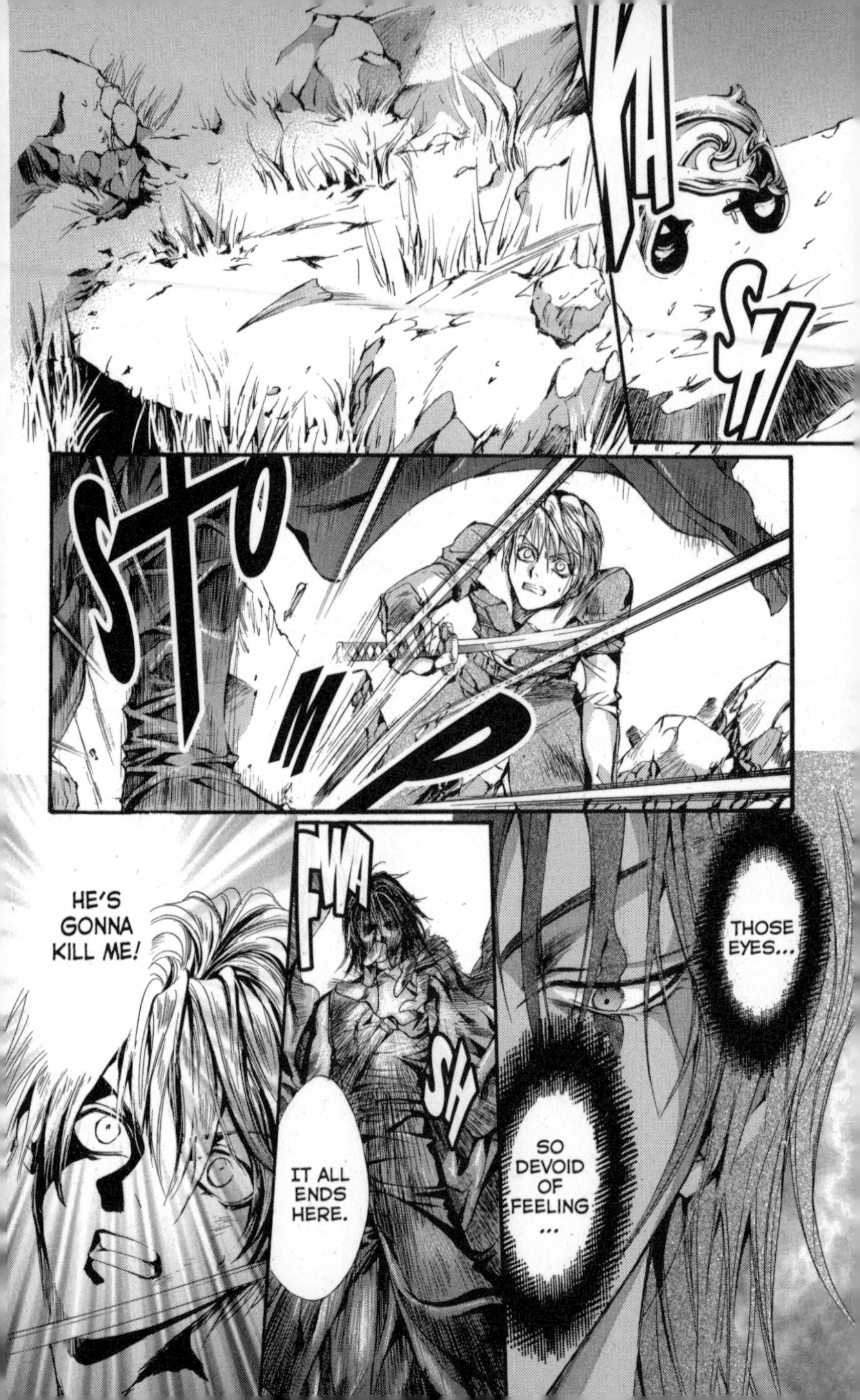
WHOOSH
STOMP
THOSE EYES...
SO DEVOID OF FEELING...
FWA
SH
IT ALL ENDS HERE.
HE'S GONNA KILL ME!

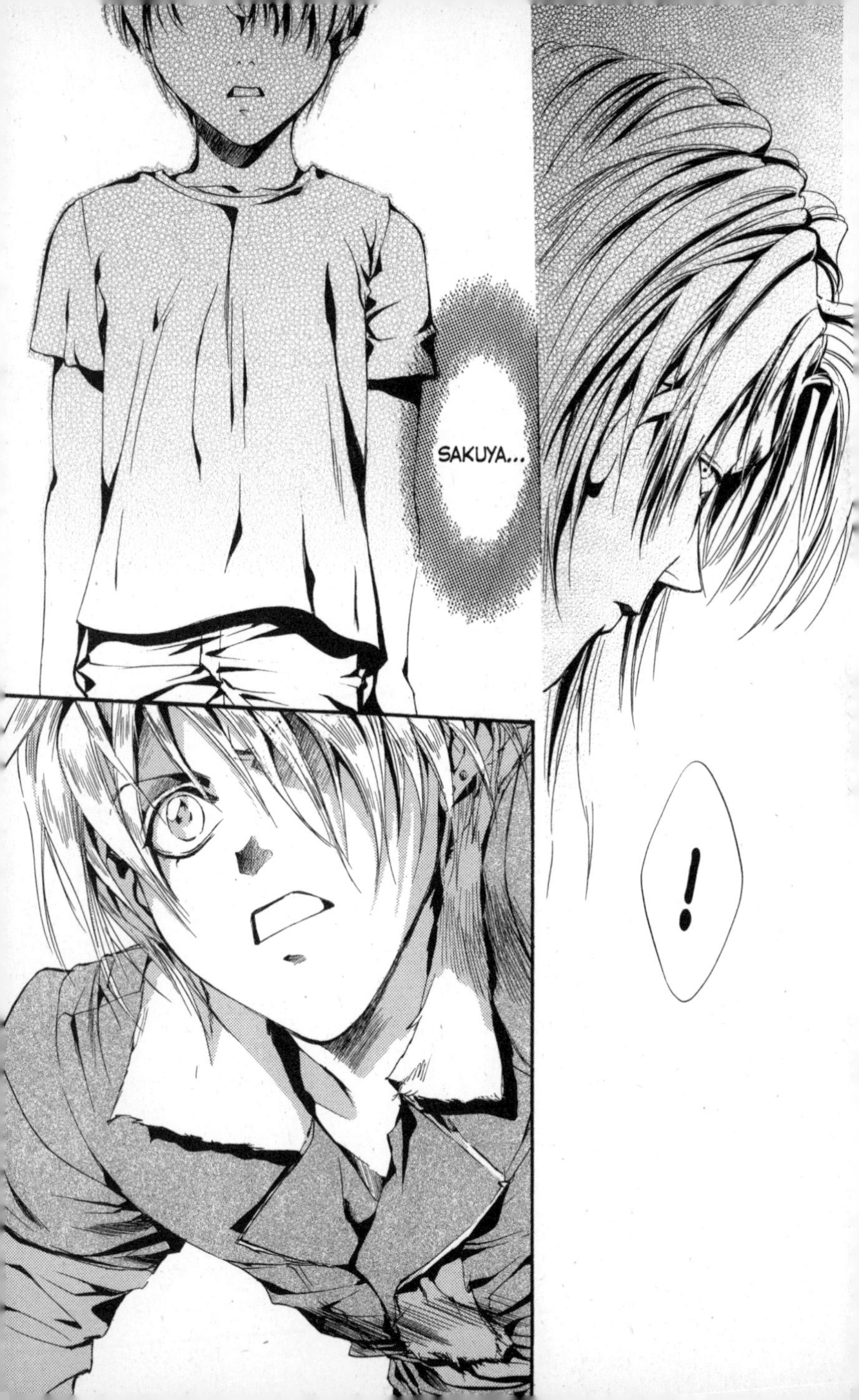
!
SAKUYA...

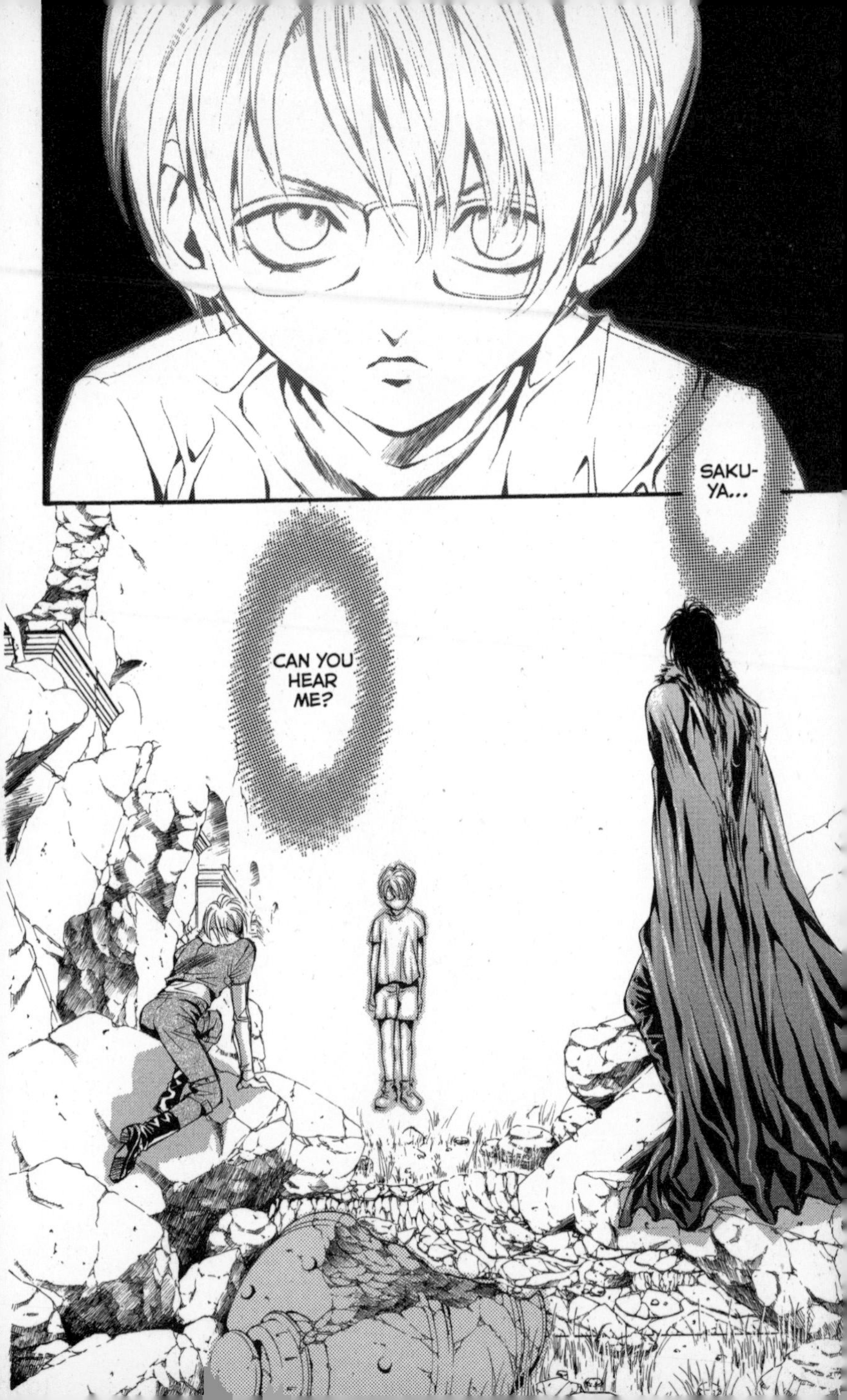
SAKU-YA...
CAN YOU HEAR ME?

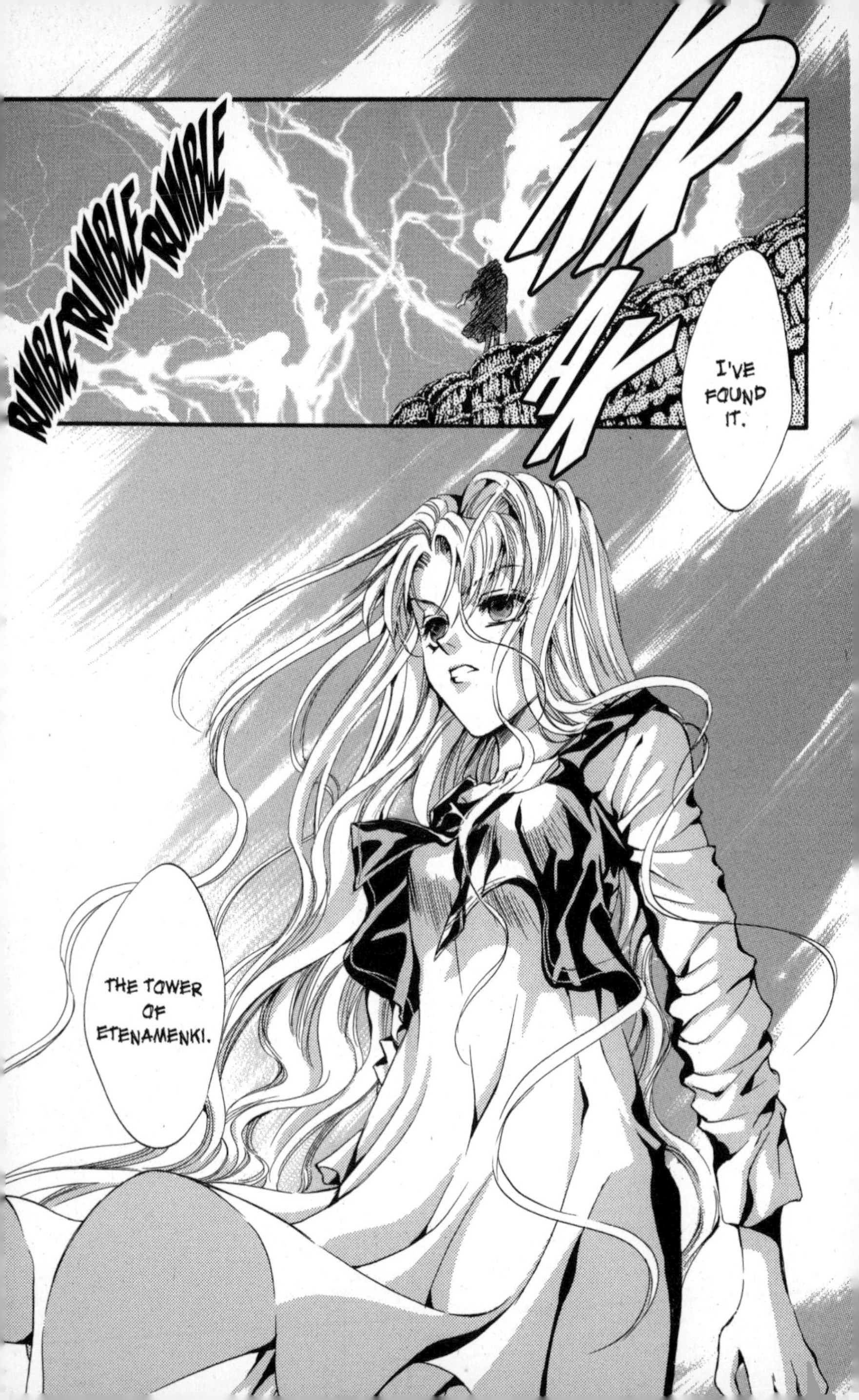
KRAK
RUMBLE RUMBLE RUMBLE
I'VE FOUND IT.
THE TOWER OF ETENAMENKI.

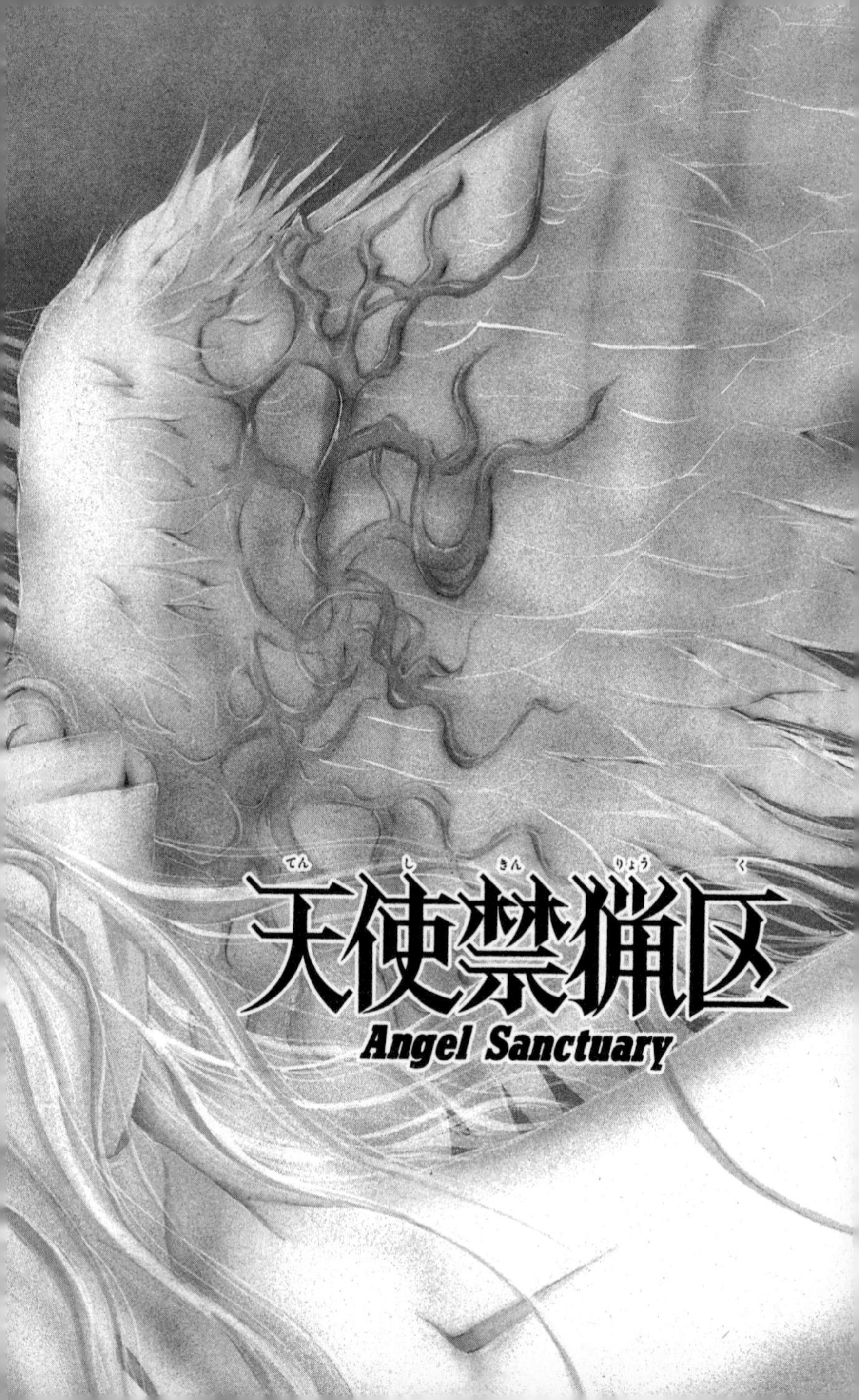
天使禁猟区
Angel Sanctuary

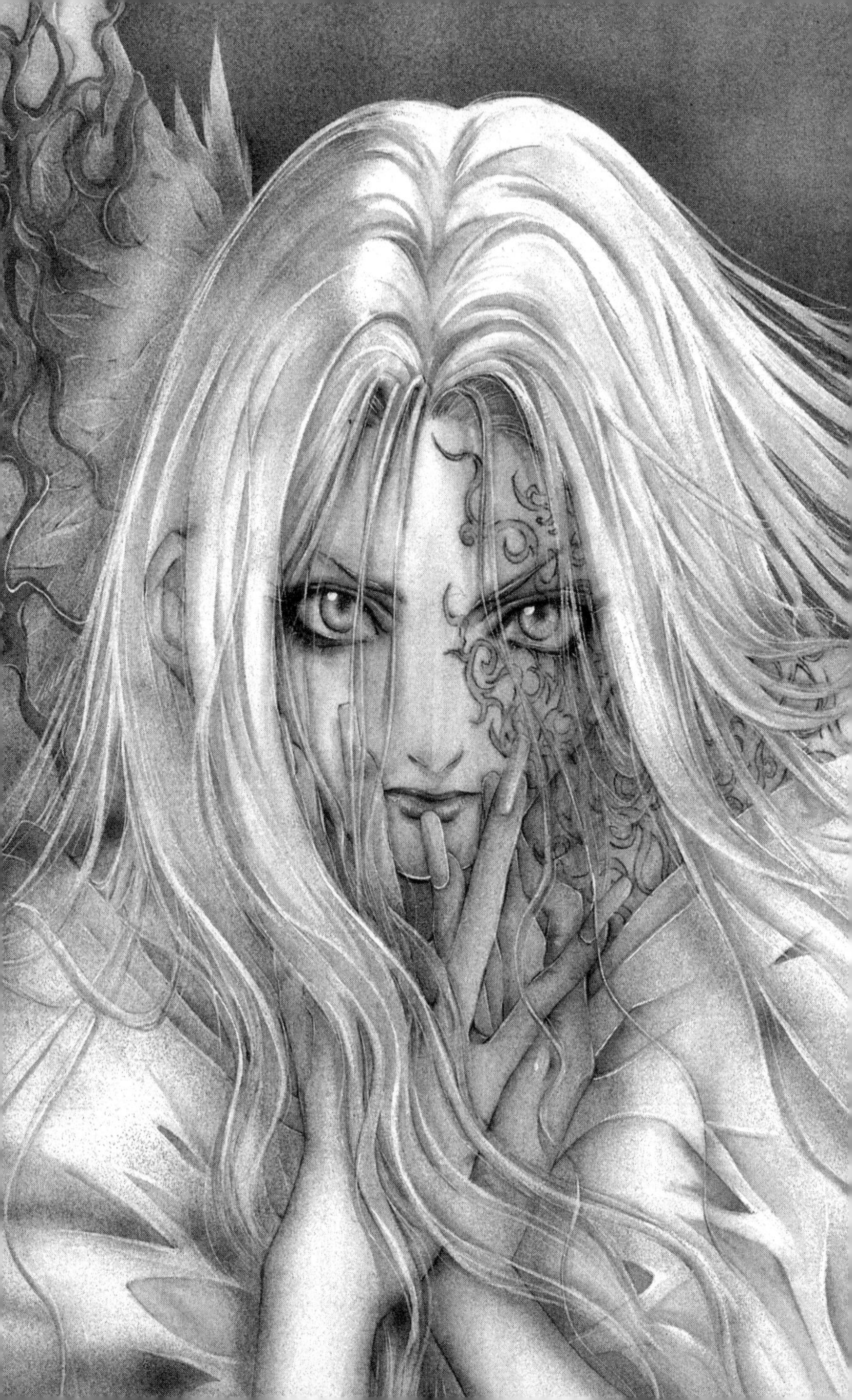

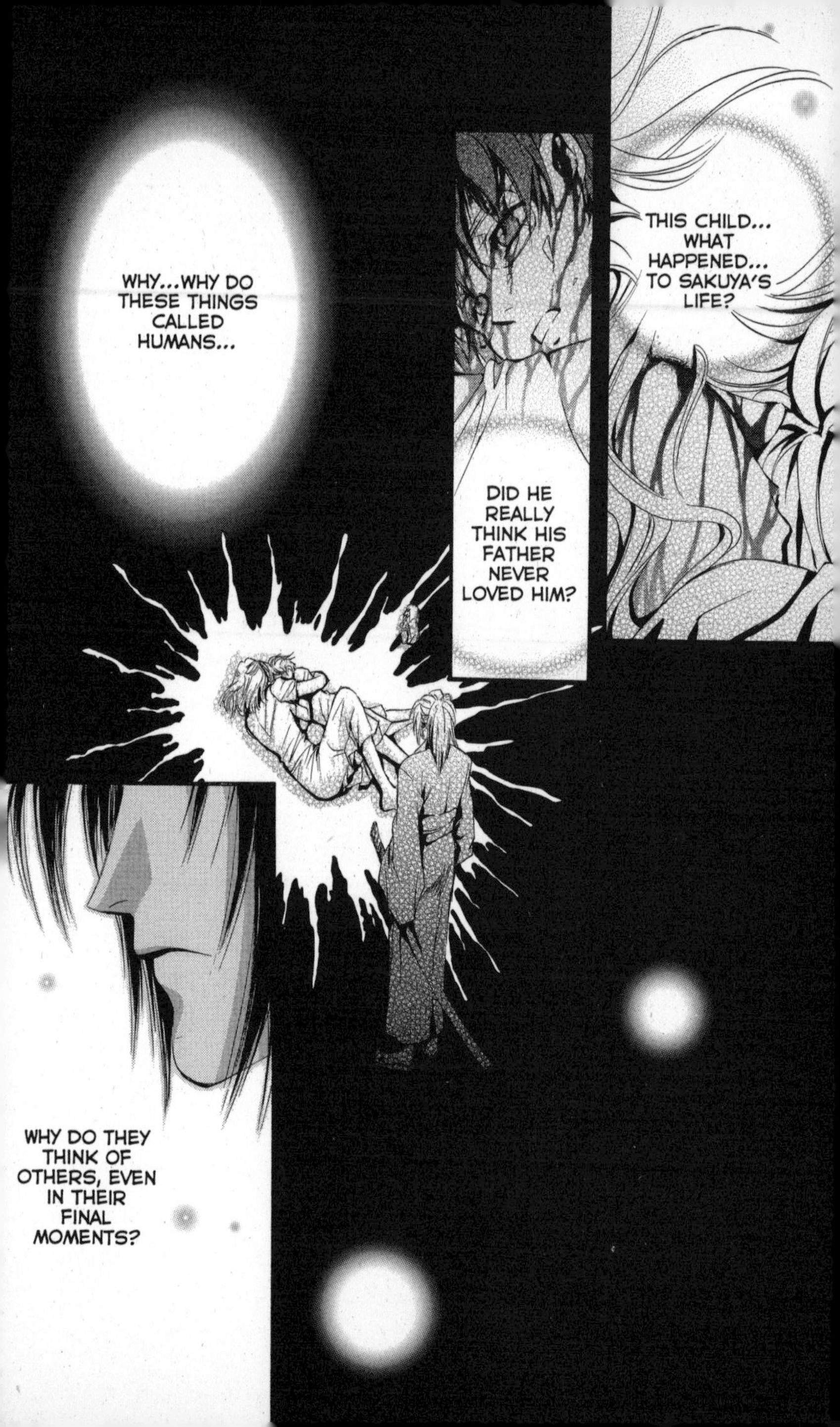
THIS CHILD... WHAT HAPPENED... TO SAKUYA'S LIFE?
DID HE REALLY THINK HIS FATHER NEVER LOVED HIM?
WHY...WHY DO THESE THINGS CALLED HUMANS...
WHY DO THEY THINK OF OTHERS, EVEN IN THEIR FINAL MOMENTS?

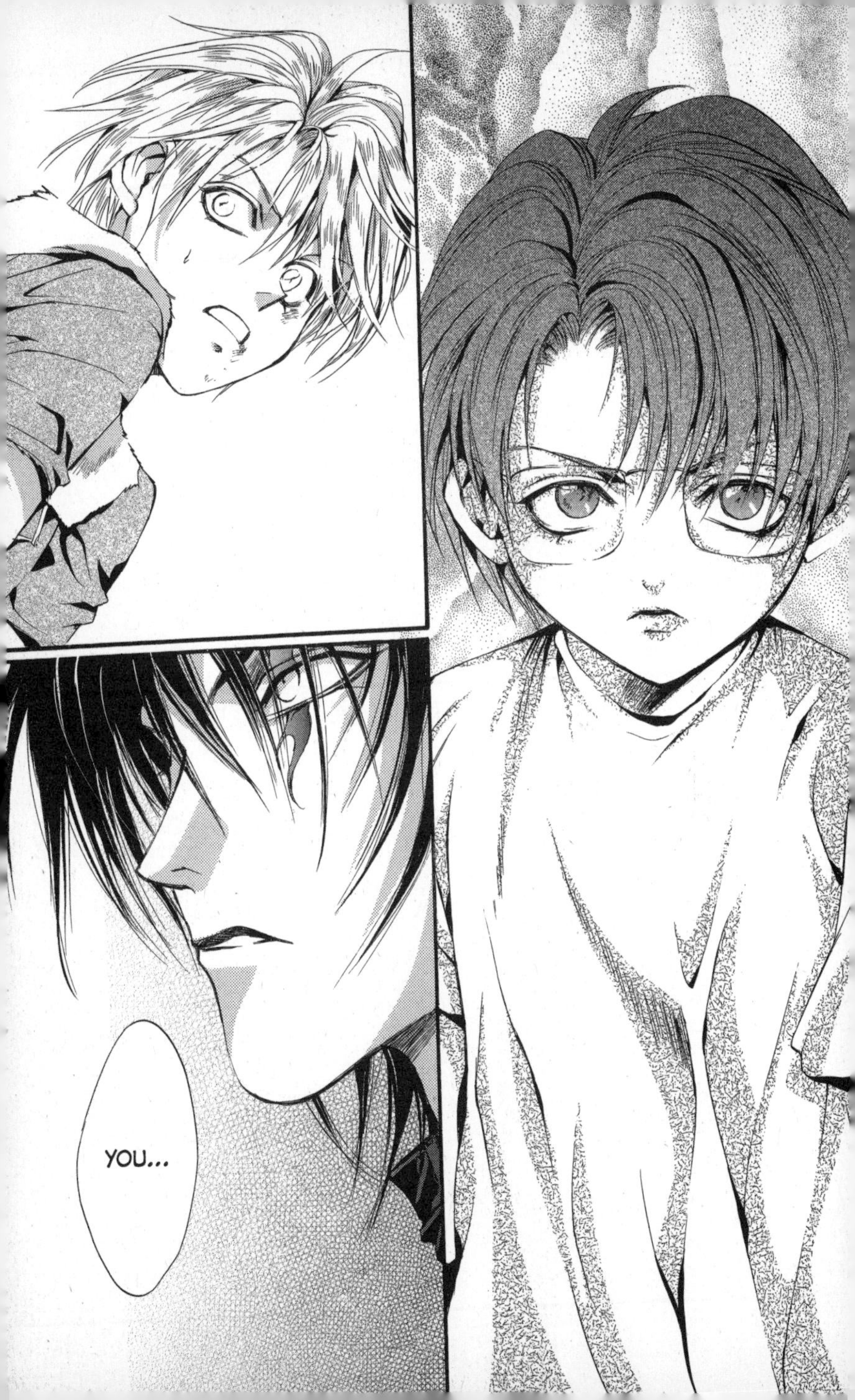
YOU...

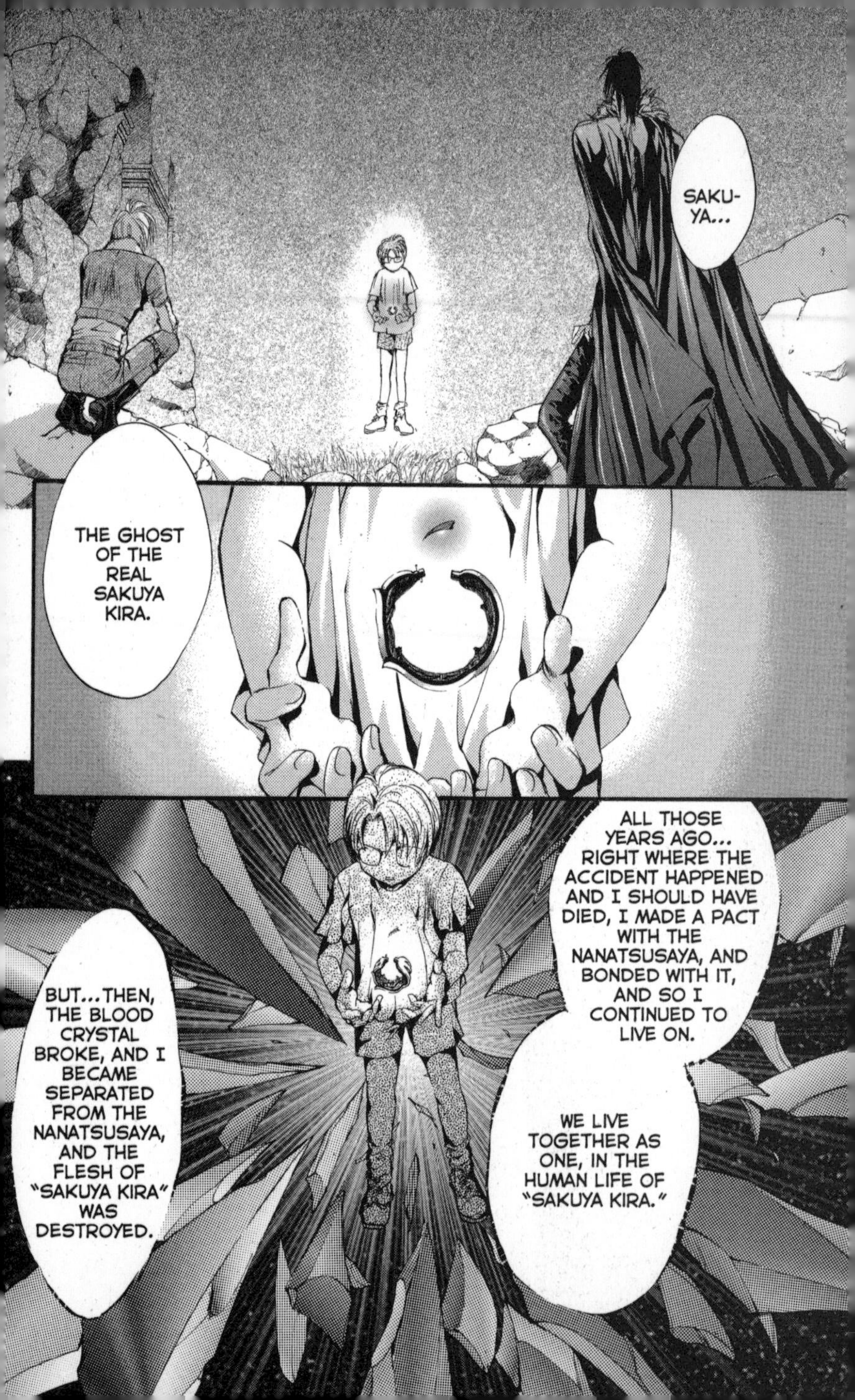
SAKU-YA...
THE GHOST OF THE REAL SAKUYA KIRA.
ALL THOSE YEARS AGO... RIGHT WHERE THE ACCIDENT HAPPENED AND I SHOULD HAVE DIED, I MADE A PACT WITH THE NANATSUSAYA, AND BONDED WITH IT, AND SO I CONTINUED TO LIVE ON.
WE LIVE TOGETHER AS ONE, IN THE HUMAN LIFE OF "SAKUYA KIRA."
BUT...THEN, THE BLOOD CRYSTAL BROKE, AND I BECAME SEPARATED FROM THE NANATSUSAYA, AND THE FLESH OF "SAKUYA KIRA" WAS DESTROYED.

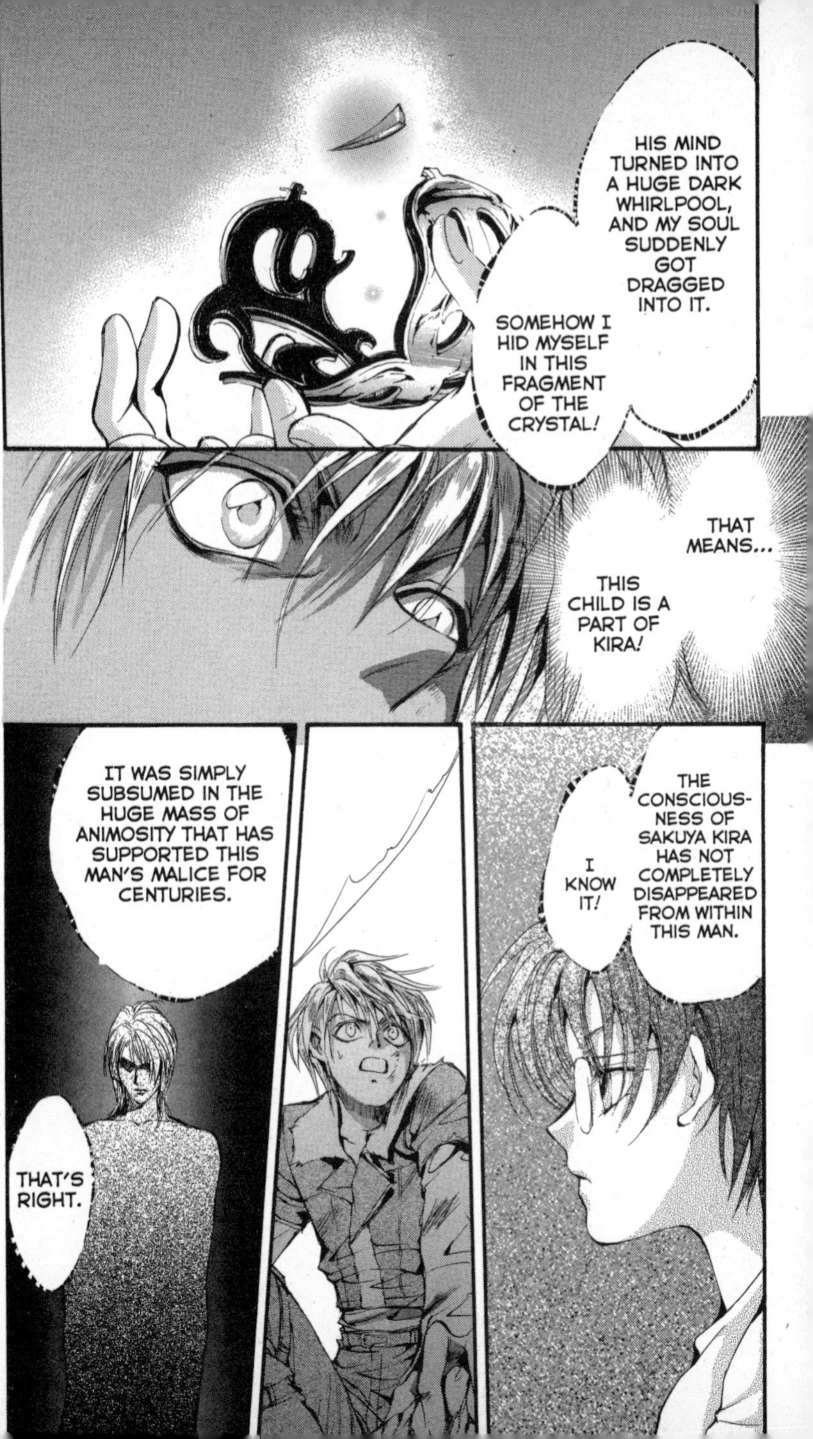
HIS MIND TURNED INTO A HUGE DARK WHIRLPOOL, AND MY SOUL SUDDENLY GOT DRAGGED INTO IT.
SOMEHOW I HID MYSELF IN THIS FRAGMENT OF THE CRYSTAL!
THAT MEANS...
THIS CHILD IS A PART OF KIRA!
THE CONSCIOUSNESS OF SAKUYA KIRA HAS NOT COMPLETELY DISAPPEARED FROM WITHIN THIS MAN.
I KNOW IT!
IT WAS SIMPLY SUBSUMED IN THE HUGE MASS OF ANIMOSITY THAT HAS SUPPORTED THIS MAN'S MALICE FOR CENTURIES.
THAT'S RIGHT.

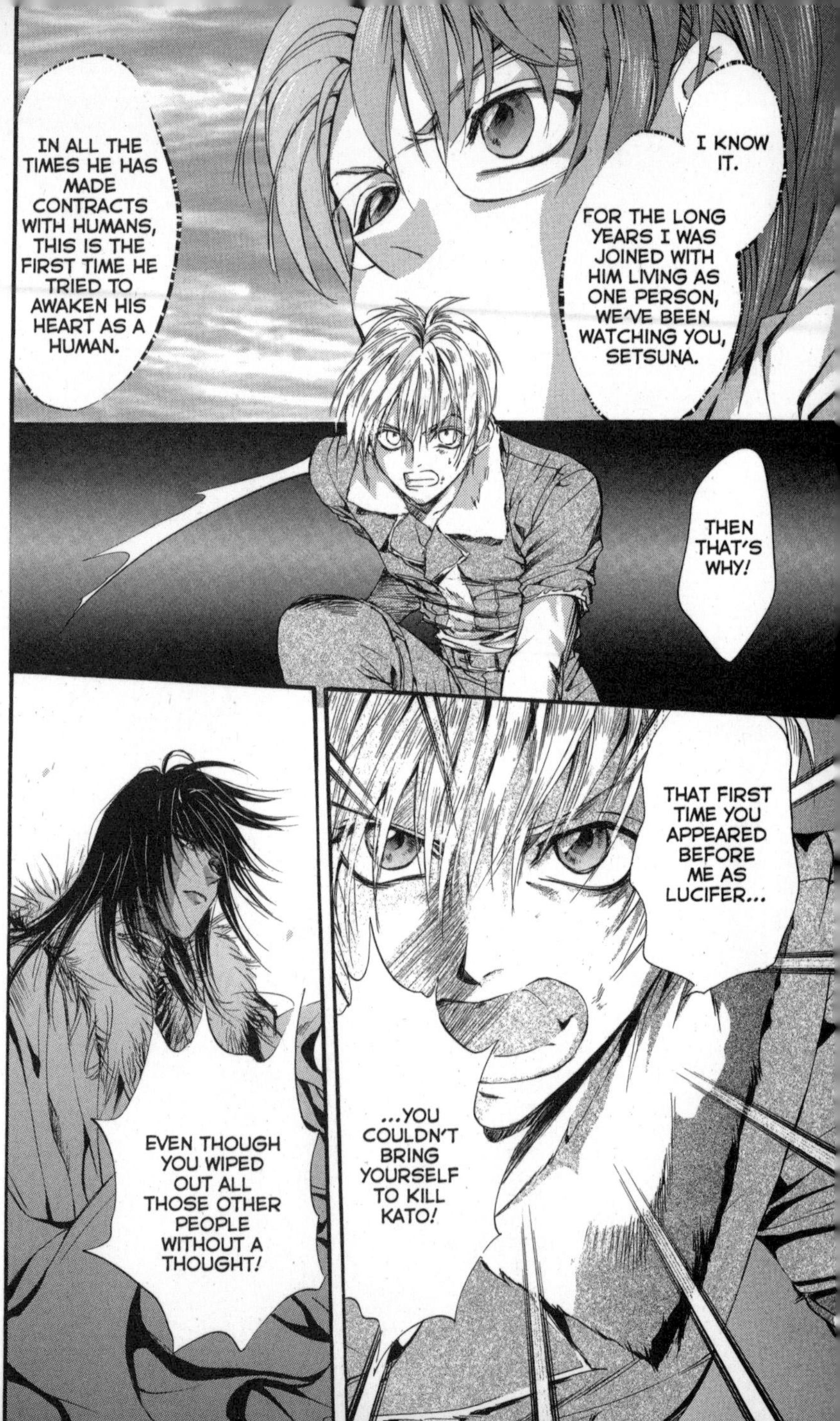
I KNOW IT.
FOR THE LONG YEARS I WAS JOINED WITH HIM LIVING AS ONE PERSON, WE'VE BEEN WATCHING YOU, SETSUNA.
IN ALL THE TIMES HE HAS MADE CONTRACTS WITH HUMANS, THIS IS THE FIRST TIME HE TRIED TO AWAKEN HIS HEART AS A HUMAN.
THEN THAT'S WHY!
THAT FIRST TIME YOU APPEARED BEFORE ME AS LUCIFER...
...YOU COULDN'T BRING YOURSELF TO KILL KATO!
EVEN THOUGH YOU WIPED OUT ALL THOSE OTHER PEOPLE WITHOUT A THOUGHT!

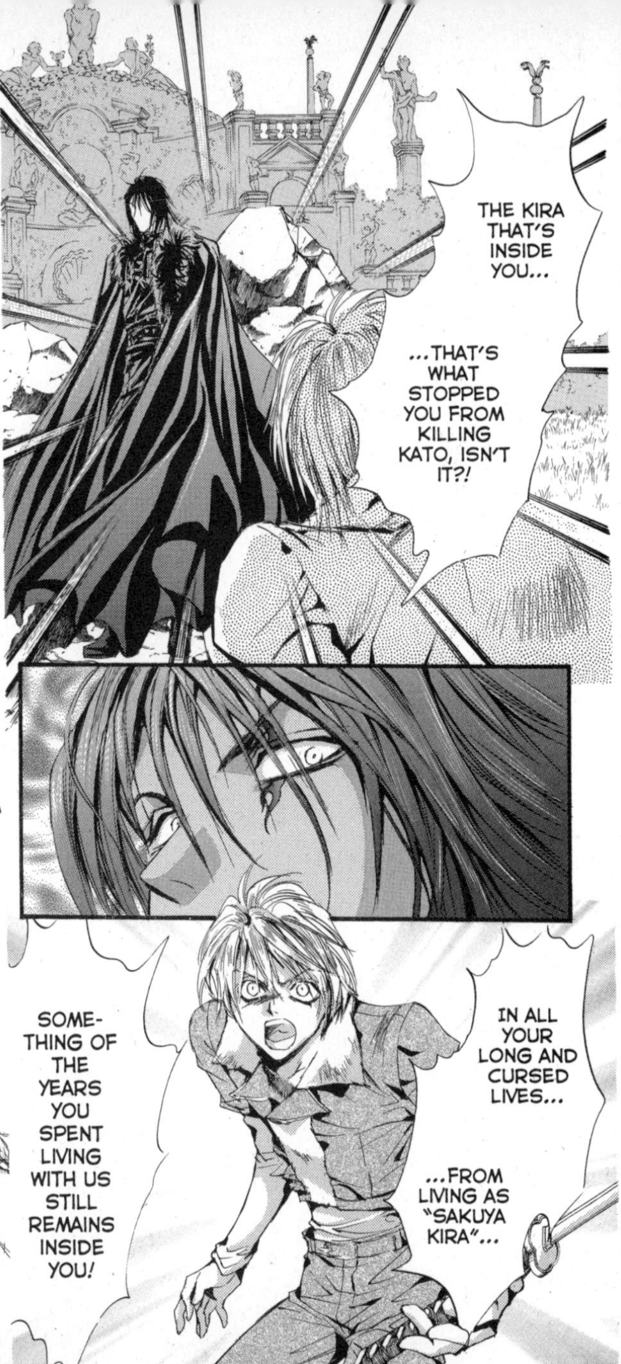
THE KIRA THAT'S INSIDE YOU...
...THAT'S WHAT STOPPED YOU FROM KILLING KATO, ISN'T IT?!
IN ALL YOUR LONG AND CURSED LIVES...
...FROM LIVING AS "SAKUYA KIRA"...
SOME-THING OF THE YEARS YOU SPENT LIVING WITH US STILL REMAINS INSIDE YOU!

In the Katan-in-the-coffin scene, the music and the sound effects really gave it a good cinematic mood. When Meta gets caught by the fake nun, he makes this flapping sound, which was really cute. I want to hear Michael and Raphael and the Hatter's voices really soon. Then in the Book of Hades section, when Setsuna is inside Alexiel's body, the voice was Alexiel's (of course).

So it looks like the CDs will keep coming out, so I hope people get interested in them. I'm sorry I keep trying to get you to buy things, like the OVA and the CD, etc.

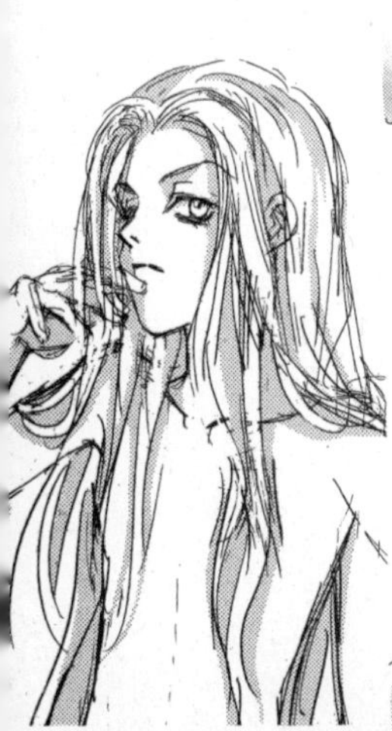

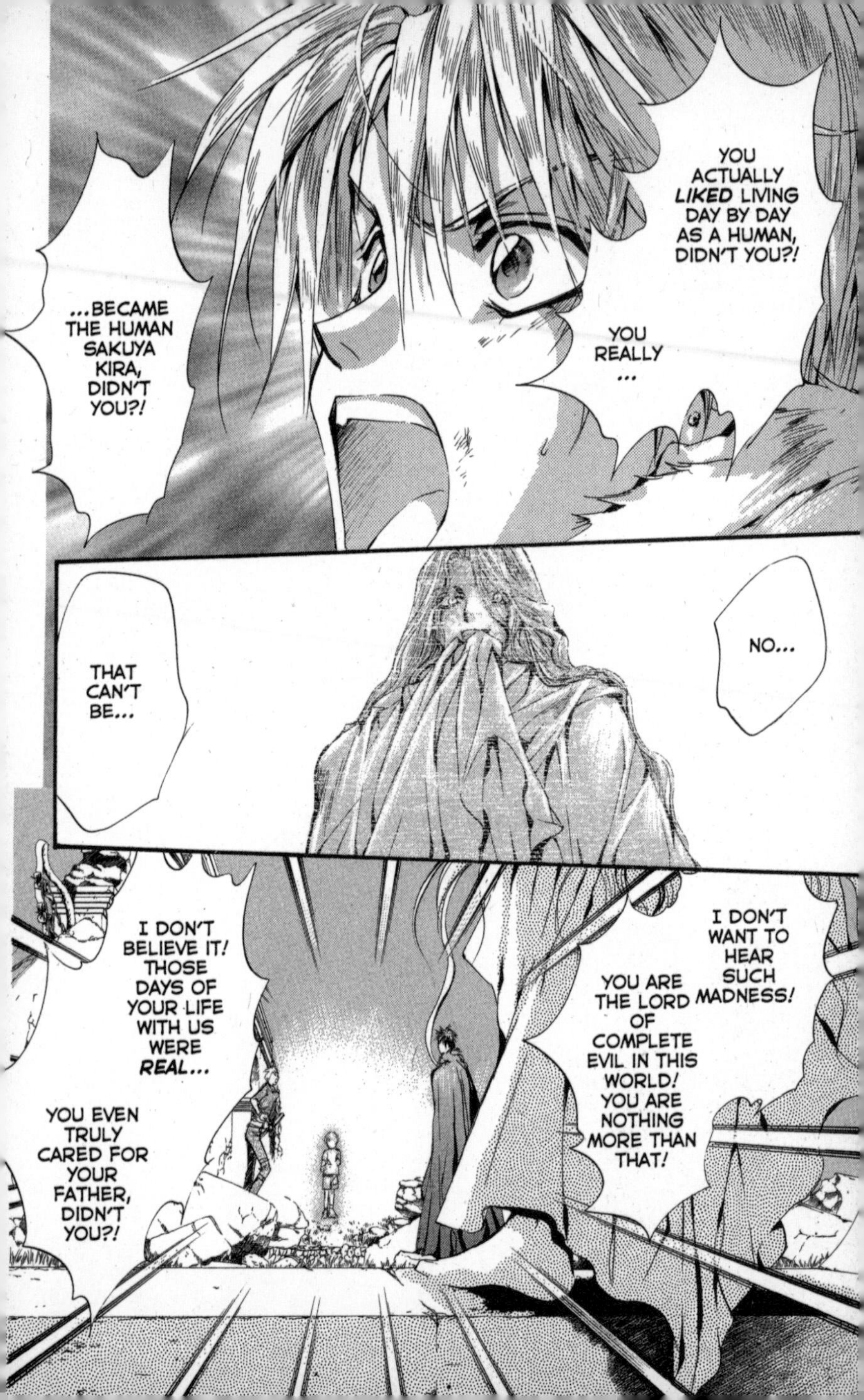
YOU ACTUALLY *LIKED* LIVING DAY BY DAY AS A HUMAN, DIDN'T YOU?!
YOU REALLY ...
...BECAME THE HUMAN SAKUYA KIRA, DIDN'T YOU?!
NO...
THAT CAN'T BE...
I DON'T WANT TO HEAR SUCH MADNESS!
YOU ARE THE LORD OF COMPLETE EVIL IN THIS WORLD! YOU ARE NOTHING MORE THAN THAT!
I DON'T BELIEVE IT! THOSE DAYS OF YOUR LIFE WITH US WERE *REAL*...
YOU EVEN TRULY CARED FOR YOUR FATHER, DIDN'T YOU?!

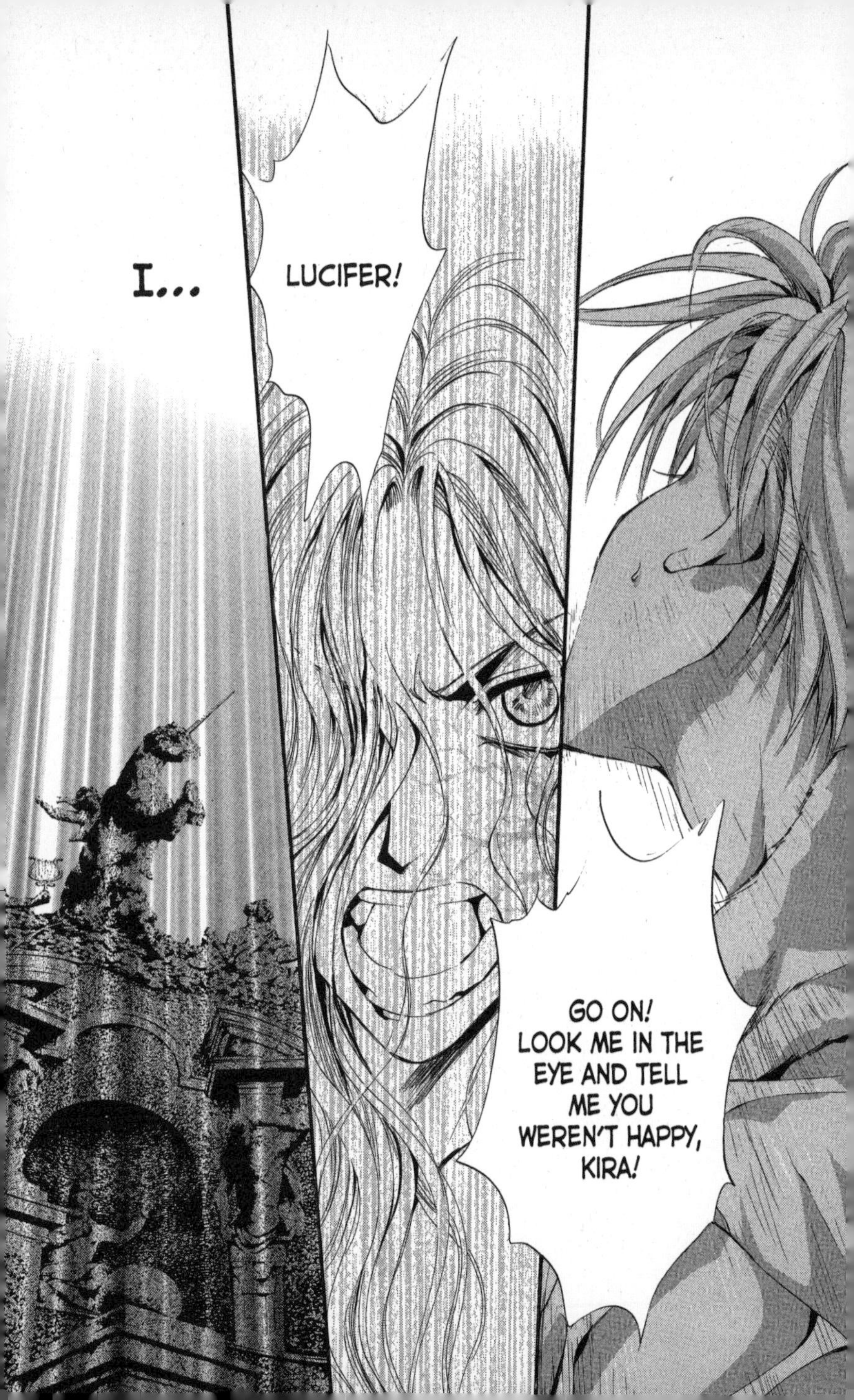
GO ON! LOOK ME IN THE EYE AND TELL ME YOU WEREN'T HAPPY, KIRA!
LUCIFER!
I...

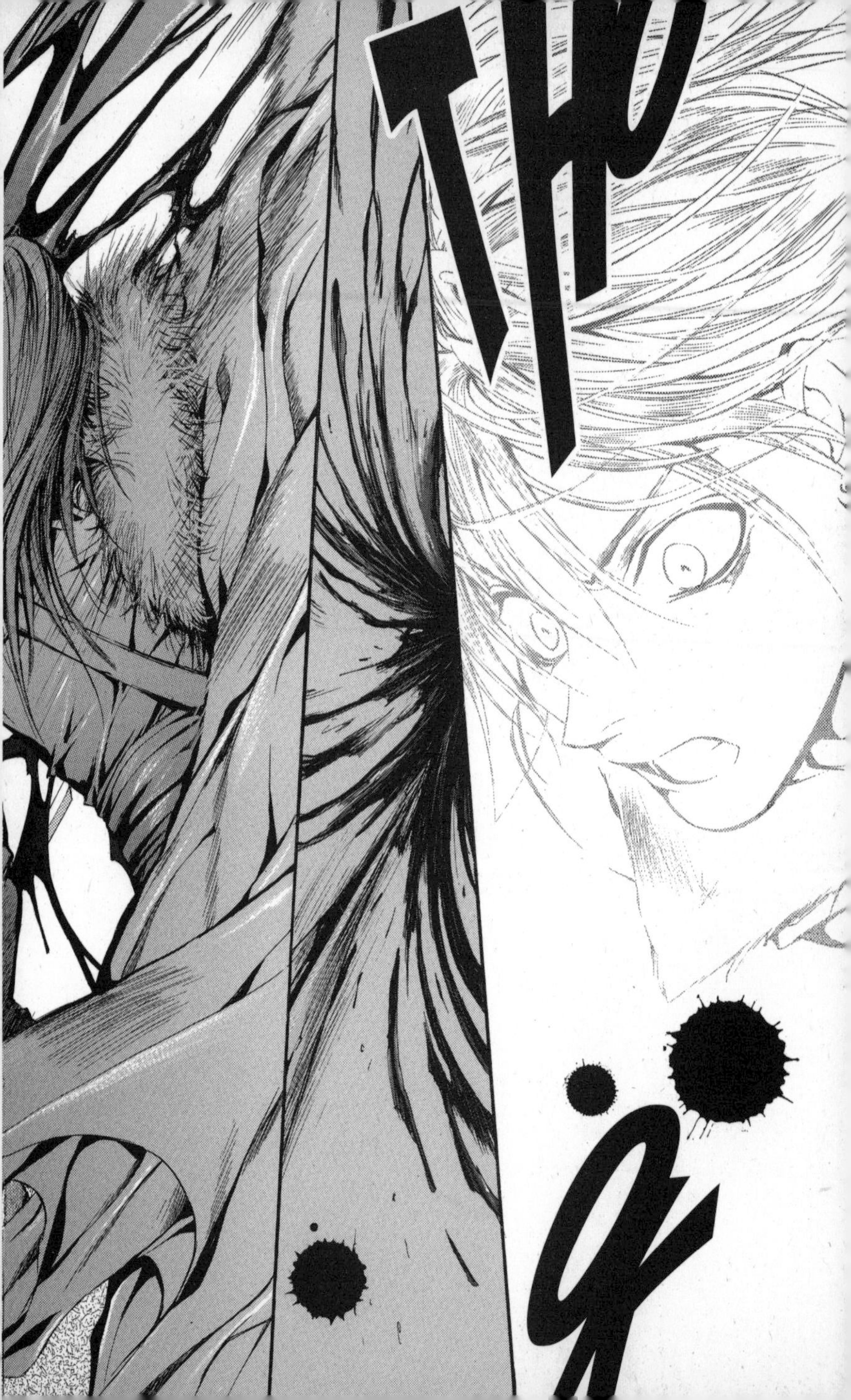

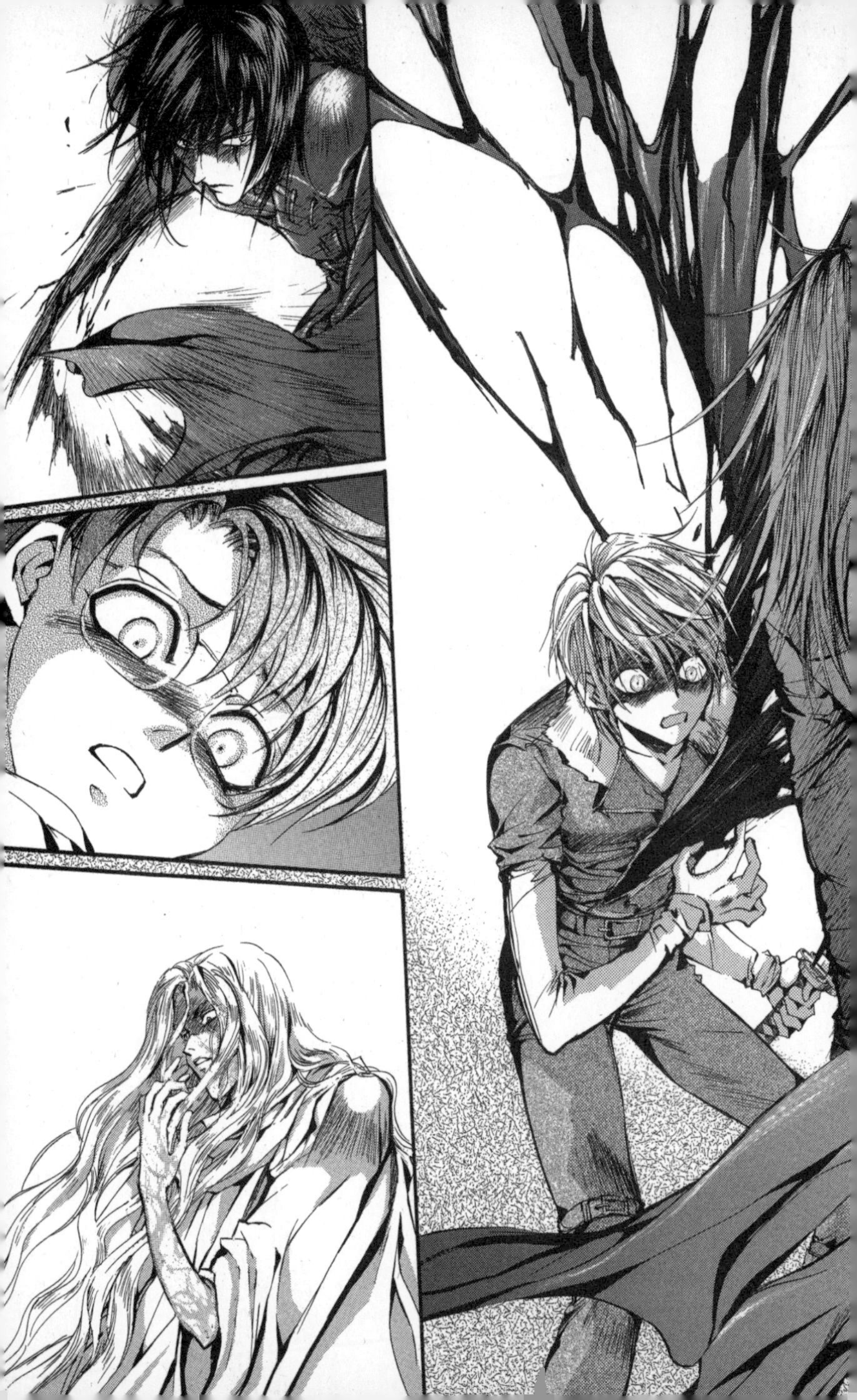

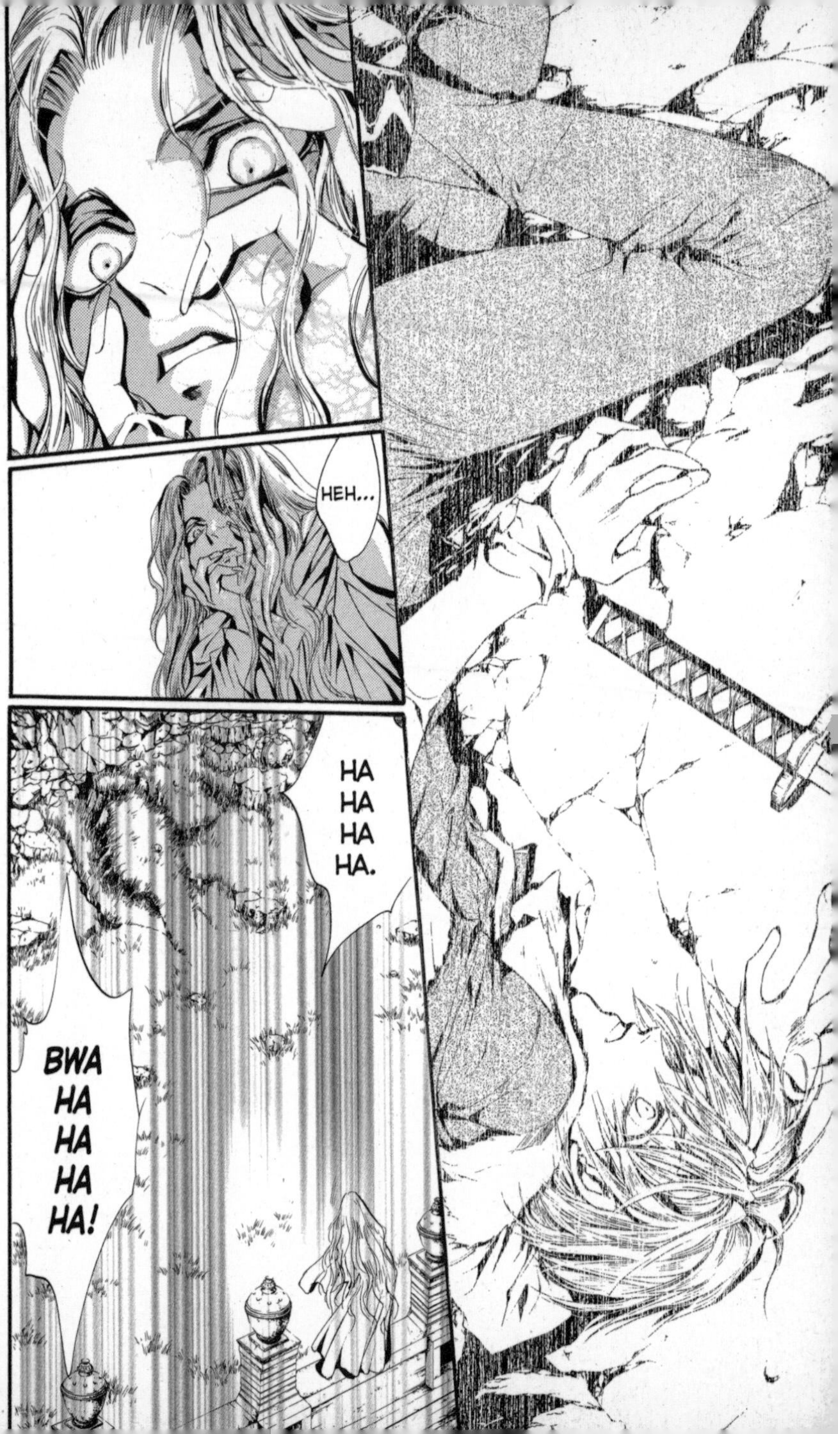
HEH...
HA HA HA HA.
BWA HA HA HA HA!

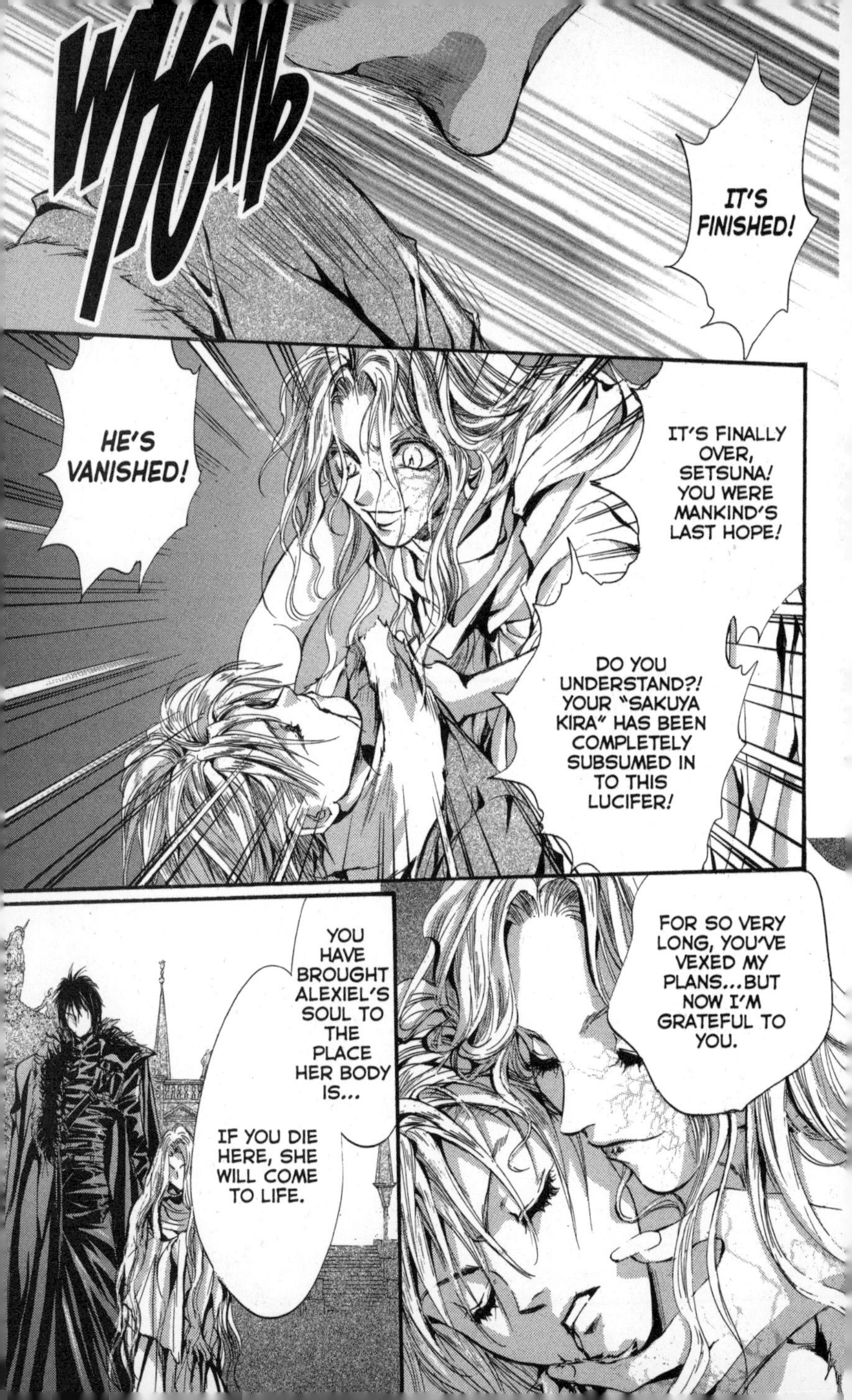
WHOOM
IT'S FINISHED!
IT'S FINALLY OVER, SETSUNA! YOU WERE MANKIND'S LAST HOPE!
HE'S VANISHED!
DO YOU UNDERSTAND?! YOUR "SAKUYA KIRA" HAS BEEN COMPLETELY SUBSUMED IN TO THIS LUCIFER!
FOR SO VERY LONG, YOU'VE VEXED MY PLANS...BUT NOW I'M GRATEFUL TO YOU.
YOU HAVE BROUGHT ALEXIEL'S SOUL TO THE PLACE HER BODY IS...
IF YOU DIE HERE, SHE WILL COME TO LIFE.

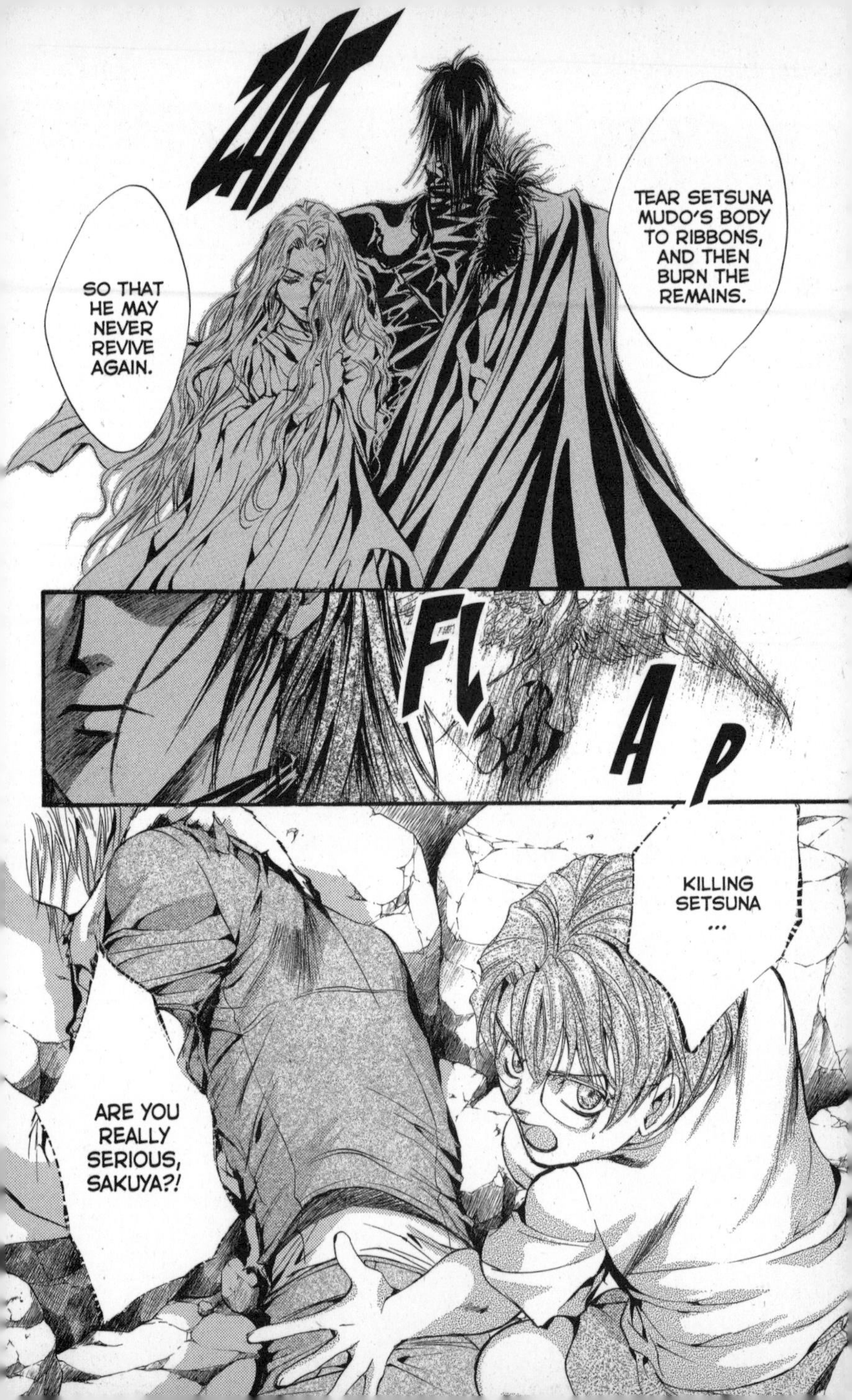
TEAR SETSUNA MUDO'S BODY TO RIBBONS, AND THEN BURN THE REMAINS.
ZAN
SO THAT HE MAY NEVER REVIVE AGAIN.
FLAP
KILLING SETSUNA ...
ARE YOU REALLY SERIOUS, SAKUYA?!

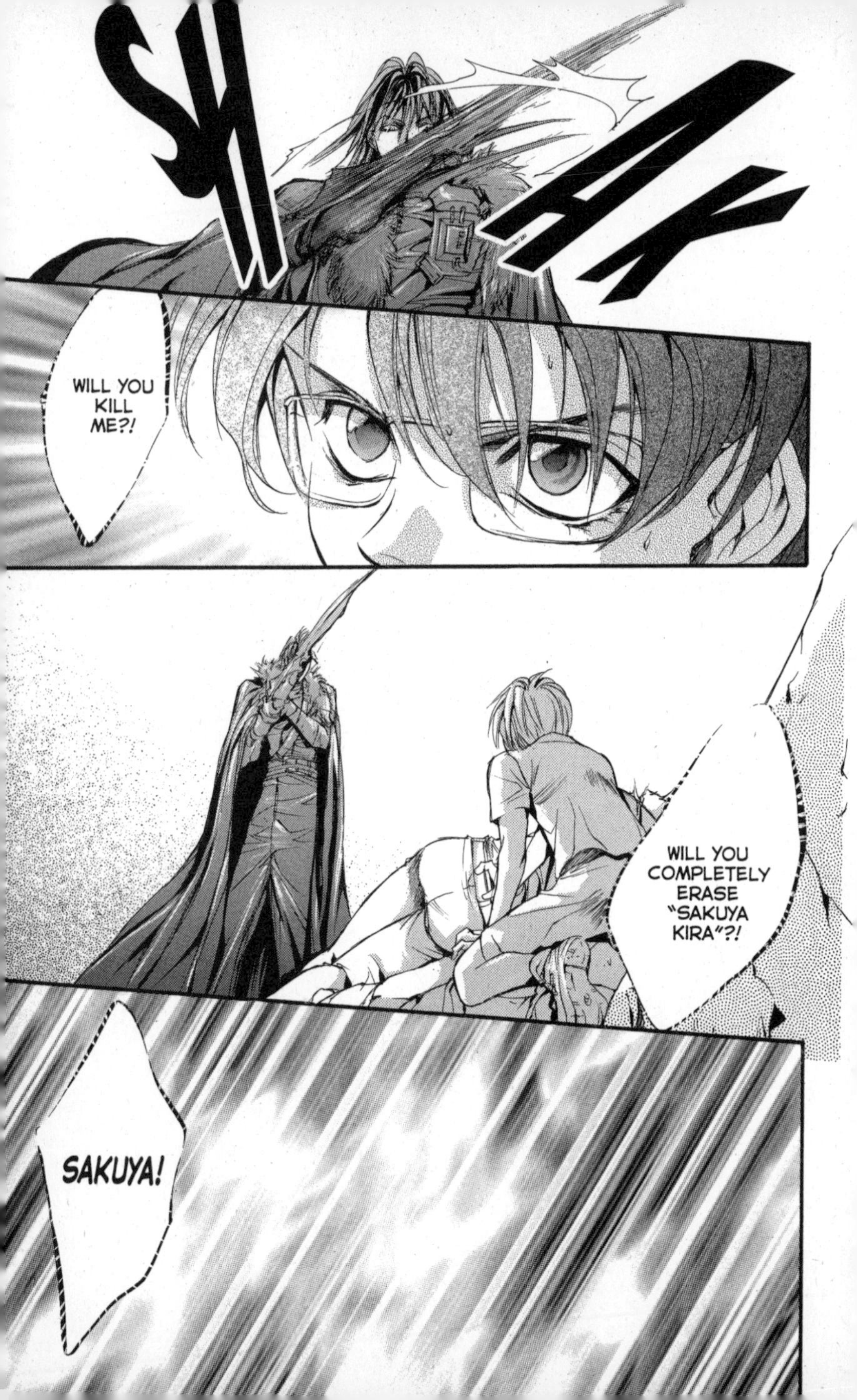
SHAK
WILL YOU KILL ME?!
WILL YOU COMPLETELY ERASE "SAKUYA KIRA"?!
SAKUYA!

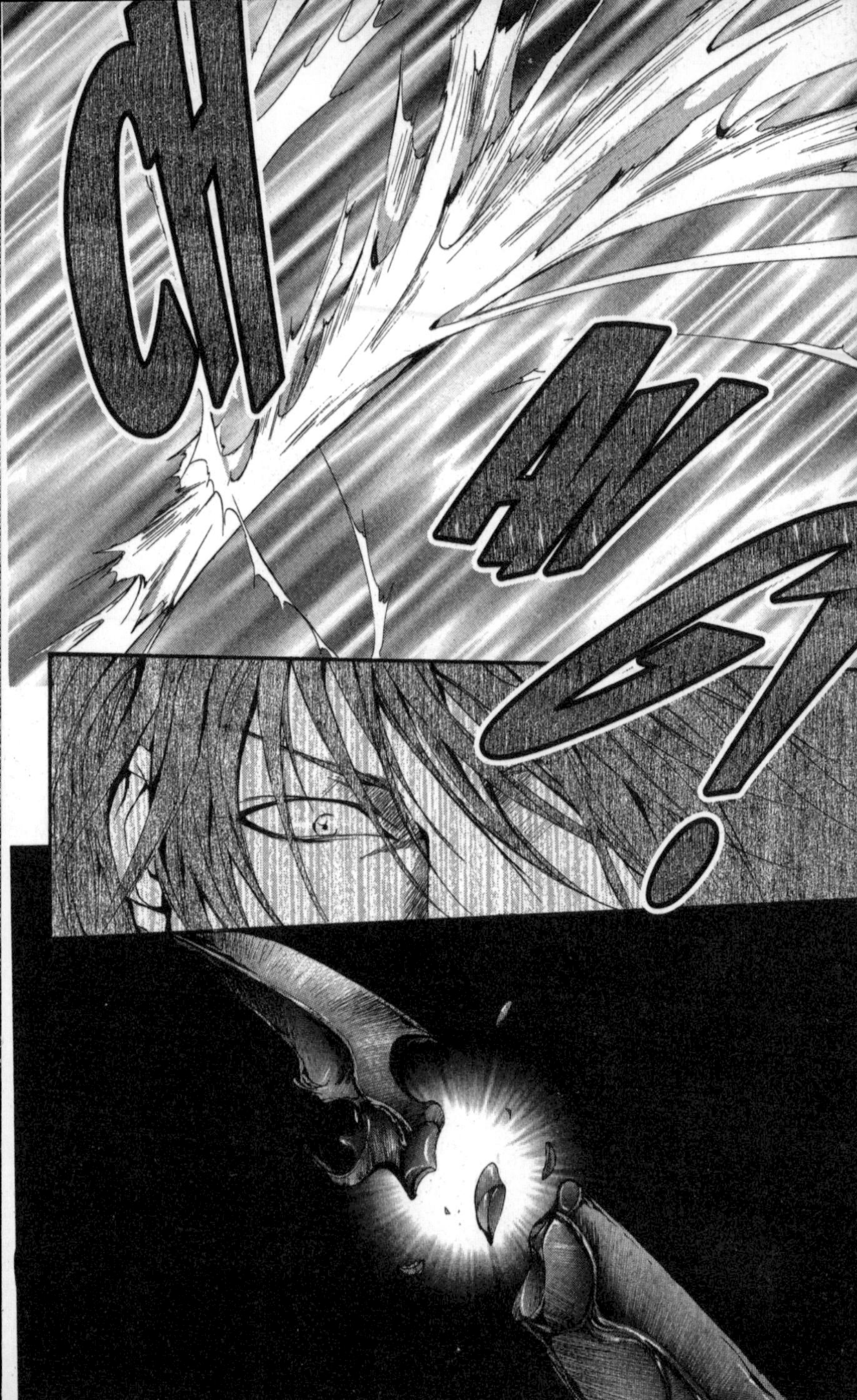
CHANG!

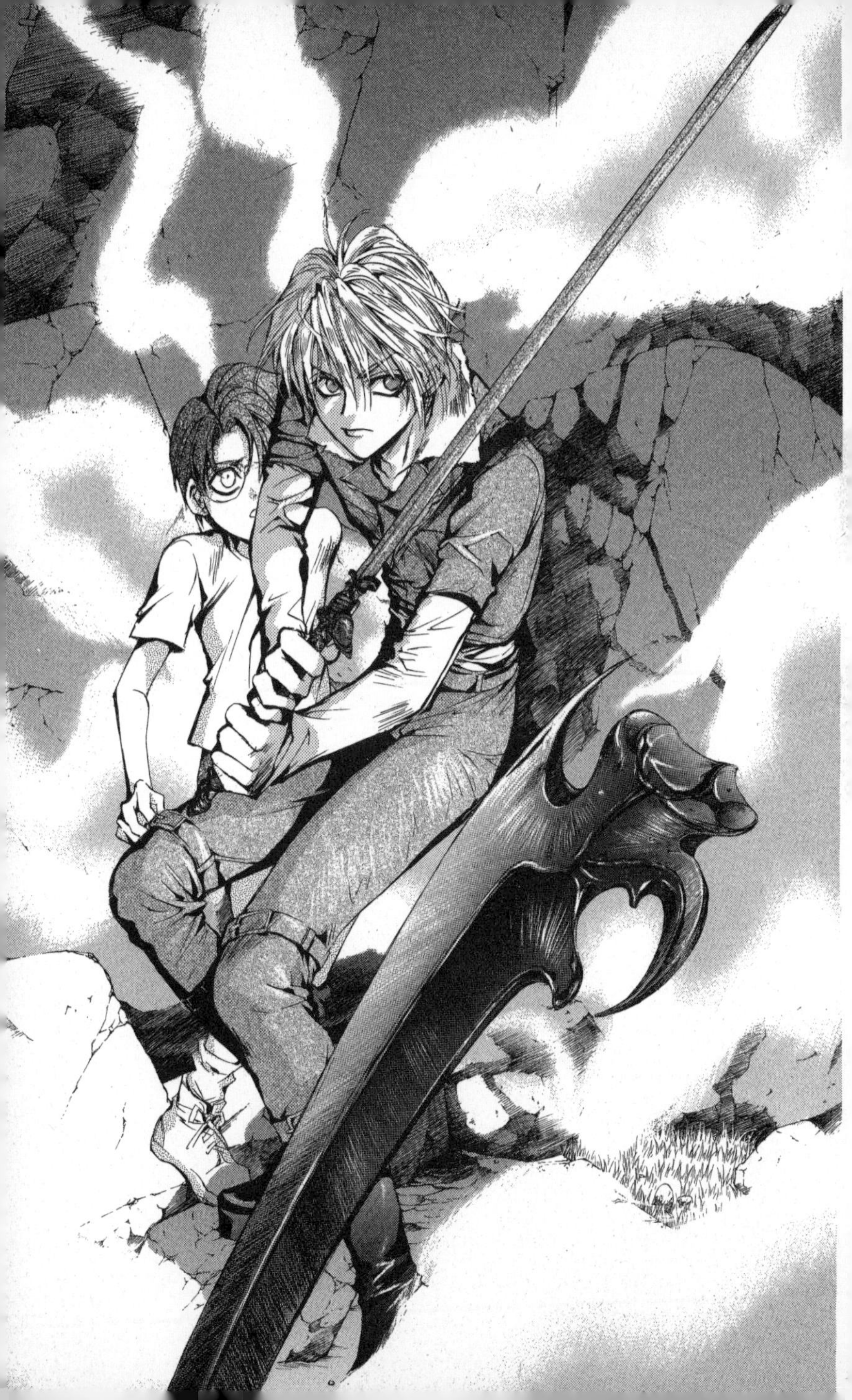

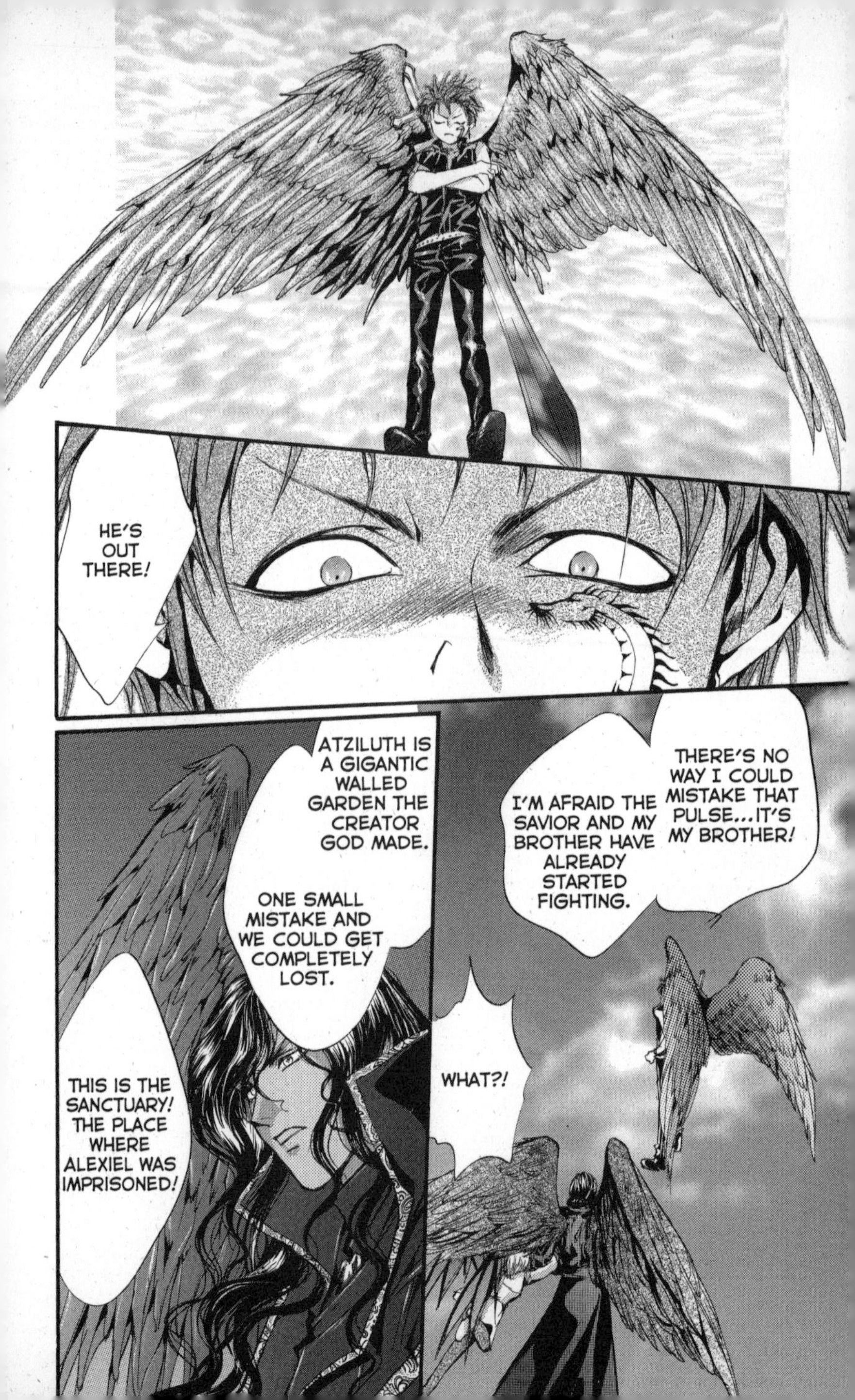
HE'S OUT THERE!
THERE'S NO WAY I COULD MISTAKE THAT PULSE...IT'S MY BROTHER!
I'M AFRAID THE SAVIOR AND MY BROTHER HAVE ALREADY STARTED FIGHTING.
WHAT?!
ATZILUTH IS A GIGANTIC WALLED GARDEN THE CREATOR GOD MADE.
ONE SMALL MISTAKE AND WE COULD GET COMPLETELY LOST.
THIS IS THE SANCTUARY! THE PLACE WHERE ALEXIEL WAS IMPRISONED!

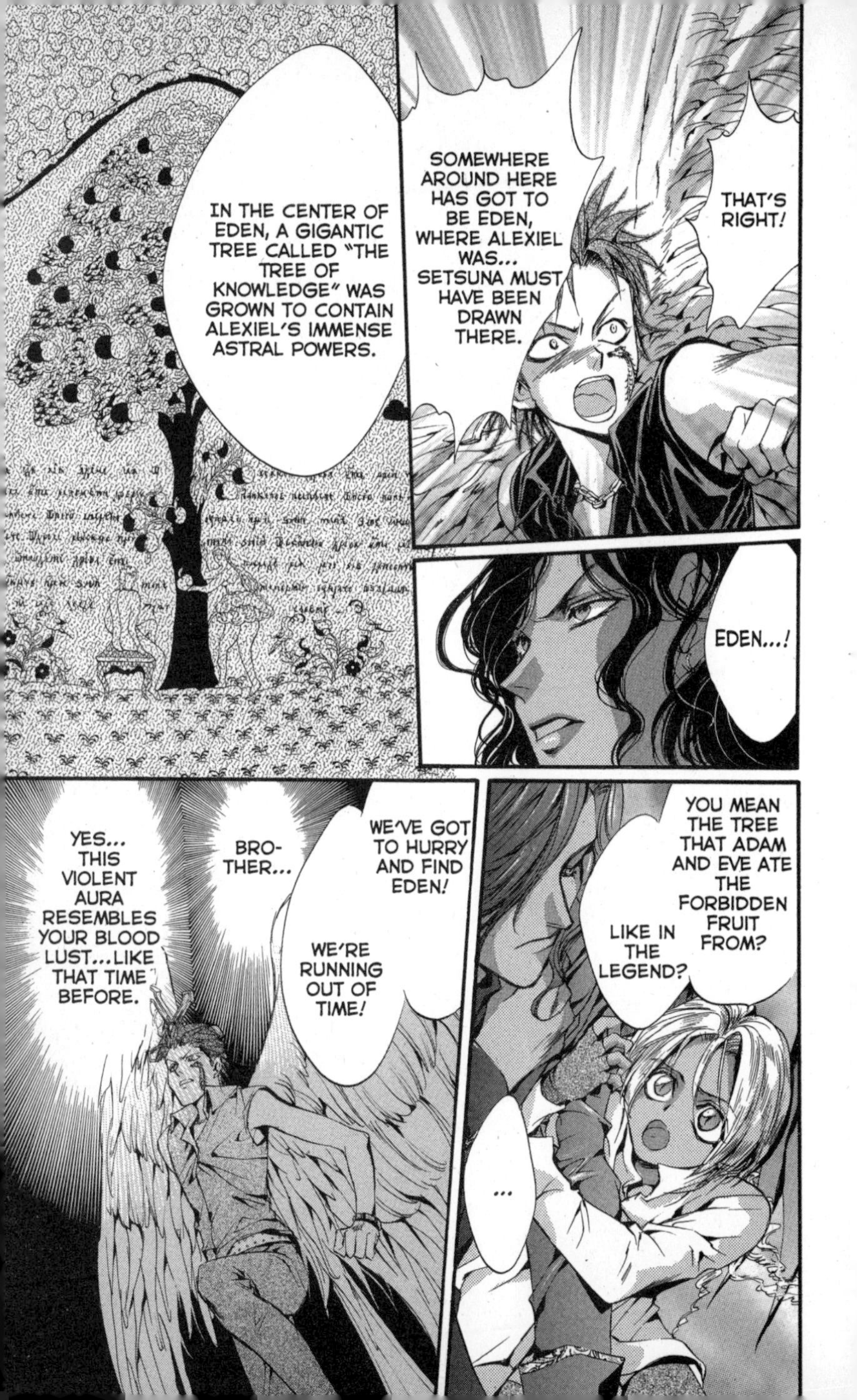
THAT'S RIGHT!
SOMEWHERE AROUND HERE HAS GOT TO BE EDEN, WHERE ALEXIEL WAS... SETSUNA MUST HAVE BEEN DRAWN THERE.
EDEN...!
IN THE CENTER OF EDEN, A GIGANTIC TREE CALLED "THE TREE OF KNOWLEDGE" WAS GROWN TO CONTAIN ALEXIEL'S IMMENSE ASTRAL POWERS.
YOU MEAN THE TREE THAT ADAM AND EVE ATE THE FORBIDDEN FRUIT FROM?
LIKE IN THE LEGEND?
...
WE'VE GOT TO HURRY AND FIND EDEN!
WE'RE RUNNING OUT OF TIME!
BRO-THER...
YES... THIS VIOLENT AURA RESEMBLES YOUR BLOOD LUST...LIKE THAT TIME BEFORE.

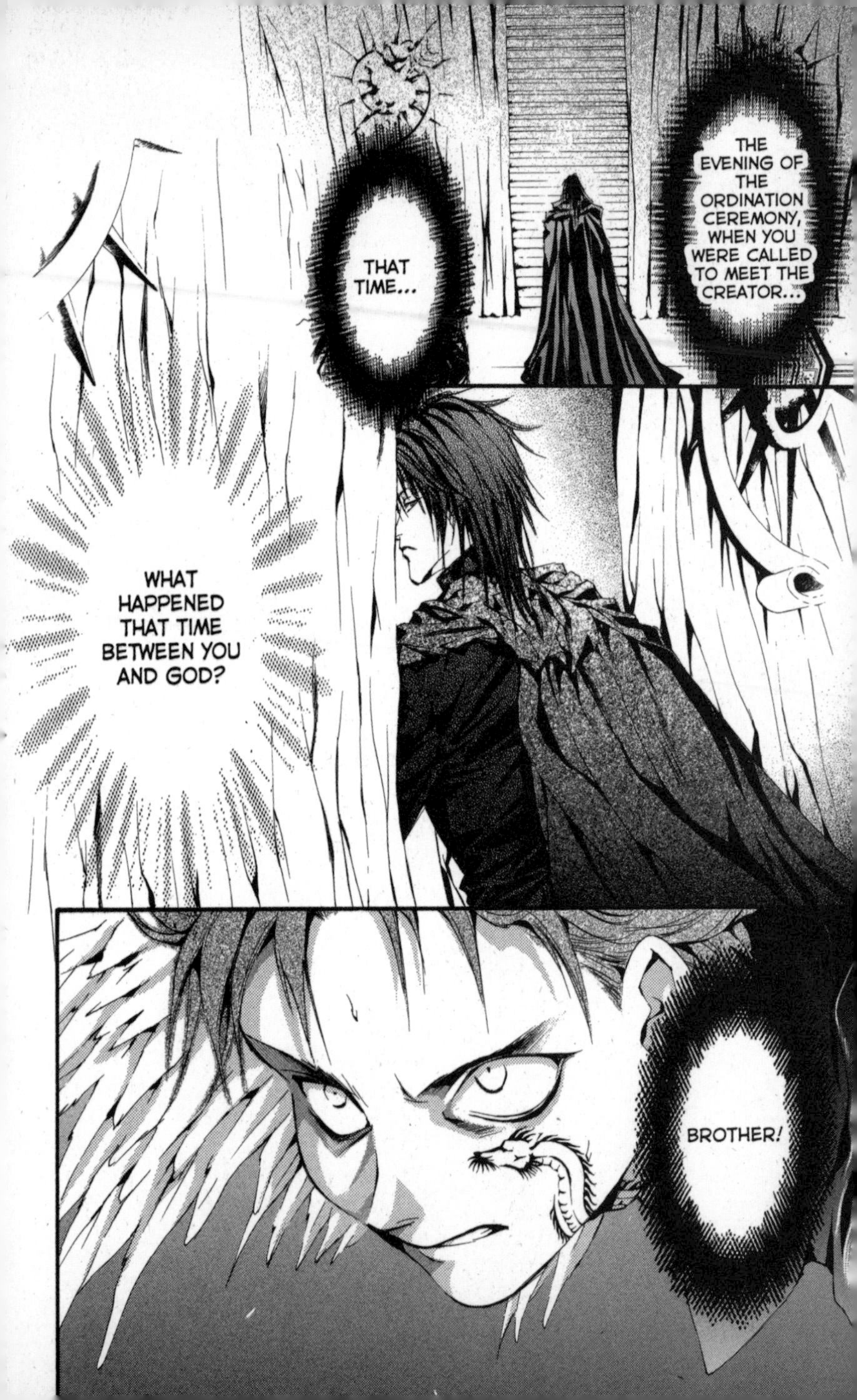
THE EVENING OF THE ORDINATION CEREMONY, WHEN YOU WERE CALLED TO MEET THE CREATOR...
THAT TIME...
WHAT HAPPENED THAT TIME BETWEEN YOU AND GOD?
BROTHER!

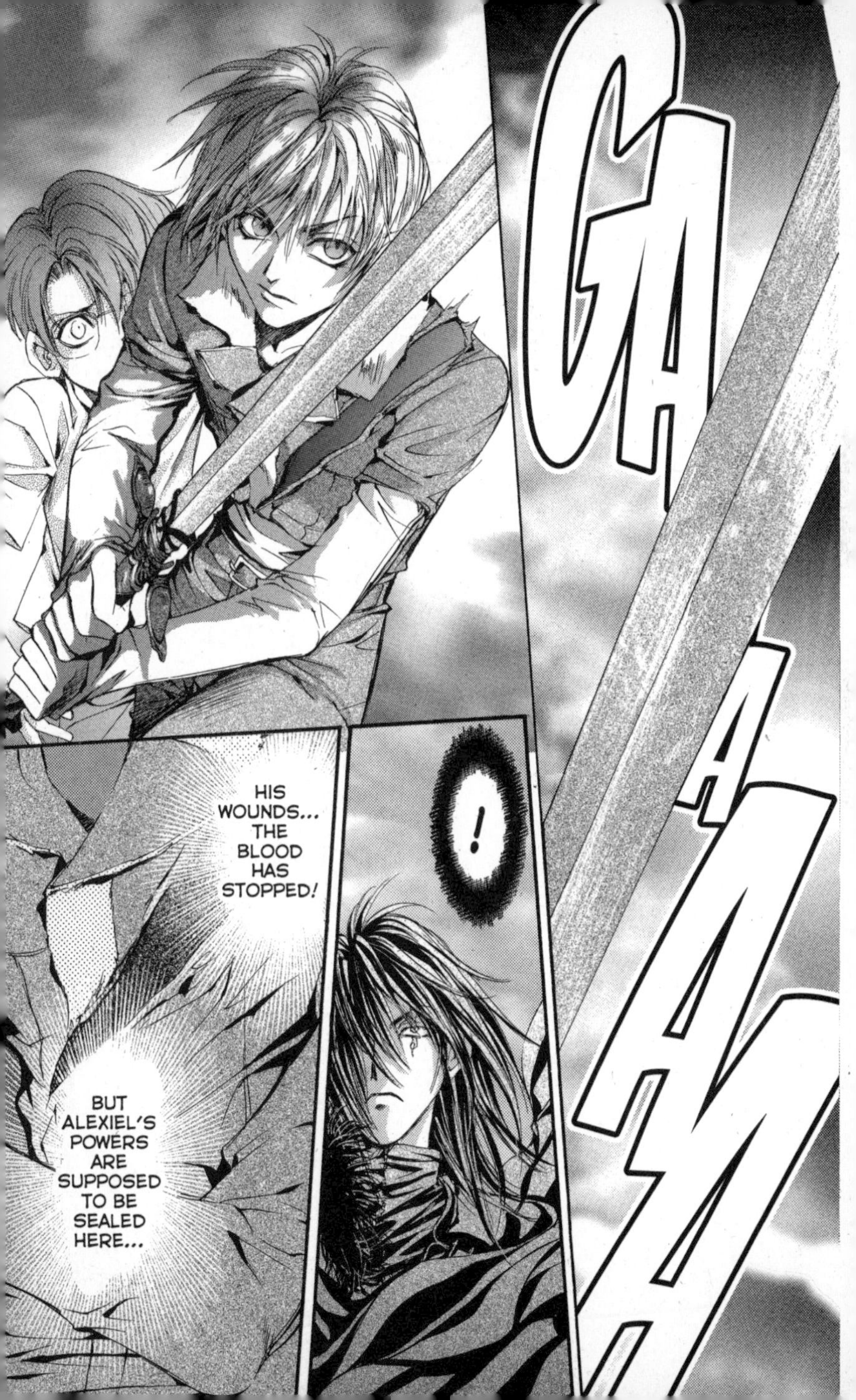
GA
!
HIS WOUNDS... THE BLOOD HAS STOPPED!
BUT ALEXIEL'S POWERS ARE SUPPOSED TO BE SEALED HERE...

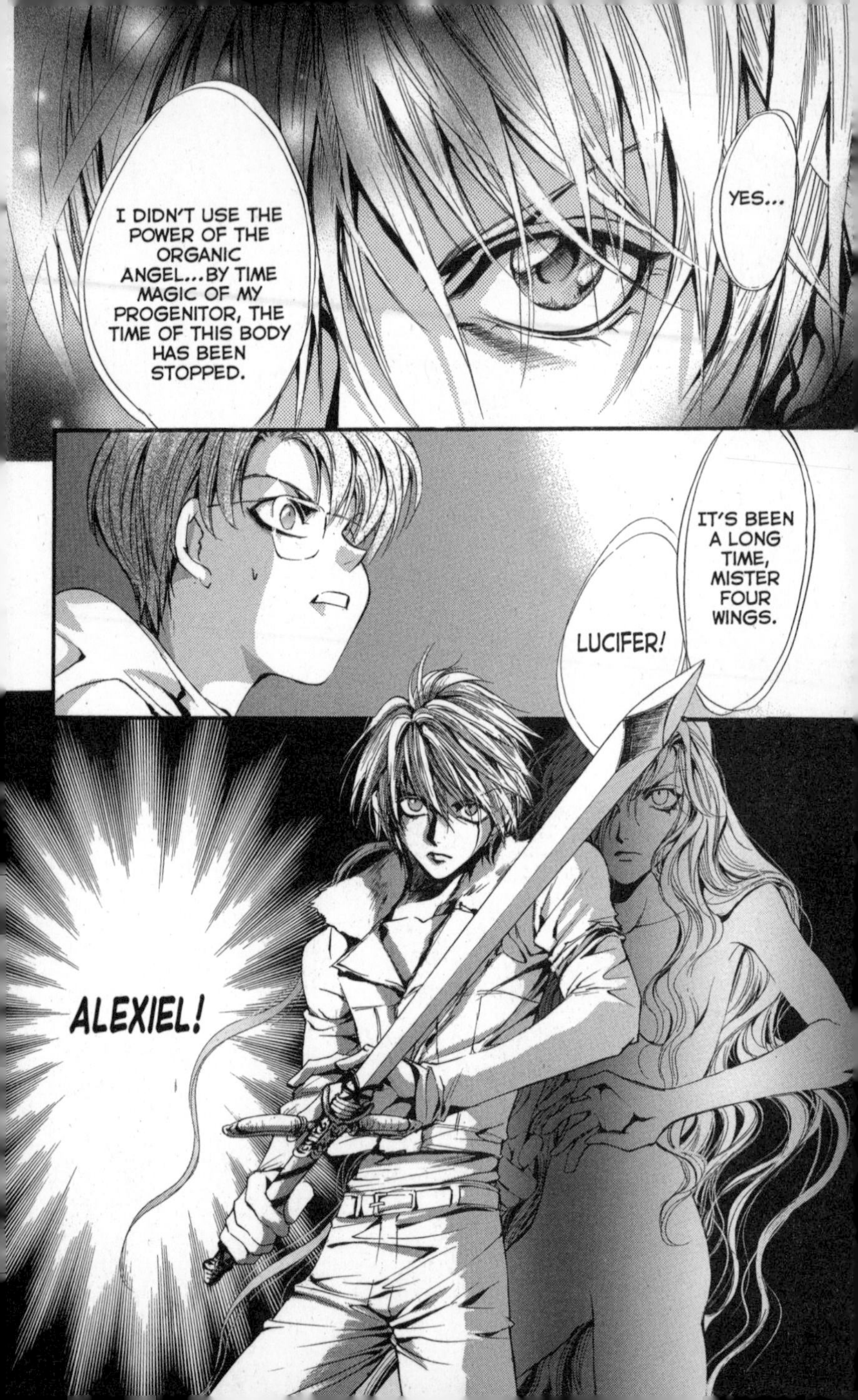
YES...
I DIDN'T USE THE POWER OF THE ORGANIC ANGEL...BY TIME MAGIC OF MY PROGENITOR, THE TIME OF THIS BODY HAS BEEN STOPPED.
IT'S BEEN A LONG TIME, MISTER FOUR WINGS.
LUCIFER!
ALEXIEL!

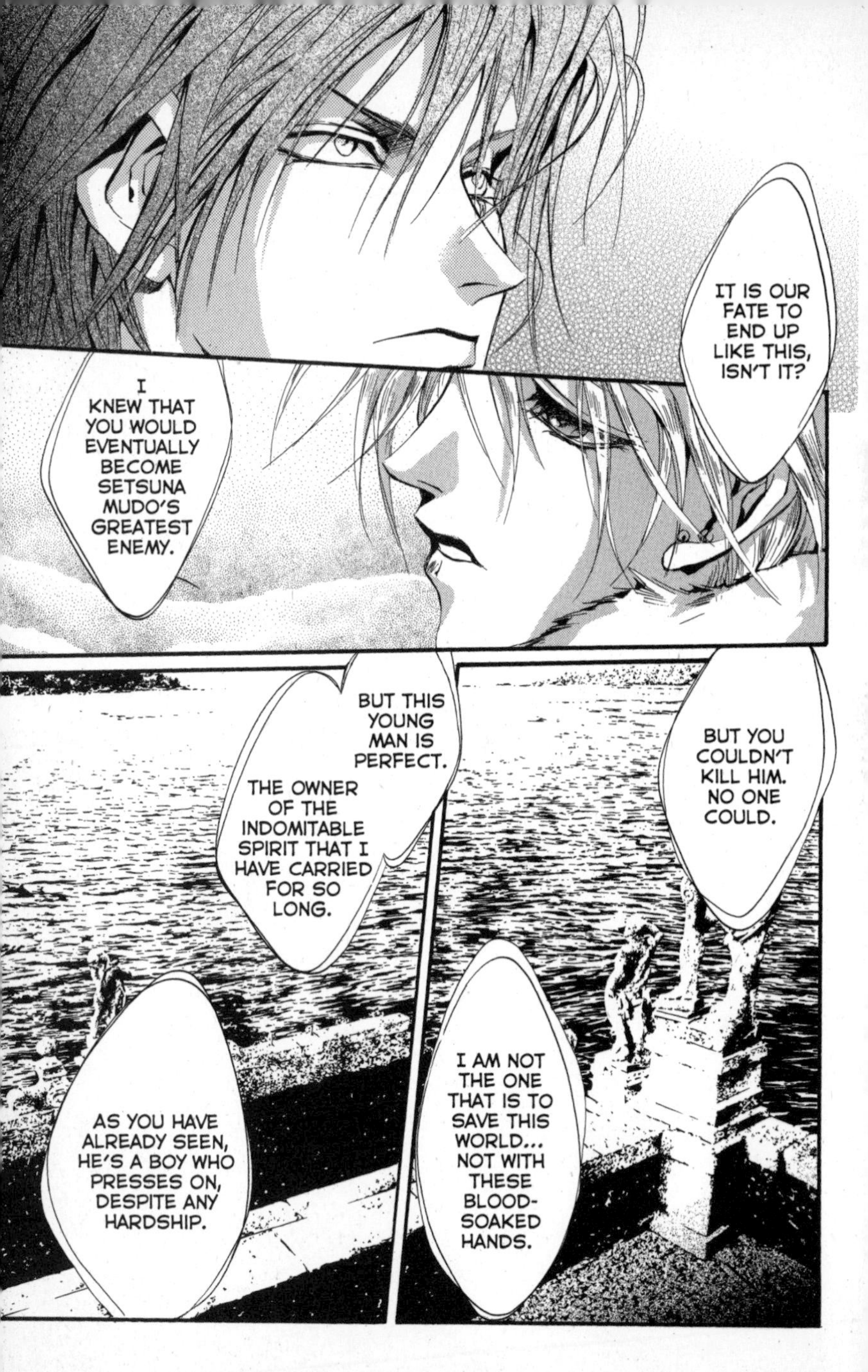
IT IS OUR FATE TO END UP LIKE THIS, ISN'T IT?
I KNEW THAT YOU WOULD EVENTUALLY BECOME SETSUNA MUDO'S GREATEST ENEMY.
BUT YOU COULDN'T KILL HIM. NO ONE COULD.
I AM NOT THE ONE THAT IS TO SAVE THIS WORLD... NOT WITH THESE BLOOD-SOAKED HANDS.
BUT THIS YOUNG MAN IS PERFECT.
THE OWNER OF THE INDOMITABLE SPIRIT THAT I HAVE CARRIED FOR SO LONG.
AS YOU HAVE ALREADY SEEN, HE'S A BOY WHO PRESSES ON, DESPITE ANY HARDSHIP.

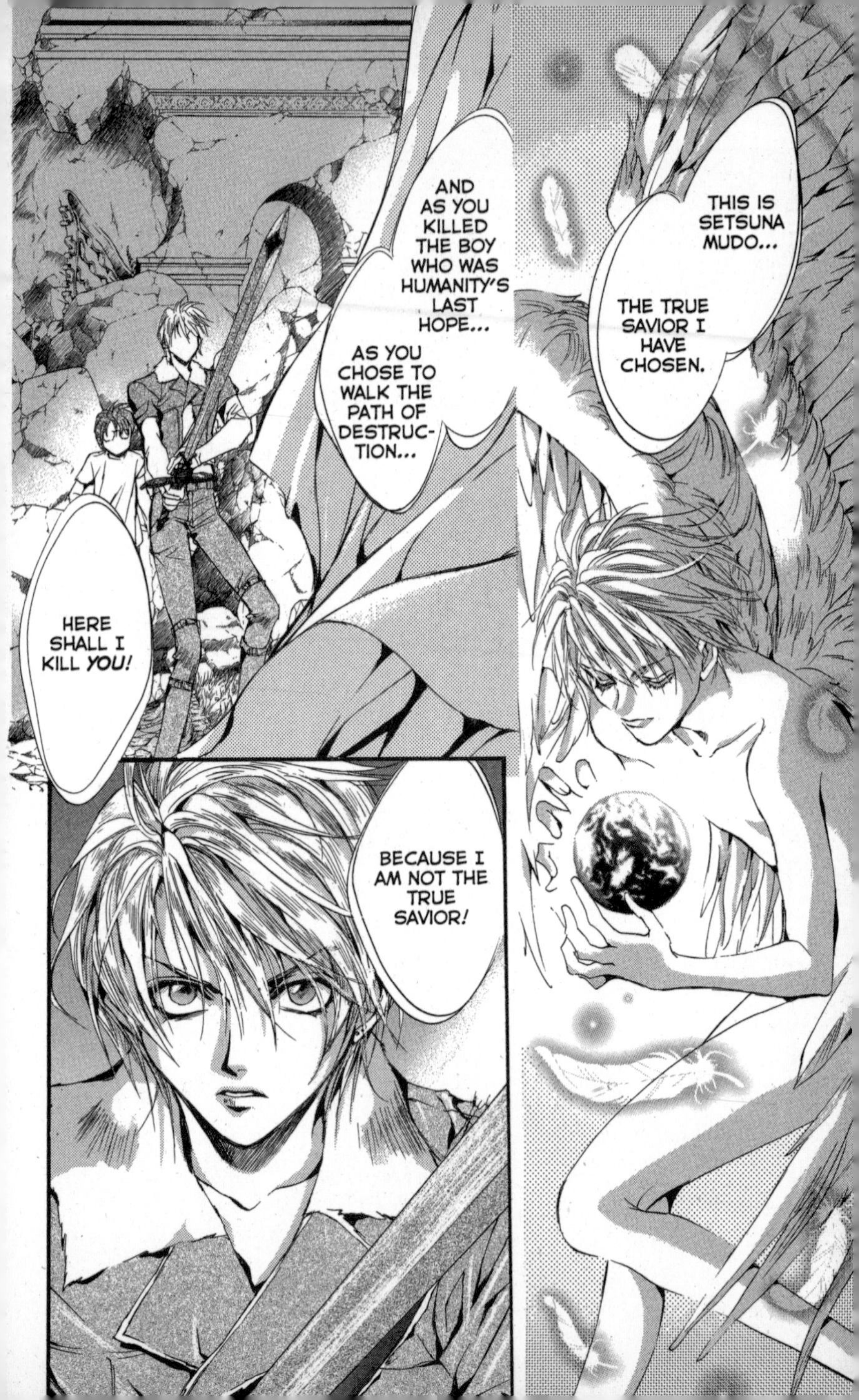
THIS IS SETSUNA MUDO...
THE TRUE SAVIOR I HAVE CHOSEN.
AND AS YOU KILLED THE BOY WHO WAS HUMANITY'S LAST HOPE...
AS YOU CHOSE TO WALK THE PATH OF DESTRUC-TION...
HERE SHALL I KILL *YOU!*
BECAUSE I AM NOT THE TRUE SAVIOR!

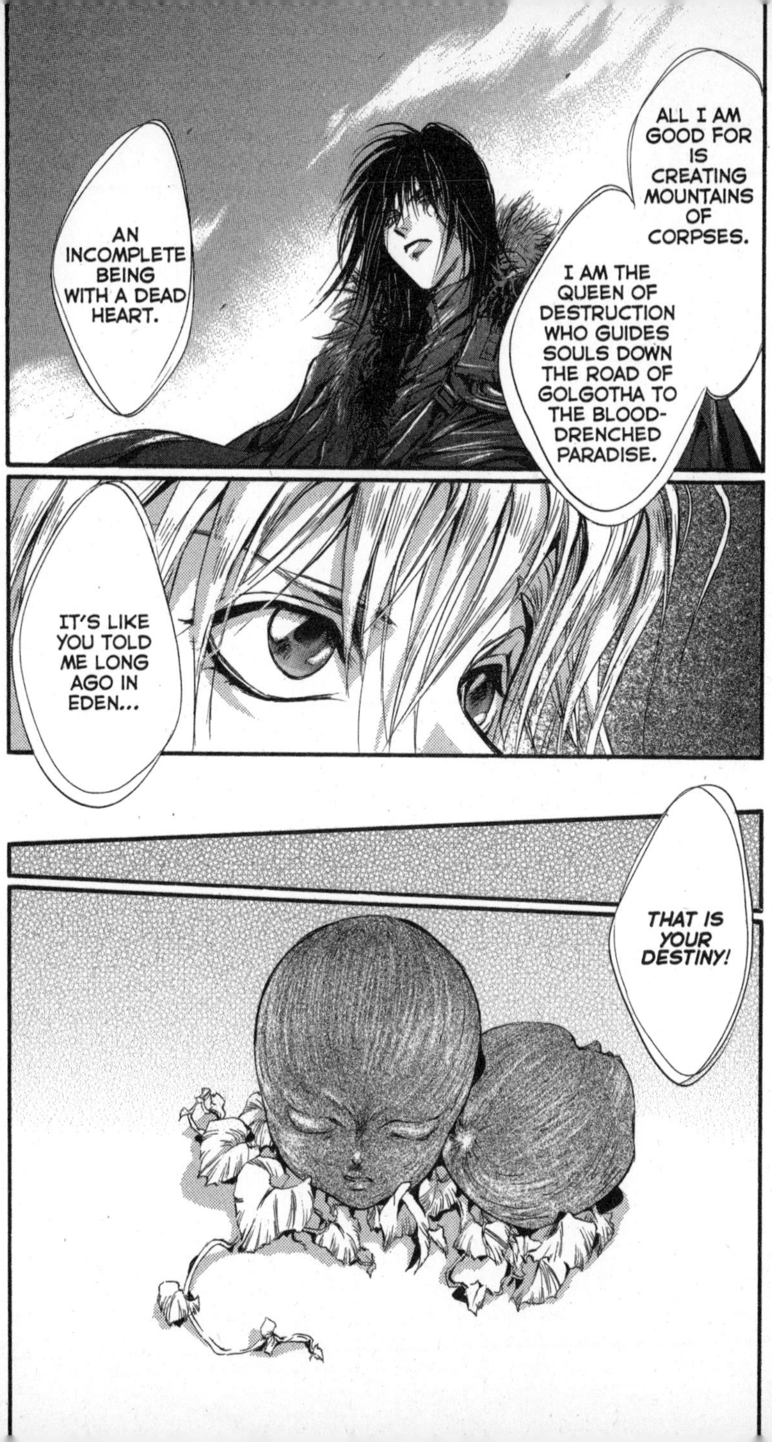
ALL I AM GOOD FOR IS CREATING MOUNTAINS OF CORPSES.
I AM THE QUEEN OF DESTRUCTION WHO GUIDES SOULS DOWN THE ROAD OF GOLGOTHA TO THE BLOOD-DRENCHED PARADISE.
AN INCOMPLETE BEING WITH A DEAD HEART.
IT'S LIKE YOU TOLD ME LONG AGO IN EDEN...
THAT IS YOUR DESTINY!

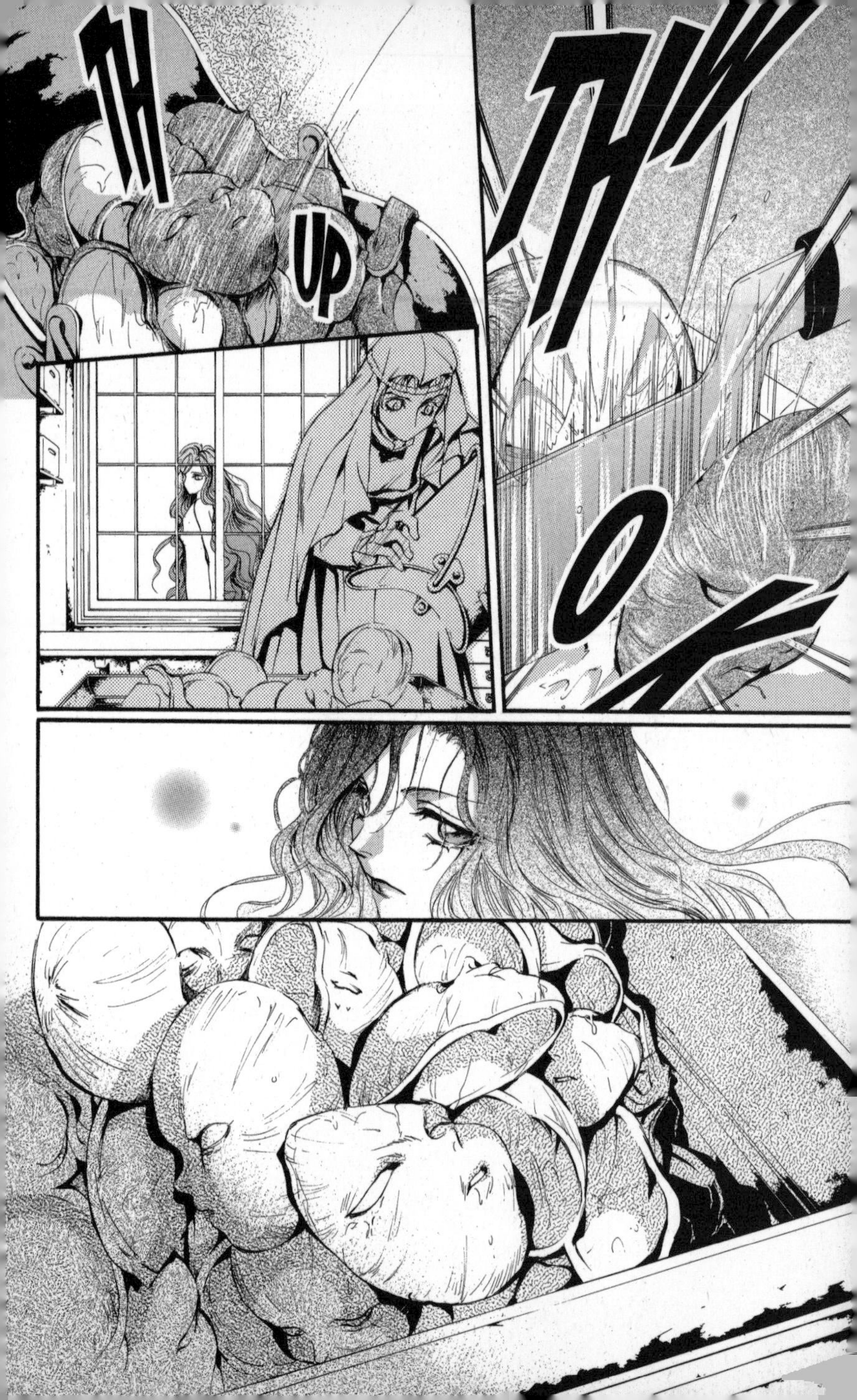
THWOK
THUP

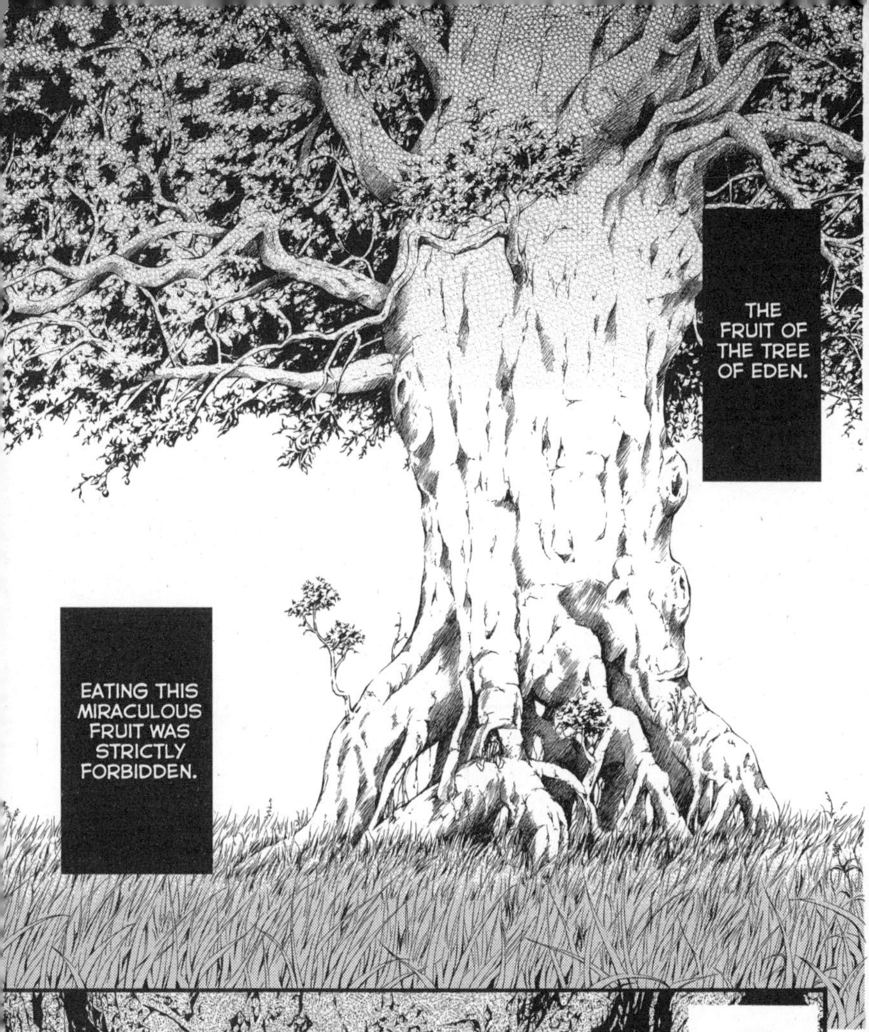
THE FRUIT OF THE TREE OF EDEN.
EATING THIS MIRACULOUS FRUIT WAS STRICTLY FORBIDDEN.

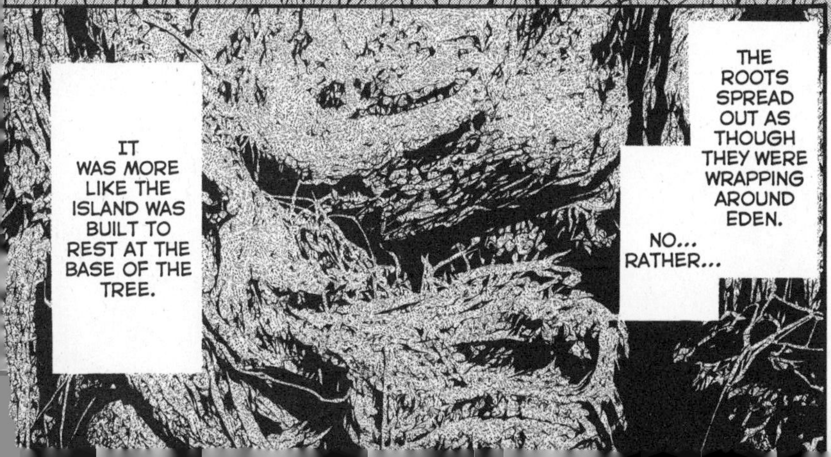
THE ROOTS SPREAD OUT AS THOUGH THEY WERE WRAPPING AROUND EDEN.
NO... RATHER...
IT WAS MORE LIKE THE ISLAND WAS BUILT TO REST AT THE BASE OF THE TREE.

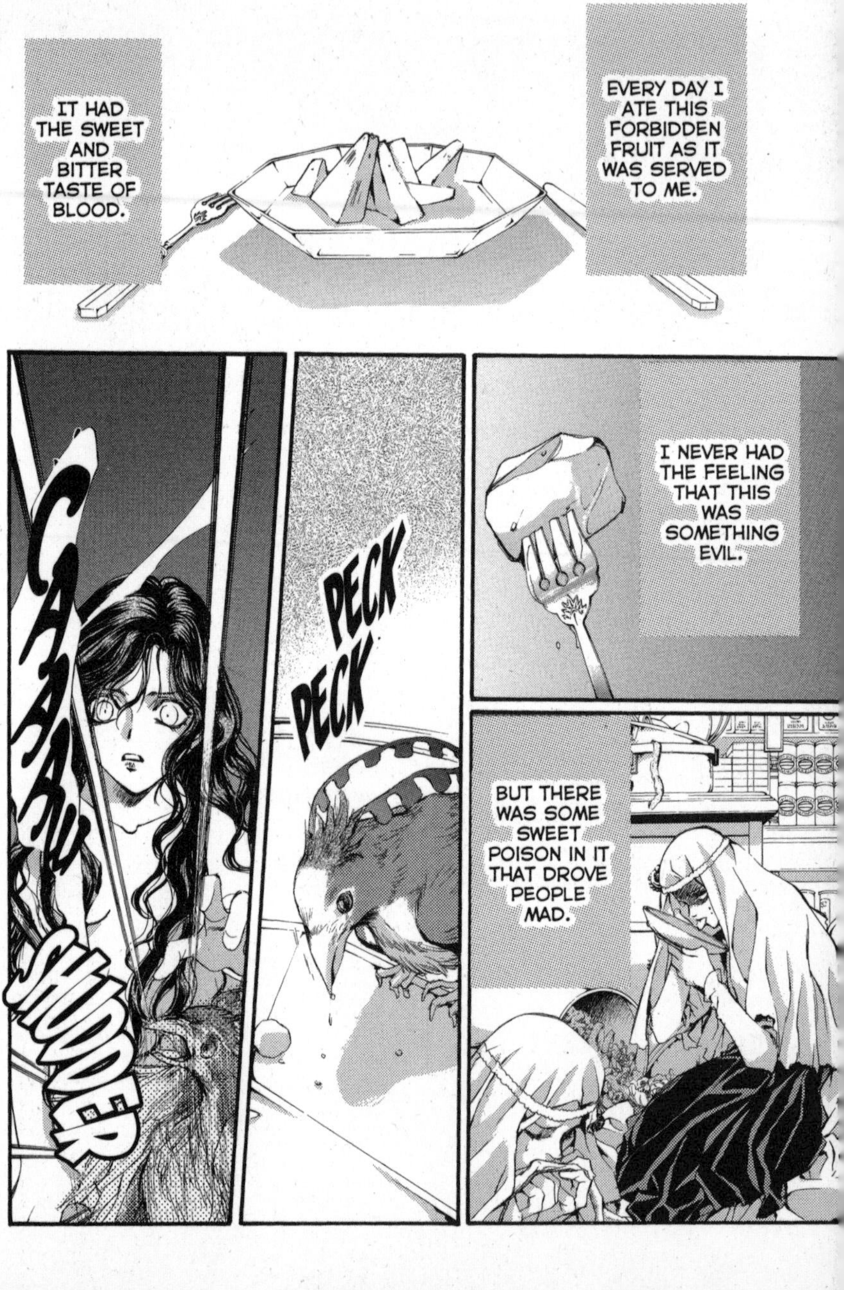
EVERY DAY I ATE THIS FORBIDDEN FRUIT AS IT WAS SERVED TO ME.
IT HAD THE SWEET AND BITTER TASTE OF BLOOD.
I NEVER HAD THE FEELING THAT THIS WAS SOMETHING EVIL.
BUT THERE WAS SOME SWEET POISON IN IT THAT DROVE PEOPLE MAD.
PECK
PECK
CAAAW
SHUDDER

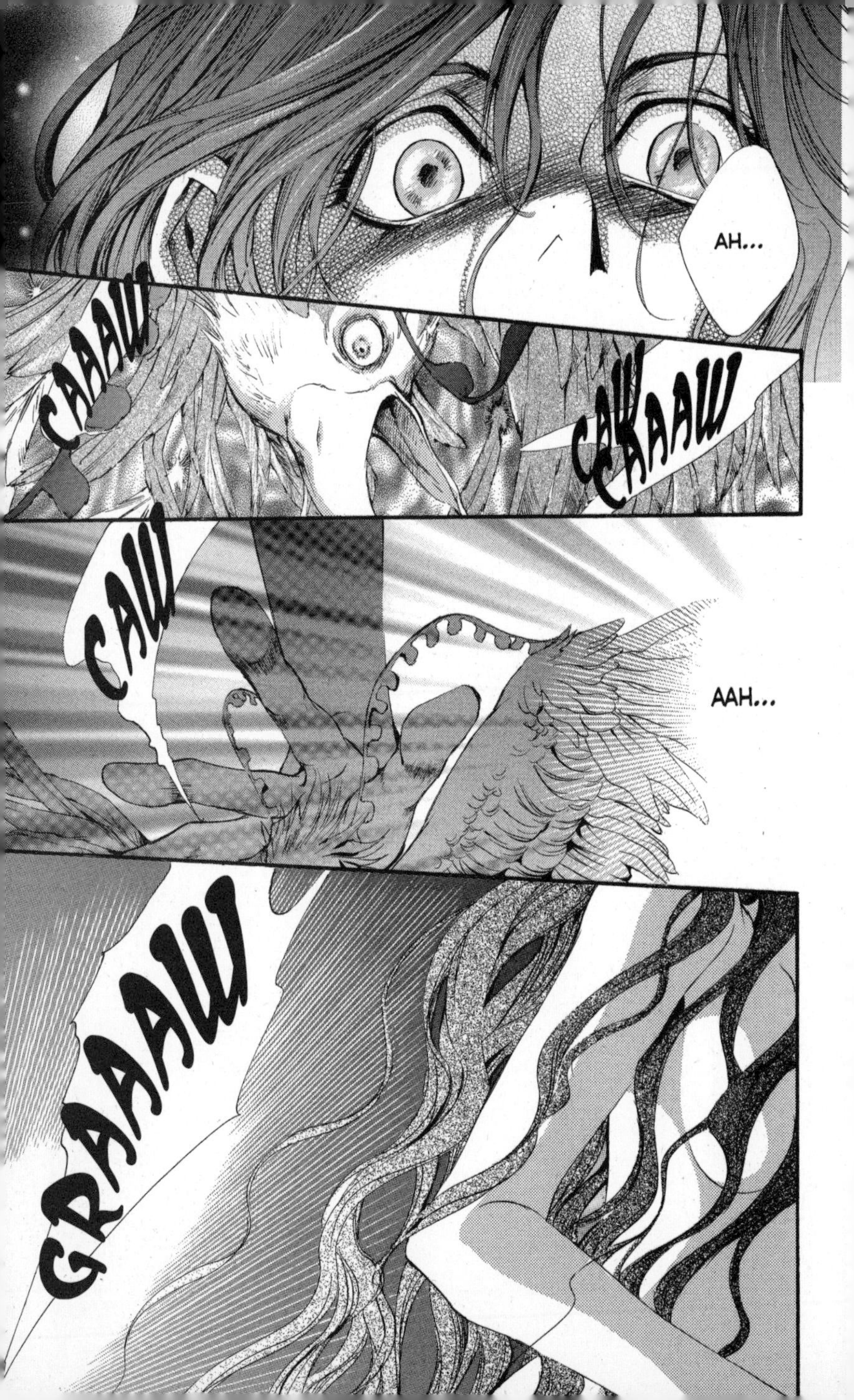
AH...
CAW
CAAAW
CAAAW
AAH...
CAW
GRAAAW

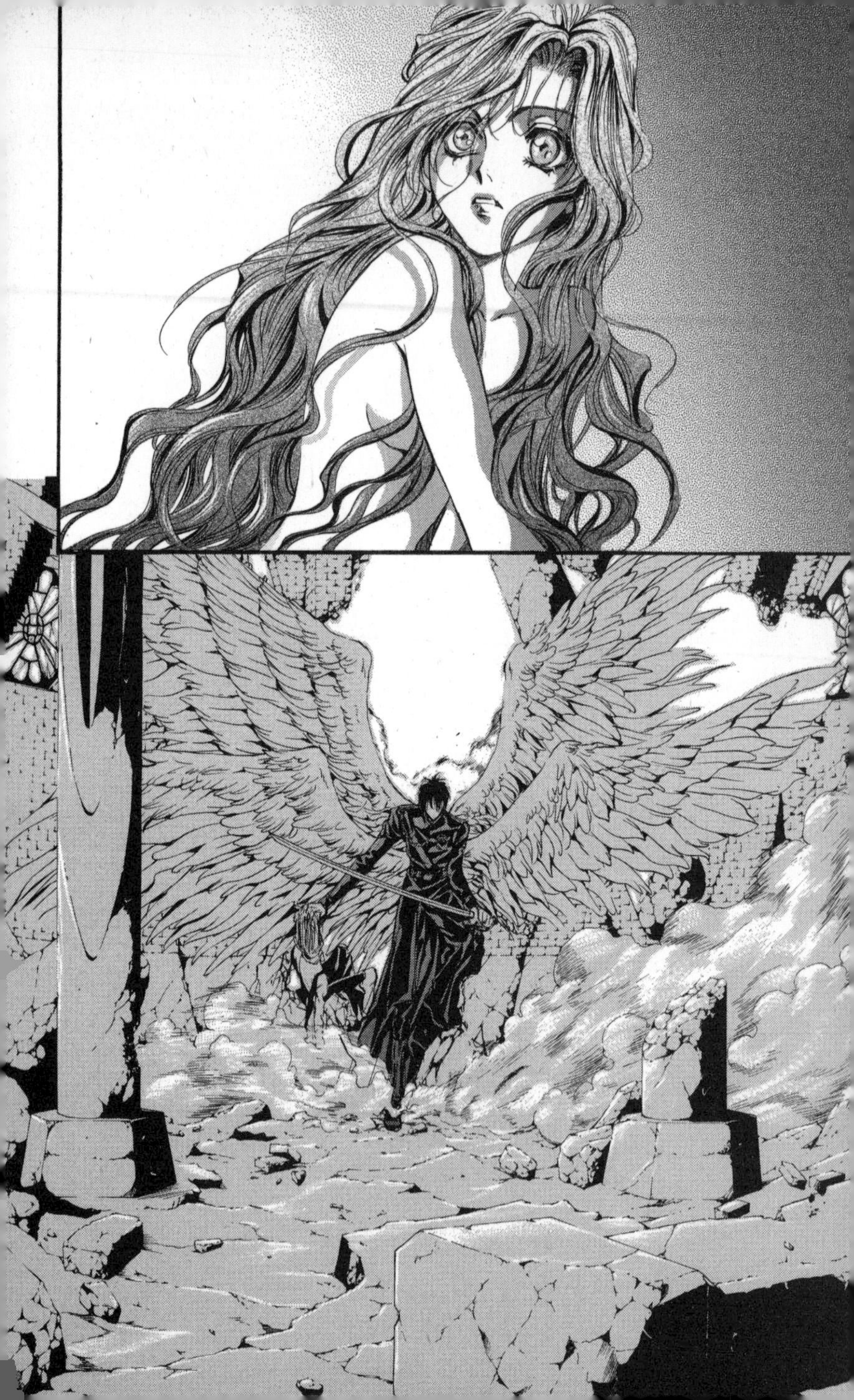

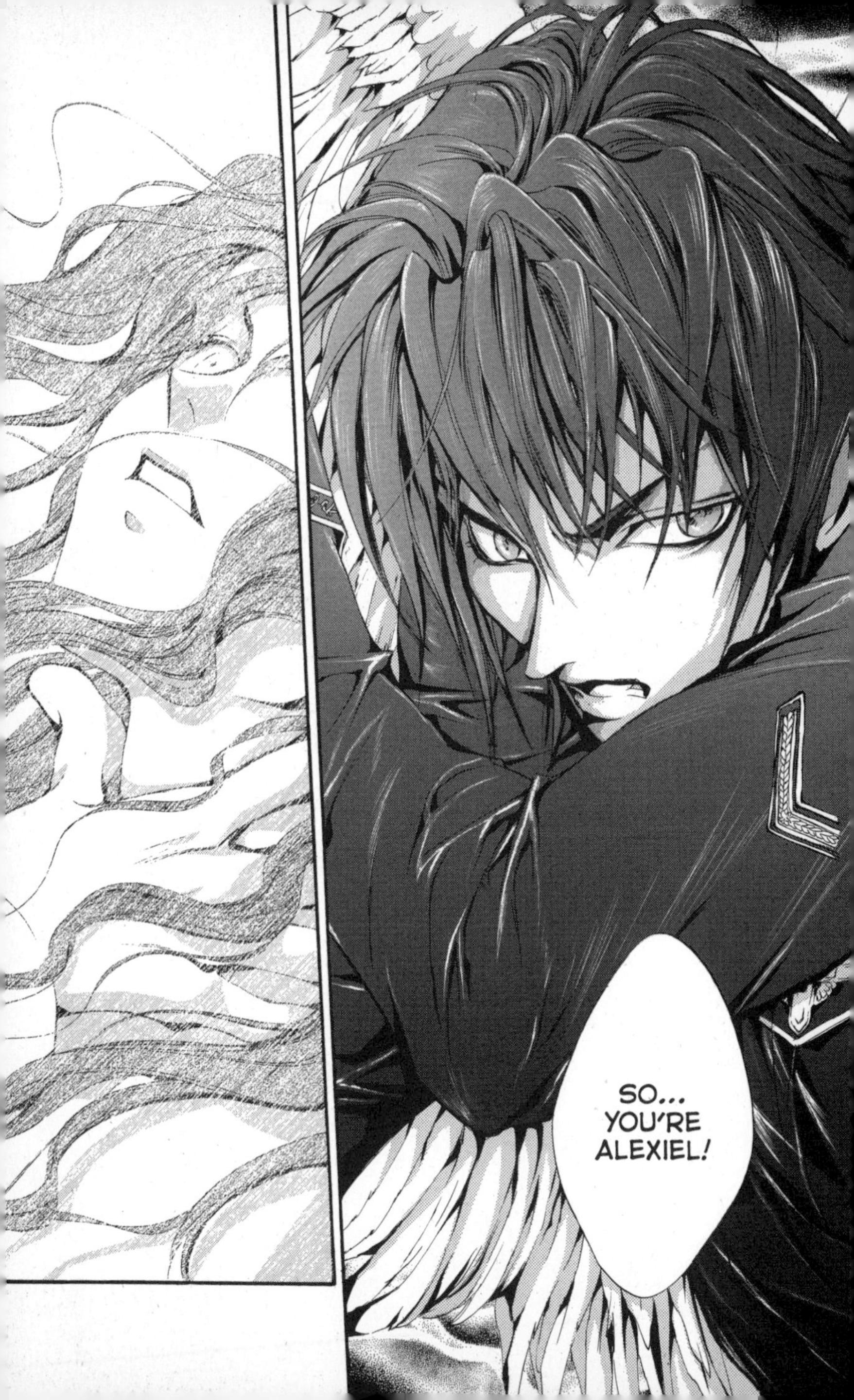
SO... YOU'RE ALEXIEL!

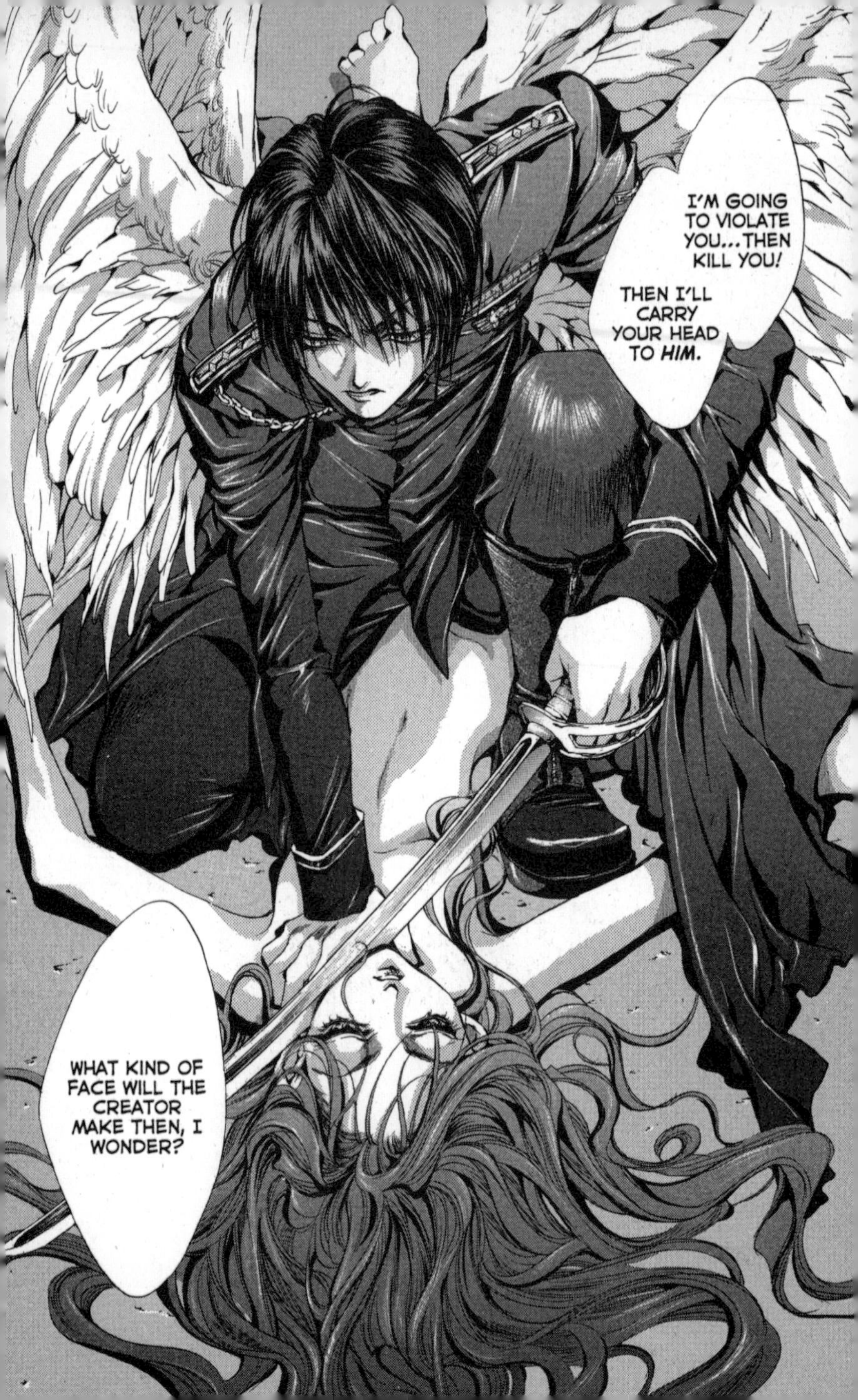
I'M GOING TO VIOLATE YOU...THEN KILL YOU!
THEN I'LL CARRY YOUR HEAD TO *HIM*.
WHAT KIND OF FACE WILL THE CREATOR MAKE THEN, I WONDER?

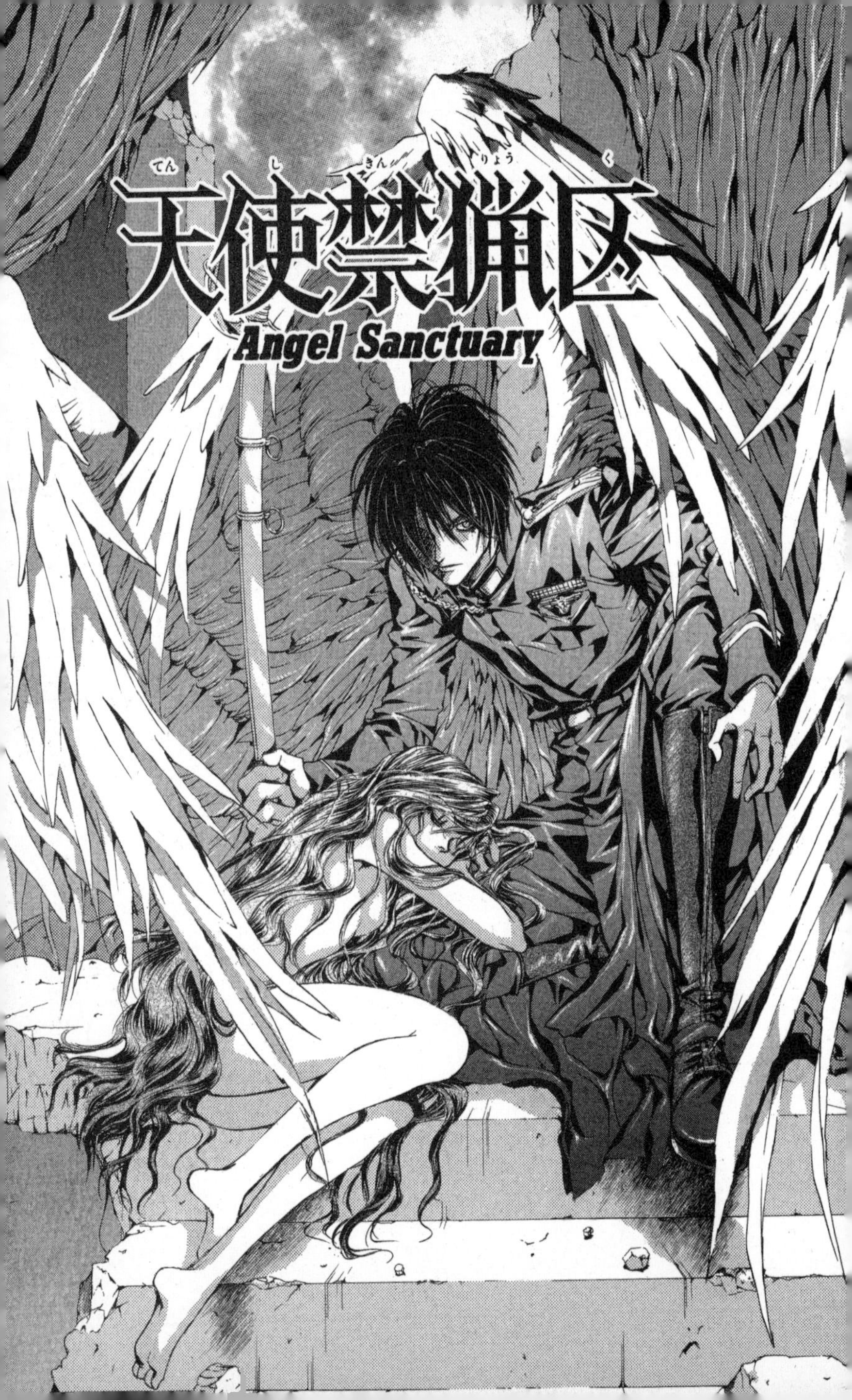
天使禁猟区
Angel Sanctuary

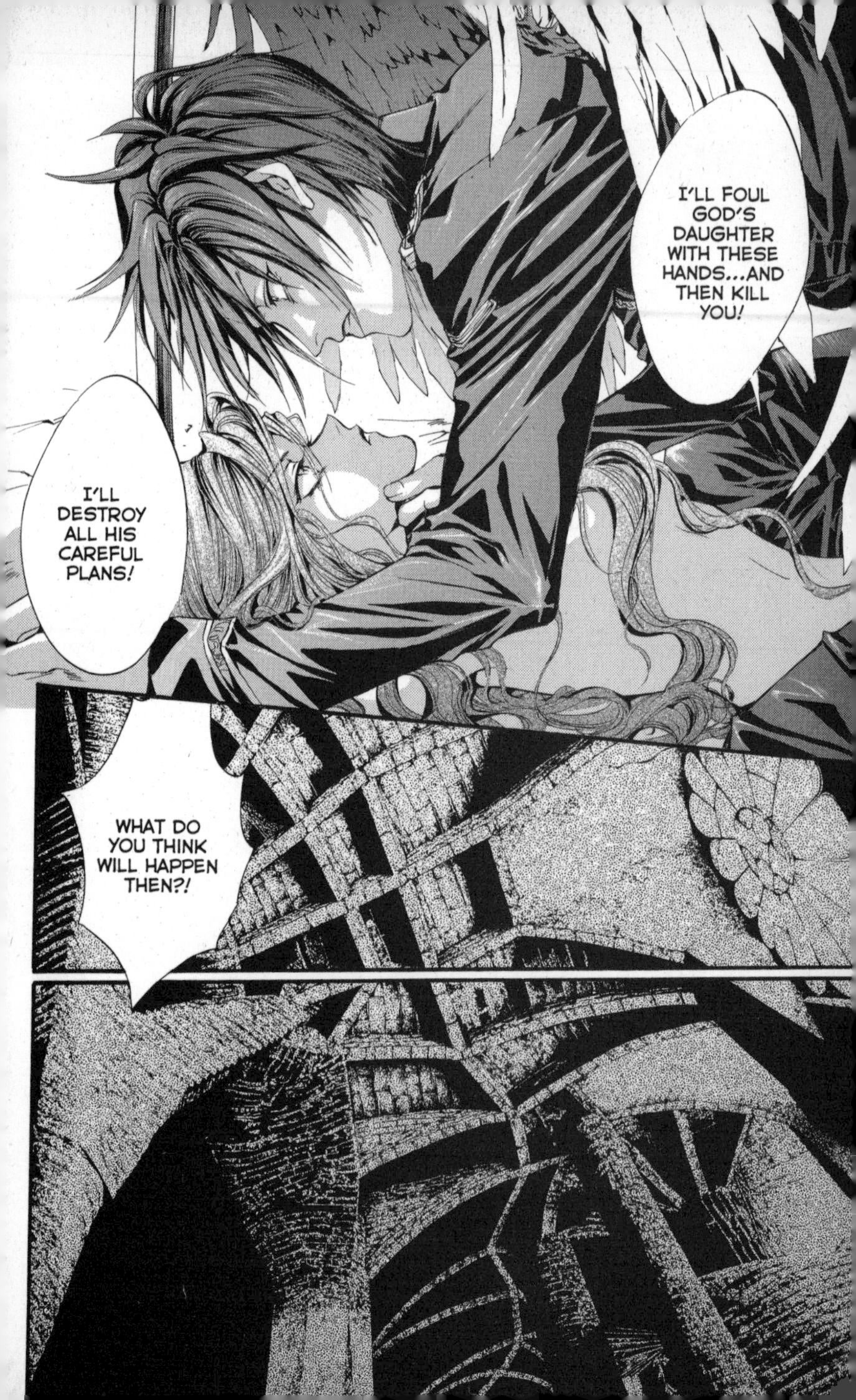
I'LL FOUL GOD'S DAUGHTER WITH THESE HANDS...AND THEN KILL YOU!
I'LL DESTROY ALL HIS CAREFUL PLANS!
WHAT DO YOU THINK WILL HAPPEN THEN?!

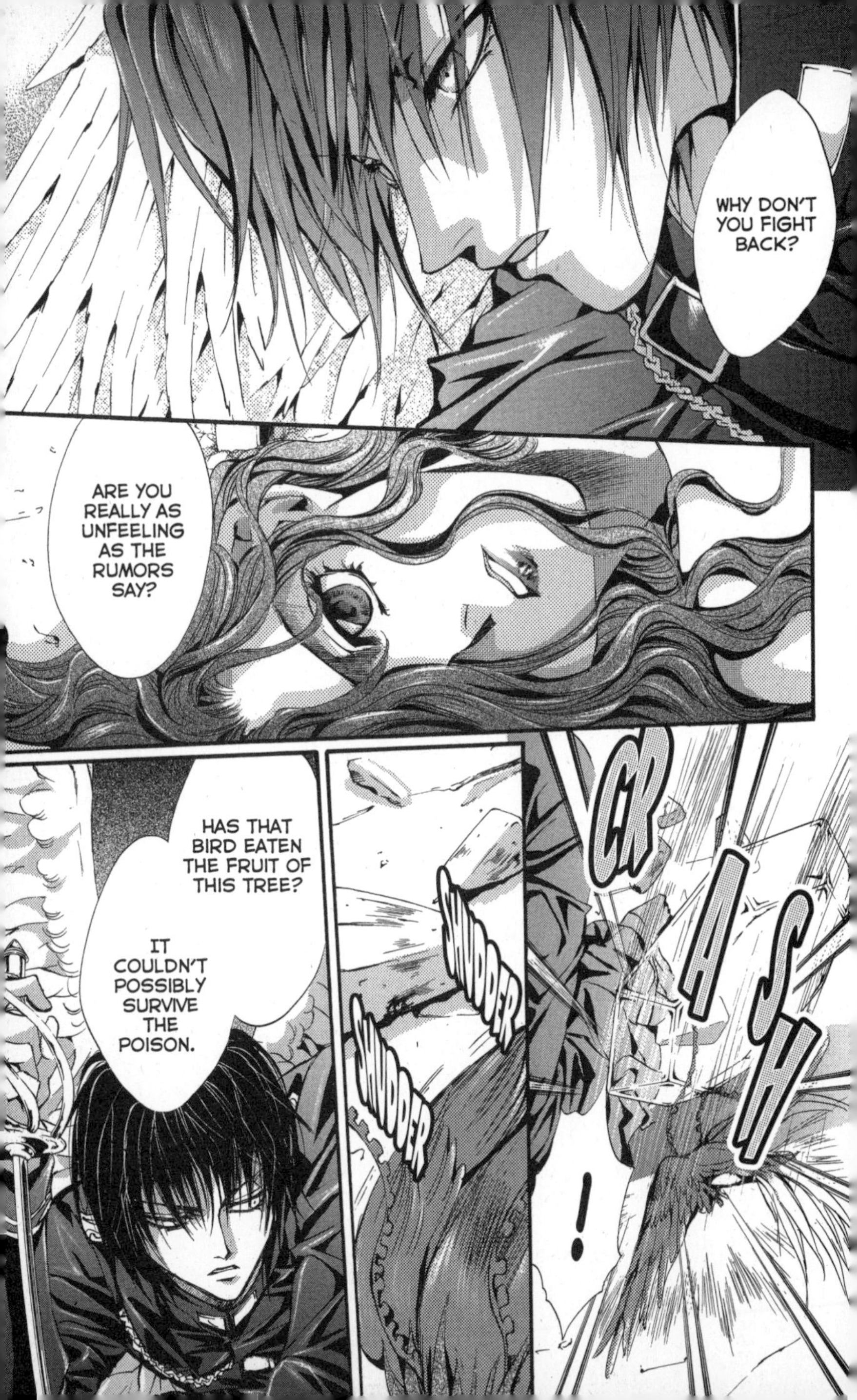
WHY DON'T YOU FIGHT BACK?
ARE YOU REALLY AS UNFEELING AS THE RUMORS SAY?
CRASH
!
SHUDDER
SHUDDER
HAS THAT BIRD EATEN THE FRUIT OF THIS TREE?
IT COULDN'T POSSIBLY SURVIVE THE POISON.

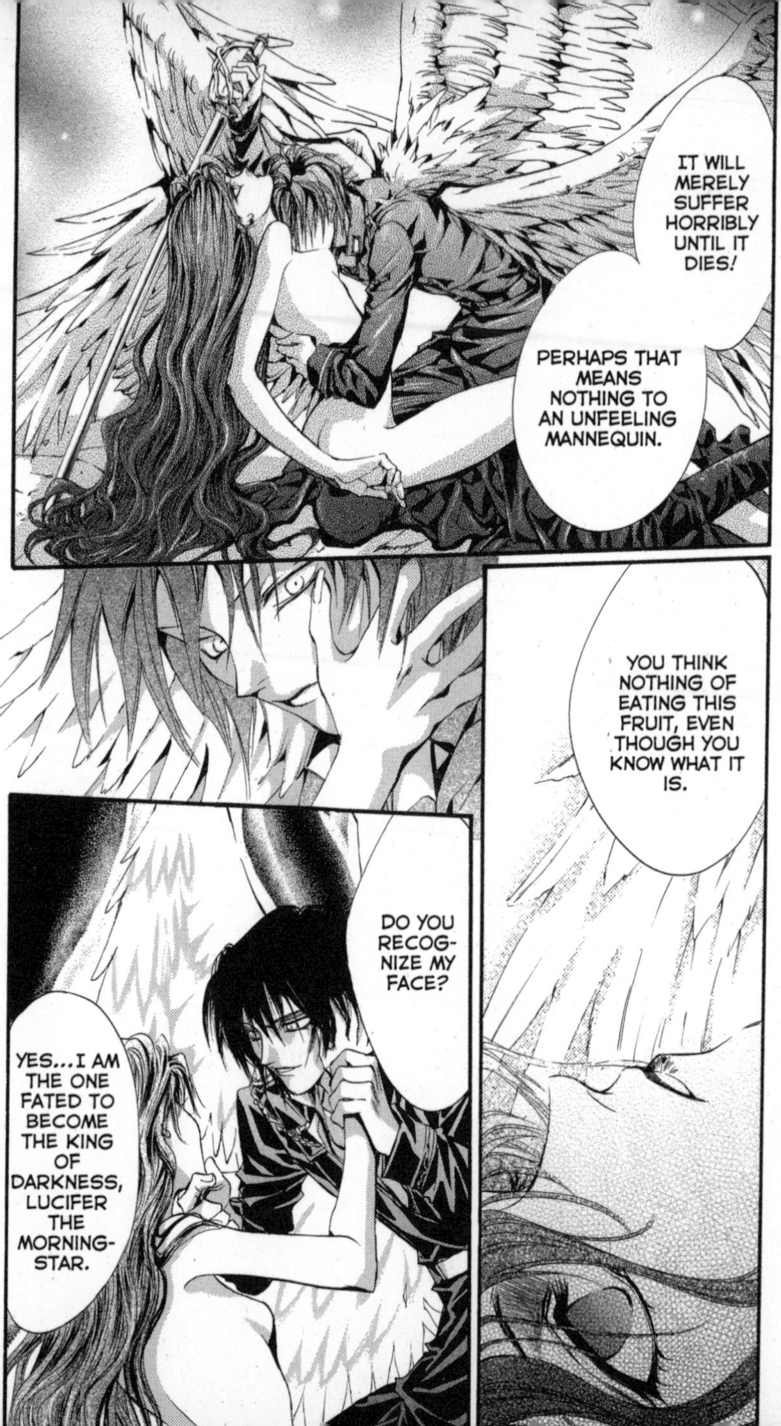
IT WILL MERELY SUFFER HORRIBLY UNTIL IT DIES!
PERHAPS THAT MEANS NOTHING TO AN UNFEELING MANNEQUIN.
YOU THINK NOTHING OF EATING THIS FRUIT, EVEN THOUGH YOU KNOW WHAT IT IS.
DO YOU RECOG-NIZE MY FACE?
YES...I AM THE ONE FATED TO BECOME THE KING OF DARKNESS, LUCIFER THE MORNING-STAR.

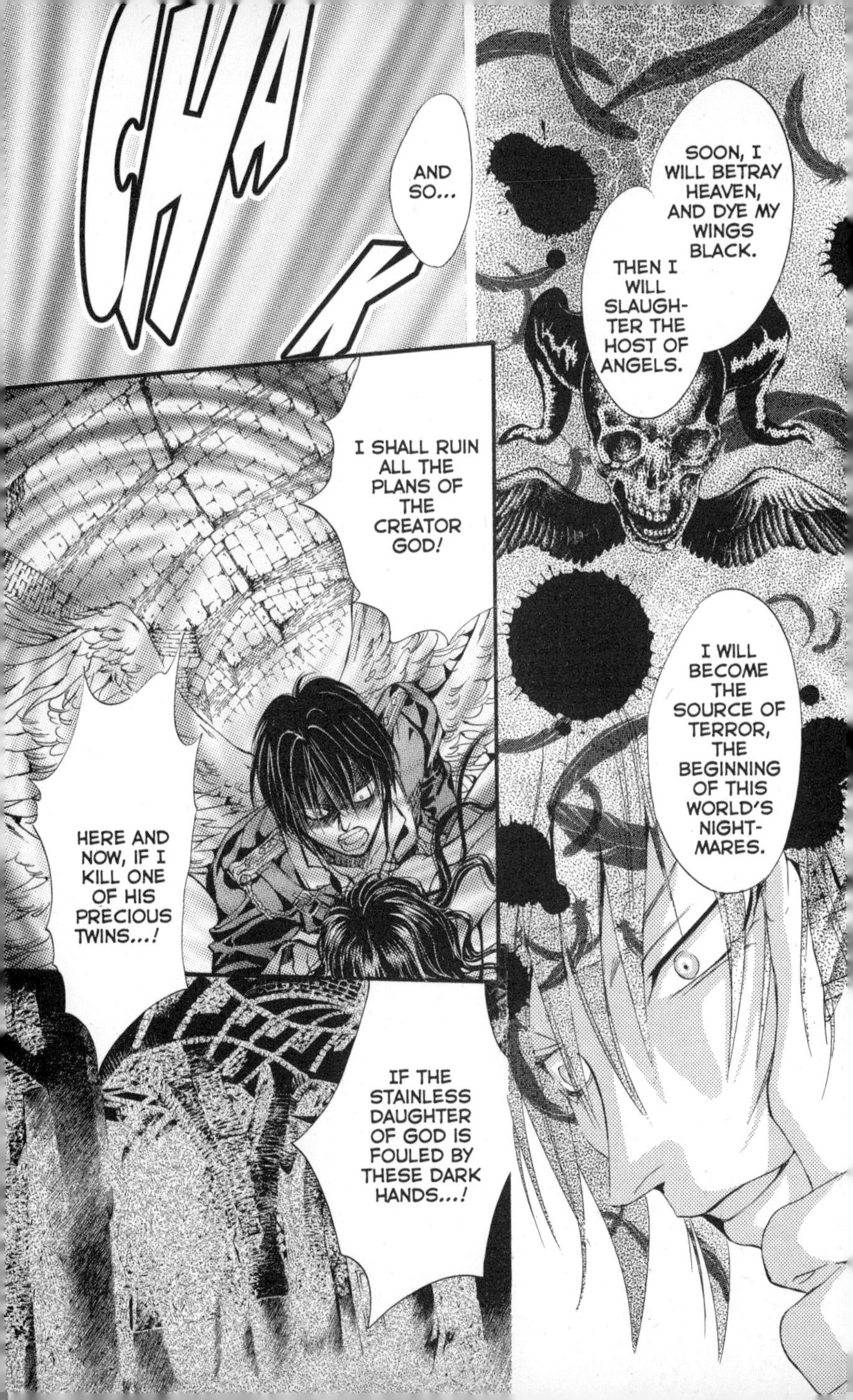
SOON, I WILL BETRAY HEAVEN, AND DYE MY WINGS BLACK.
THEN I WILL SLAUGHTER THE HOST OF ANGELS.
I WILL BECOME THE SOURCE OF TERROR, THE BEGINNING OF THIS WORLD'S NIGHTMARES.
AND SO...
CHA
I SHALL RUIN ALL THE PLANS OF THE CREATOR GOD!
HERE AND NOW, IF I KILL ONE OF HIS PRECIOUS TWINS...!
IF THE STAINLESS DAUGHTER OF GOD IS FOULED BY THESE DARK HANDS...!

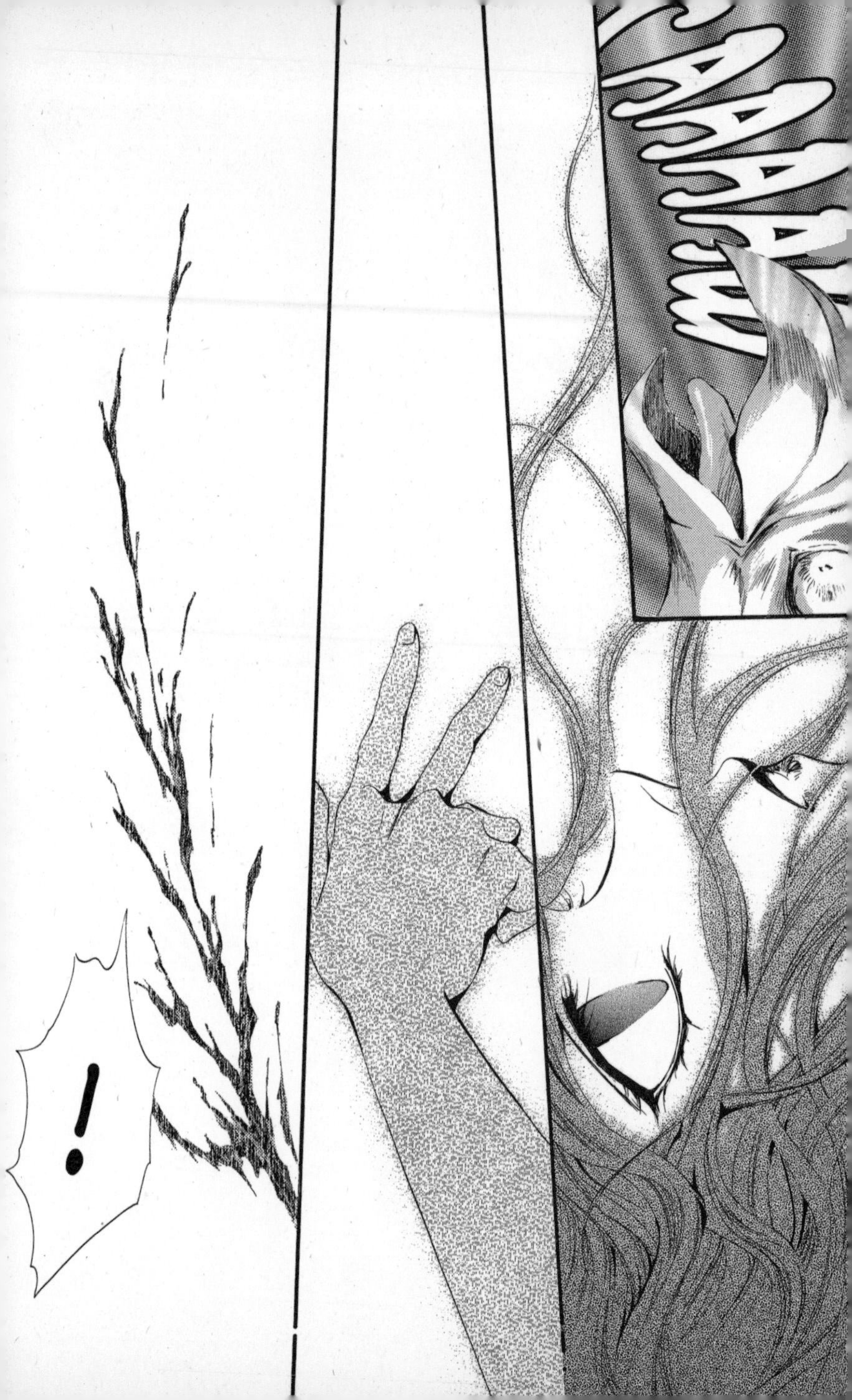
!

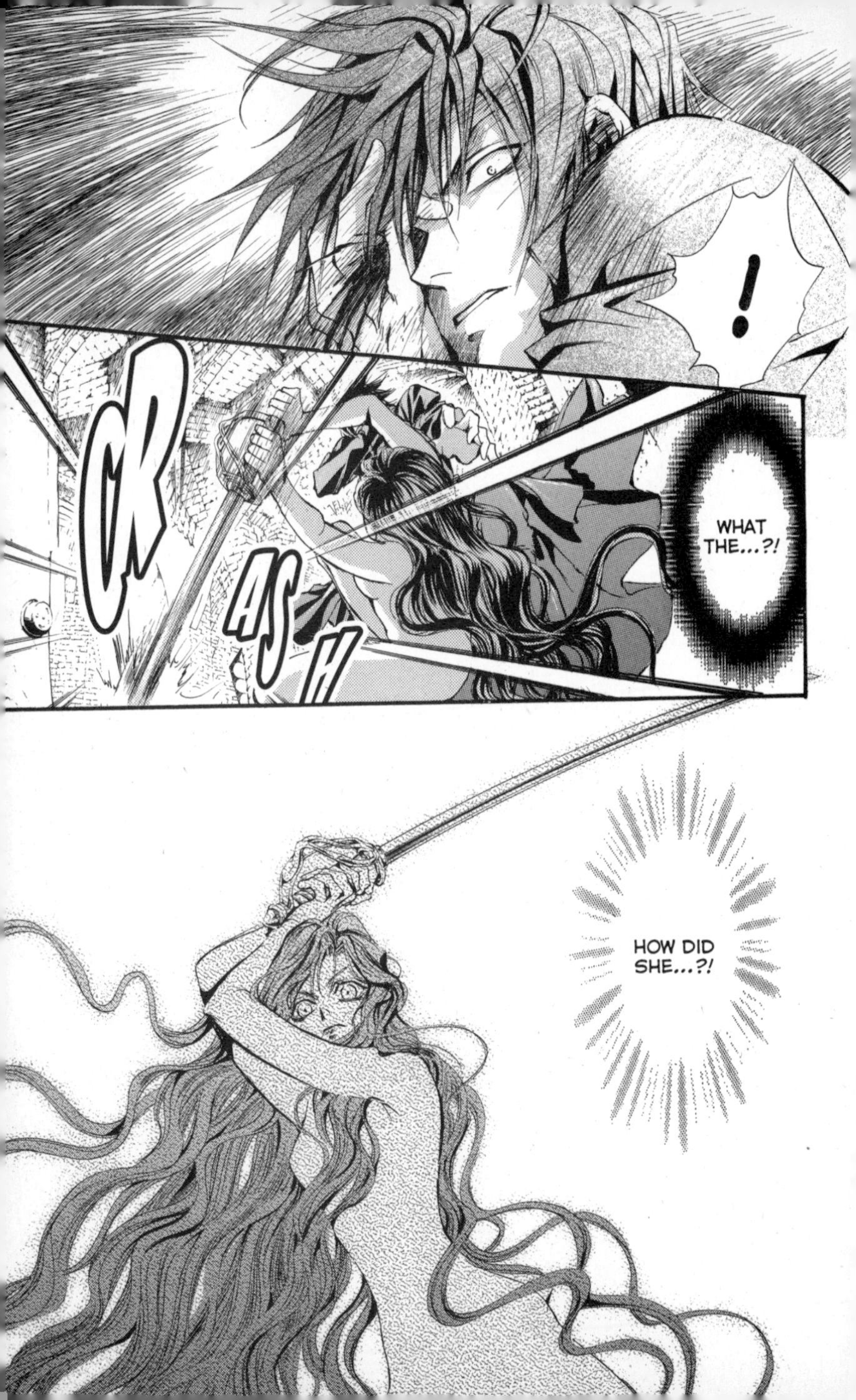
!
CRASH
WHAT THE...?!
HOW DID SHE...?!

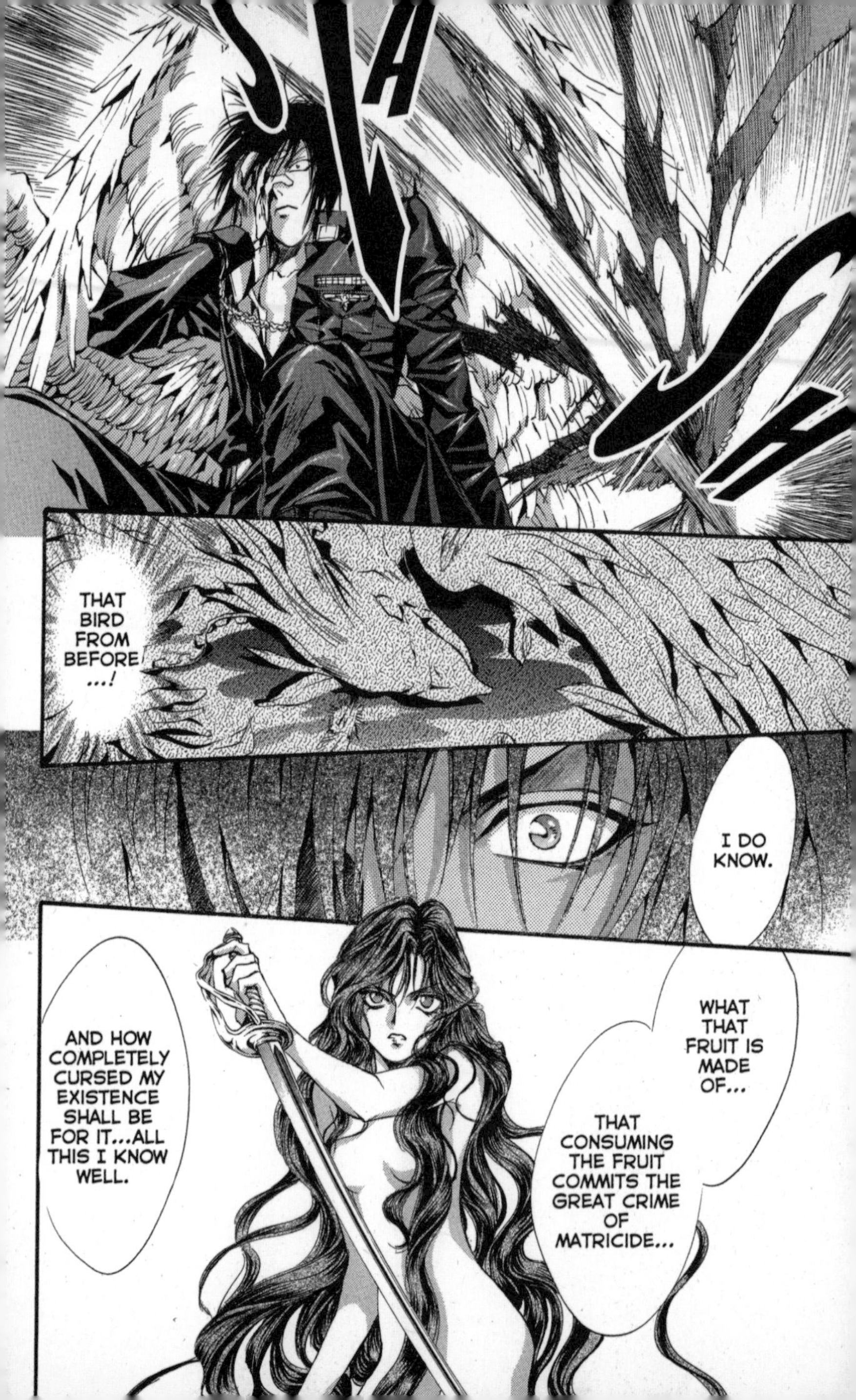
THAT BIRD FROM BEFORE...!
I DO KNOW.
WHAT THAT FRUIT IS MADE OF...
THAT CONSUMING THE FRUIT COMMITS THE GREAT CRIME OF MATRICIDE...
AND HOW COMPLETELY CURSED MY EXISTENCE SHALL BE FOR IT...ALL THIS I KNOW WELL.

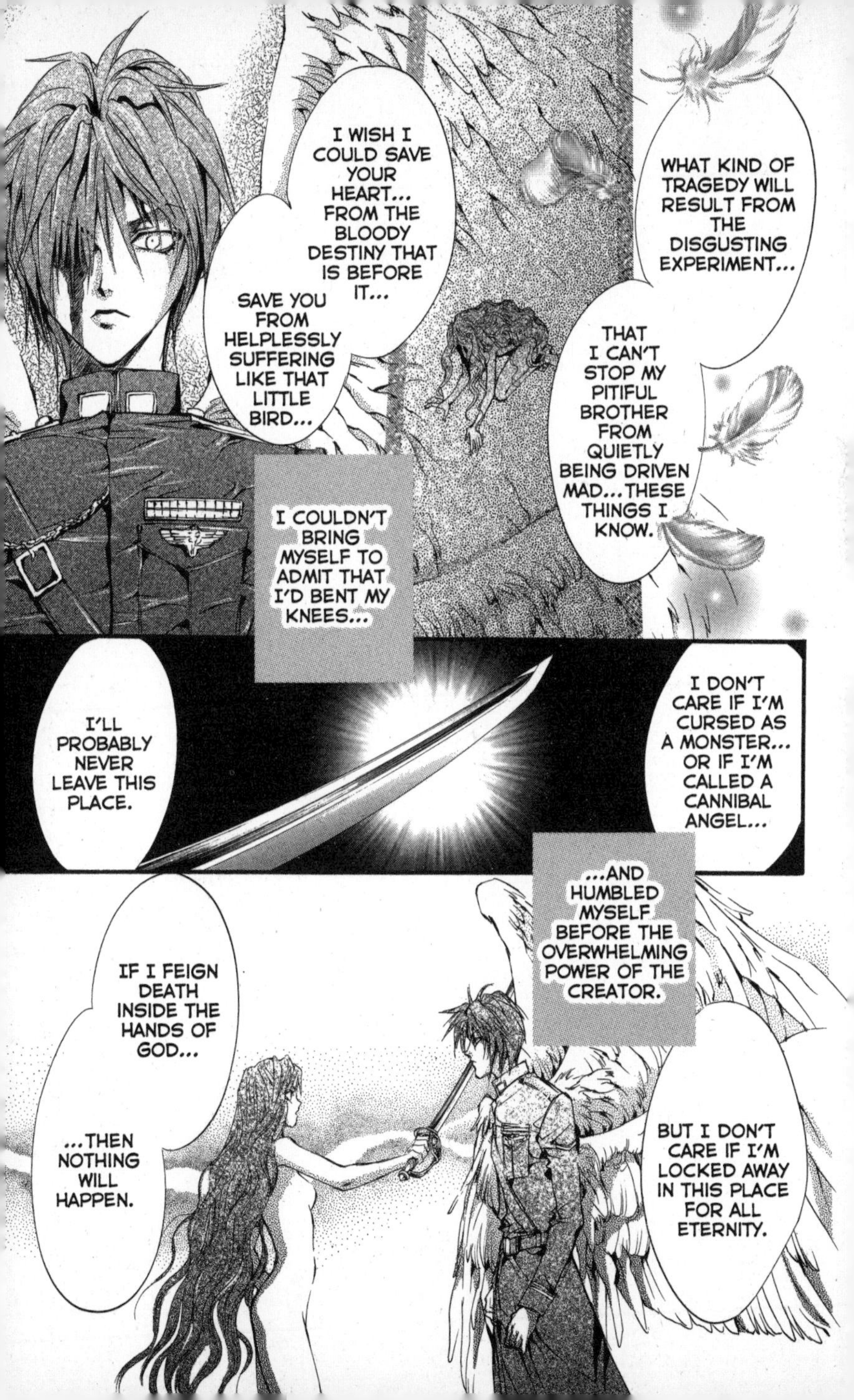
WHAT KIND OF TRAGEDY WILL RESULT FROM THE DISGUSTING EXPERIMENT...
THAT I CAN'T STOP MY PITIFUL BROTHER FROM QUIETLY BEING DRIVEN MAD... THESE THINGS I KNOW.
I WISH I COULD SAVE YOUR HEART... FROM THE BLOODY DESTINY THAT IS BEFORE IT...
SAVE YOU FROM HELPLESSLY SUFFERING LIKE THAT LITTLE BIRD...
I COULDN'T BRING MYSELF TO ADMIT THAT I'D BENT MY KNEES...
I DON'T CARE IF I'M CURSED AS A MONSTER... OR IF I'M CALLED A CANNIBAL ANGEL...
I'LL PROBABLY NEVER LEAVE THIS PLACE.
...AND HUMBLED MYSELF BEFORE THE OVERWHELMING POWER OF THE CREATOR.
BUT I DON'T CARE IF I'M LOCKED AWAY IN THIS PLACE FOR ALL ETERNITY.
IF I FEIGN DEATH INSIDE THE HANDS OF GOD...
...THEN NOTHING WILL HAPPEN.

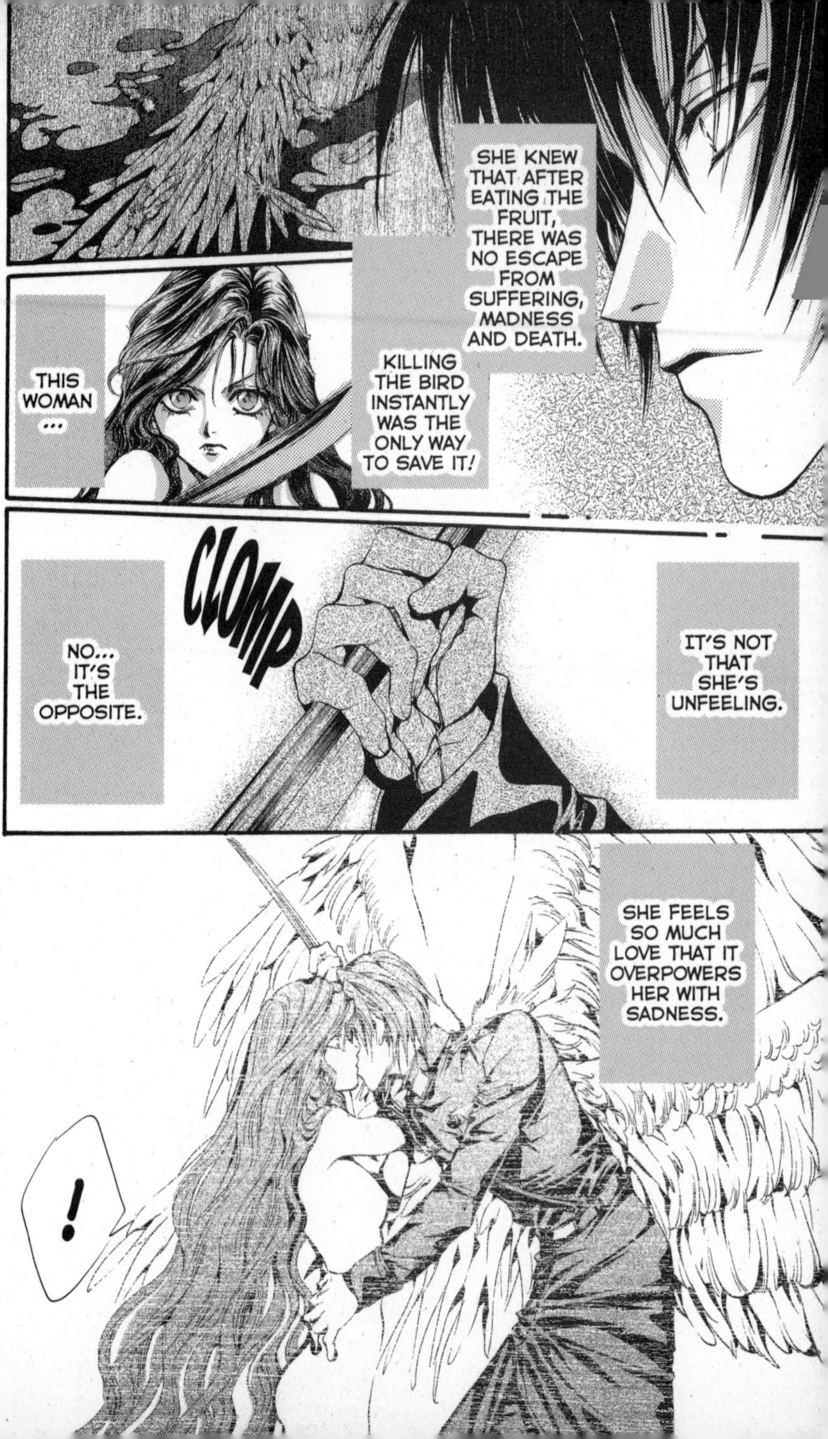
SHE KNEW THAT AFTER EATING THE FRUIT, THERE WAS NO ESCAPE FROM SUFFERING, MADNESS AND DEATH.
KILLING THE BIRD INSTANTLY WAS THE ONLY WAY TO SAVE IT!
THIS WOMAN ...
IT'S NOT THAT SHE'S UNFEELING.
CLOMP
NO... IT'S THE OPPOSITE.
SHE FEELS SO MUCH LOVE THAT IT OVERPOWERS HER WITH SADNESS.
!

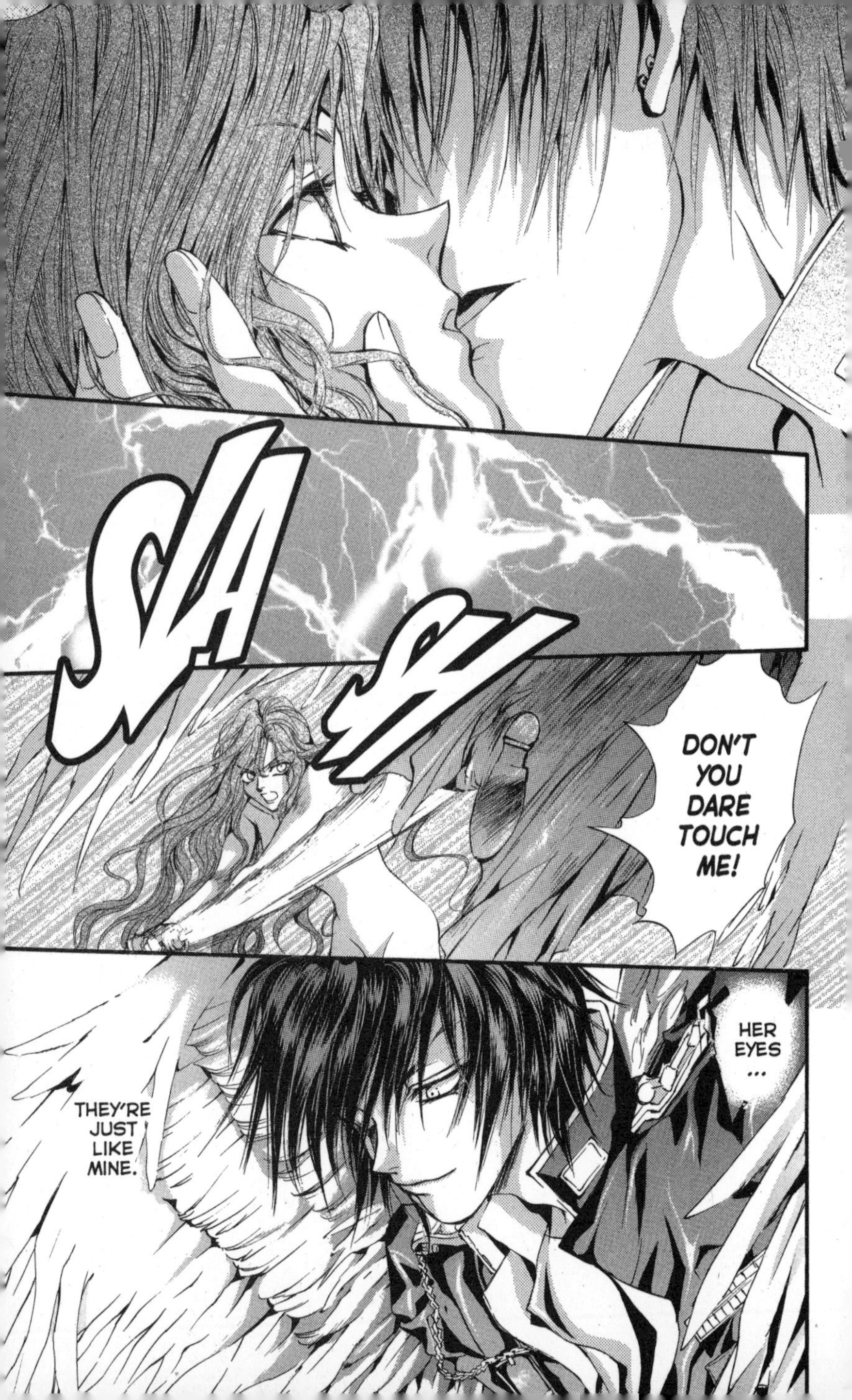
SLASH
DON'T YOU DARE TOUCH ME!
HER EYES ...
THEY'RE JUST LIKE MINE.

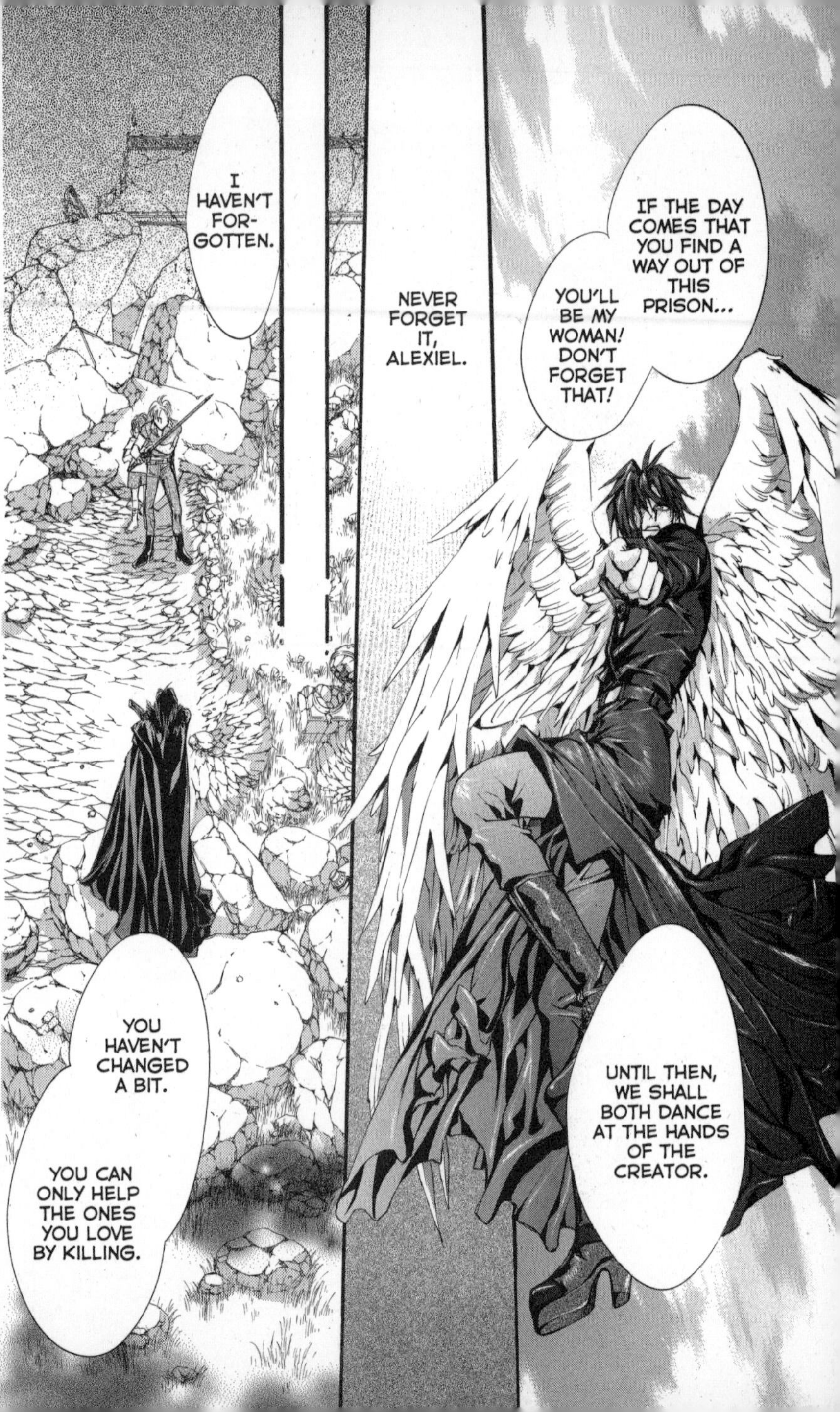
IF THE DAY COMES THAT YOU FIND A WAY OUT OF THIS PRISON...
YOU'LL BE MY WOMAN! DON'T FORGET THAT!
UNTIL THEN, WE SHALL BOTH DANCE AT THE HANDS OF THE CREATOR.
NEVER FORGET IT, ALEXIEL.
I HAVEN'T FOR-GOTTEN.
YOU HAVEN'T CHANGED A BIT.
YOU CAN ONLY HELP THE ONES YOU LOVE BY KILLING.

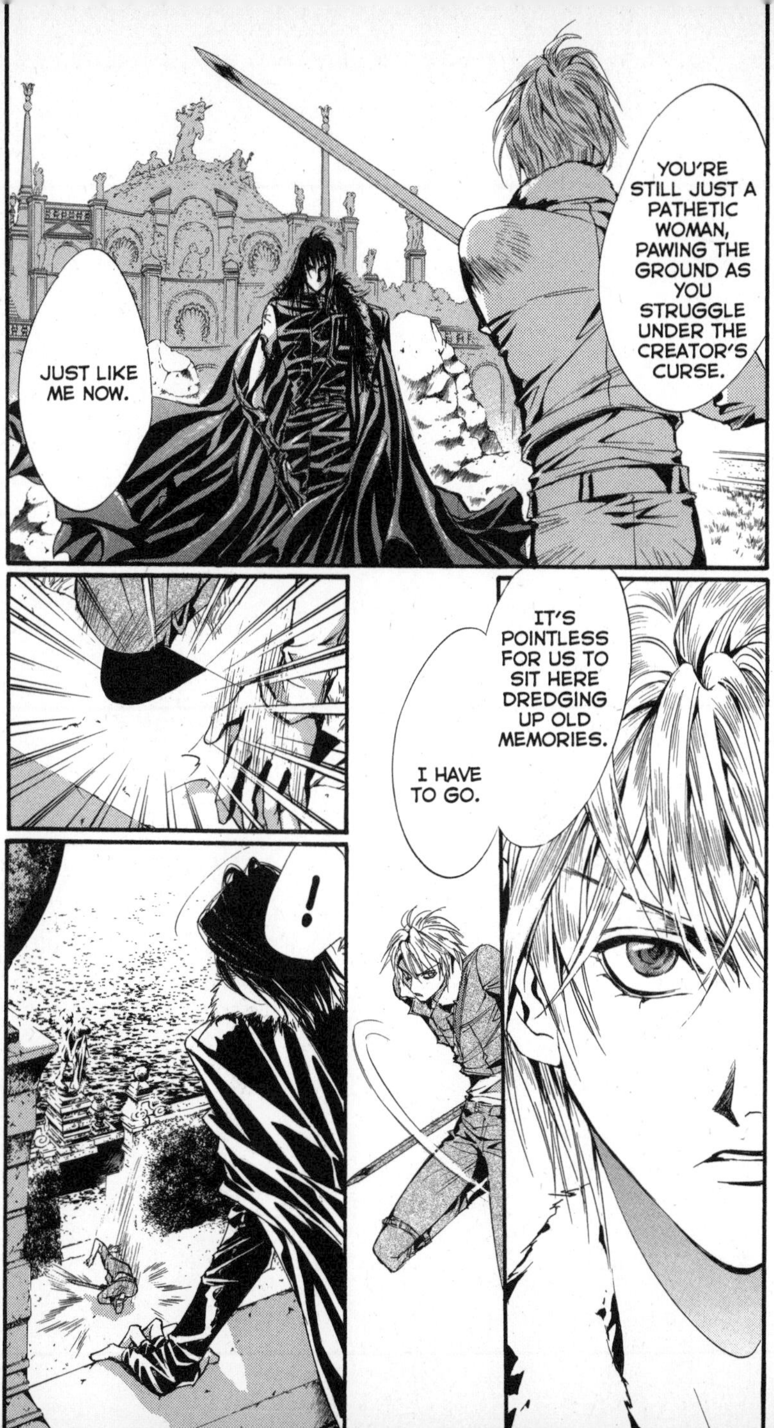
YOU'RE STILL JUST A PATHETIC WOMAN, PAWING THE GROUND AS YOU STRUGGLE UNDER THE CREATOR'S CURSE.
JUST LIKE ME NOW.
IT'S POINTLESS FOR US TO SIT HERE DREDGING UP OLD MEMORIES.
I HAVE TO GO.
!

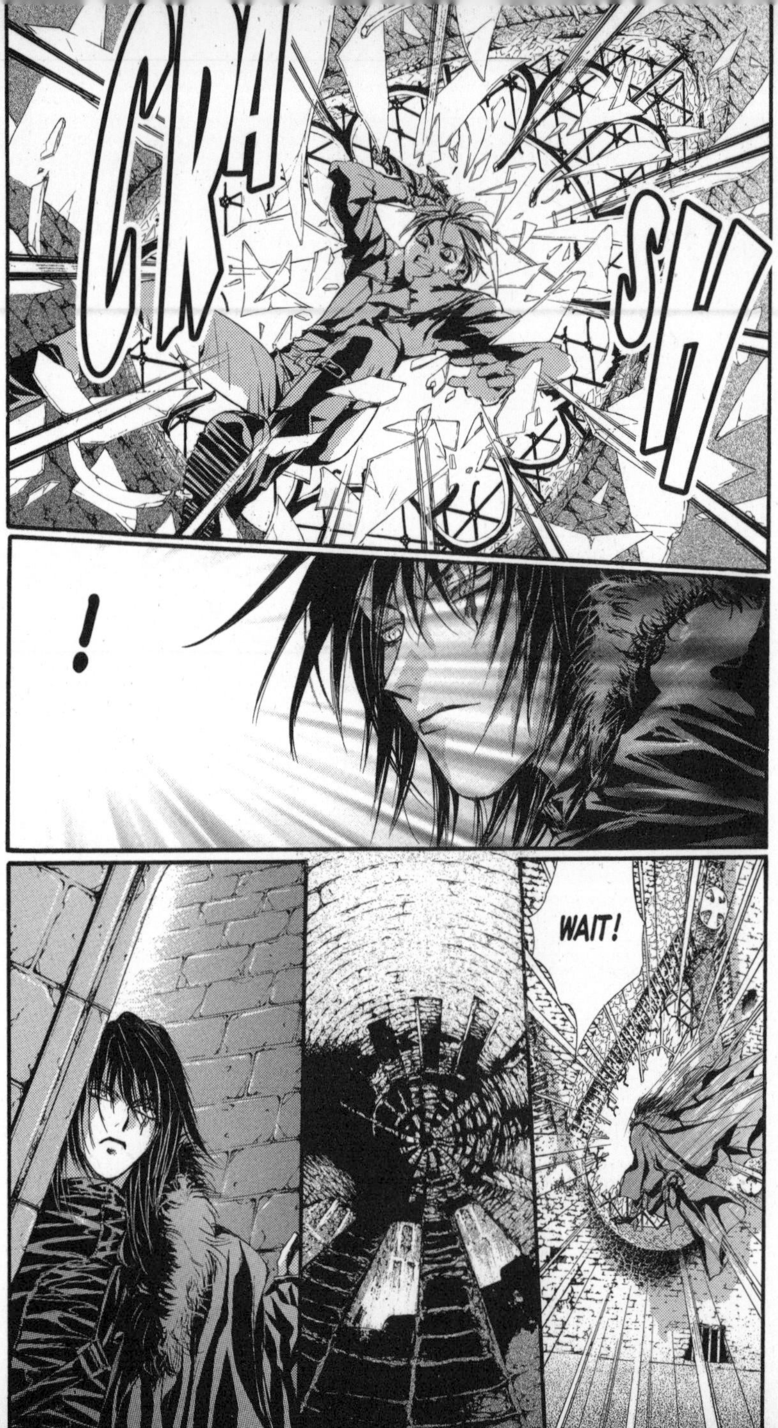
CRASH
!
WAIT!

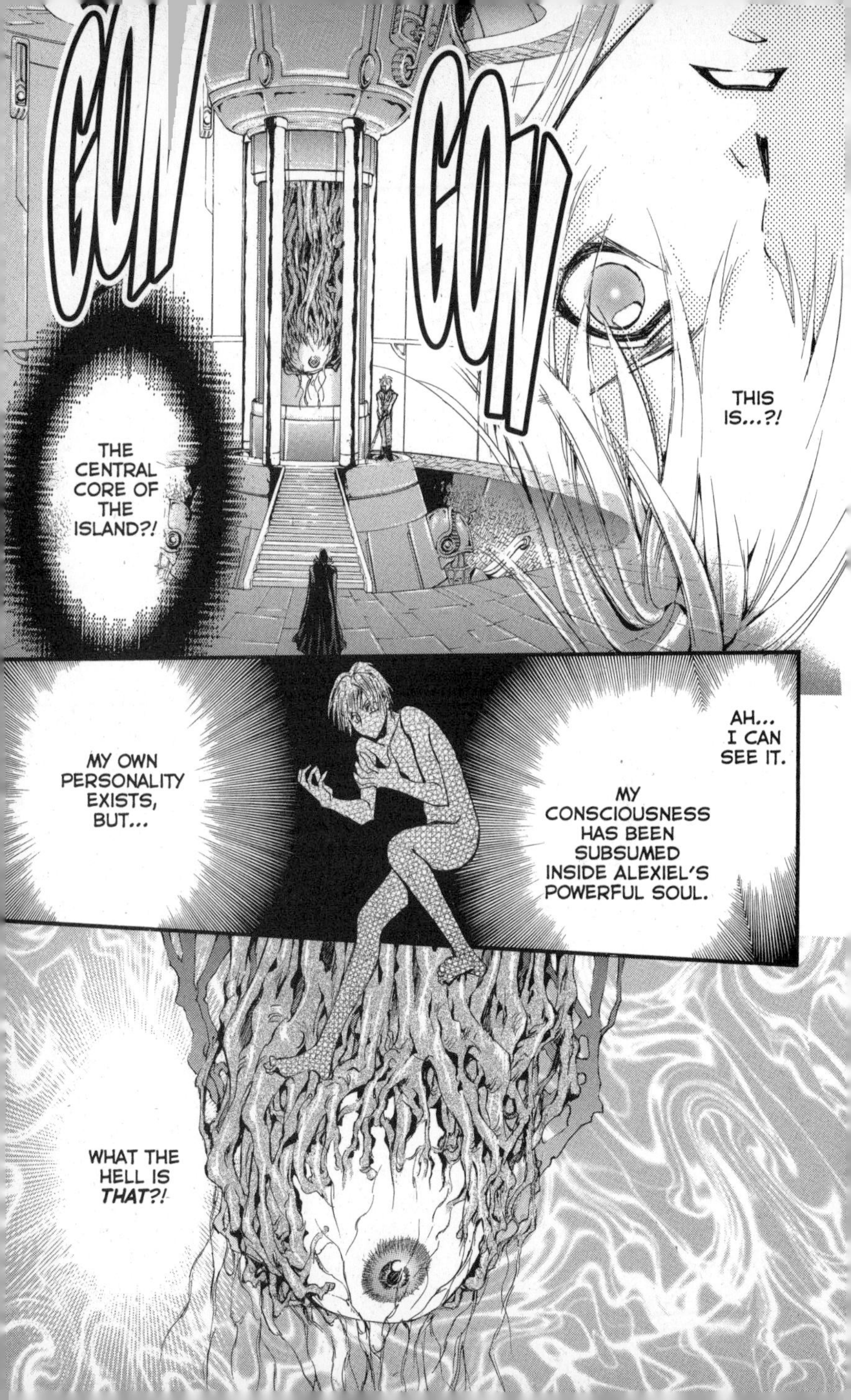
GON
GON
THIS IS...?!
THE CENTRAL CORE OF THE ISLAND?!
AH... I CAN SEE IT.
MY CONSCIOUSNESS HAS BEEN SUBSUMED INSIDE ALEXIEL'S POWERFUL SOUL.
MY OWN PERSONALITY EXISTS, BUT...
WHAT THE HELL IS *THAT*?!

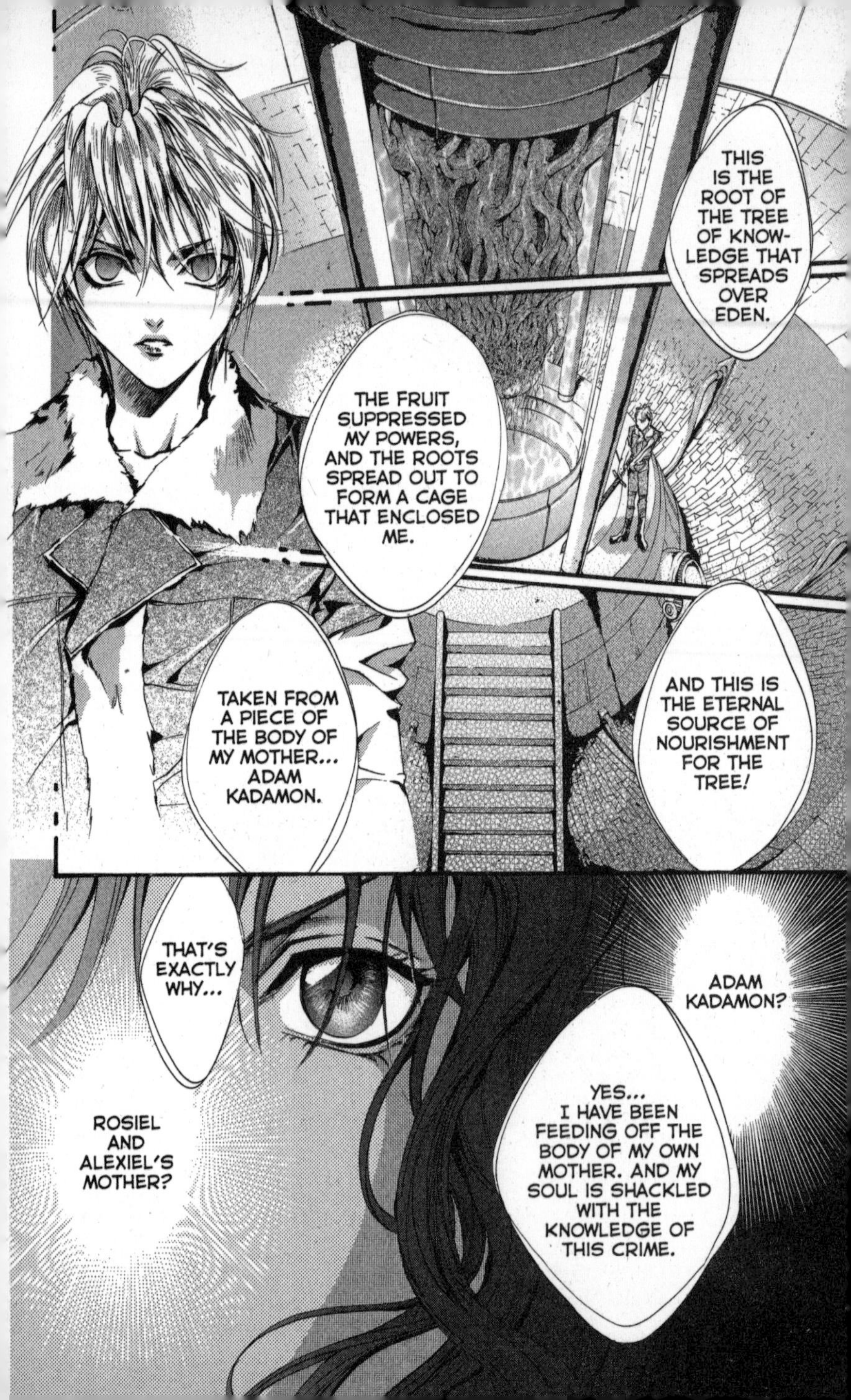
THIS IS THE ROOT OF THE TREE OF KNOW-LEDGE THAT SPREADS OVER EDEN.
THE FRUIT SUPPRESSED MY POWERS, AND THE ROOTS SPREAD OUT TO FORM A CAGE THAT ENCLOSED ME.
AND THIS IS THE ETERNAL SOURCE OF NOURISHMENT FOR THE TREE!
TAKEN FROM A PIECE OF THE BODY OF MY MOTHER... ADAM KADAMON.
ADAM KADAMON?
YES... I HAVE BEEN FEEDING OFF THE BODY OF MY OWN MOTHER. AND MY SOUL IS SHACKLED WITH THE KNOWLEDGE OF THIS CRIME.
ROSIEL AND ALEXIEL'S MOTHER?
THAT'S EXACTLY WHY...

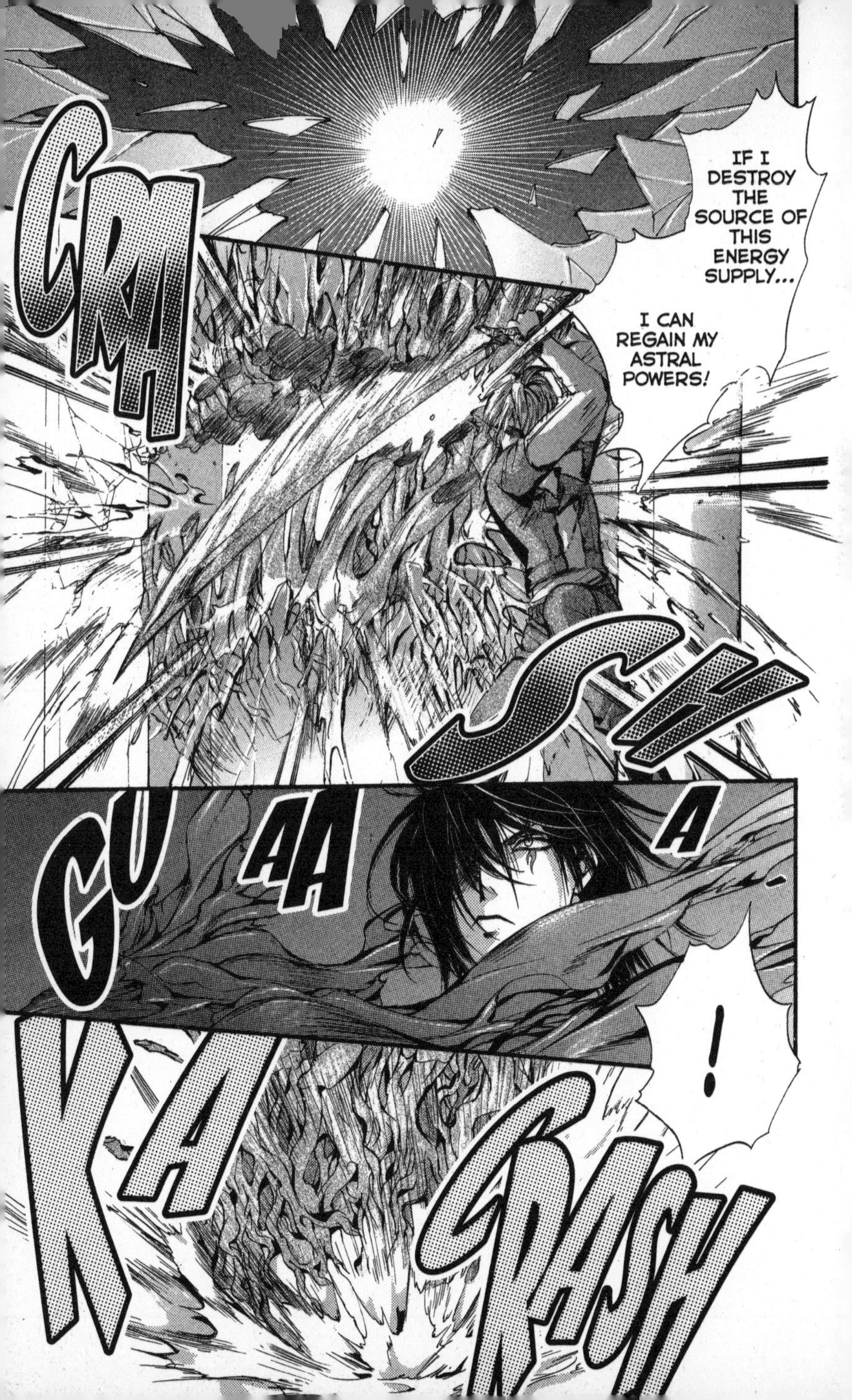
IF I DESTROY THE SOURCE OF THIS ENERGY SUPPLY...
I CAN REGAIN MY ASTRAL POWERS!
CRA
SH
GU AA A
!
KA
CRASH

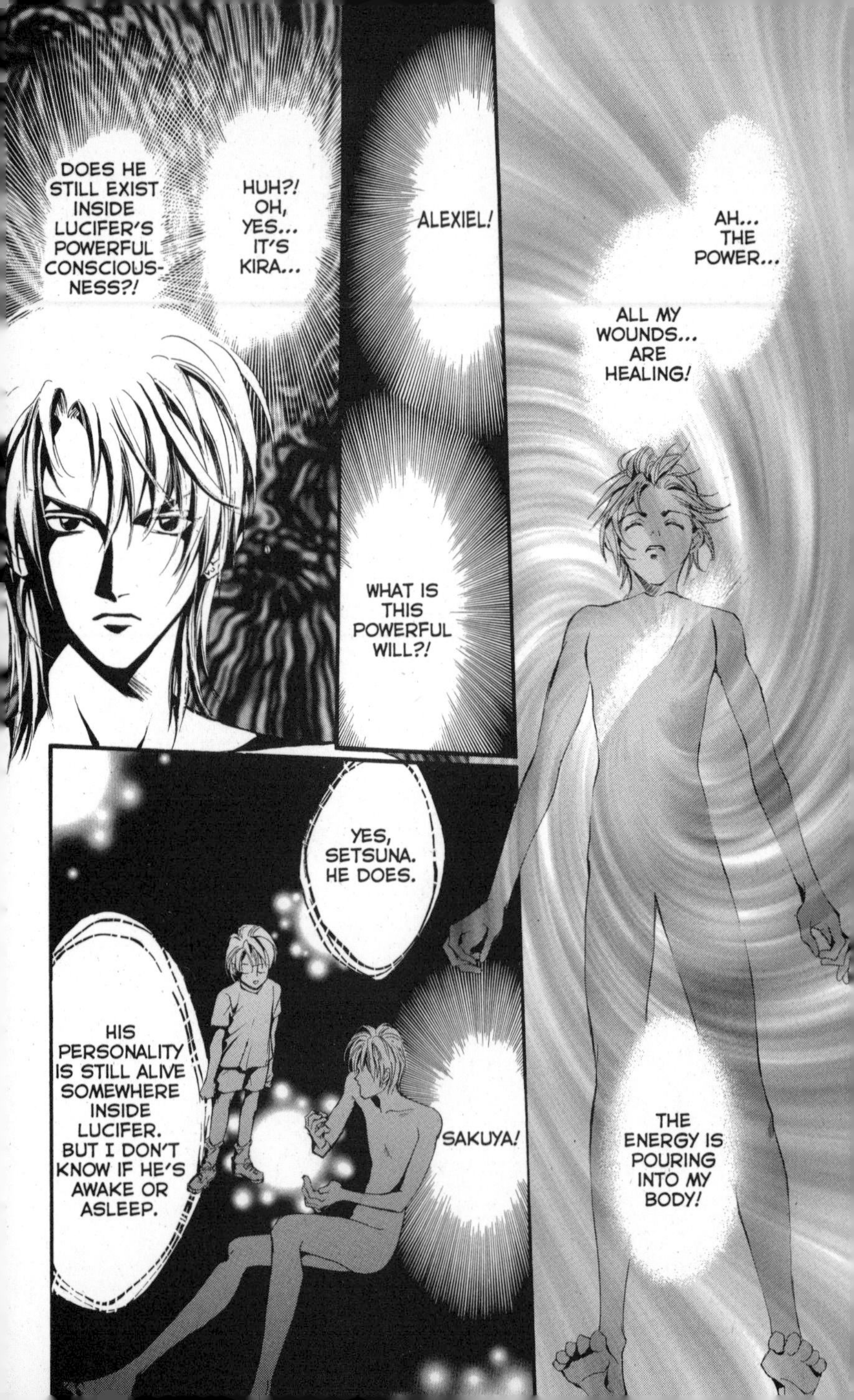
AH... THE POWER...
ALL MY WOUNDS... ARE HEALING!
THE ENERGY IS POURING INTO MY BODY!
ALEXIEL!
WHAT IS THIS POWERFUL WILL?!
HUH?! OH, YES... IT'S KIRA...
DOES HE STILL EXIST INSIDE LUCIFER'S POWERFUL CONSCIOUS-NESS?!
SAKUYA!
YES, SETSUNA. HE DOES.
HIS PERSONALITY IS STILL ALIVE SOMEWHERE INSIDE LUCIFER. BUT I DON'T KNOW IF HE'S AWAKE OR ASLEEP.

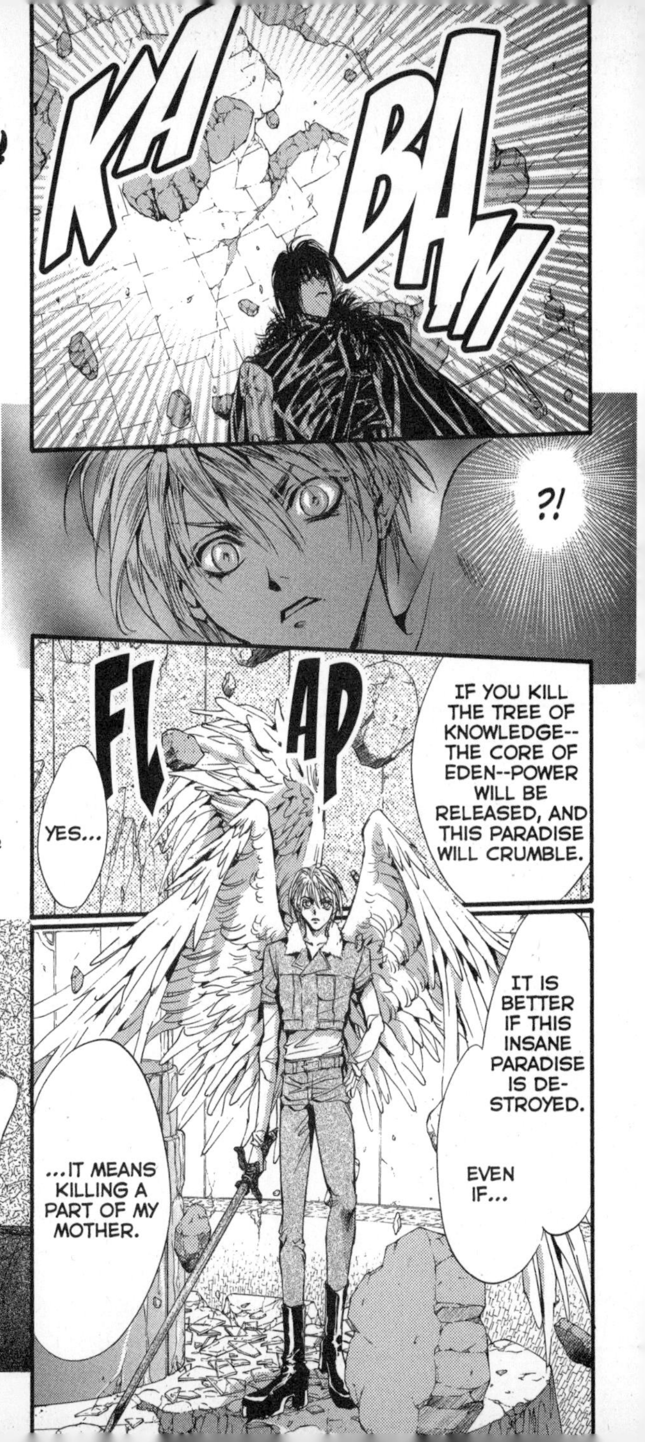
KA
BAM
?!
FLAP
IF YOU KILL THE TREE OF KNOWLEDGE--THE CORE OF EDEN--POWER WILL BE RELEASED, AND THIS PARADISE WILL CRUMBLE.
YES...
IT IS BETTER IF THIS INSANE PARADISE IS DE-STROYED.
EVEN IF...
...IT MEANS KILLING A PART OF MY MOTHER.

Even though we're near the end, the workload has increased, what with coloring and drawing...I never have a moment's rest! The fun I can have is at home. I have some video games at home, which I keep ending up playing. Actually, a day never goes by without me cranking up the games. I play "Persona," "Final Fantasy" and "Dragon Quest" a lot. "Koudleka" is also a scary game, with a pretty main character that I like. My PC got tired of me chatting, so it broke down. So now all I do with it is look up game advice pages. But when I look on the cheat web sites, I think "I can't do all that wild stuff." They're pretty impressive.

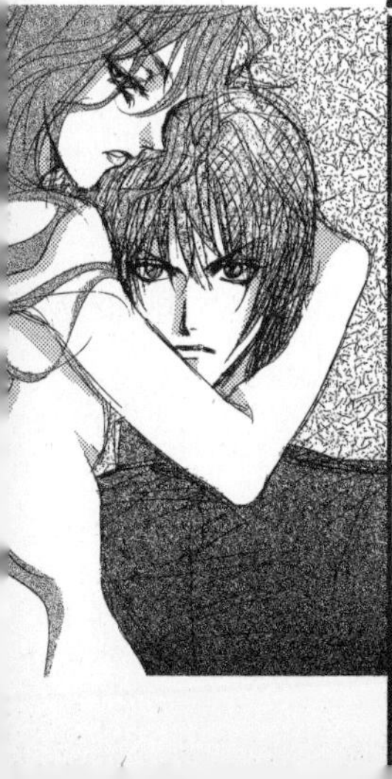

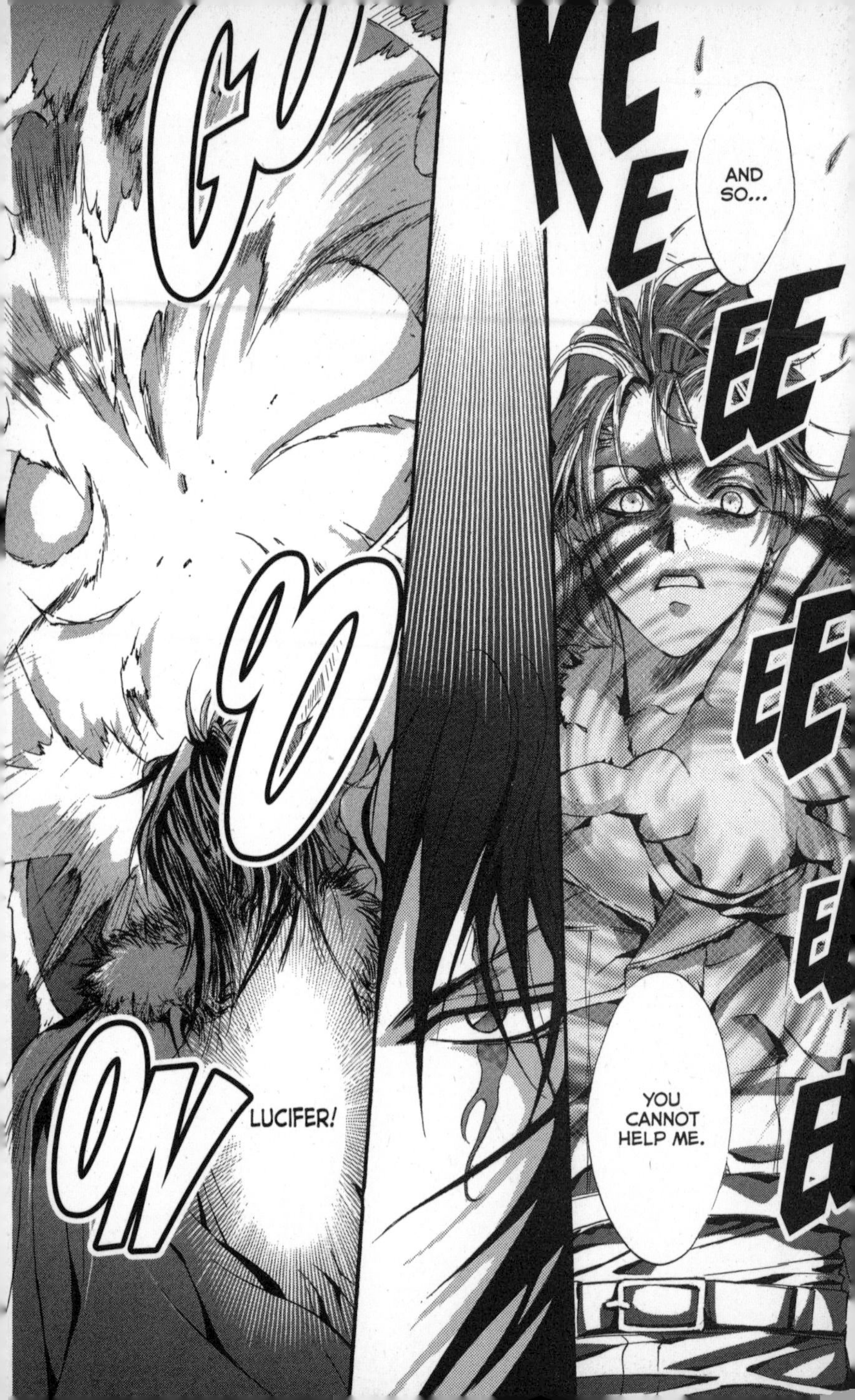
AND SO...
YOU CANNOT HELP ME.
LUCIFER!

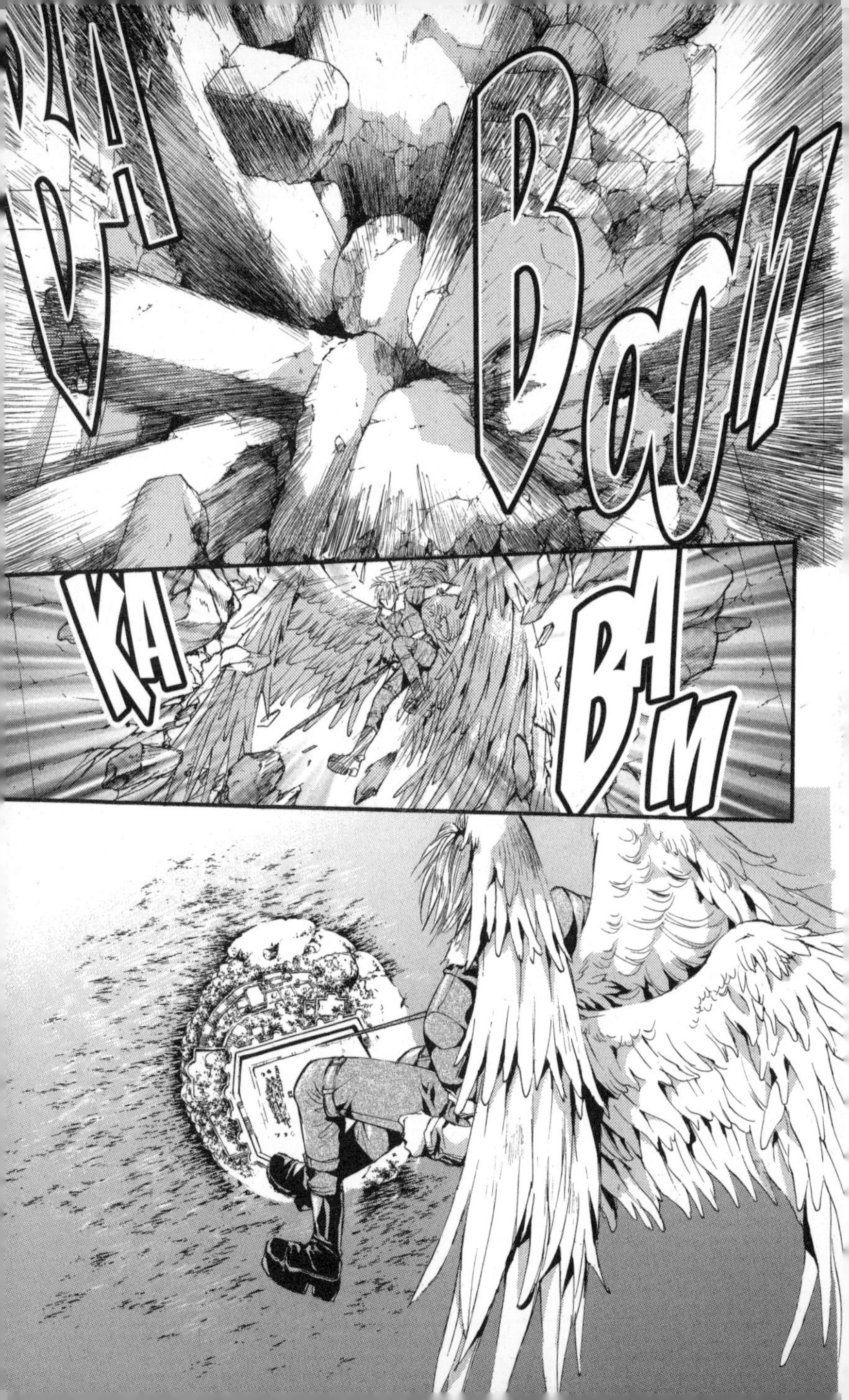
Boom
KA
BAM

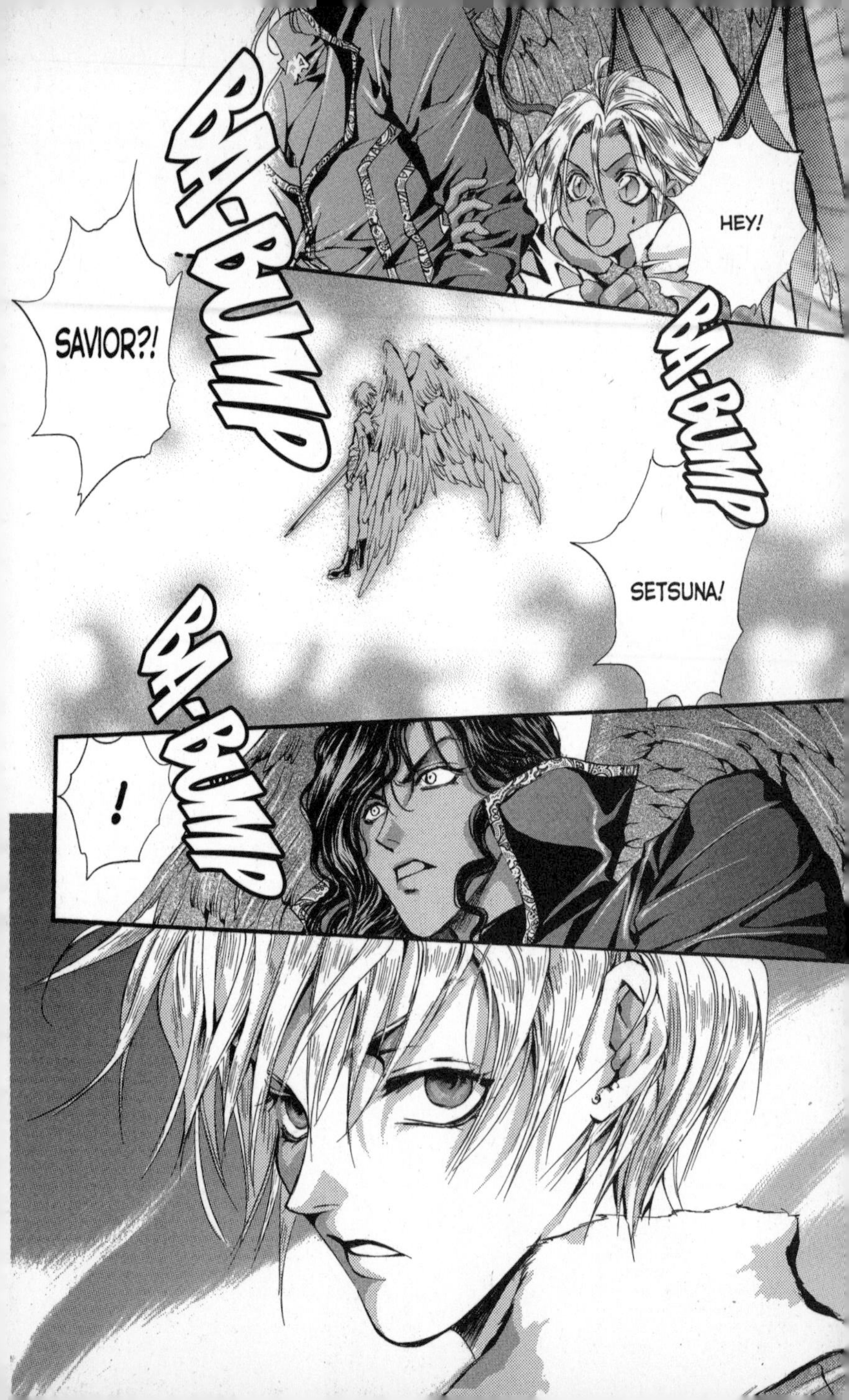
HEY!
SAVIOR?!
BA-BUMP
BA-BUMP
SETSUNA!
BA-BUMP
!

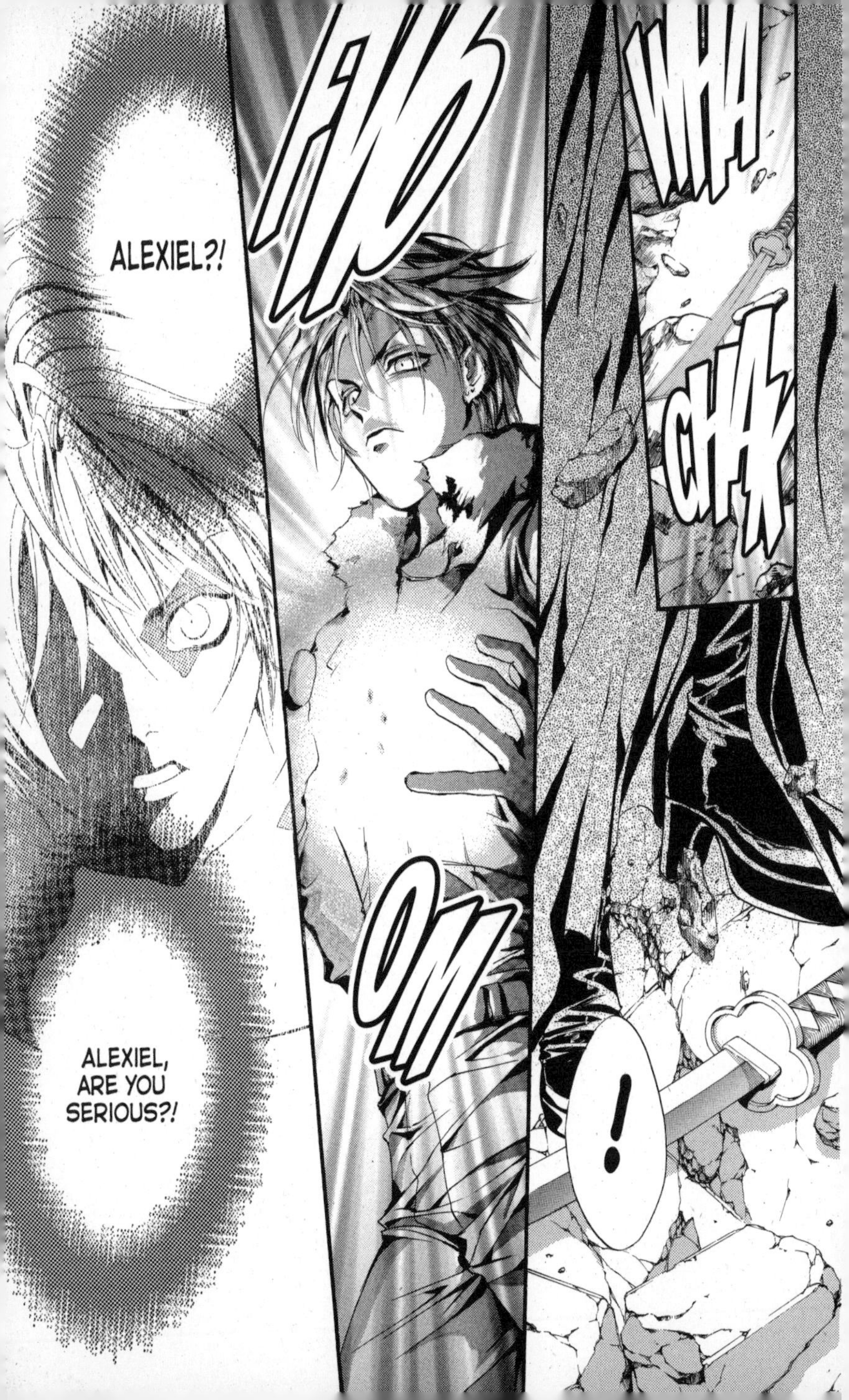
WHA
CHA
!
ALEXIEL?!
ALEXIEL, ARE YOU SERIOUS?!

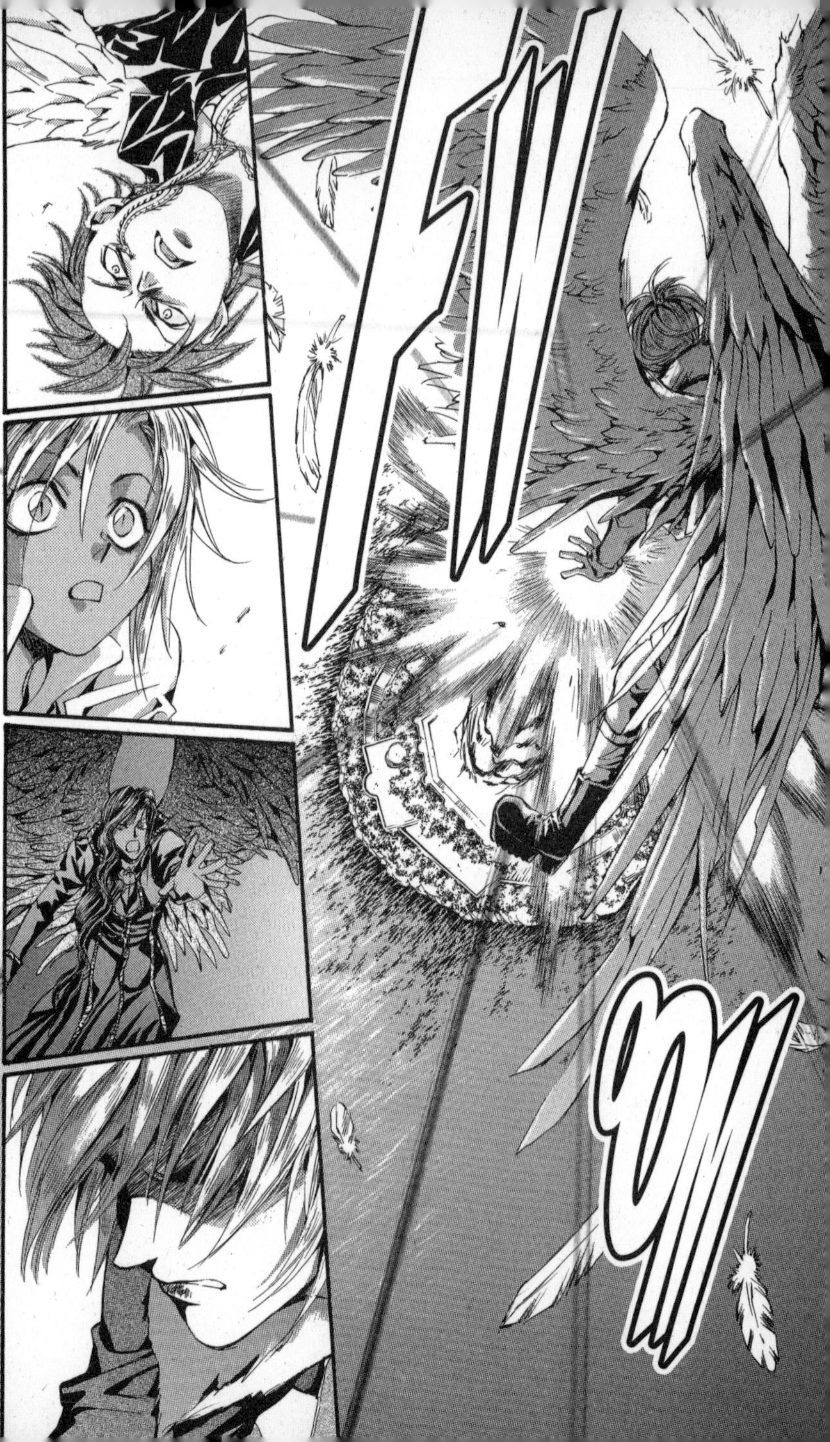

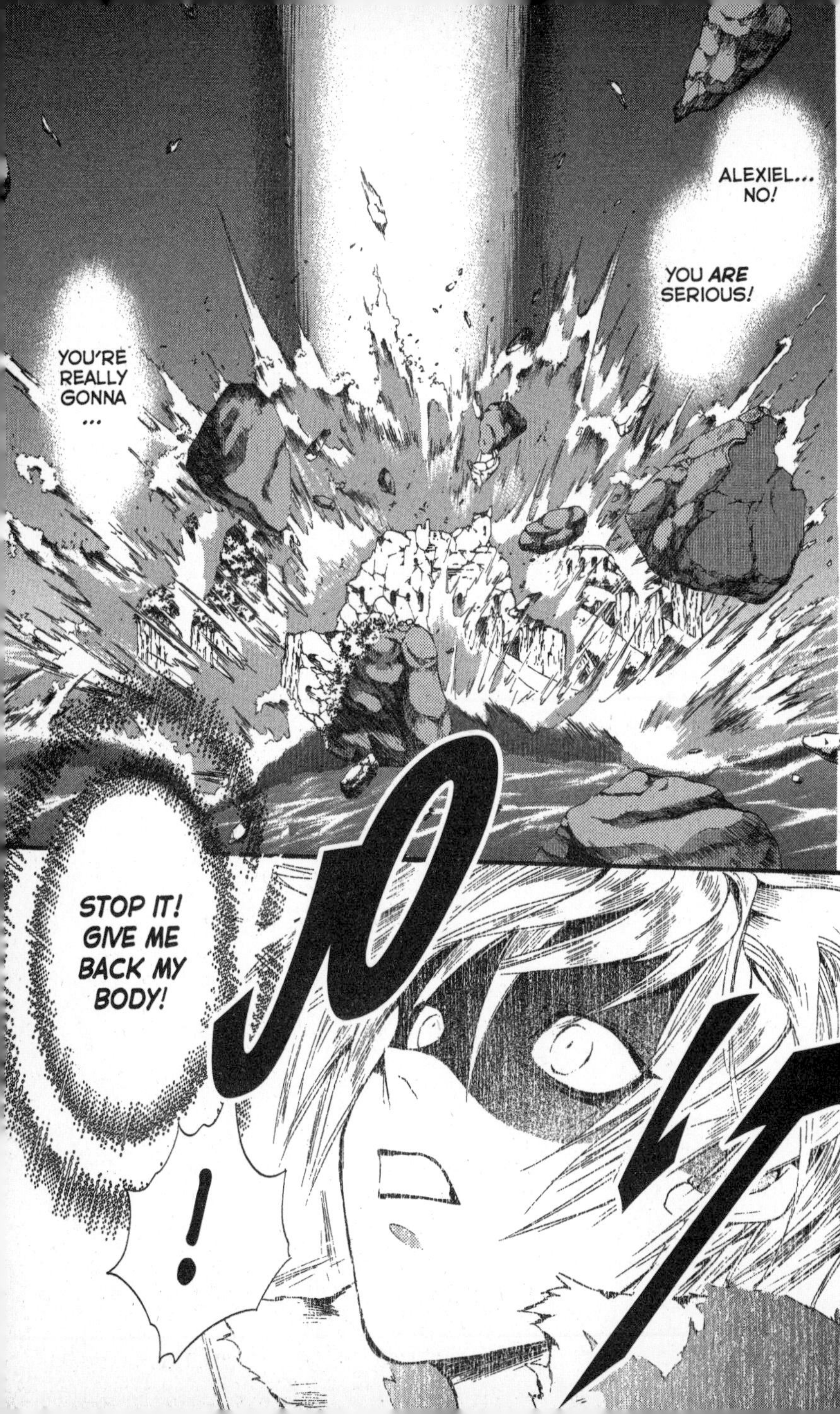
ALEXIEL... NO!
YOU ARE SERIOUS!
YOU'RE REALLY GONNA ...
STOP IT! GIVE ME BACK MY BODY!
!

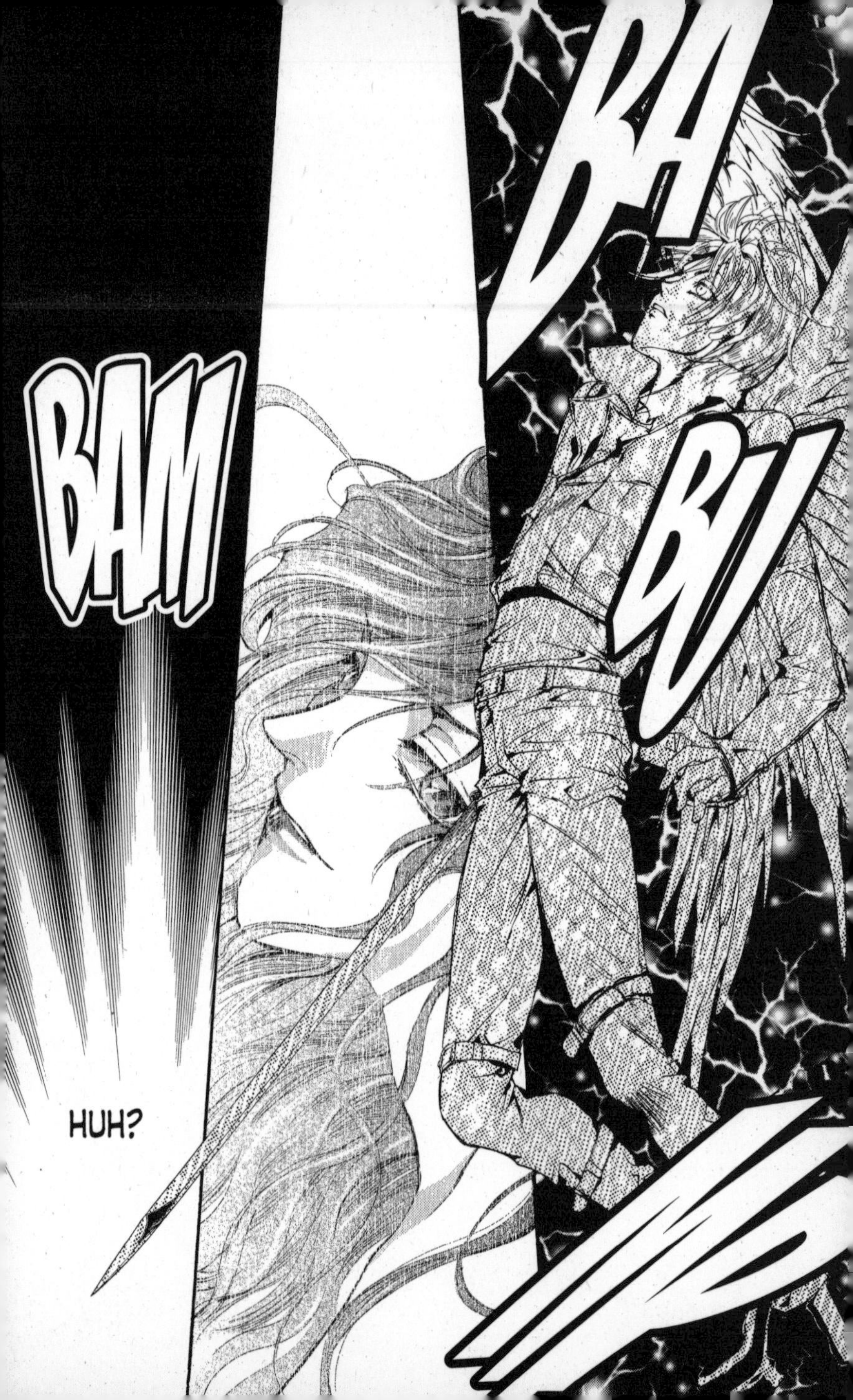
BA
BI
BAM
HUH?

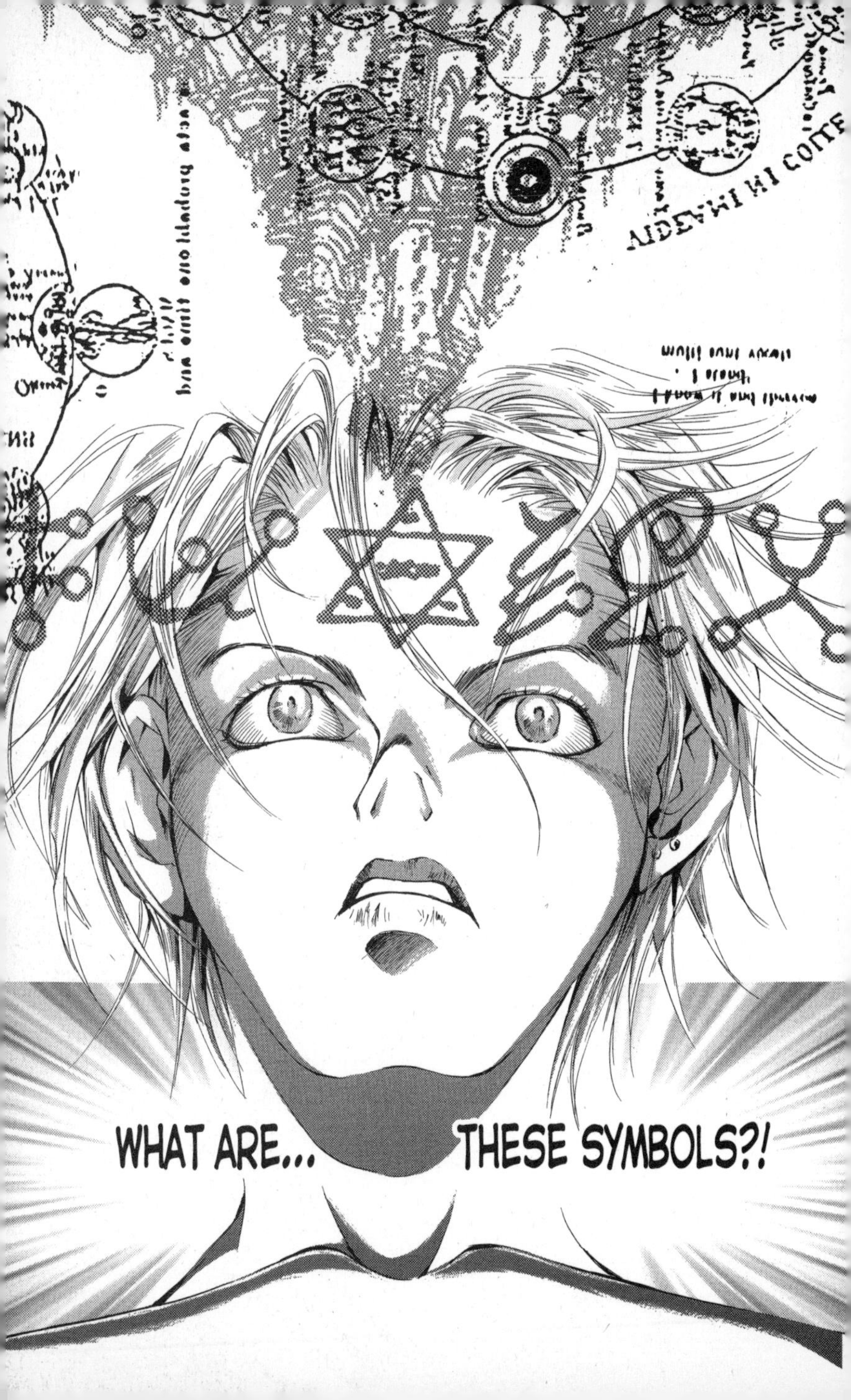
WHAT ARE...
THESE SYMBOLS?!

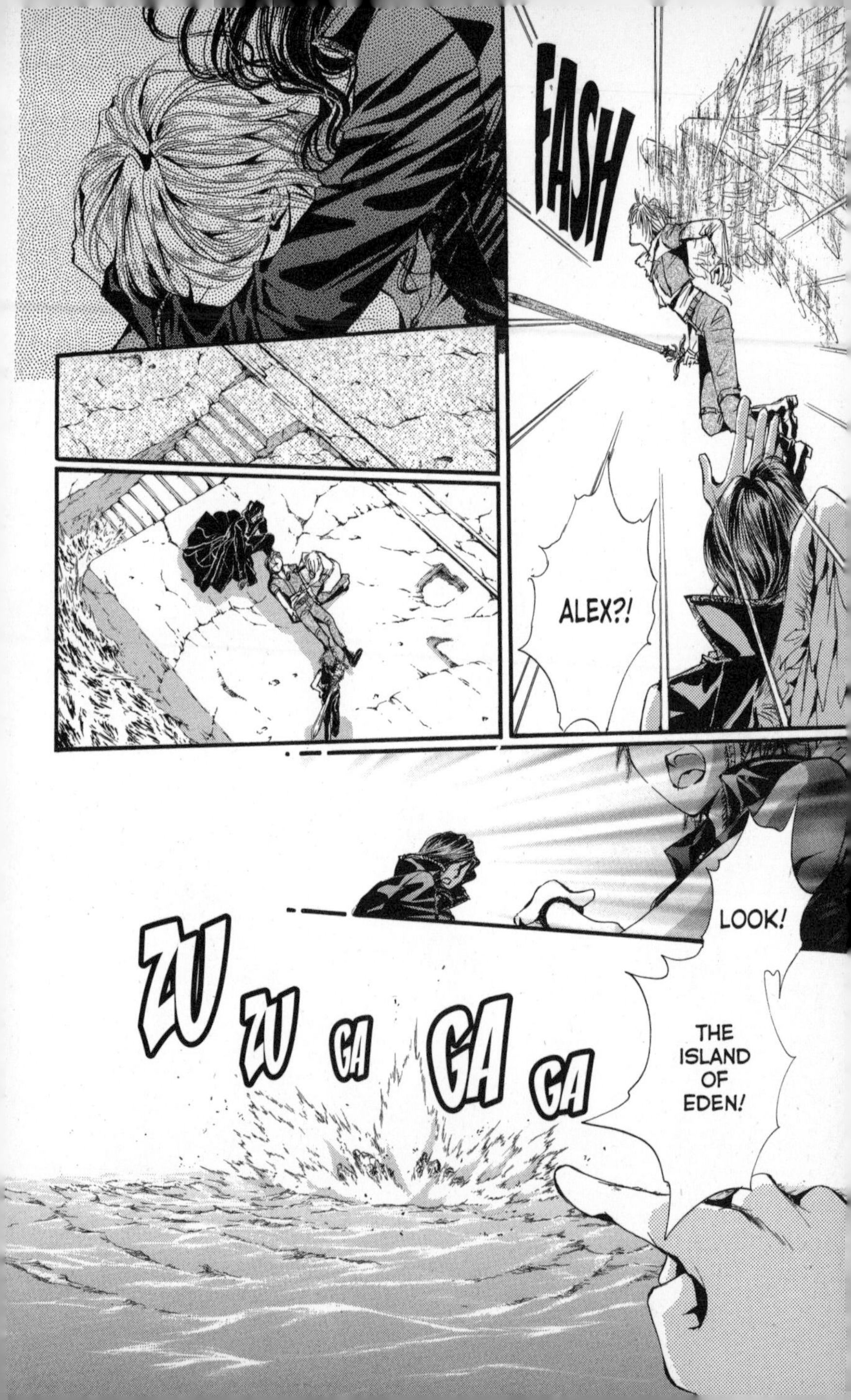
FASH
ALEX?!
LOOK!
THE ISLAND OF EDEN!
ZU ZU GA GA GA

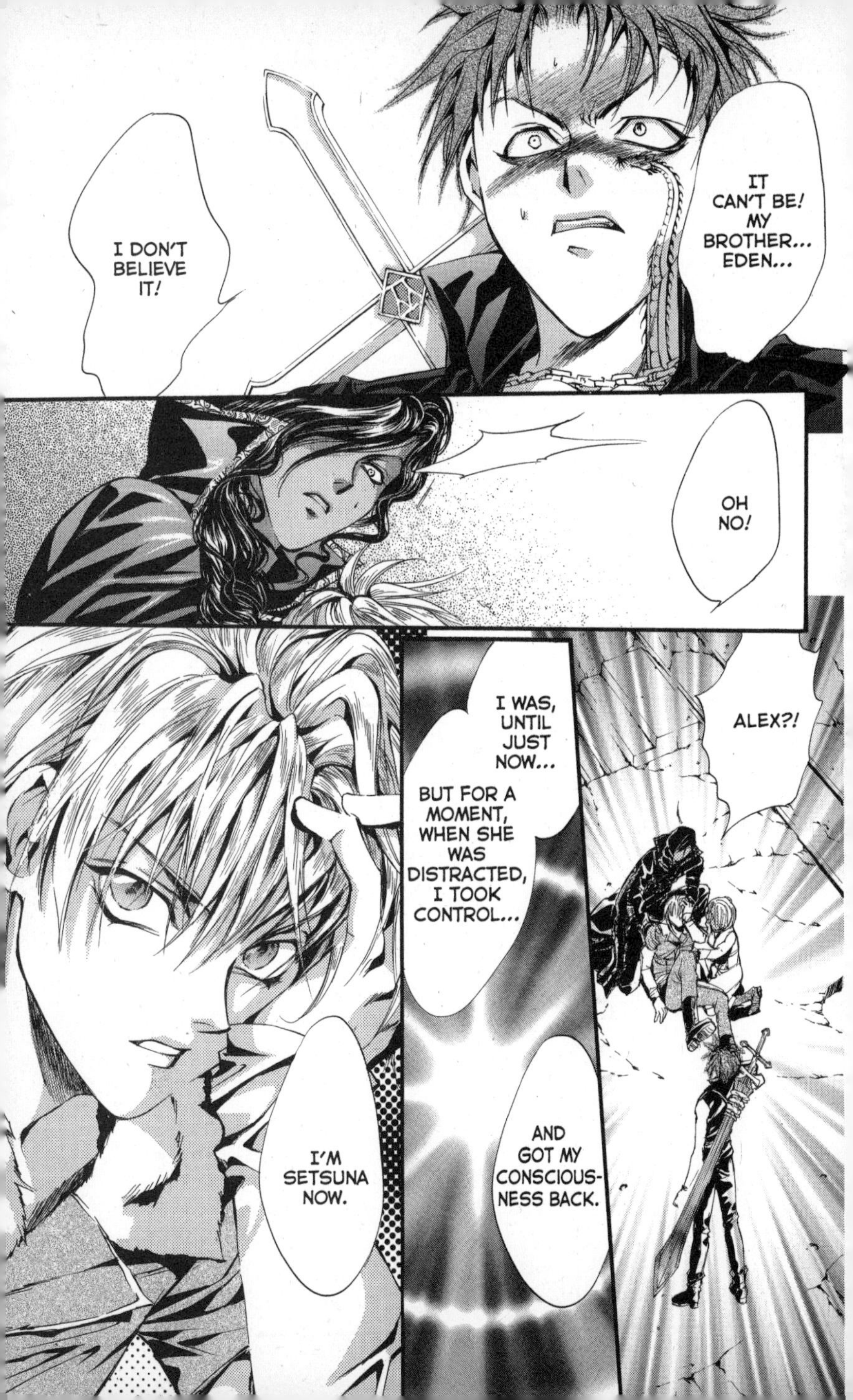

IT CAN'T BE! MY BROTHER... EDEN...
I DON'T BELIEVE IT!
OH NO!
ALEX?!
I WAS, UNTIL JUST NOW...
BUT FOR A MOMENT, WHEN SHE WAS DISTRACTED, I TOOK CONTROL...
AND GOT MY CONSCIOUS-NESS BACK.
I'M SETSUNA NOW.

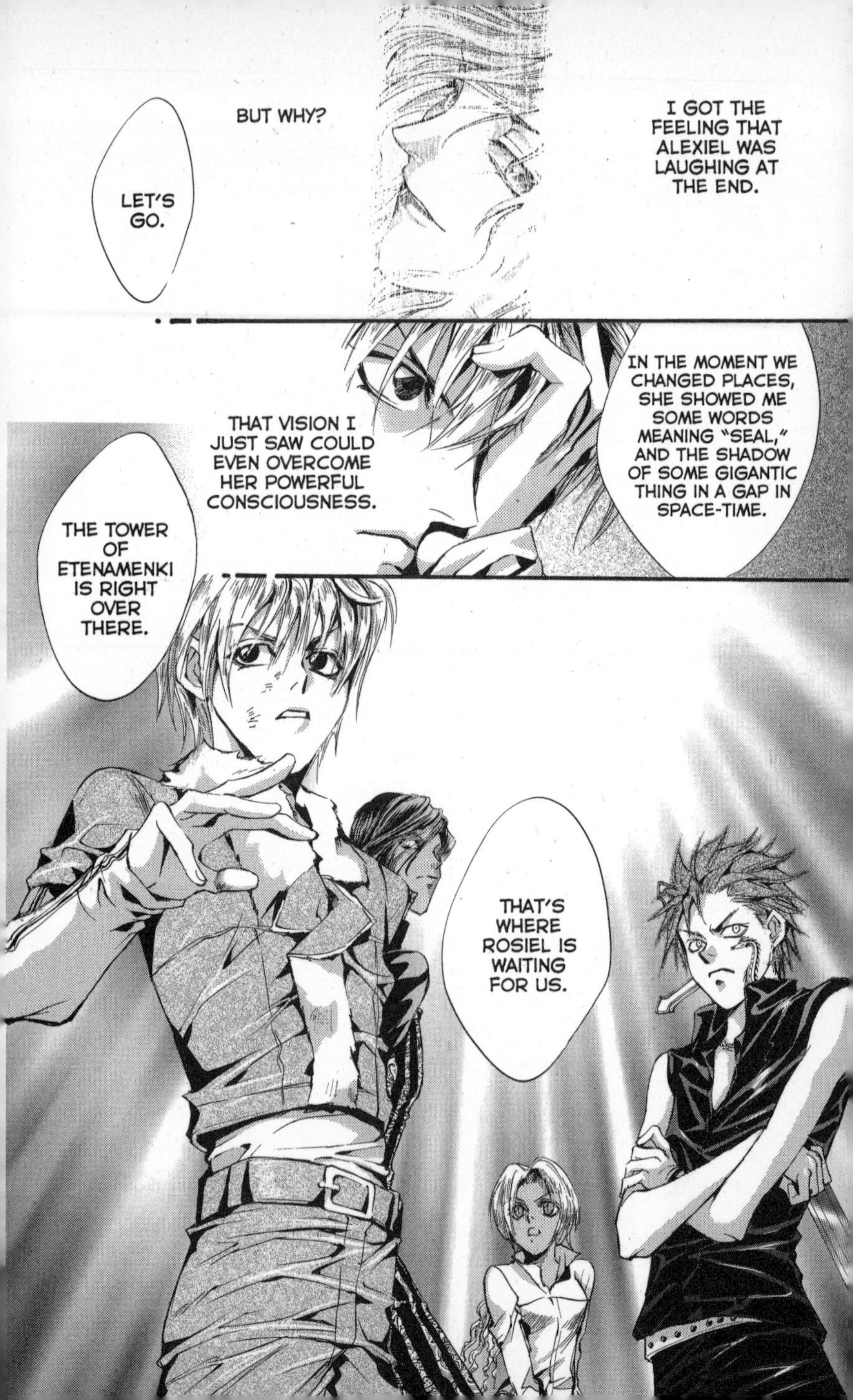
I GOT THE FEELING THAT ALEXIEL WAS LAUGHING AT THE END.
BUT WHY?
LET'S GO.
IN THE MOMENT WE CHANGED PLACES, SHE SHOWED ME SOME WORDS MEANING "SEAL," AND THE SHADOW OF SOME GIGANTIC THING IN A GAP IN SPACE-TIME.
THAT VISION I JUST SAW COULD EVEN OVERCOME HER POWERFUL CONSCIOUSNESS.
THE TOWER OF ETENAMENKI IS RIGHT OVER THERE.
THAT'S WHERE ROSIEL IS WAITING FOR US.

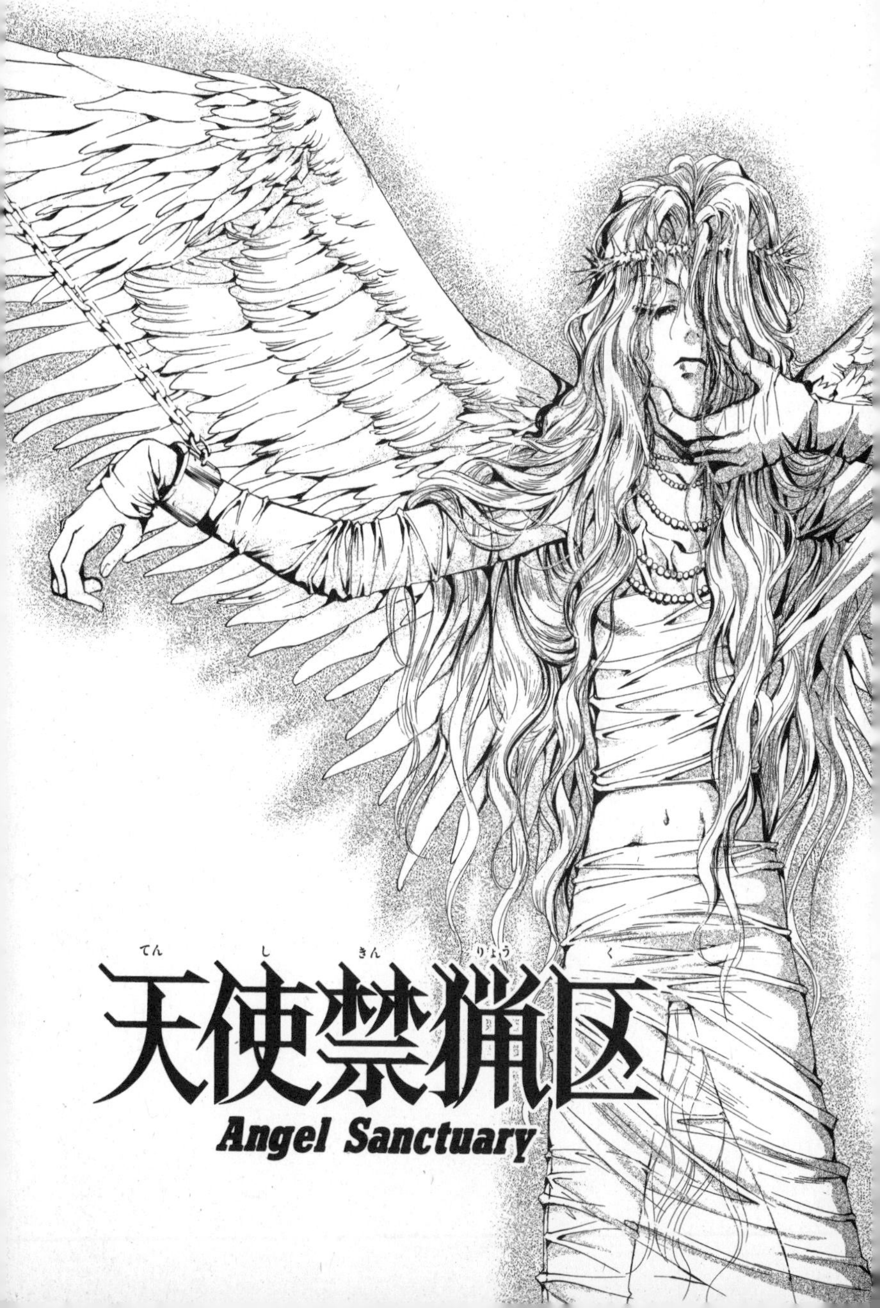
天使禁猟区
Angel Sanctuary

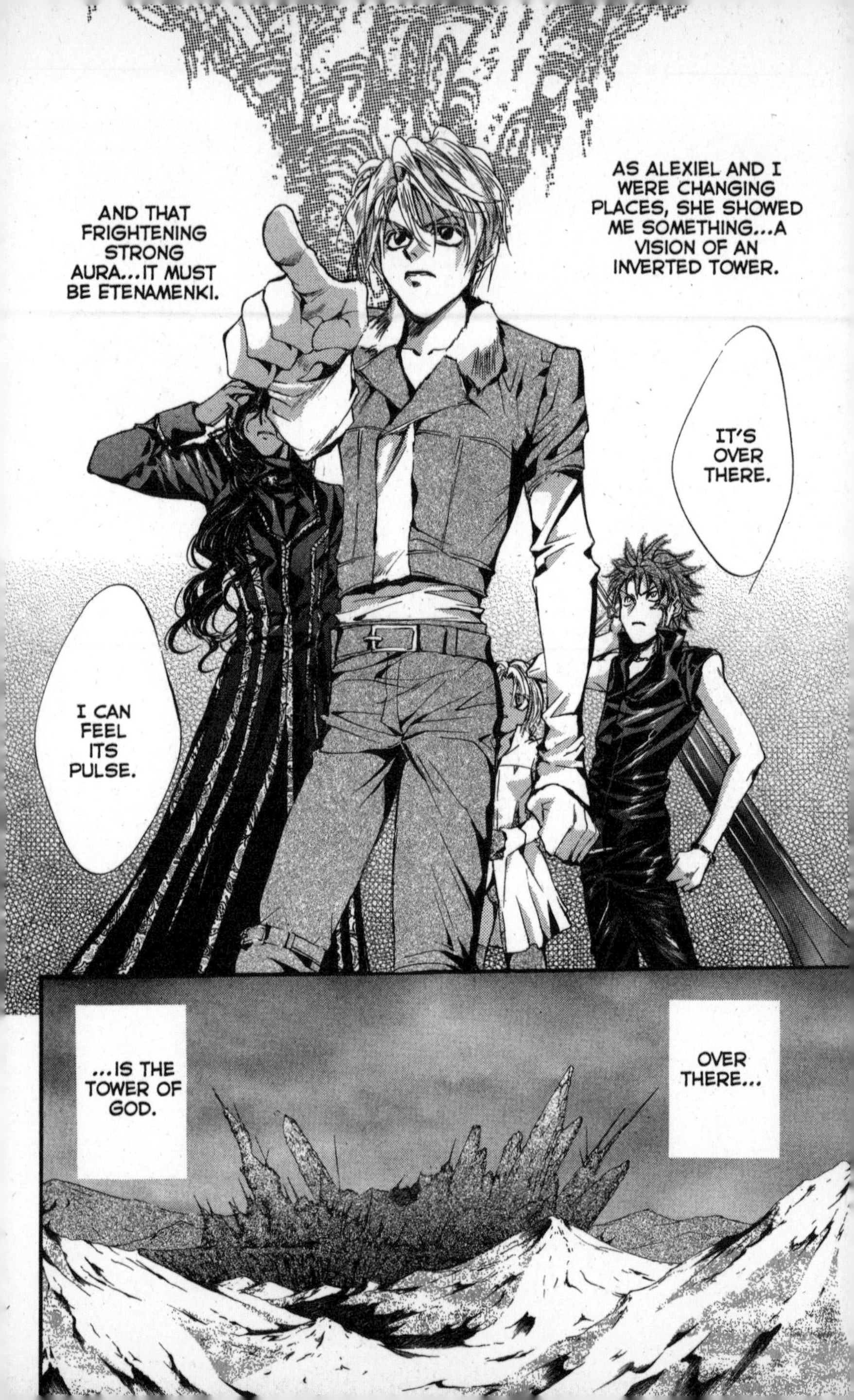
AS ALEXIEL AND I WERE CHANGING PLACES, SHE SHOWED ME SOMETHING...A VISION OF AN INVERTED TOWER.
AND THAT FRIGHTENING STRONG AURA...IT MUST BE ETENAMENKI.
IT'S OVER THERE.
I CAN FEEL ITS PULSE.
OVER THERE...
...IS THE TOWER OF GOD.

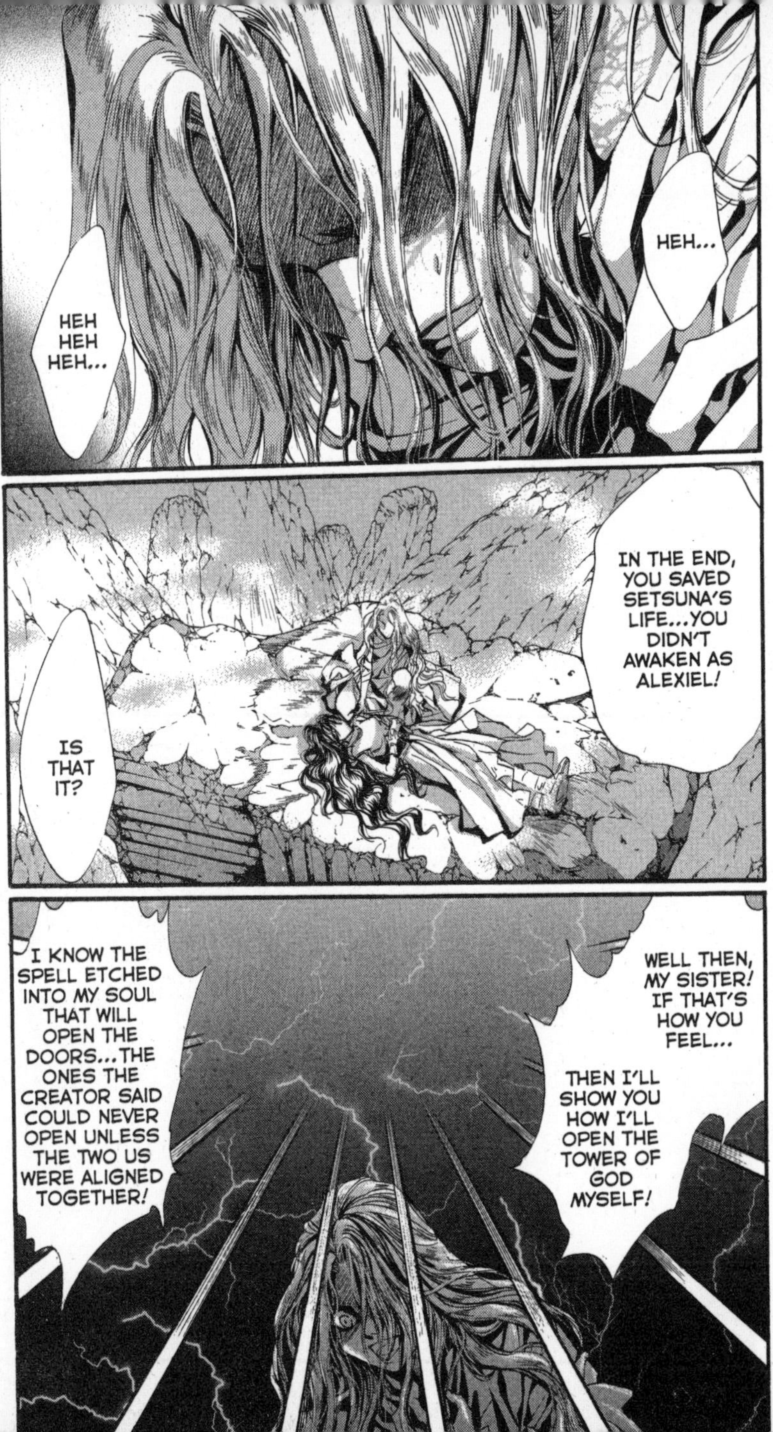
HEH...
HEH HEH HEH...
IN THE END, YOU SAVED SETSUNA'S LIFE...YOU DIDN'T AWAKEN AS ALEXIEL!
IS THAT IT?
WELL THEN, MY SISTER! IF THAT'S HOW YOU FEEL...
THEN I'LL SHOW YOU HOW I'LL OPEN THE TOWER OF GOD MYSELF!
I KNOW THE SPELL ETCHED INTO MY SOUL THAT WILL OPEN THE DOORS...THE ONES THE CREATOR SAID COULD NEVER OPEN UNLESS THE TWO US WERE ALIGNED TOGETHER!

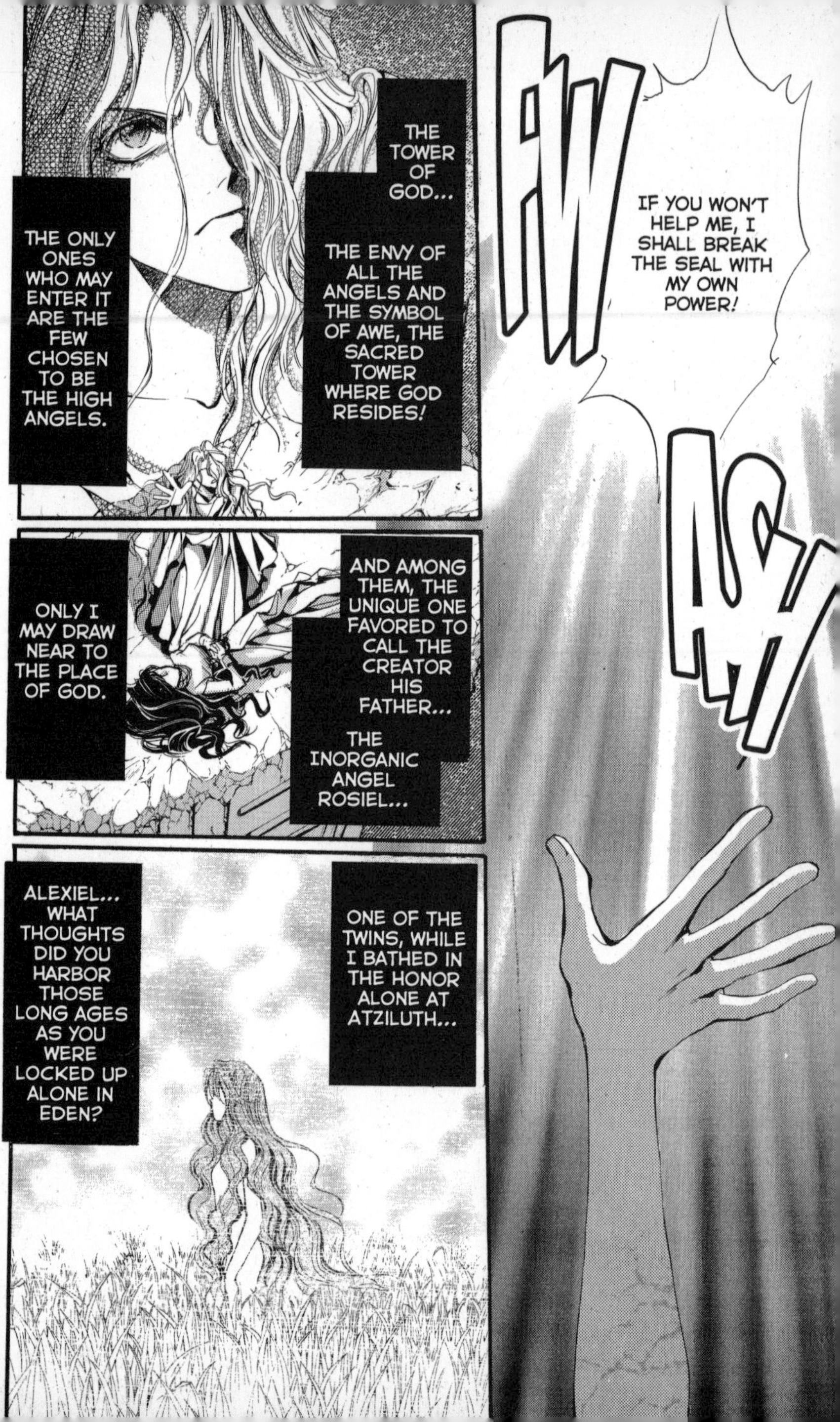

IF YOU WON'T HELP ME, I SHALL BREAK THE SEAL WITH MY OWN POWER!
FWASH
THE TOWER OF GOD...
THE ENVY OF ALL THE ANGELS AND THE SYMBOL OF AWE, THE SACRED TOWER WHERE GOD RESIDES!
THE ONLY ONES WHO MAY ENTER IT ARE THE FEW CHOSEN TO BE THE HIGH ANGELS.
AND AMONG THEM, THE UNIQUE ONE FAVORED TO CALL THE CREATOR HIS FATHER...
THE INORGANIC ANGEL ROSIEL...
ONLY I MAY DRAW NEAR TO THE PLACE OF GOD.
ONE OF THE TWINS, WHILE I BATHED IN THE HONOR ALONE AT ATZILUTH...
ALEXIEL... WHAT THOUGHTS DID YOU HARBOR THOSE LONG AGES AS YOU WERE LOCKED UP ALONE IN EDEN?

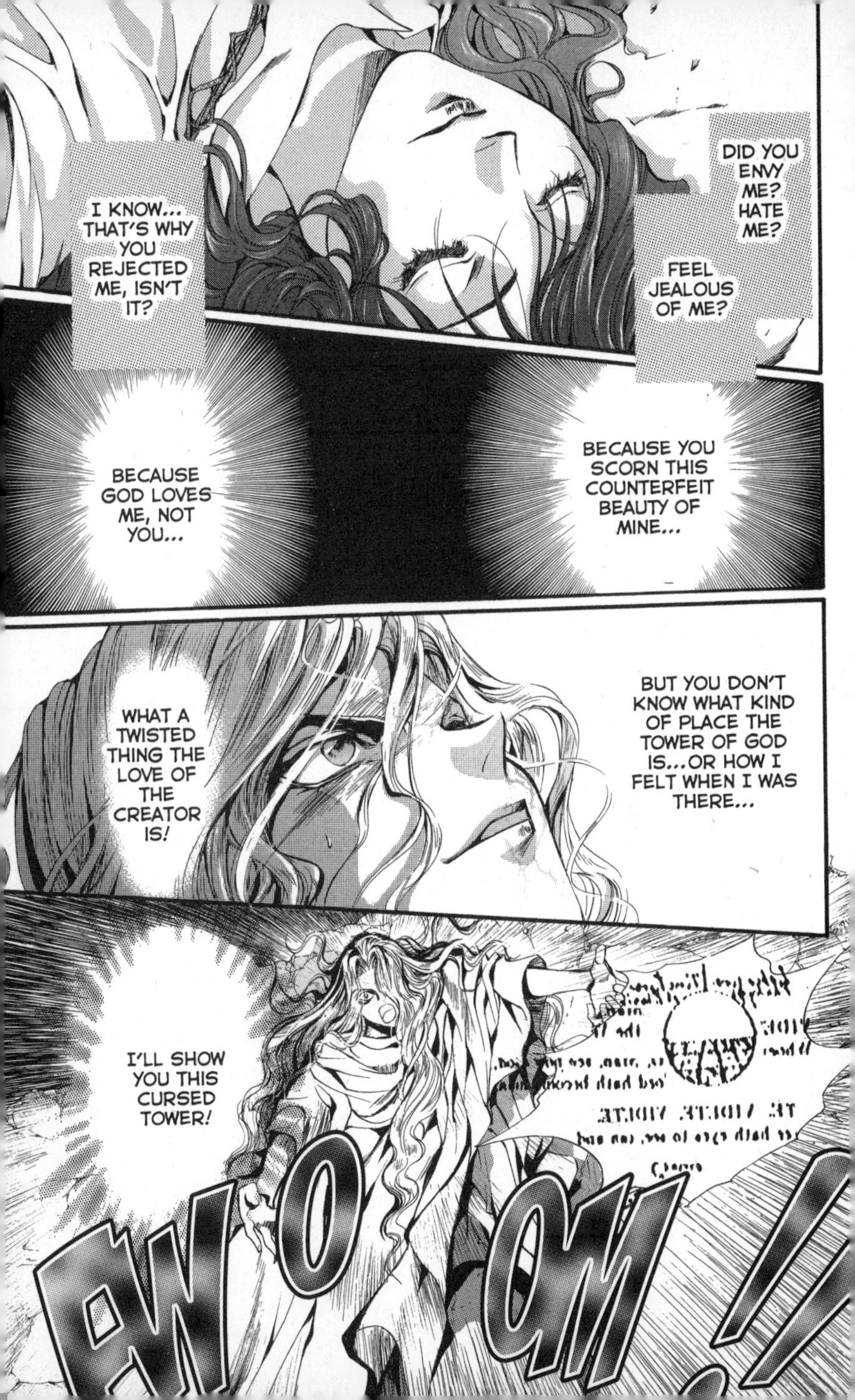
DID YOU ENVY ME? HATE ME?
FEEL JEALOUS OF ME?
I KNOW... THAT'S WHY YOU REJECTED ME, ISN'T IT?
BECAUSE YOU SCORN THIS COUNTERFEIT BEAUTY OF MINE...
BECAUSE GOD LOVES ME, NOT YOU...
BUT YOU DON'T KNOW WHAT KIND OF PLACE THE TOWER OF GOD IS...OR HOW I FELT WHEN I WAS THERE...
WHAT A TWISTED THING THE LOVE OF THE CREATOR IS!
I'LL SHOW YOU THIS CURSED TOWER!
AWOOM!!

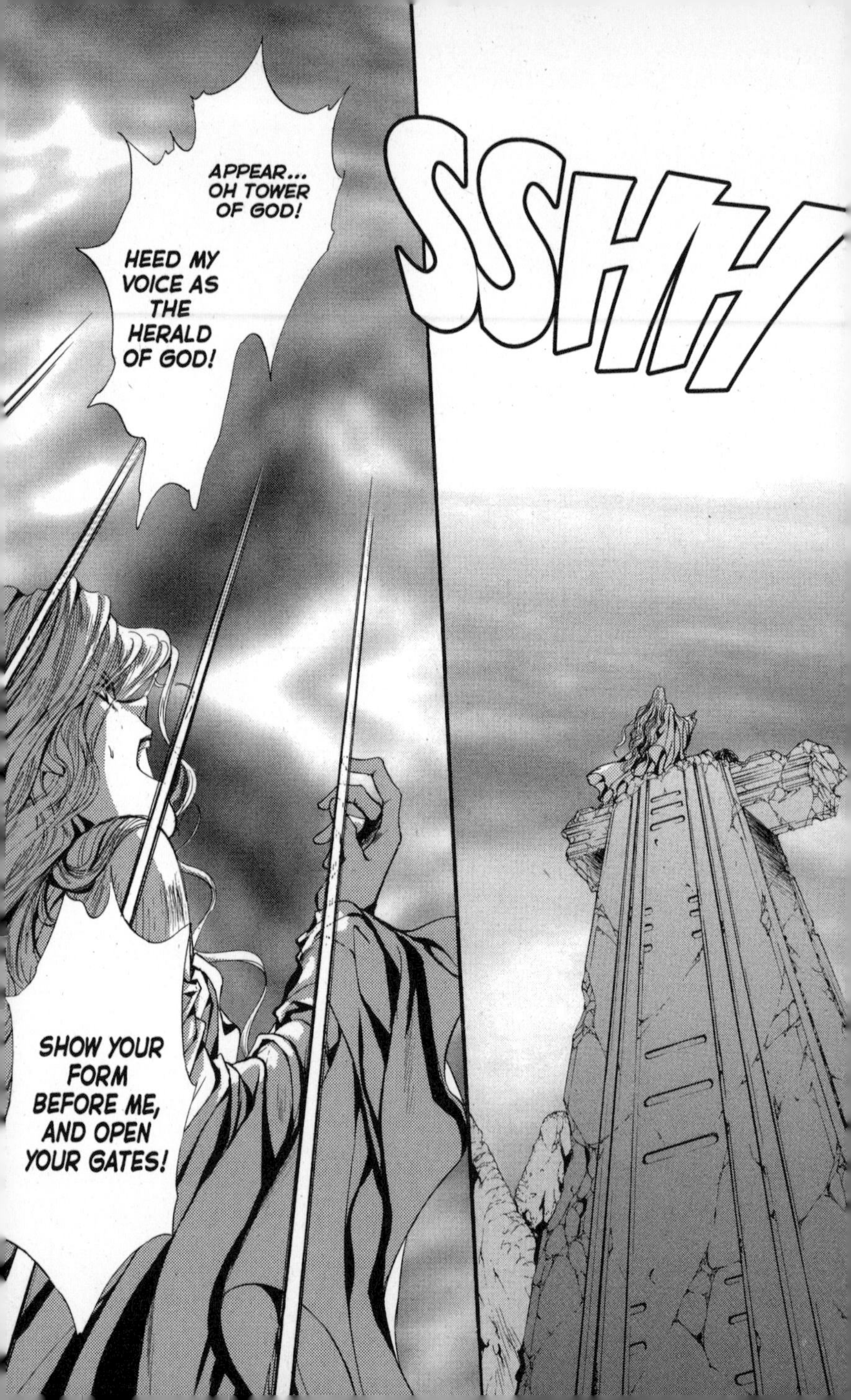
SSHH
APPEAR... OH TOWER OF GOD!
HEED MY VOICE AS THE HERALD OF GOD!
SHOW YOUR FORM BEFORE ME, AND OPEN YOUR GATES!

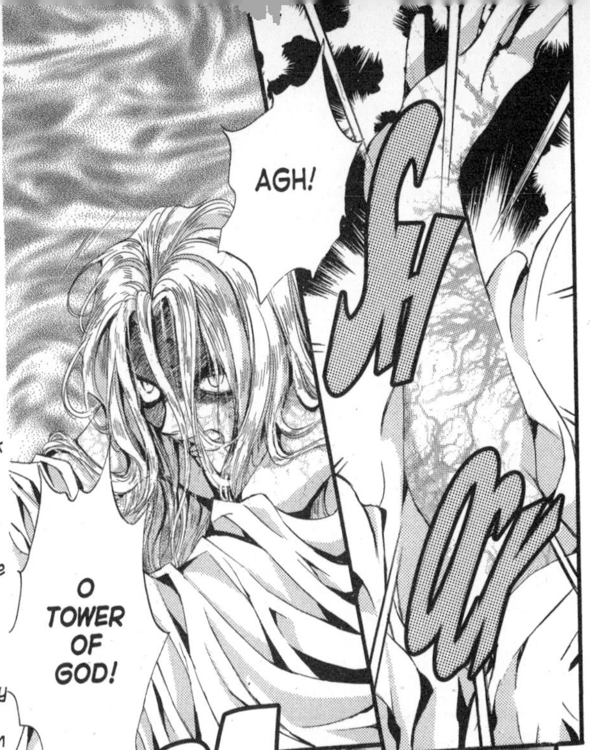
AGH!
O TOWER OF GOD!

I haven't said anything about this book. Kato had a big impact on the previous volume. Thanks for all your letters. I wanted to have Setsuna mourn him a little more, but there just weren't enough pages. I got a lot of letters from Rosiel fans about how pathetic he looks. It's been a real pain to stick on all the screen tones for his injuries. Lately he's been almost naked. I enjoyed dressing him up before. Recently I've been getting a lot of letters from fans overseas. Readers from Korea and Taiwan have been writing in very nice Japanese...I'm impressed! There's even been some letters in English.

And thanks for all the presents!

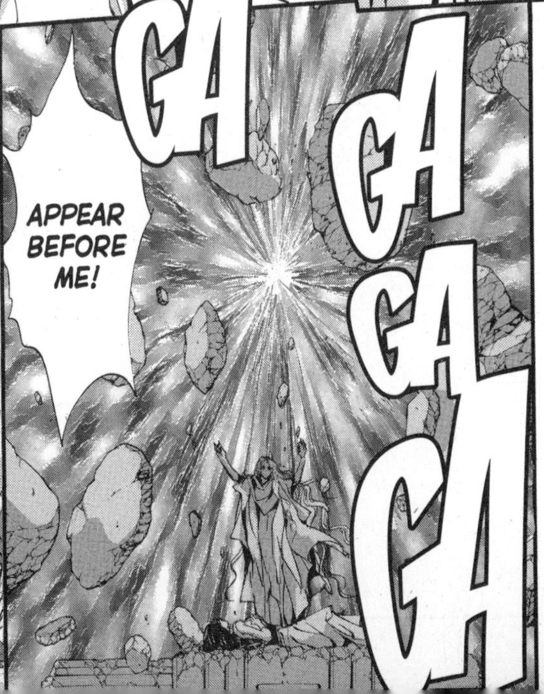
GA
GA
GA
GA
APPEAR BEFORE ME!

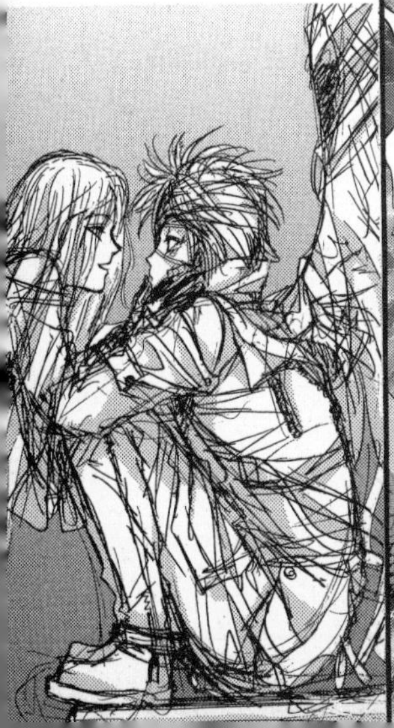

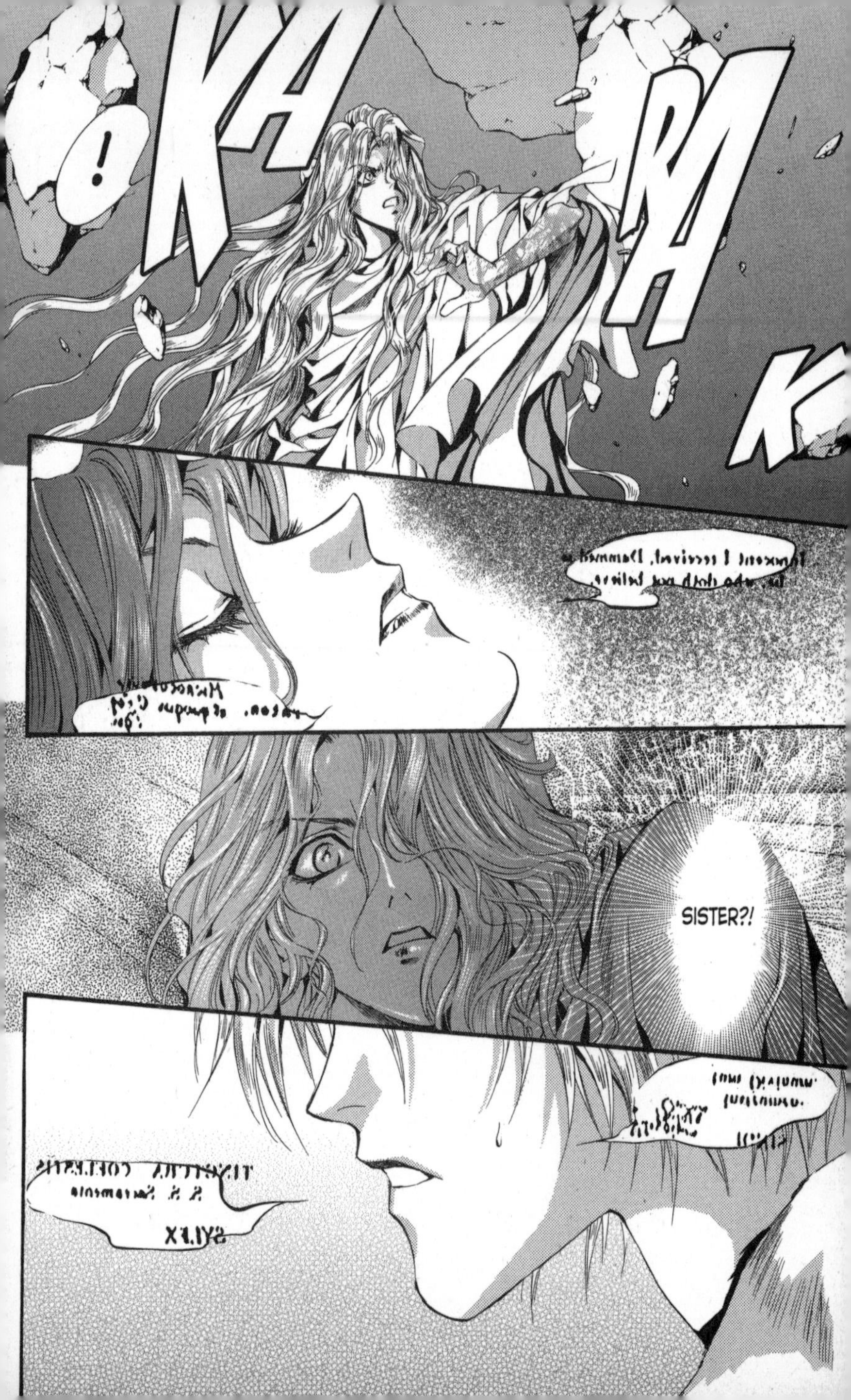

!
KA
RA
K
SISTER?!

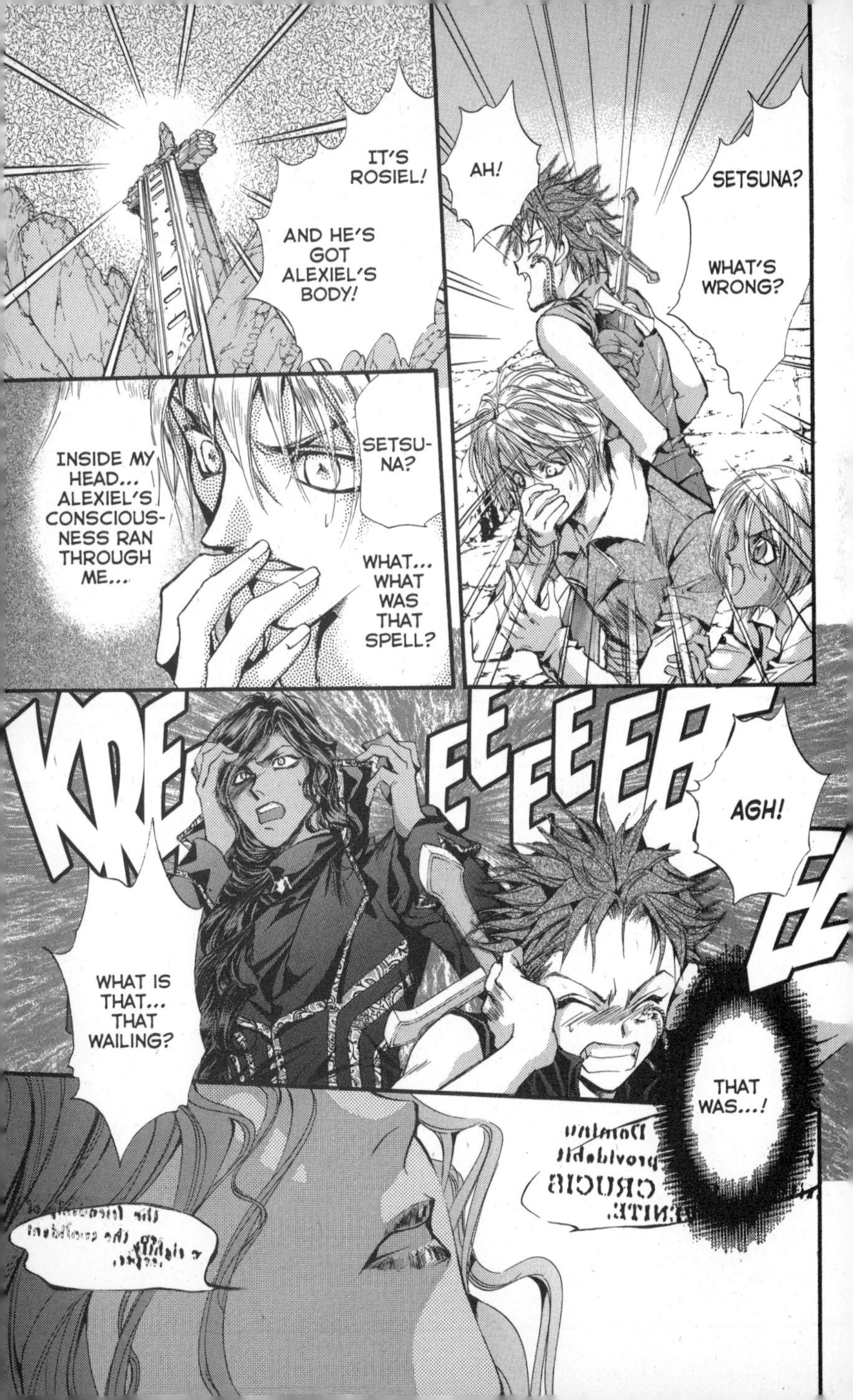
SETSUNA?
WHAT'S WRONG?
AH!
IT'S ROSIEL!
AND HE'S GOT ALEXIEL'S BODY!
SETSU-NA?
WHAT... WHAT WAS THAT SPELL?
INSIDE MY HEAD... ALEXIEL'S CONSCIOUS-NESS RAN THROUGH ME...
KREEEEEEEER
AGH!
WHAT IS THAT... THAT WAILING?
THAT WAS...!

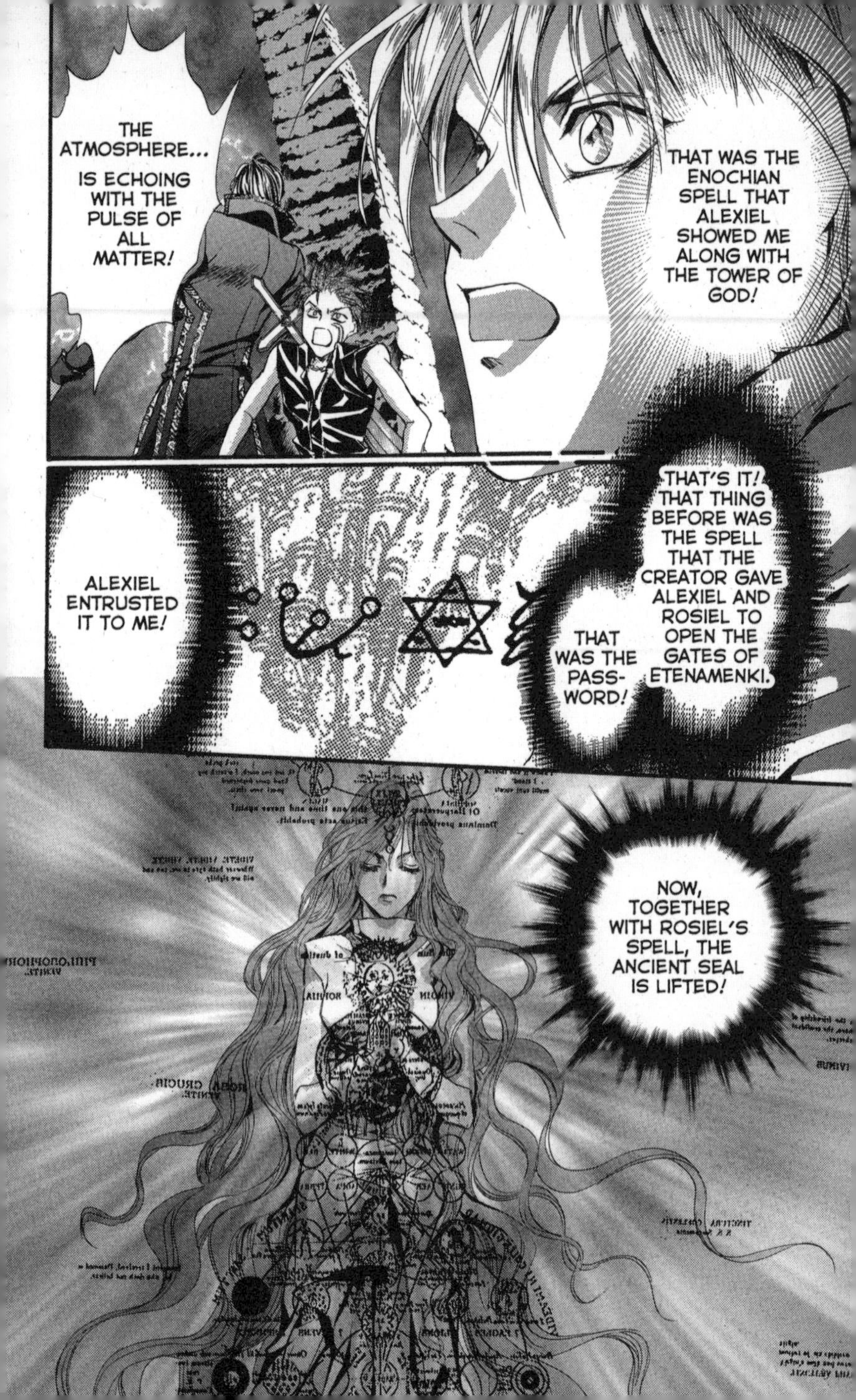
THAT WAS THE ENOCHIAN SPELL THAT ALEXIEL SHOWED ME ALONG WITH THE TOWER OF GOD!
THE ATMOSPHERE...
IS ECHOING WITH THE PULSE OF ALL MATTER!
THAT'S IT! THAT THING BEFORE WAS THE SPELL THAT THE CREATOR GAVE ALEXIEL AND ROSIEL TO OPEN THE GATES OF ETENAMENKI.
THAT WAS THE PASS-WORD!
ALEXIEL ENTRUSTED IT TO ME!
NOW, TOGETHER WITH ROSIEL'S SPELL, THE ANCIENT SEAL IS LIFTED!

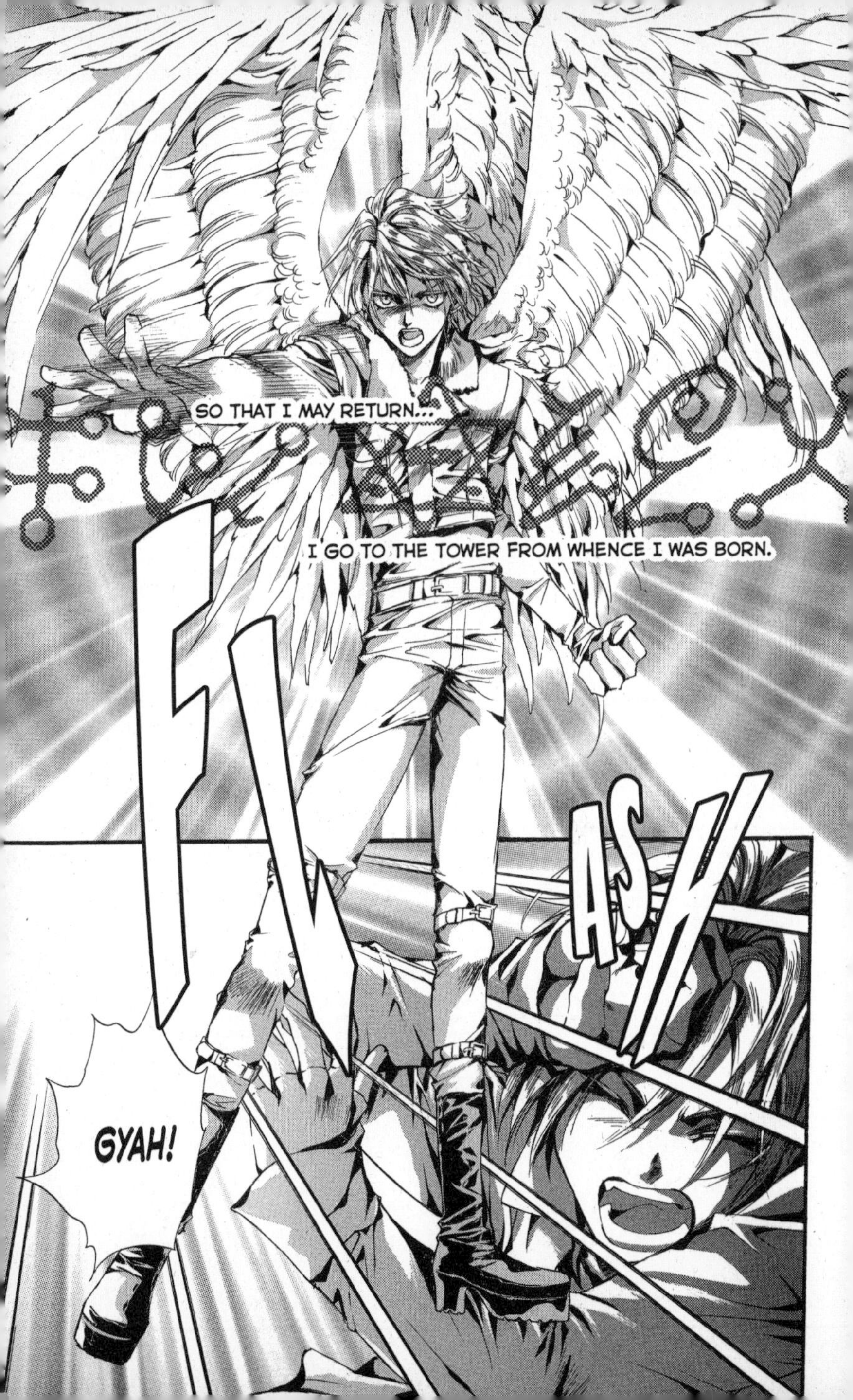
SO THAT I MAY RETURN...
I GO TO THE TOWER FROM WHENCE I WAS BORN.
FLASH
GYAH!

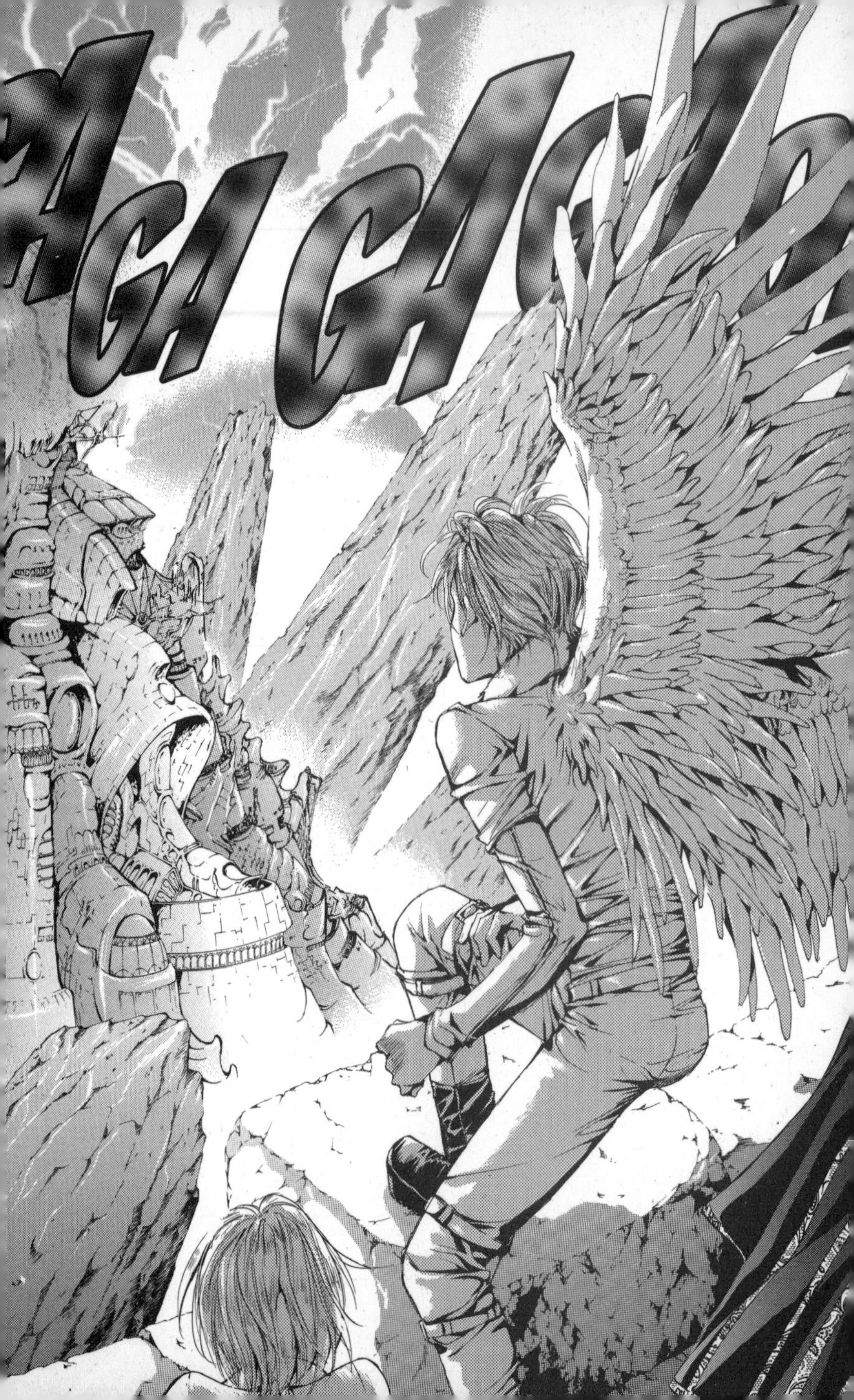
GA GA

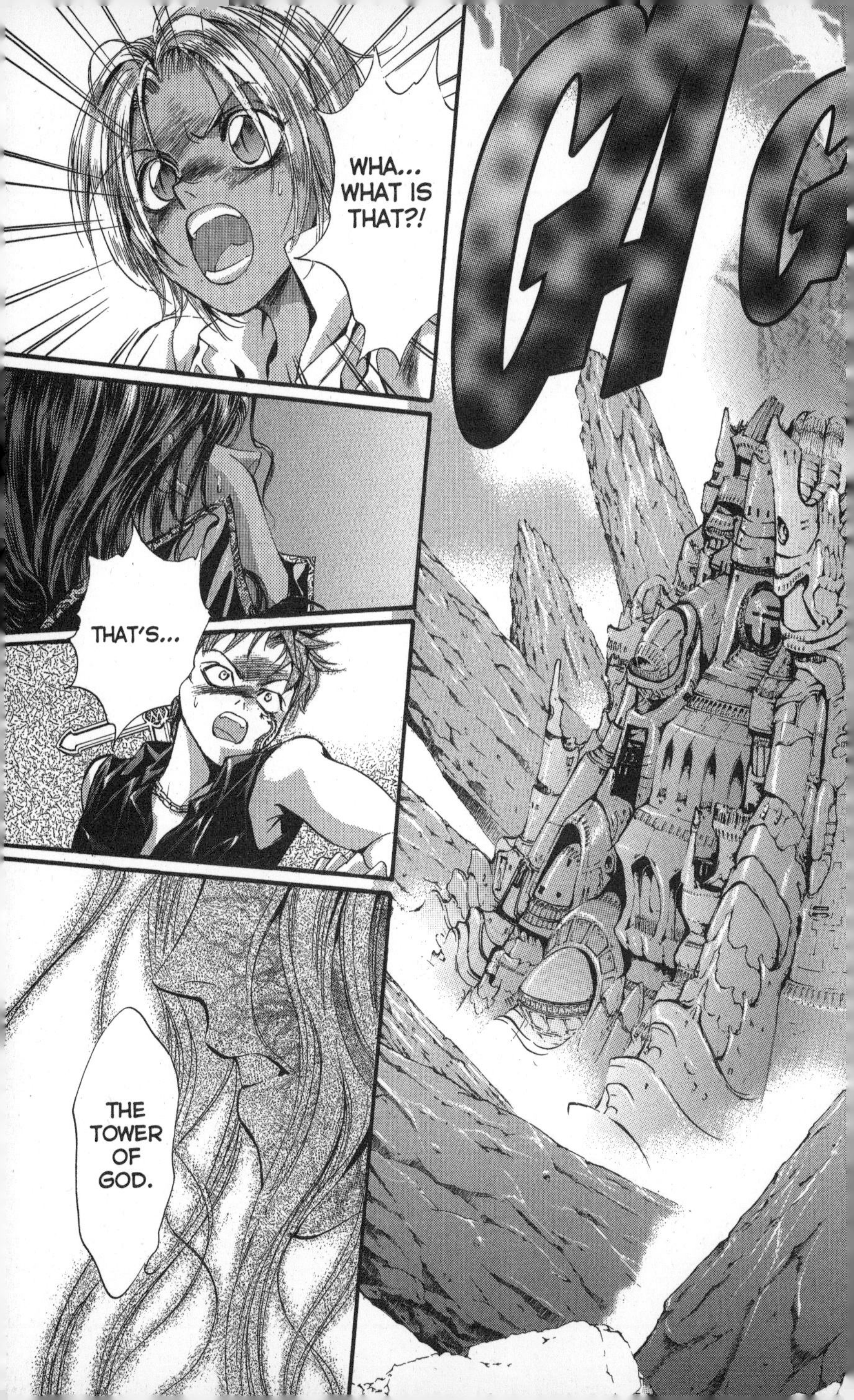
GAG
WHA... WHAT IS THAT?!
THAT'S...
THE TOWER OF GOD.

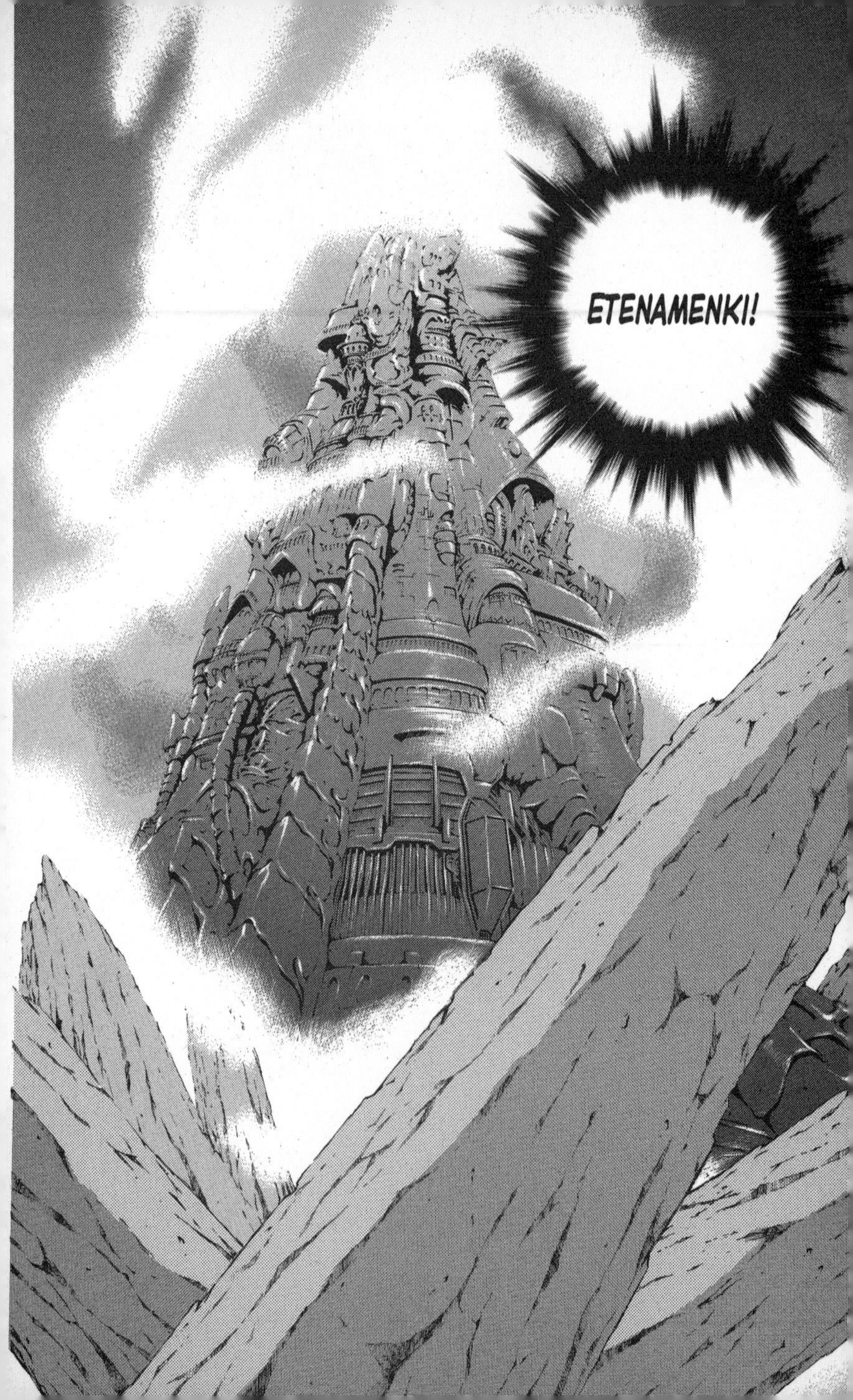
ETENAMENKI!

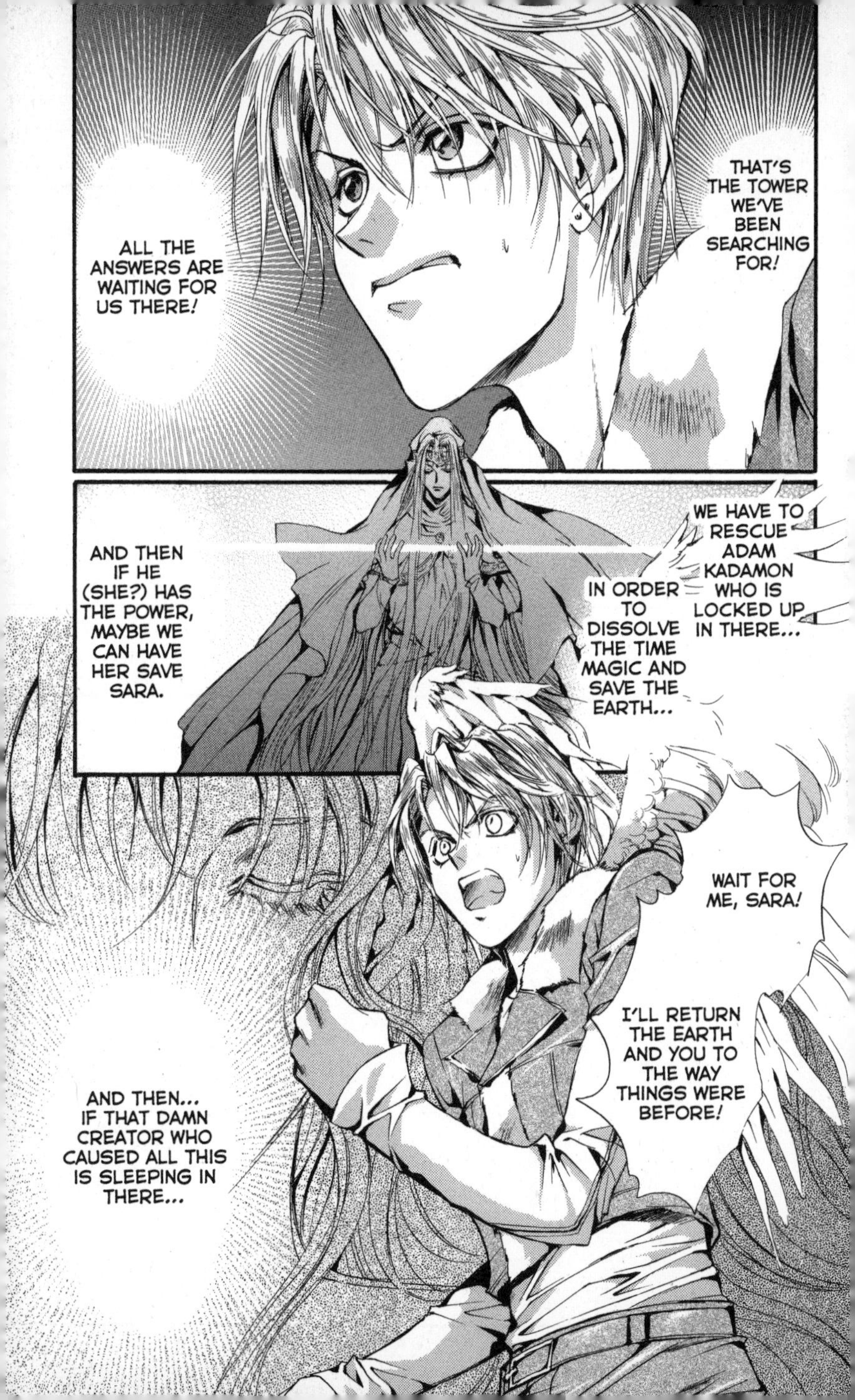
THAT'S THE TOWER WE'VE BEEN SEARCHING FOR!
ALL THE ANSWERS ARE WAITING FOR US THERE!
WE HAVE TO RESCUE ADAM KADAMON WHO IS LOCKED UP IN THERE...
IN ORDER TO DISSOLVE THE TIME MAGIC AND SAVE THE EARTH...
AND THEN IF HE (SHE?) HAS THE POWER, MAYBE WE CAN HAVE HER SAVE SARA.
WAIT FOR ME, SARA!
I'LL RETURN THE EARTH AND YOU TO THE WAY THINGS WERE BEFORE!
AND THEN... IF THAT DAMN CREATOR WHO CAUSED ALL THIS IS SLEEPING IN THERE...

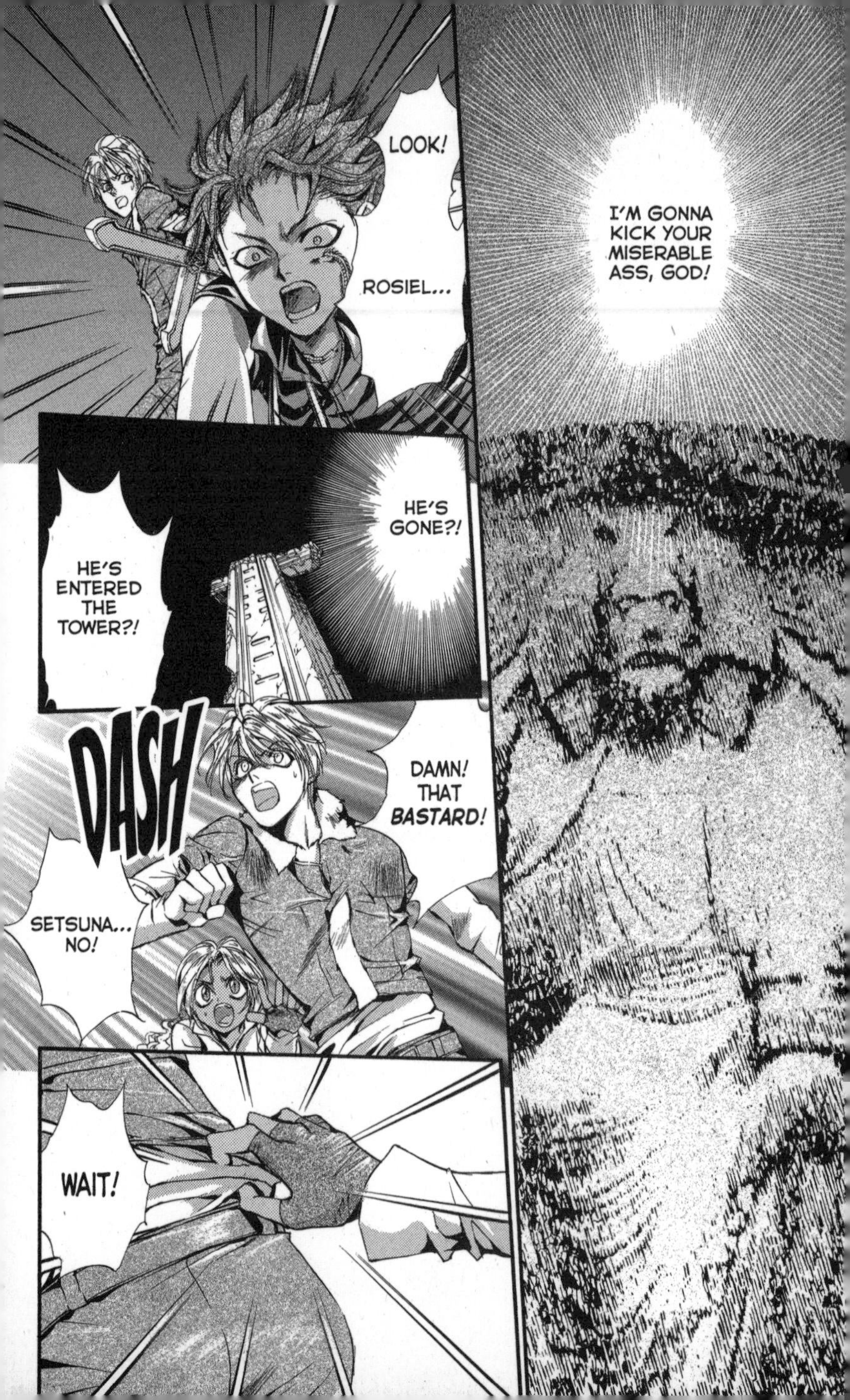
I'M GONNA KICK YOUR MISERABLE ASS, GOD!
LOOK!
ROSIEL...
HE'S GONE?!
HE'S ENTERED THE TOWER?!
DASH
DAMN! THAT BASTARD!
SETSUNA... NO!
WAIT!

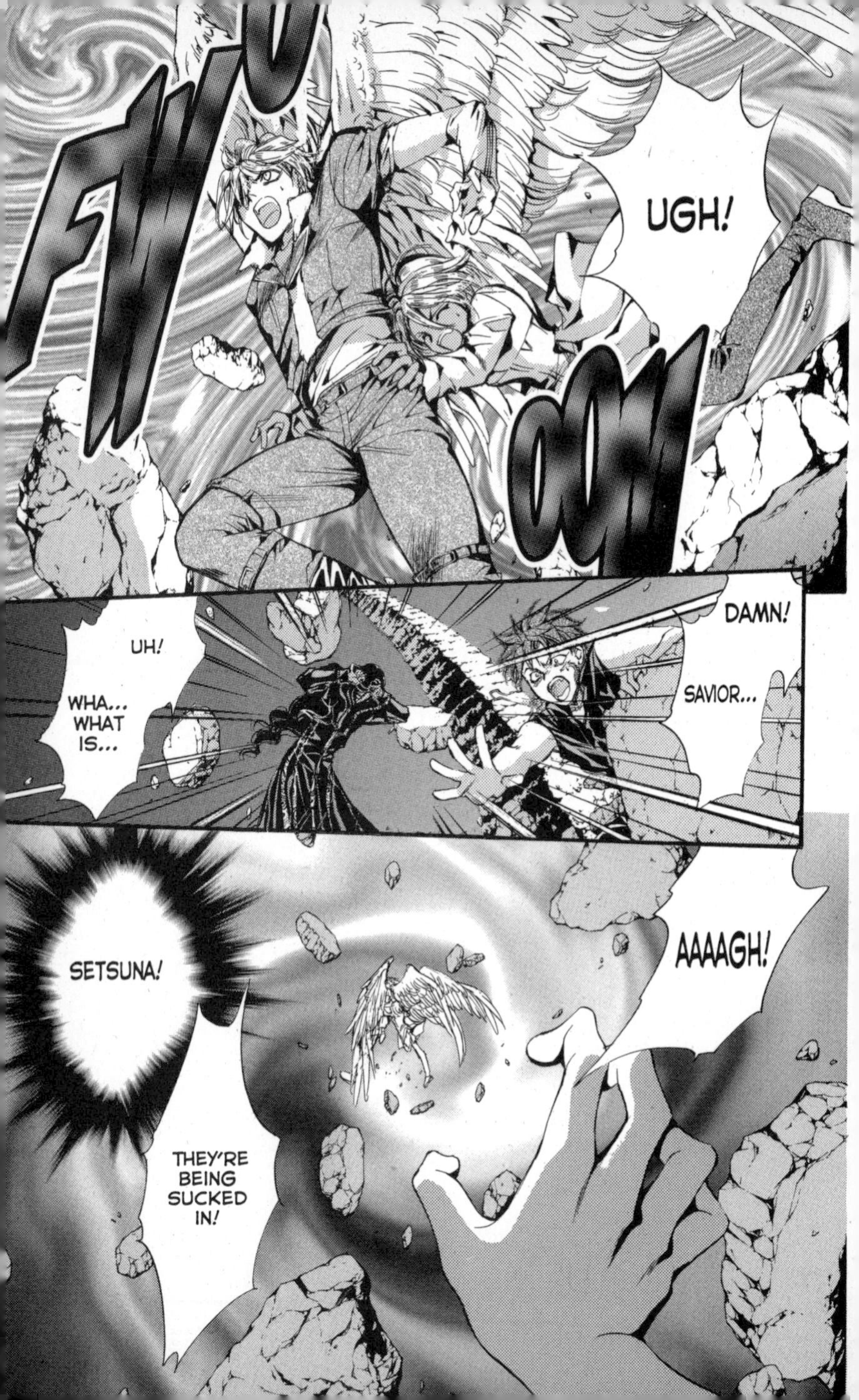
UGH!
DAMN!
SAVIOR...
UH!
WHA... WHAT IS...
AAAAGH!
SETSUNA!
THEY'RE BEING SUCKED IN!

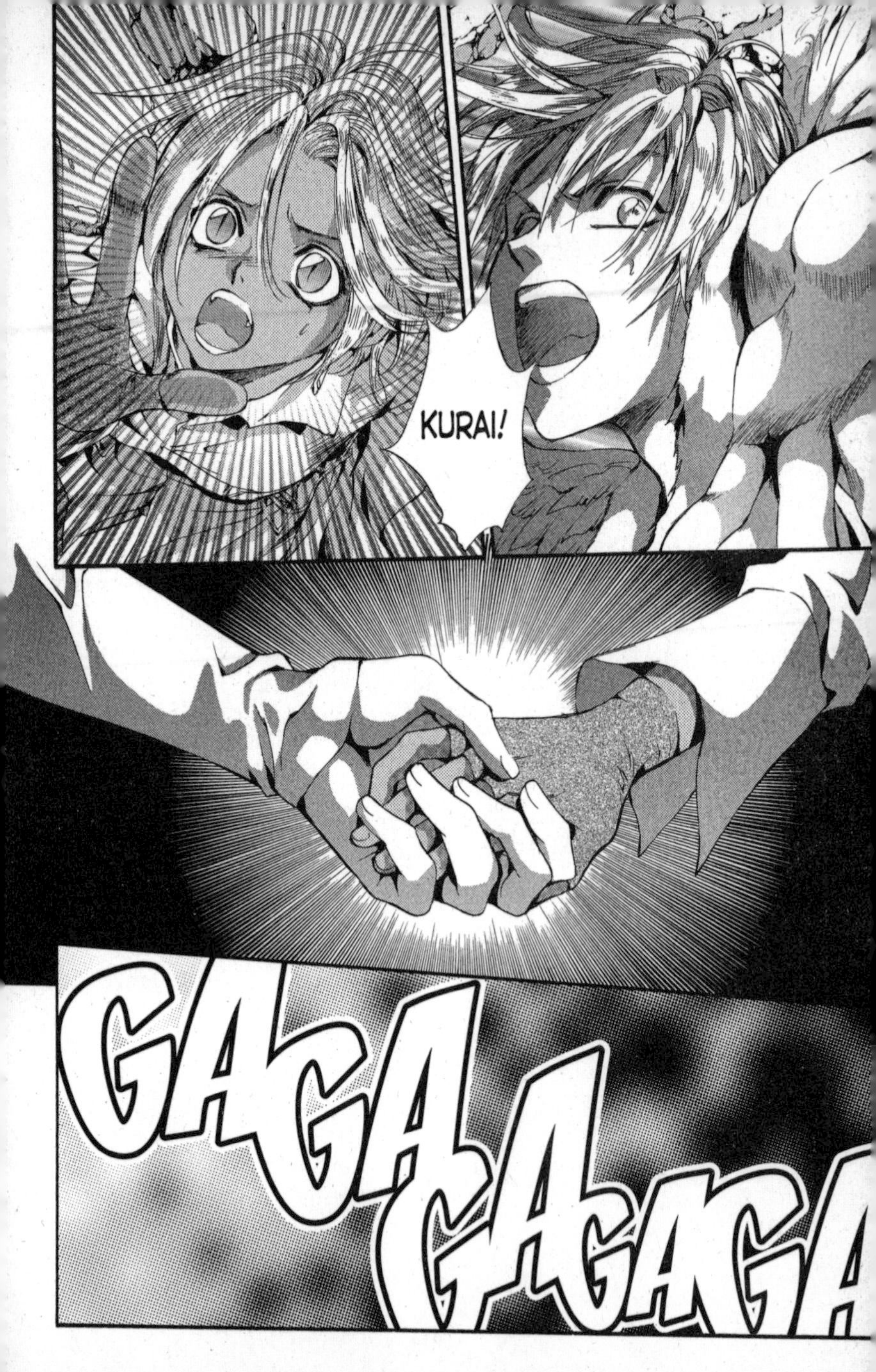
KURAI!
GAGA
GAGAGA

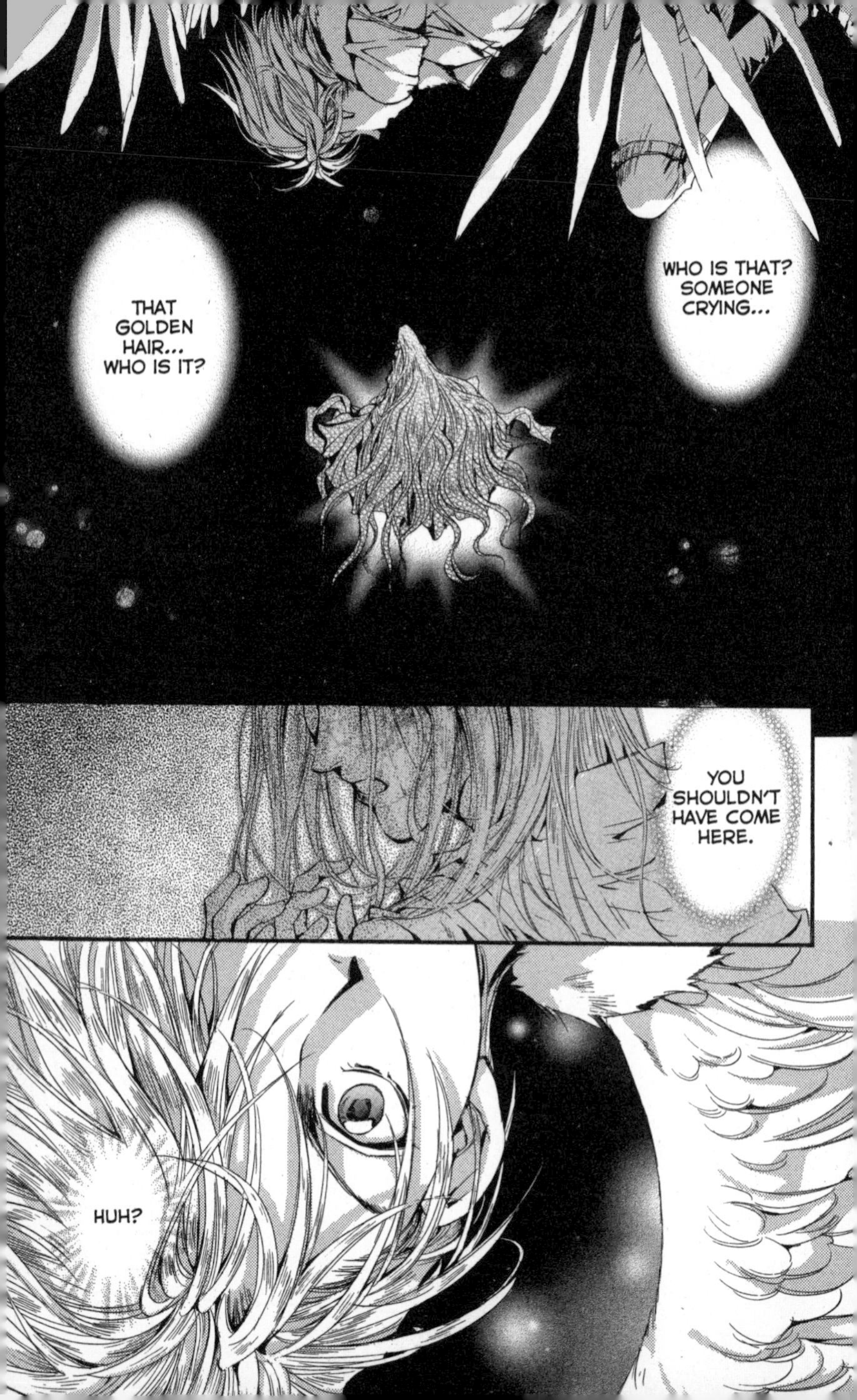
WHO IS THAT? SOMEONE CRYING...
THAT GOLDEN HAIR... WHO IS IT?
YOU SHOULDN'T HAVE COME HERE.
HUH?

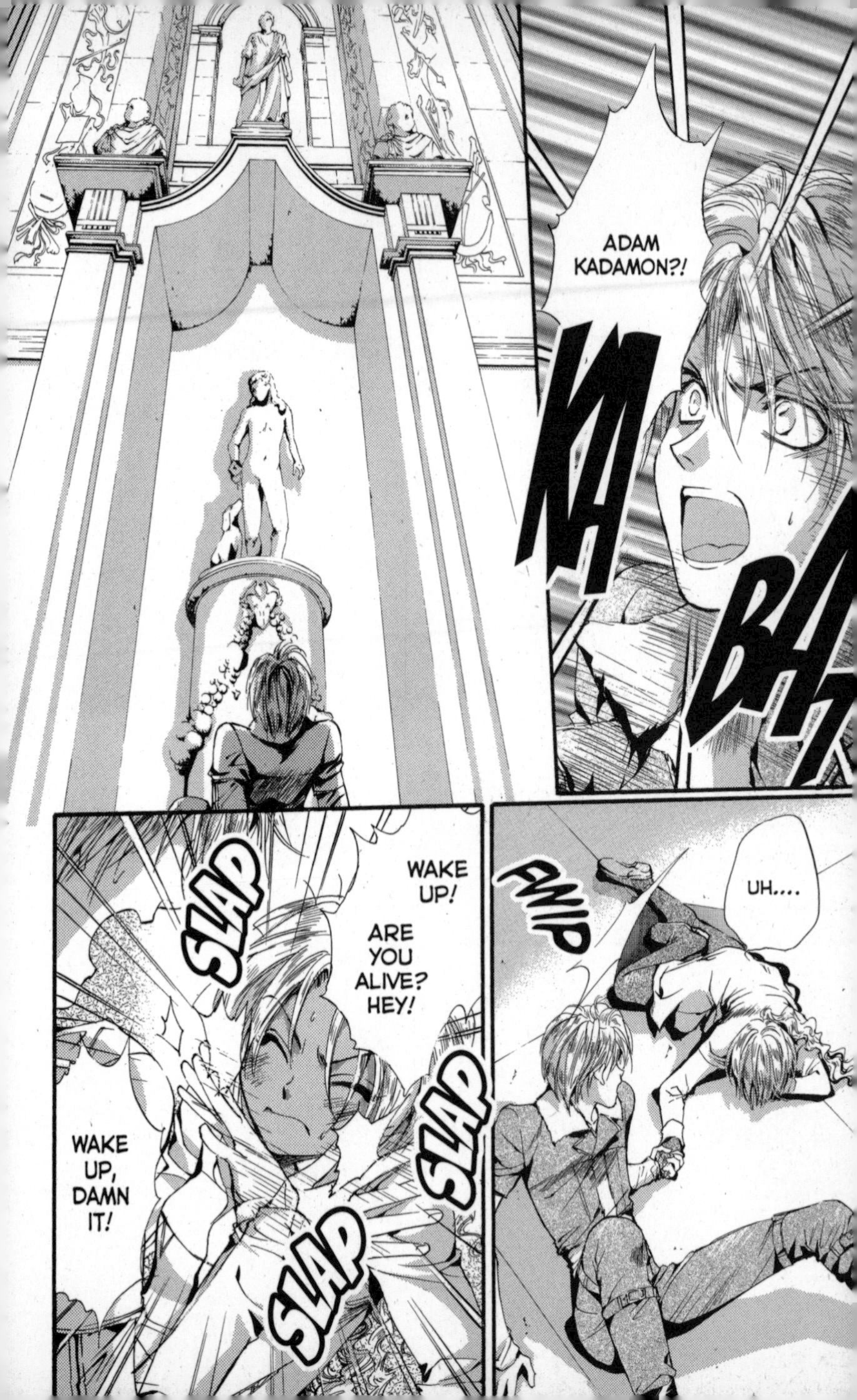
ADAM KADAMON?!
KA
BA
FWIP
UH....
WAKE UP!
ARE YOU ALIVE? HEY!
SLAP
SLAP
WAKE UP, DAMN IT!
SLAP

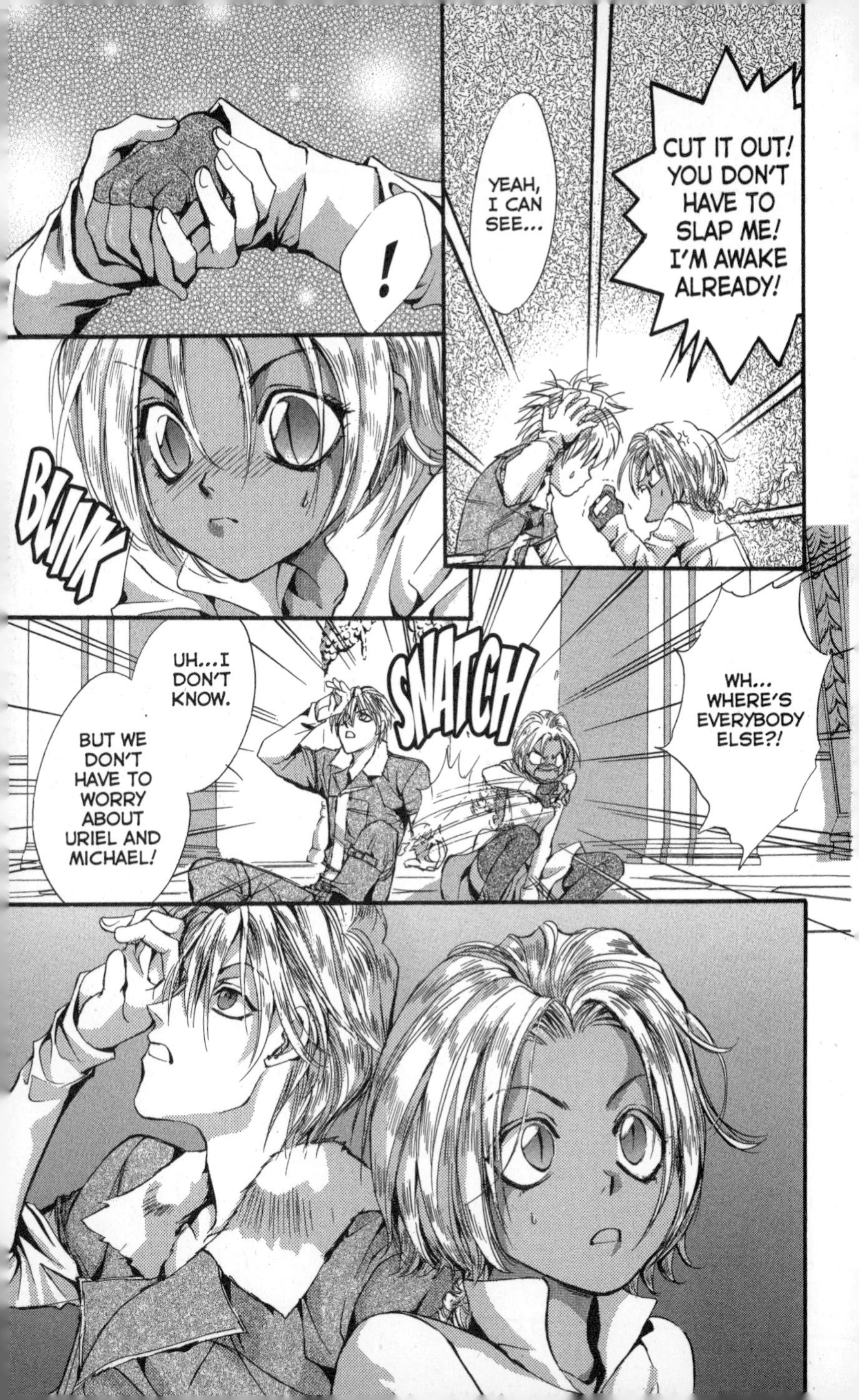
CUT IT OUT! YOU DON'T HAVE TO SLAP ME! I'M AWAKE ALREADY!
YEAH, I CAN SEE...
!
BLINK
WH... WHERE'S EVERYBODY ELSE?!
SNATCH
UH...I DON'T KNOW.
BUT WE DON'T HAVE TO WORRY ABOUT URIEL AND MICHAEL!

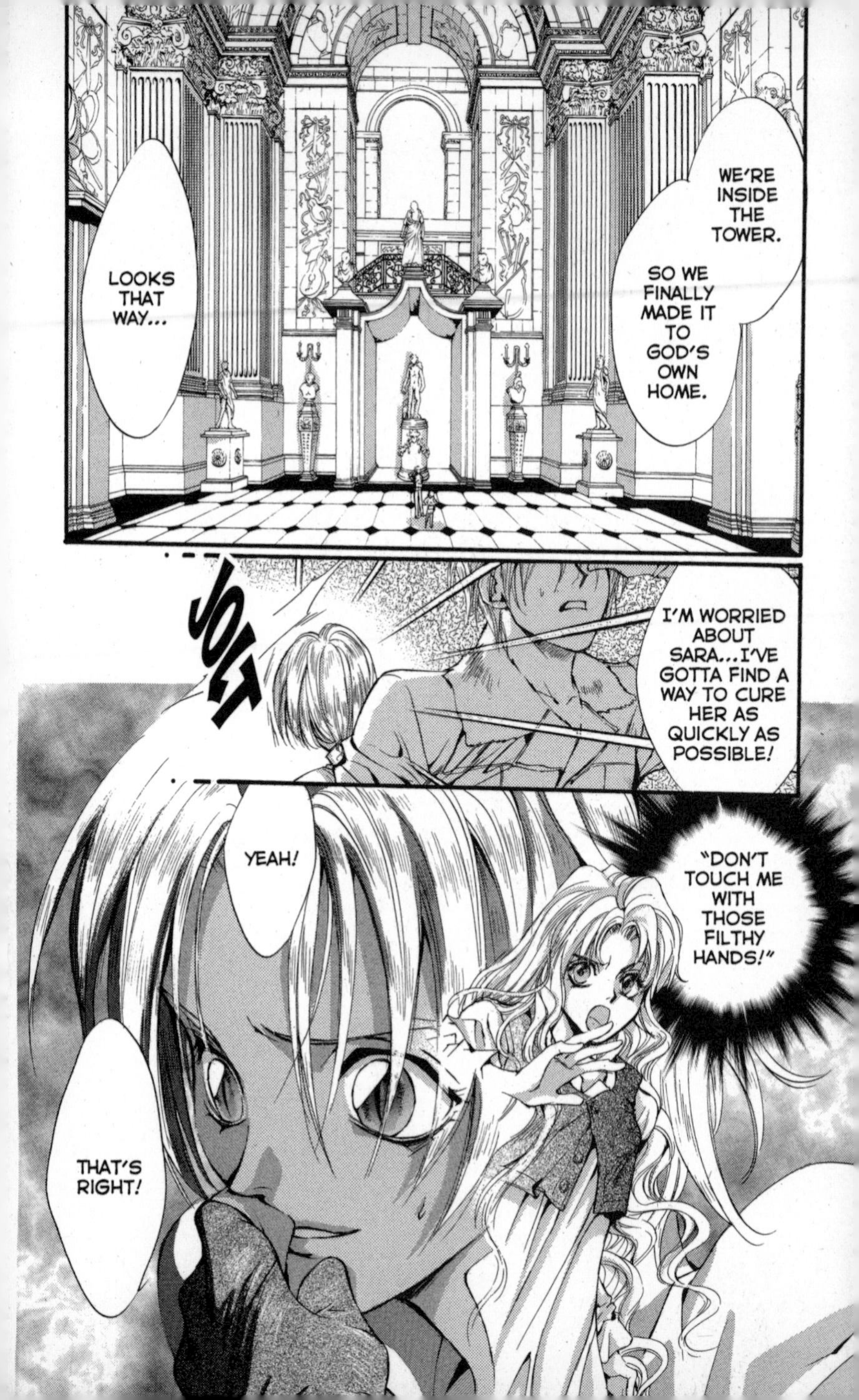
WE'RE INSIDE THE TOWER.
SO WE FINALLY MADE IT TO GOD'S OWN HOME.
LOOKS THAT WAY...
I'M WORRIED ABOUT SARA...I'VE GOTTA FIND A WAY TO CURE HER AS QUICKLY AS POSSIBLE!
JOLT
"DON'T TOUCH ME WITH THOSE FILTHY HANDS!"
YEAH!
THAT'S RIGHT!

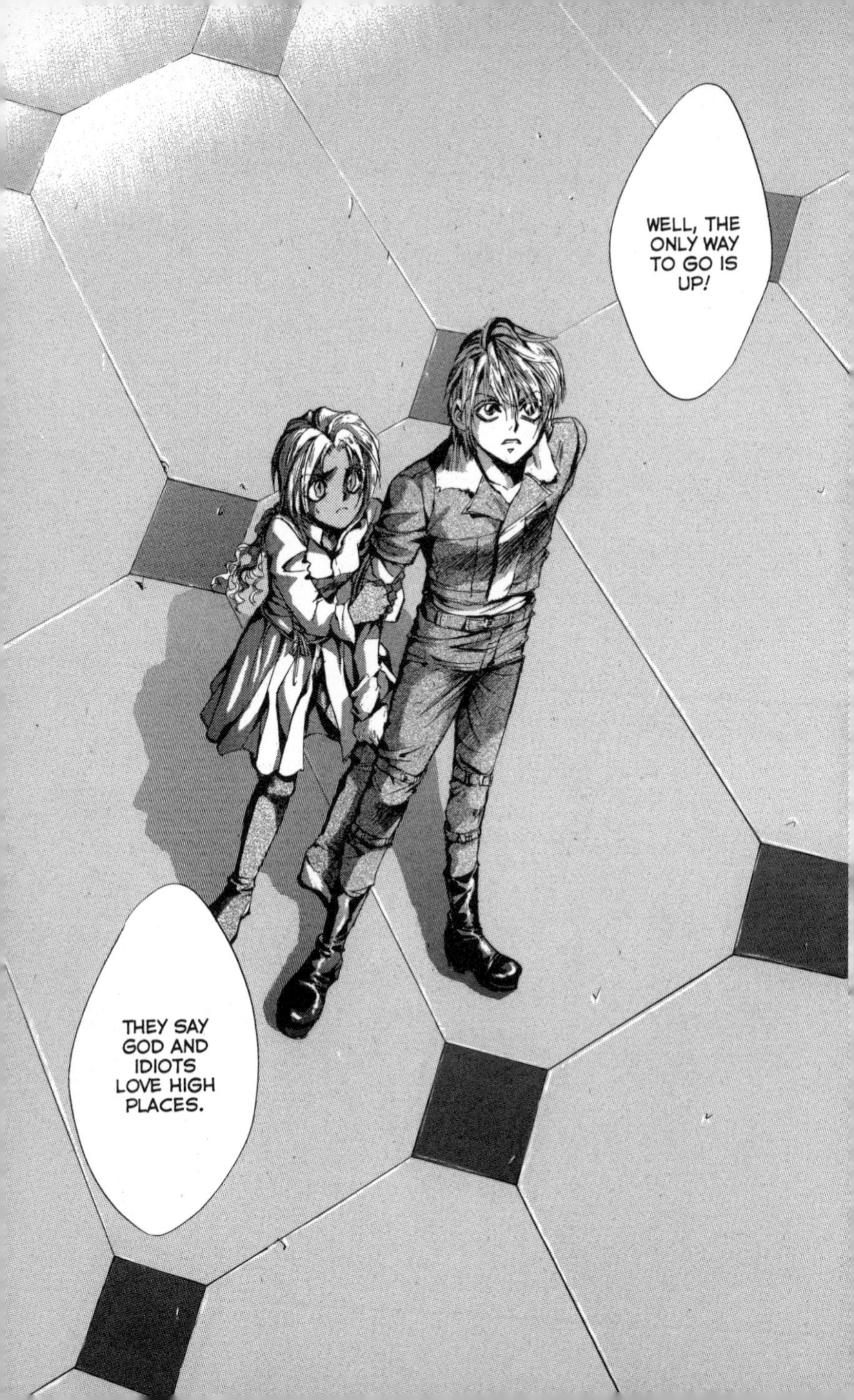
WELL, THE ONLY WAY TO GO IS UP!
THEY SAY GOD AND IDIOTS LOVE HIGH PLACES.

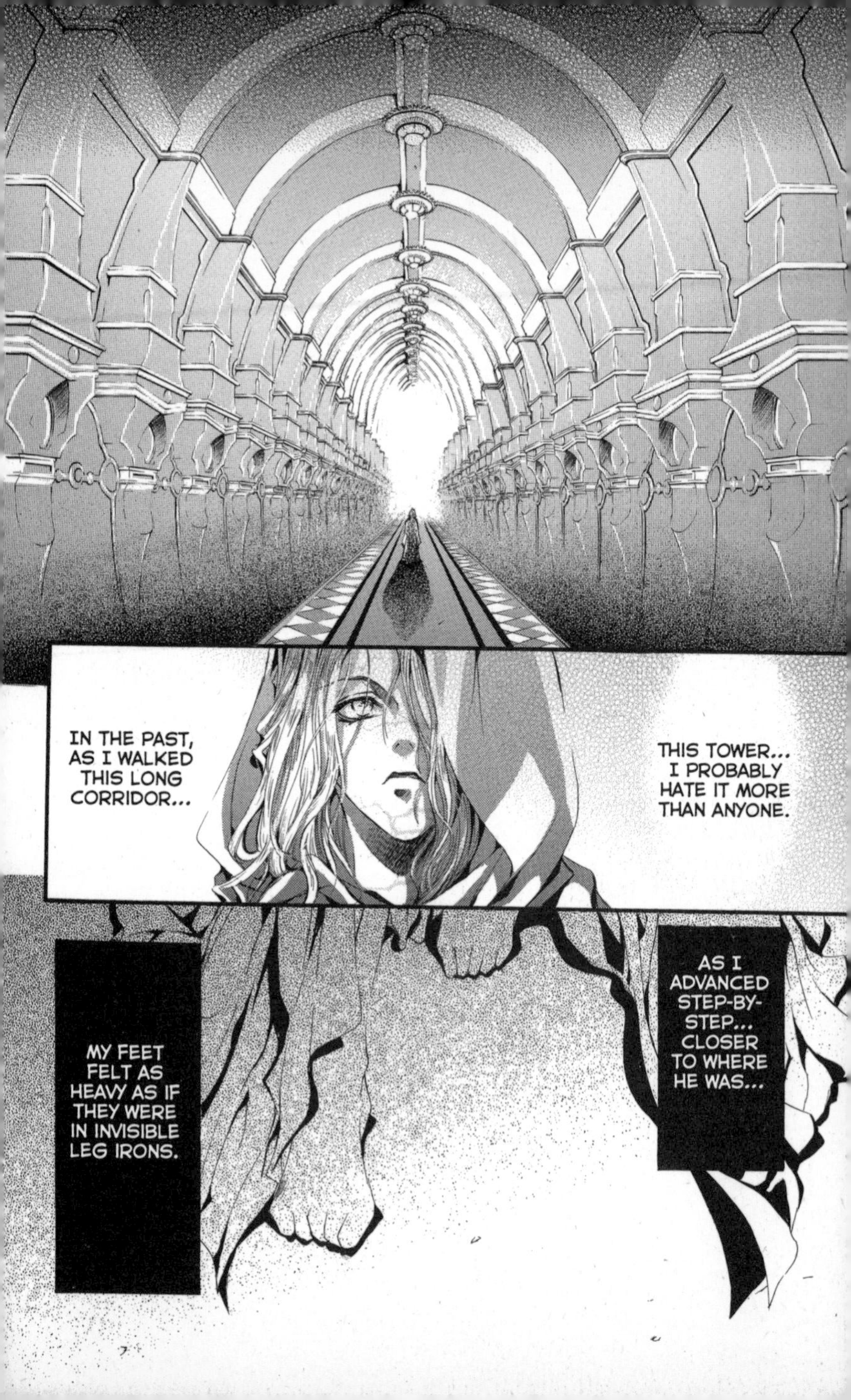
THIS TOWER... I PROBABLY HATE IT MORE THAN ANYONE.
IN THE PAST, AS I WALKED THIS LONG CORRIDOR...
AS I ADVANCED STEP-BY-STEP... CLOSER TO WHERE HE WAS...
MY FEET FELT AS HEAVY AS IF THEY WERE IN INVISIBLE LEG IRONS.

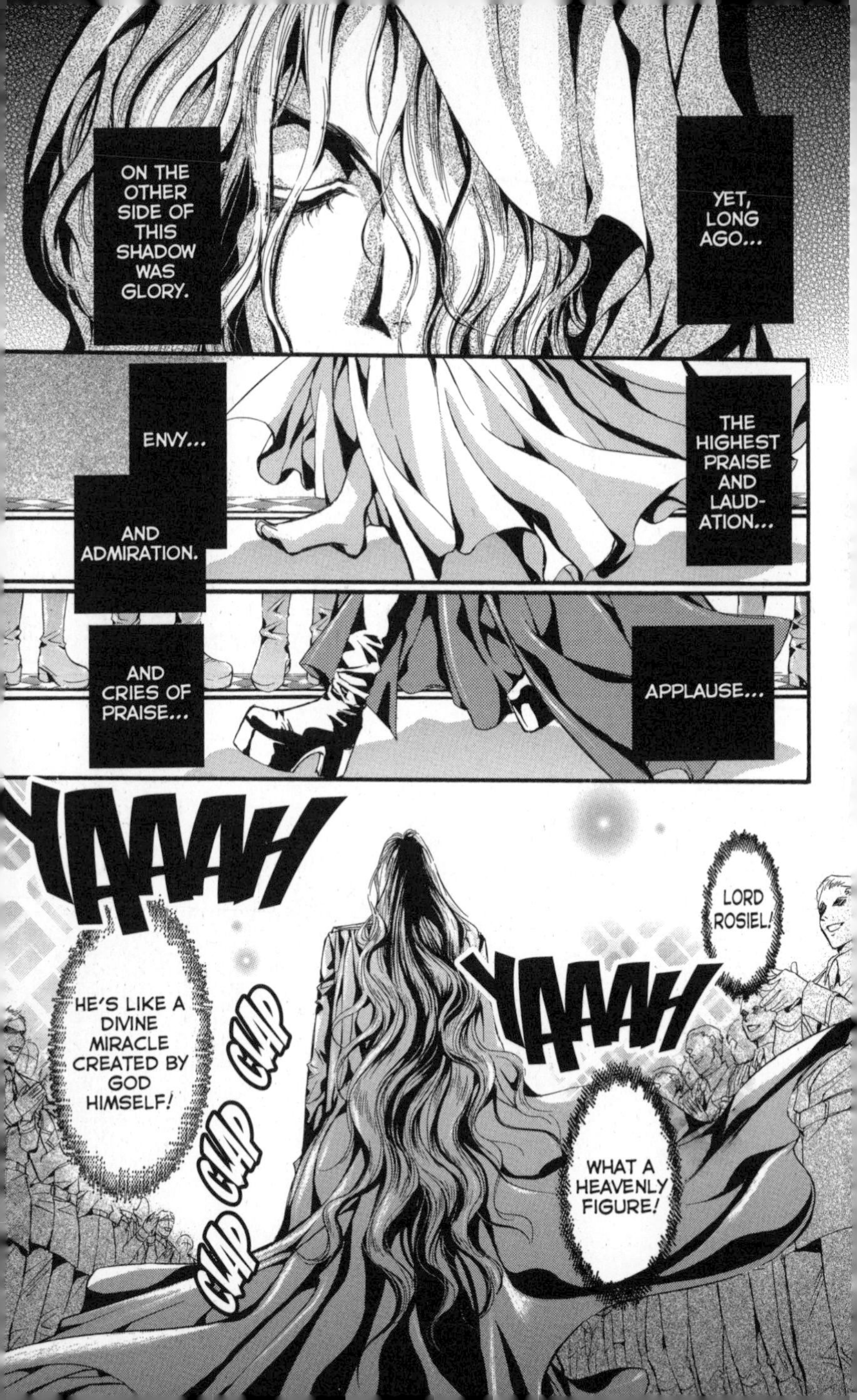
YET, LONG AGO...
ON THE OTHER SIDE OF THIS SHADOW WAS GLORY.
THE HIGHEST PRAISE AND LAUD-ATION...
ENVY...
AND ADMIRATION.
APPLAUSE...
AND CRIES OF PRAISE...
LORD ROSIEL!
YAAAH
YAAAH
HE'S LIKE A DIVINE MIRACLE CREATED BY GOD HIMSELF!
CLAP CLAP
WHAT A HEAVENLY FIGURE!
CLAP CLAP CLAP

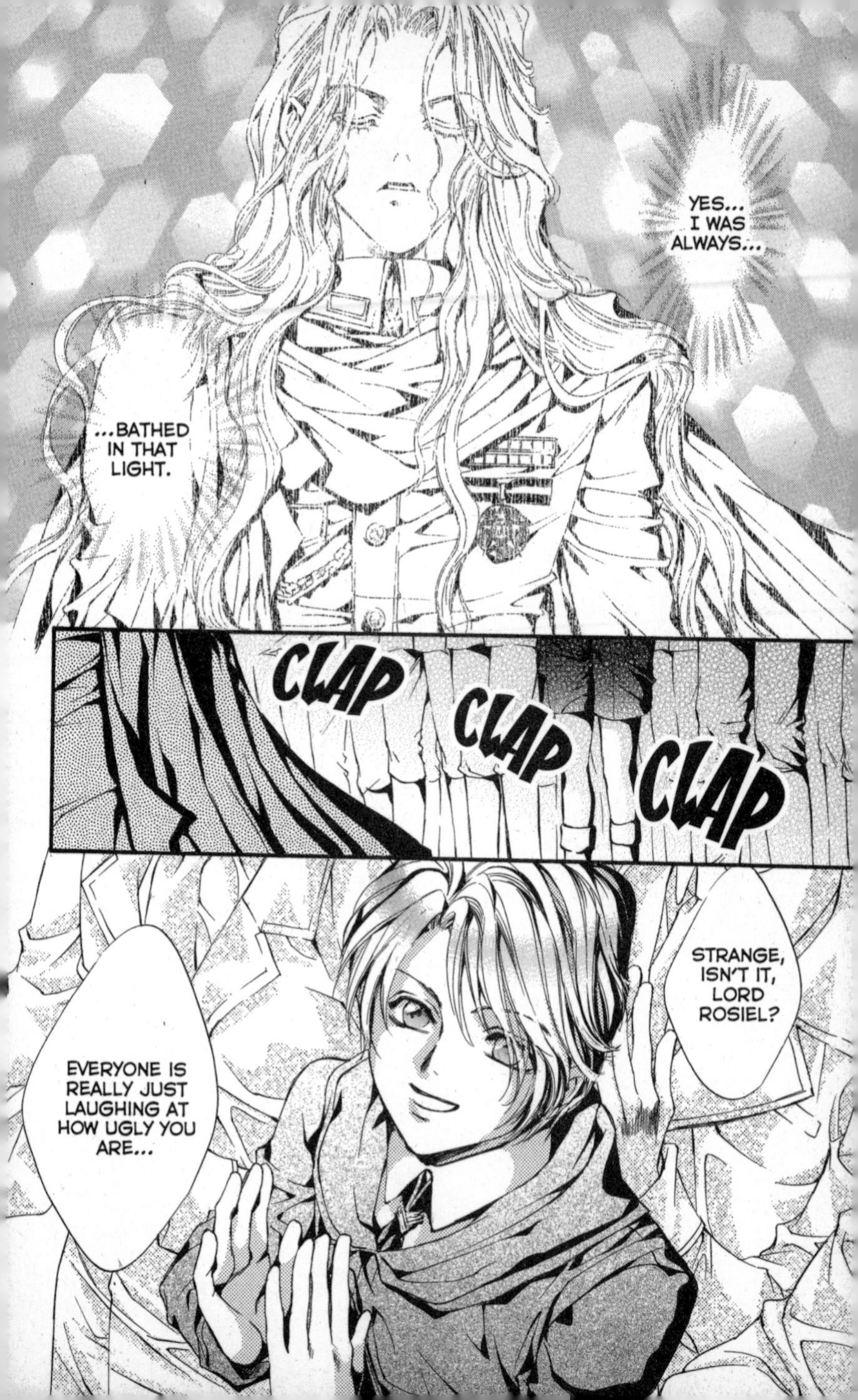
YES... I WAS ALWAYS...
...BATHED IN THAT LIGHT.
CLAP
CLAP
CLAP
STRANGE, ISN'T IT, LORD ROSIEL?
EVERYONE IS REALLY JUST LAUGHING AT HOW UGLY YOU ARE...

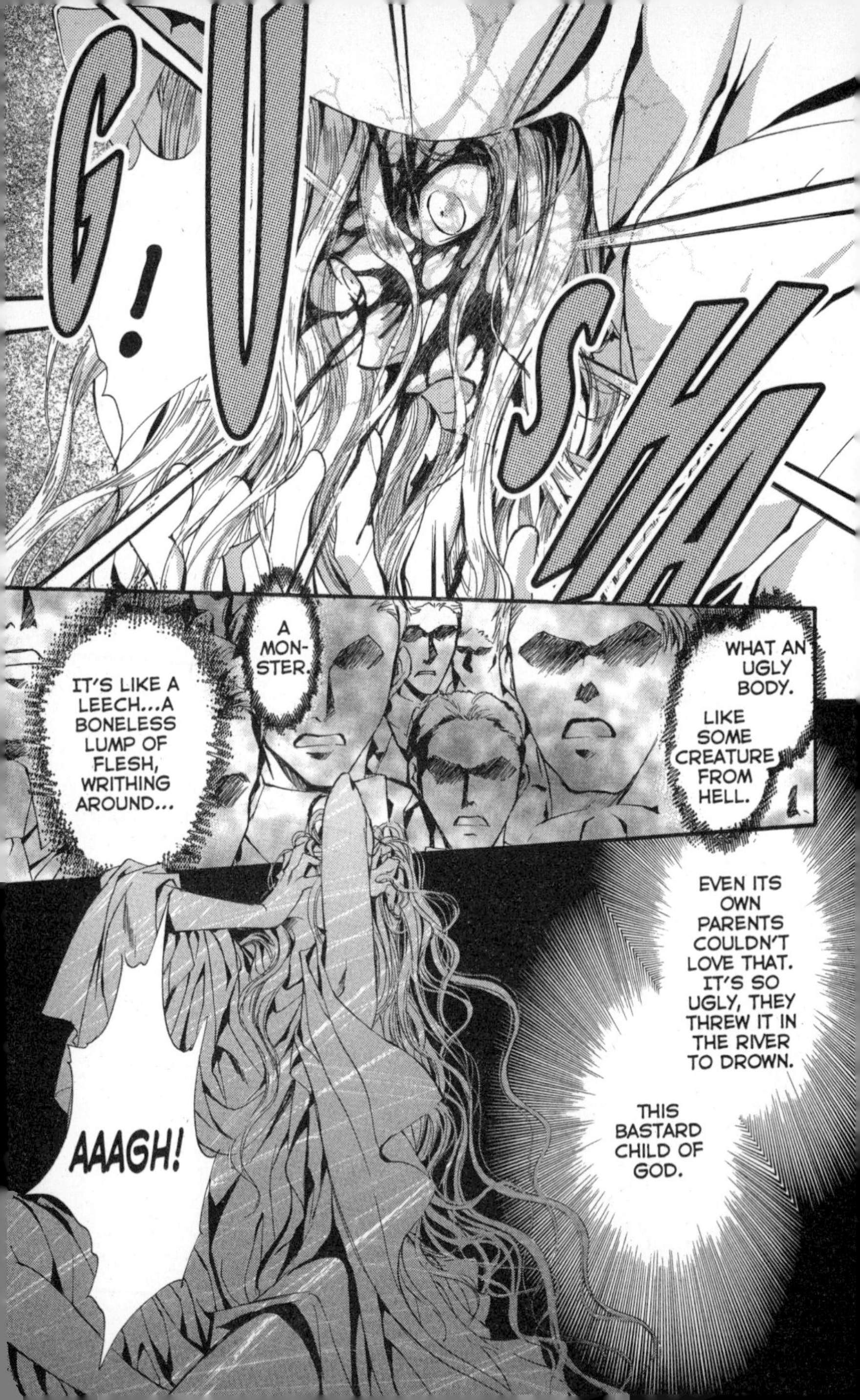
G! GUSHA
WHAT AN UGLY BODY.
LIKE SOME CREATURE FROM HELL.
A MON-STER.
IT'S LIKE A LEECH...A BONELESS LUMP OF FLESH, WRITHING AROUND...
EVEN ITS OWN PARENTS COULDN'T LOVE THAT. IT'S SO UGLY, THEY THREW IT IN THE RIVER TO DROWN.
THIS BASTARD CHILD OF GOD.
AAAGH!

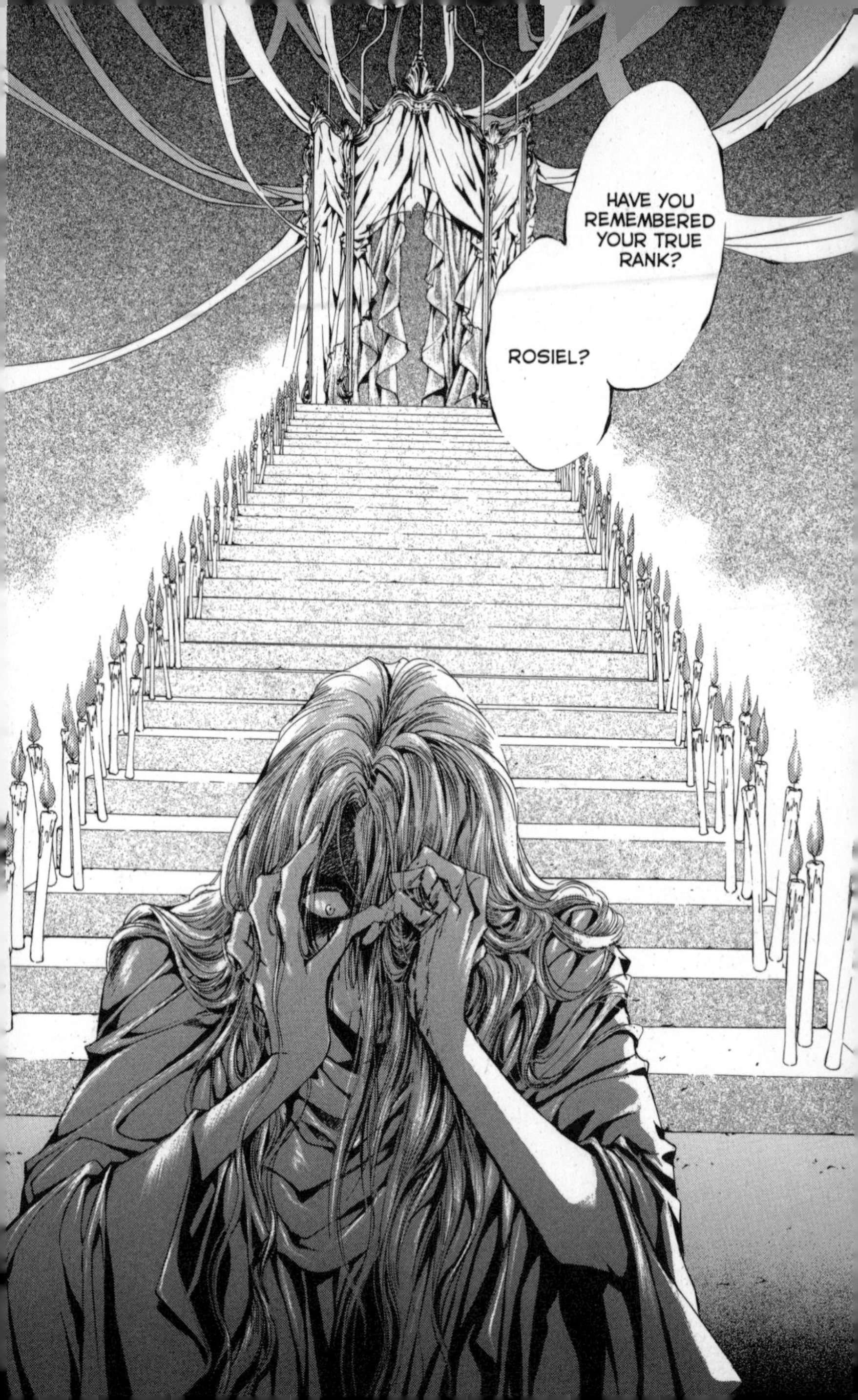
HAVE YOU REMEMBERED YOUR TRUE RANK?
ROSIEL?

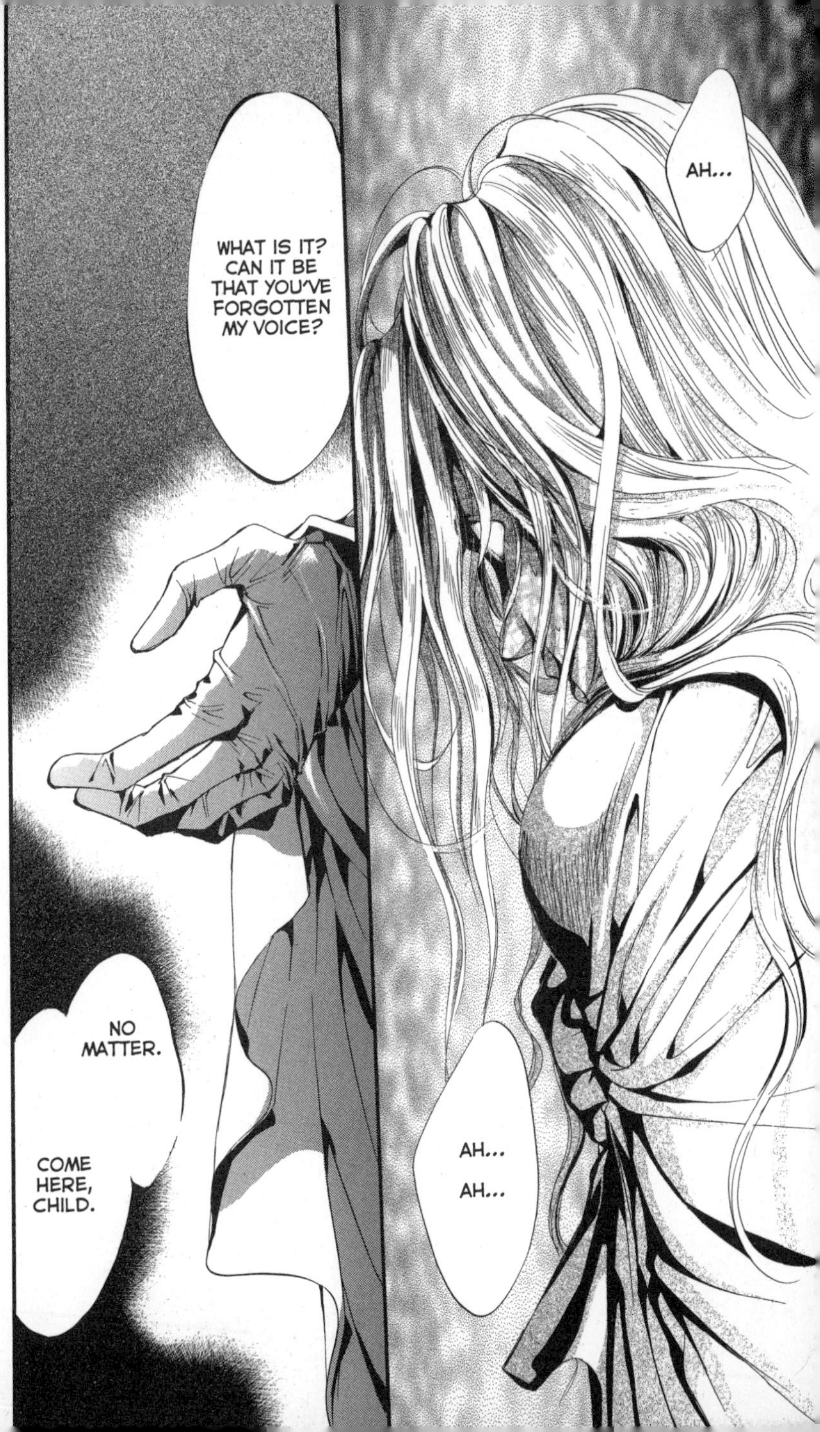
AH...
AH... AH...
WHAT IS IT? CAN IT BE THAT YOU'VE FORGOTTEN MY VOICE?
NO MATTER.
COME HERE, CHILD.

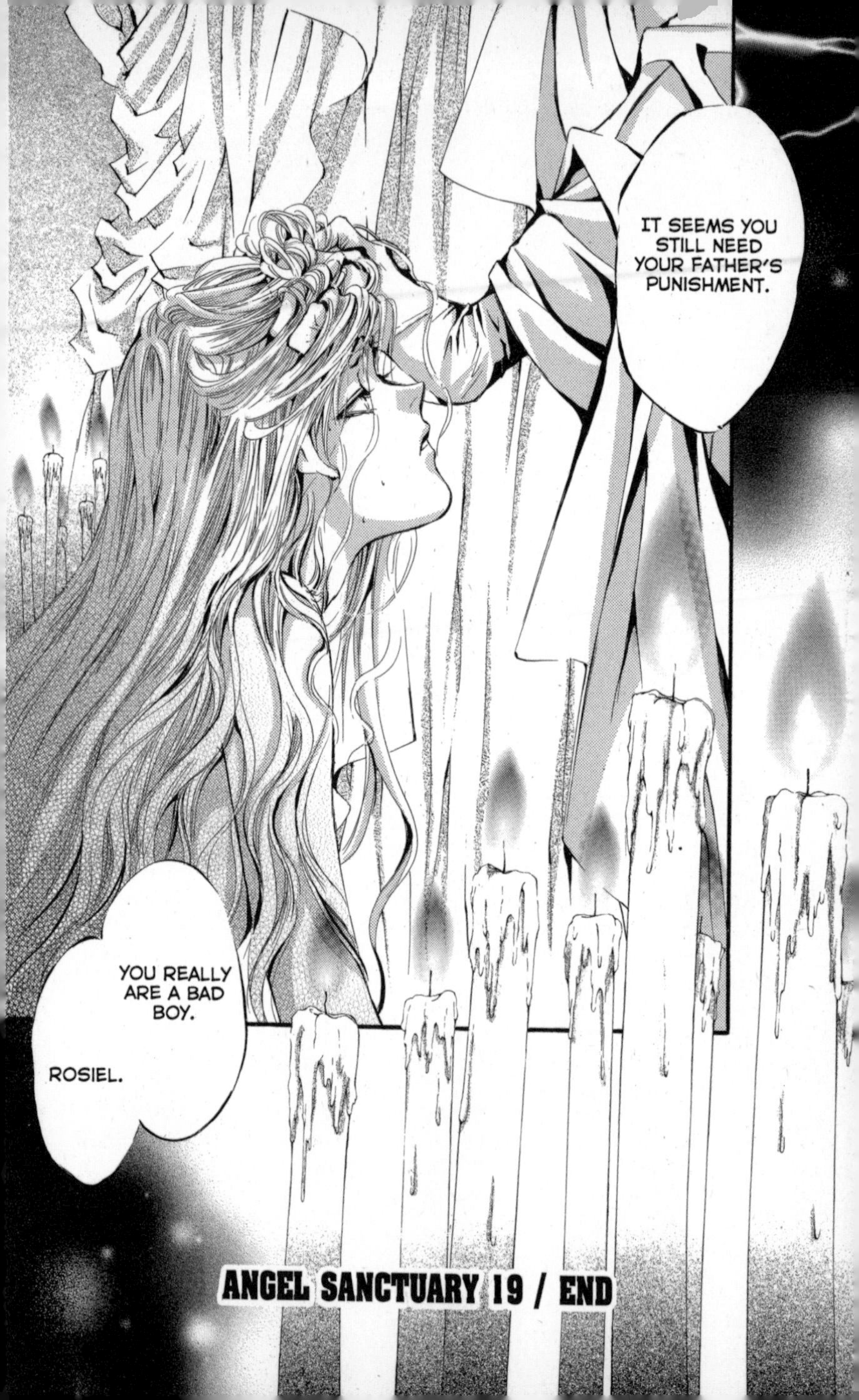
IT SEEMS YOU STILL NEED YOUR FATHER'S PUNISHMENT.
YOU REALLY ARE A BAD BOY.
ROSIEL.
ANGEL SANCTUARY 19 / END

By the time this comic comes out, it will have already been published, but my "Angel Sanct" art book "Lost Angel" is going on sale. It started out as a character book, but we added character introductions, with lots of new detail. It includes characters that only spoke a word, and enough article pages to make it feel like an "Angel Sanct Research Index." It's designed down to the fine details, so please take a look at it. Inside, there are some extremely rare early design sketches. They were selected from old notebooks and materials I dug up from six or so years ago. They were drawn just to work up my own ideas, not to show people, so I'm kind of embarrassed by them. Somehow, they are character designs I couldn't possibly come up with now. Some people will probably find them interesting. (But there are some *bishonen* versions of Astoroth and others that I couldn't find). The interviews were done right after I finished doing a lot of work, so I think I rambled on incoherently. Anyway, it's a good art book, I think! (This is kind of a trite ending.) Oh, wow, look at what time it is! Well, see in volume 20 of "Angel Sanct," the final volume. I hope it lives up to everyone's expectations!

Sep. 8, 2000
Kaori Yuki

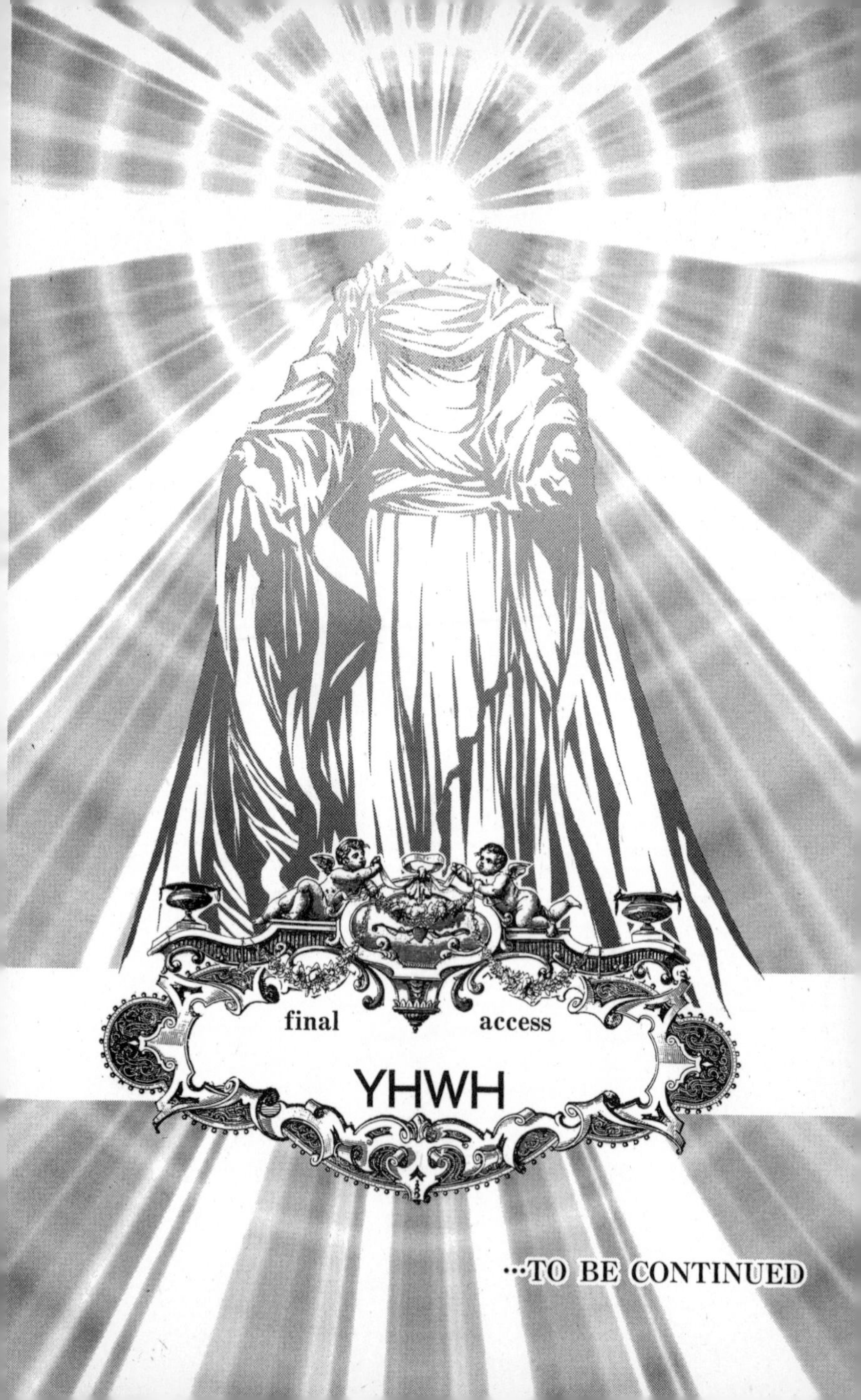
final access
YHWH
…TO BE CONTINUED

Angel Sanctuary

Vol. 19
Shōjo Edition

STORY AND ART BY KAORI YUKI

English Adaptation/Arashi Productions
Translation/Arashi Productions
Touch-up Art & Lettering/Bill Schuch
Design/Izumi Evers
Editor/Jonathan Tarbox

Managing Editor/Megan Bates
Editorial Director/Elizabeth Kawasaki
Editor in Chief/Alvin Lu
Sr. Director of Acquisitions/Rika Inouye
Sr. VP of Marketing/Liza Coppola
Exec. VP of Sales & Marketing/John Easum
Publisher/Hyoe Narita

Tenshi Kinryou Ku by Kaori Yuki © Kaori Yuki 2000
All rights reserved. First published in Japan in 2000 by HAKUSENSHA, Inc., Tokyo.
English language translation rights in America and Canada arranged with HAKUSENSHA,
Inc., Tokyo. New and adapted artwork and text © 2007 VIZ Media, LLC. The ANGEL
SANCTUARY logo is a trademark of VIZ Media, LLC. The stories, characters and incidents
mentioned in this publication are entirely fictional.

Printed in the U.S.A.

Published by VIZ Media, LLC
P.O. Box 77010
San Francisco, CA 94107

Shōjo Edition
10 9 8 7 6 5 4 3 2 1
First printing, April 2007

www.viz.com
store.viz.com

PARENTAL ADVISORY
ANGEL SANCTUARY is rated T+ for Older Teen
and is recommended for ages 16 and up. This
volume contains violence and mature situations.

Love Shojo Manga?

Let us know what you think!

Our shojo survey is now available online. Please visit **viz.com/shojosurvey**

Help us make the manga you love better!